Surface Decoration Techniques

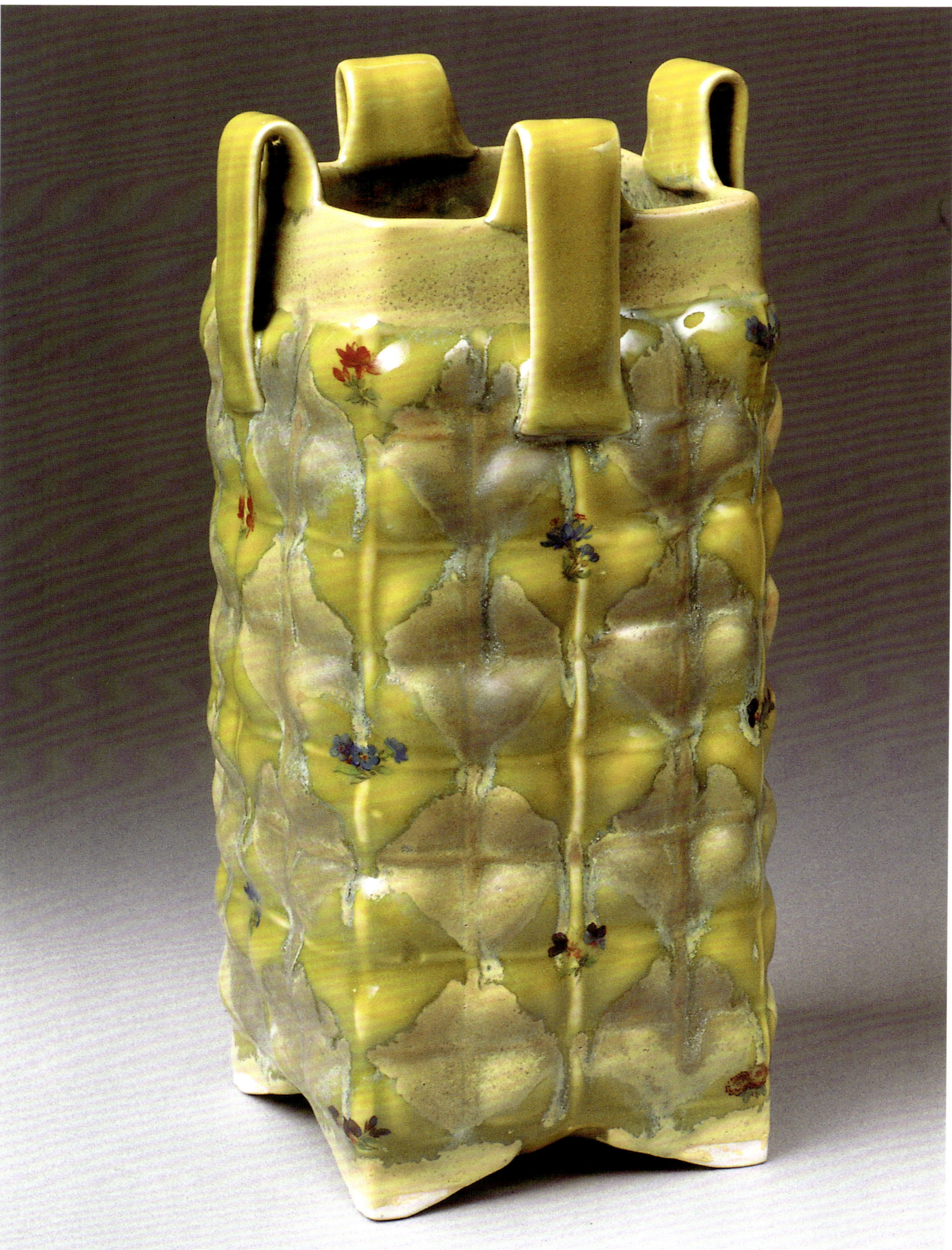

Ceramic
Arts
Handbook
Series

Surface Decoration Techniques

Edited by Anderson Turner

The American Ceramic Society
600 N. Cleveland Ave., Suite 210
Westerville, Ohio 43082
www.CeramicArtsDaily.org

The American Ceramic Society
600 N. Cleveland Ave., Suite 210
Westerville, OH 43082

ISBN: 978-1-57498-344-9 (Paperback)

ISBN: 978-1-57498-579-5 (PDF)

Publisher: Charles Spahr, Executive Director, The American Ceramic Society

Managing Director: Sherman Hall

Editor: Bill Jones

Graphic Production: Pamela S. Woodworth

Series Design: Melissa Bury

Cover Image: *Barn Salt Cellar*, earthenware with terra sigillata, crackle slip, copper oxide wash, steel carpet tacks, and nichrome wire, by Jeremy Randall. *Photo by Sarah Panzarella.*

Frontispiece: *Multi-Flower Vase*, 10½ inches in height, porcelain, handbuilt using press-molded slabs, by Margaret Bohls.

Table of Contents

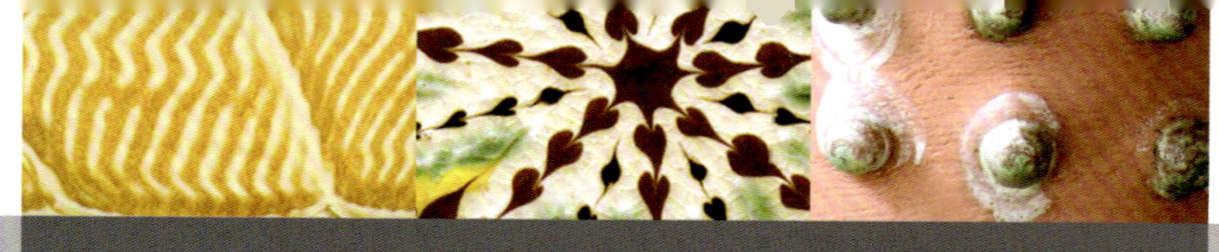

2 Layers & Inclusions

3 Carving & Etching

Preface

The surface of a piece of ware or a ceramic sculpture, while just one of the many apsects of ceramics a clay lover needs to consider, can be one of the most important parts of any creation made from clay. I've witnessed countless students and seasoned veterans struggle with the surfaces of their work. Sometimes the choice is to ignore the possibilities that texture, underglaze, glaze, slip and other decorating elements can bring to the sense of life of a piece. Or the opposite happens and the artist chooses to do too much.

This book is a book of possibilities. It's comprised of materials previously published in *Ceramics Monthly* and *Pottery Making Illustrated* over the past 15 or so years; some have been reprinted in various books or online; and others have been passed around among hundreds of potters at craft centers and schools. Where previously published materials included forming techniques or dissertations on a lifestyle or personal histories, we've selected choice processes germane to the surface treatment only.

Like anything in clay, practice makes perfect. I'd like to suggest you try a variety of techniques and see what happens. Move as much material through your studio as possible. It is only through this practice that we who work in clay can truly see all the possibilities before us. For anyone who has ever worked with a surface, results can vary from surprise to disappointment depending on a host of factors.

Surface treatment can be a lifesaver from having to consider the challenges of glazing. Perhaps Liz Smith (see page 59) said it best when she stated "After the form is constructed, I apply surface treatments at every stage of making. I think it may be my fear of the proverbial blank canvas. I can imagine almost nothing more daunting than looking at a table full of blank bisqueware without marking or color." Her primary mentor was Toshiko Takaezu, who was promoter of experimentation. When Liz asked her, as she glazed, what a piece would look like in the end she would reply, ". . . we'll see, it's all an experiment."

Anderson Turner

Forming & Texture
USING TEXTURE MOLDS
by Margaret Bohls

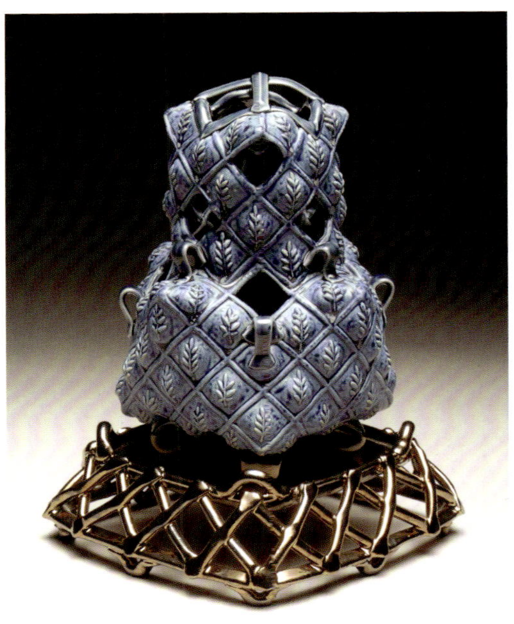

Two very different clays and forms are united by their sources of inspiration—lattice work and grid patterns. the top of this vase is made of patterned porcelain while the base is constructed of earthenware and fired separately to avoid distorting the lattice work.

I make my vessel forms using textured clay slabs pressed onto plaster molds. A textured pattern is carved into the plaster surface using a long, straightedge and the same loop tools used for carving clay. I make my molds large enough to be at least as long and as wide as the largest slab needed for any given project. My mold is about 1½ inches thick and measures about 15×30 inches.

Pouring a Plaster Slab

To make your own plaster slab you'll need a large, smooth, impermeable surface to pour on, such as glass, Plexiglas, or Formica. Make sure the work surface is level. With a Sharpie marker and a ruler, draw a rectangle on the work surface the size you want the mold to be. Either set up cottle boards on your rectangle and clamp them together to create walls to contain the plaster (figure 1) or use waste clay to build a thick, sturdy wall around your drawn rectangle. The wall should be about 2 inches high. For clay walls, reinforce the outside of the wall with a fat coil of clay to be sure it won't collapse under the weight of the liquid plaster. Use a flat-sided rib with a right angle to smooth the interior clay wall's surface. Be sure either the clay walls or the cottle boards are sealed at the joints with coils of clay so the plaster won't leak out. Determine the volume of your mold and mix up an appropriate amount of plaster.

Use #1 Pottery Plaster for casting or pressing clay. Once the plaster is mixed, pour it slowly into one spot between your clay walls, making sure not to splash or make bubbles. Jog the table several times to be sure the top of the plaster levels out. Allow it to set up thoroughly then remove the clay wall or cottle boards and lift or slide the plaster off the casting surface. Use a Surform tool to shave off any sharp edges and then sand the back of the mold (the side that was up during the casting process) using first a green kitchen scrub pad and #400 wet-or-dry sandpaper. Sand the mold under water. Until the plaster cures completely, it will be fairly fragile so handle it carefully. Sanding the back side of the mold allows you to carve texture into both sides should you want different textures or grids.

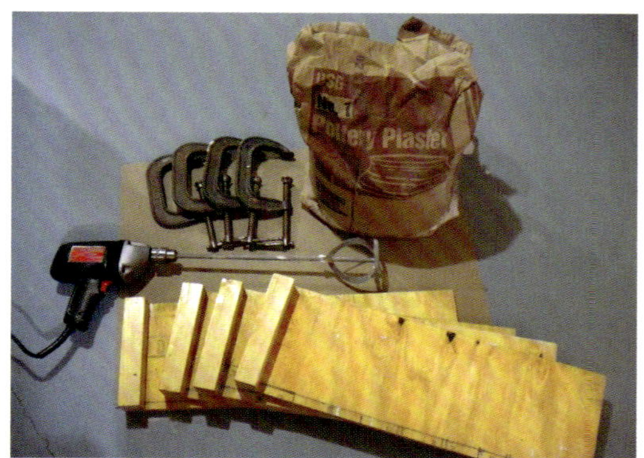

1. Build a form for your plaster mold using cottles and clamps.

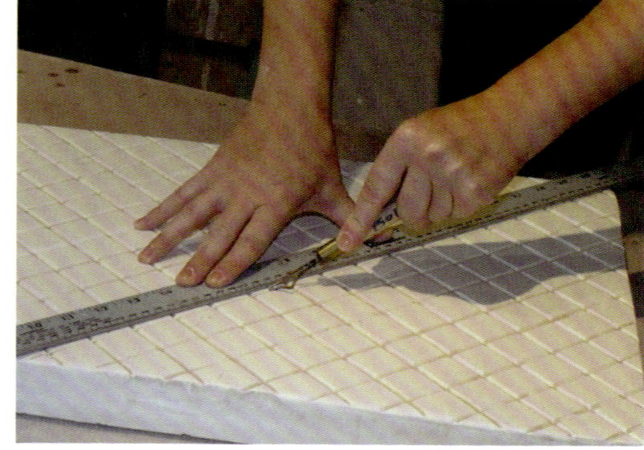

2. Create the texture grid using a loop tool and a straightedge as a guide.

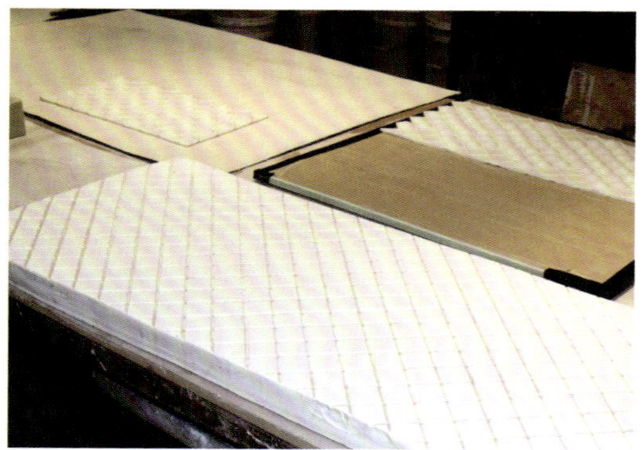

3. Finished mold with a 1-in. grid. Create several molds with different sized grids to provide design options.

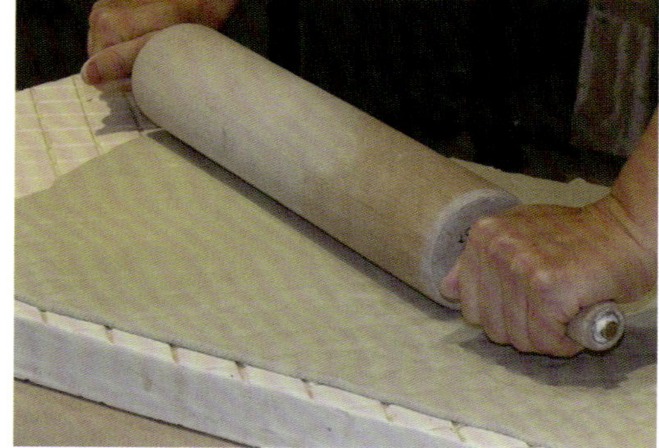

4. Use your hands, a rolling pin, and a rib, to work the clay into the slab's texture.

Carving the Plaster

Lay the plaster slab onto a smooth, level surface. I use a ruler, a square, and a pencil to draw a diagonal grid onto the plaster surface, but of course almost any drawing can be made into a carved texture. To carve long, straight lines, use a hardened-steel loop tool with a narrow loop. Lay a straightedge along the drawn line and pull the loop tool along the edge of the ruler (figure 2). It takes two or three passes to get a sufficiently deep line. Once all the lines are carved in one direction, turn the mold and carve lines in the other direction to make a grid.

Clean the mold by rinsing it under water. You may now carve the reverse side of the mold with a different pattern or grid if you choose. The size of grid squares is up to you. I have several molds with different sized grids between 1 and 2 inches (figure 3).

Caution: Remember that clay and plaster do not mix. Mix, pour, clean, and carve your plaster in an area where clay will not come in contact with it.

Texturing Clay Slabs

To texture clay, first roll out and compress a clay slab. Drop the slab onto the mold and then slap it down into the texture using your hand. Run a rolling pin over it (figure 4), and finally go over it with the plastic rib to completely smooth the back of the slab and make sure clay has filled in all the texture carved into the mold. Gently, lift the slab off of the mold, flip it over, and cut it to the appropriate size needed.

Building the First Tier of a Basket

Interior volume is a key element in functional forms because it defines the potential for contain-

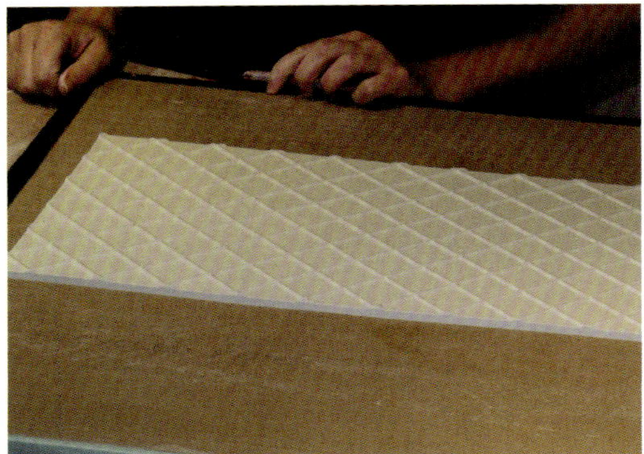

5. The trimmed slab showing the raised line formed from the carved plaster mold.

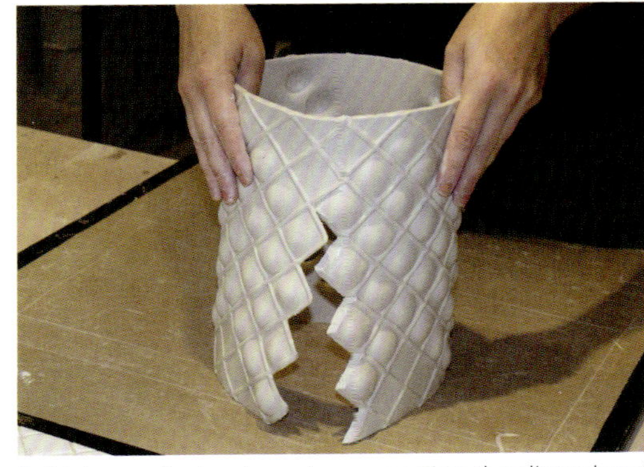

6. Make a cylinder shape by connecting the slipped and scored zigzagged edges.

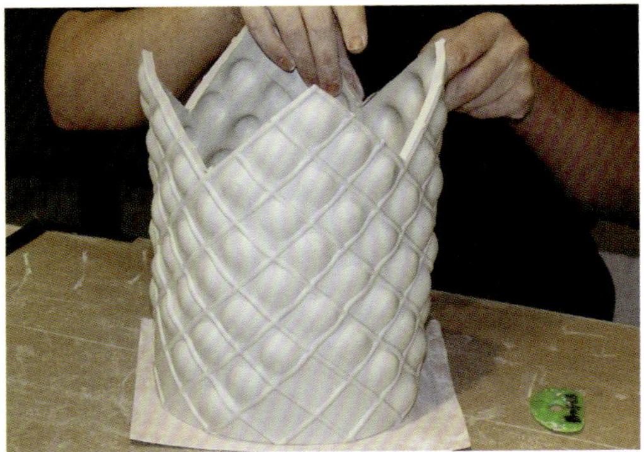

7. Cutting four equal darts from the bottom. Fold them in and join them to make a flat bottom.

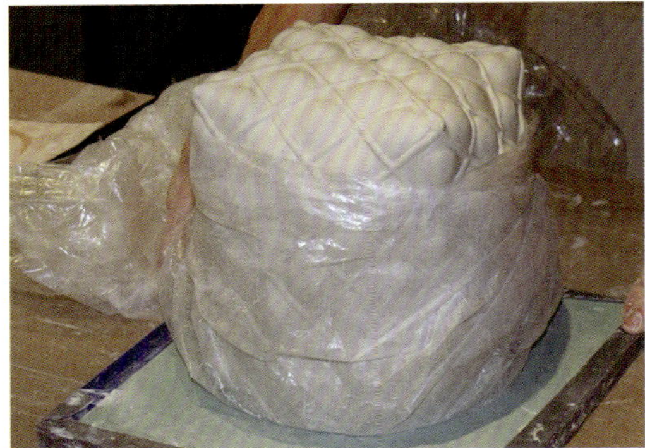

8. Wrap the body with plastic and keep the bottom exposed to become leather hard

ment. My current body of work combines a strong sense of interior volume with a grid-like surface of textural lines. The lines contain and shape that volume, creating buoyant, full, yet architectural forms with upholstered-like surfaces draped with a series of rich, complex glazes. These forms are often placed in or on earthenware baskets or trays, resulting in a layer of disparate and complex yet integrated elements.

First roll out and compress two slabs, one about 14×24 inches (figure5) and the other slightly smaller. The slabs should be between ¹/₈ and ¼ inch thick.

This vase consists of two tiers. The first tier forms the main volume and begins as a cylinder. Using a sharp knife, carefully cut the short sides of the larger slab along the raised lines of the grid pattern. This gives you a "zigzag" edge on these two sides. On one side, bevel this zigzag edge so you remove the raised line. Turn the slab over and bevel the other edge from the back. This leaves the raised line on the opposite surface. Score and slip these beveled edges and join them (figure 6). Once they're joined, the seam is hidden under the grid lines. Smooth and secure the seams with a rubber rib and a sponge.

Create the bottom of the vase by cutting darts in four places along the raised grid lines (figure 7). Fold down the flaps to enclose the form. Bevel the edge of these flaps, score and slip, then join the seams.

Wait to clean up the insides of these seams until you're able to turn the pot over. This part of the pot needs to dry to leather hard before the feet are attached, however the rest of the cylinder needs

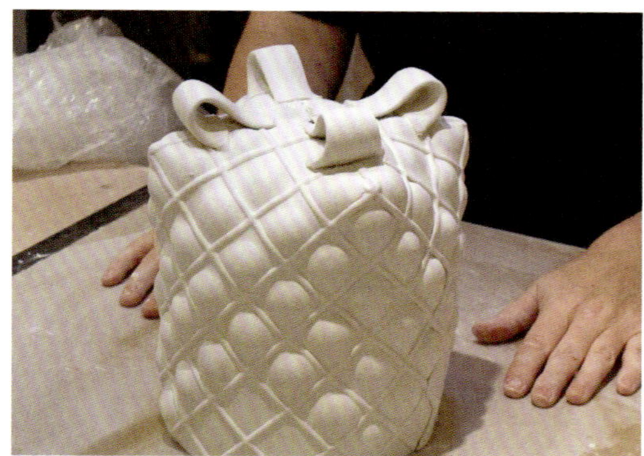

9. Pull handle-like forms and attach the feet to the bottom of the main volume.

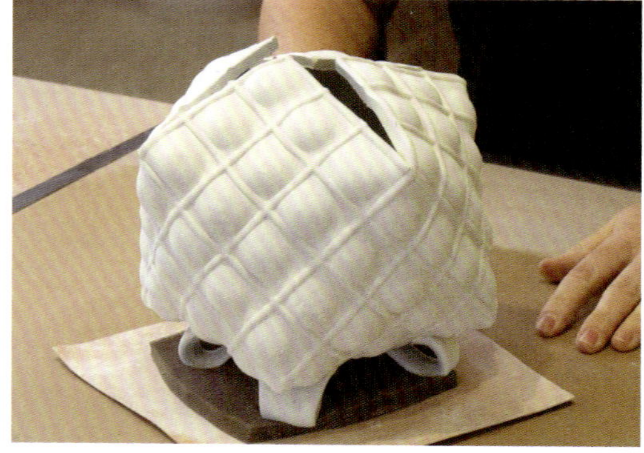

10. Dart, fold in, and join the top of the main volume. Cut a small circle in the top for stems to fit through.

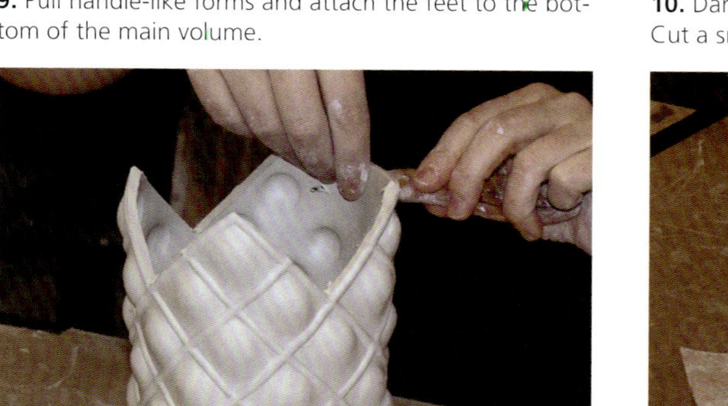

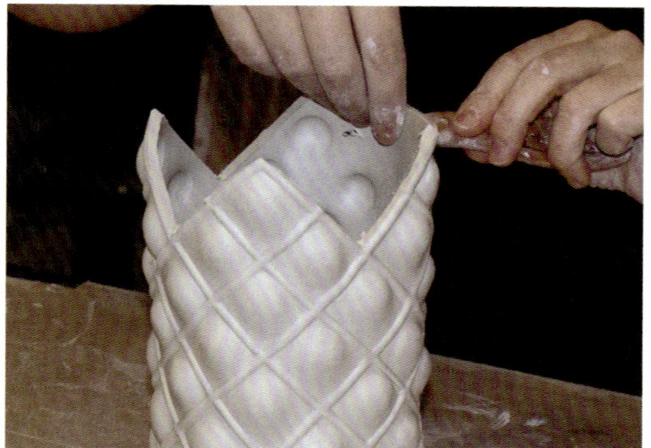

11. Form a thinner, taller cylinder for the top tier and cut darts to form the top.

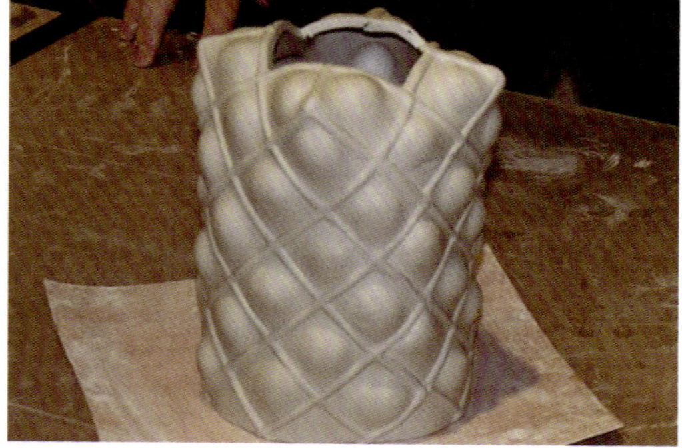

12. Cut a square from the top following the grid lines and clean and smooth the edges.

to remain soft, so that the top can be darted and folded. Wrap the form in soft plastic, leaving just the closed part exposed (figure 8).

The feet are pulled like handles. To make pulling multiple feet easier and faster, roll a long coil, flatten it with your palm, cut the coil into short lengths, and then pinch each piece to taper one end. Pull a "handle" from each of these lugs and lay them flat on the table until slightly dry. Bevel the large ends of the pulled feet and bend them. Once they stiffen a bit, score and slip them onto the vase (figure 9).

Now, re-wrap the pot in plastic leaving only the end with the attached feet exposed. Once the feet are stiff enough to support the weight of the pot, unwrap the pot and turn it over onto a thin piece of foam. Reach into the form and smooth and join the bottom seams. Once the interior is cleaned up, dart the top of the pot as you did the bottom, fold in the flaps, then bevel and join the edges (figure 10). To make these top seams easier to join, cut a 1-inch diameter hole in the top to get your fingers inside.

Adding the Second Tier

The upper tier of the vase also begins as a cylinder. Cut and join the edges as you did on the bottom tier. Cut four darts and form the top (figure 11). Cut a hole in the top of this piece. Create the opening at the top of the vase. Here, cut just inside the carved grid lines (figure 12). The two tiers are now spliced together. Cut along the textured lines at the bottom of the top tier, leaving a zigzag edge. This edge is spread out to meet the bottom tier (figure 13).

Gently set the top tier onto the bottom tier and lightly trace a line along the zigzag edge. The two

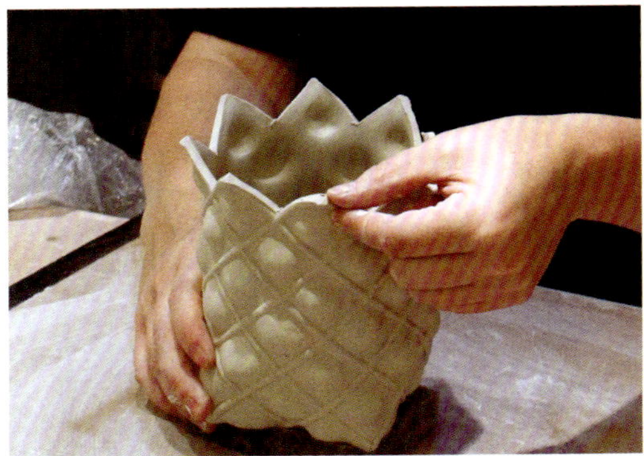

13. Open up the bottom edge and gently fold back the flaps to match up with the mail volume.

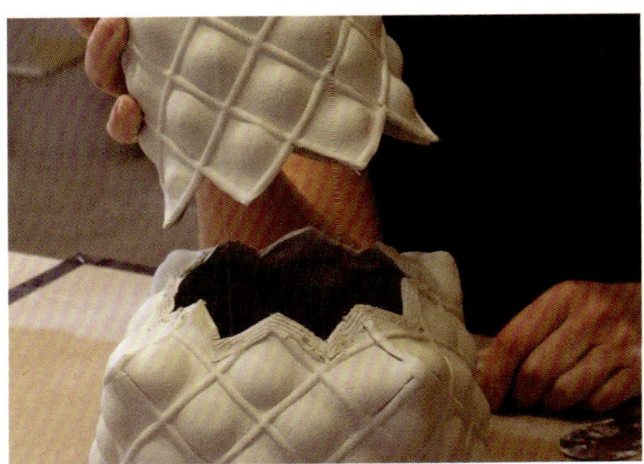

14. Attach the two tiers by matching the grid lines and scoring and slipping.

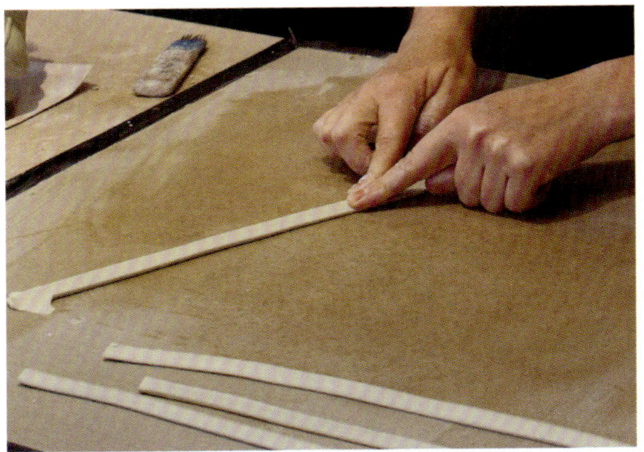

15. Roll out and flatten thin coils for the lattice and handle decorations.

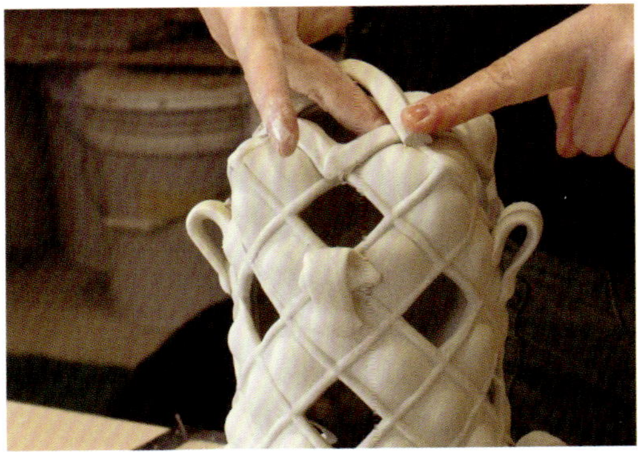

16. Attach the lattice to the top edge opening then make a crisscross pattern.

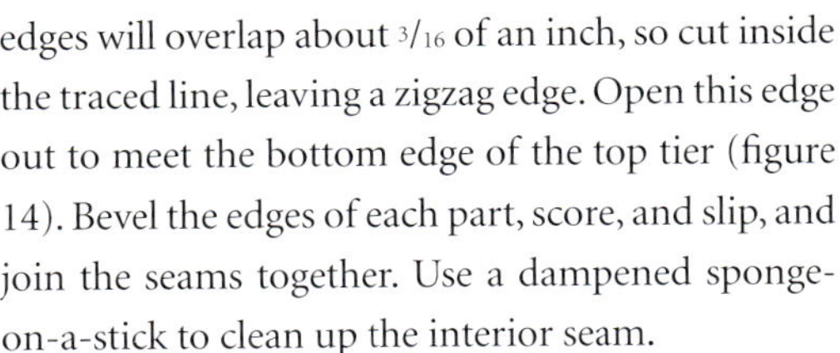

edges will overlap about 3/16 of an inch, so cut inside the traced line, leaving a zigzag edge. Open this edge out to meet the bottom edge of the top tier (figure 14). Bevel the edges of each part, score, and slip, and join the seams together. Use a dampened sponge-on-a-stick to clean up the interior seam.

Lattice and Handles

When the entire form is leather hard, cut holes in the vase for the flowers, and add a small lattice on the top of the vase. Cut the holes using a sharp knife. Once they have been cut out, trim the interior edge of each hole and smooth the edges.

To make the lattice for the top, begin with a thin coil and flatten it with a pastry roller. Now create a triangular cross section by rolling each side of the coil at an angle. This triangular cross section makes the coil stronger and less likely to warp in the firing. To make the strip smooth and consistent, tack one end of it to the table with a little water, and run a damp sponge and/or two fingers along the length of it (figure 15).

This strip acts as a lip around the edge of the top opening of the vase. It also crisscrosses the opening to form a lattice. To attach the lip, bevel the edge of the opening, cutting off the raised grid line, and score both the beveled edge and the back of the strip. Cut four pieces of the strip to lay along each side of the opening, being careful to overlap and join the corners well (this is where cracks sometimes happen). Then attach two more pieces of the strip in an "X" across the opening (figure 16).

Add decorative handles if desired. Pull, bevel, shape, and attach them exactly like the feet. Add decorative sprigs for a final touch.

Forming & Texture

DAVID GAMBLE'S WALL TILE RELIEFS

by Paul Andrew Wandless

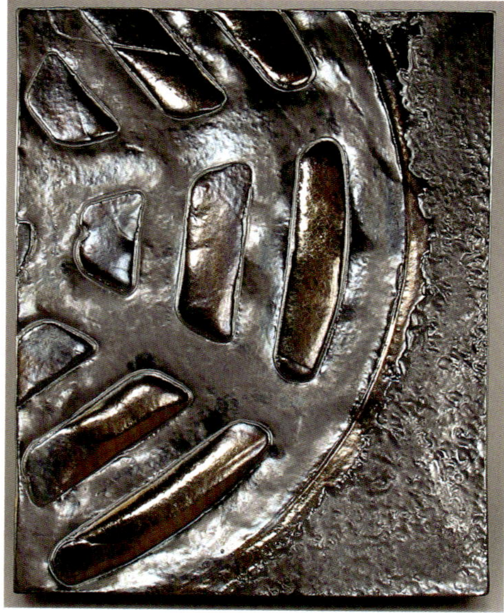

Sewer Cover Wall Relief Tile. Explore different textures and images around your home or studio to find hidden compositions. The construction process of the wall relief is the same regardless of what image you have in mind.

Artists often look for hidden compositions existing in the mundane, ordinary and commonplace objects of everyday life. It's easy to appreciate and enjoy the vibrant color of flowers, the way light sparkles on ripples in the ocean or the beauty of a summer sunset. More challenging, though, is enjoying the fascinating designs and images surrounding us in the simple form of textured surfaces. Manhole covers and storm drain grates are everyday items not immediately thought of as aesthetically pleasing surfaces. These so-called ordinary surfaces typically go unnoticed and start to become invisible unless, of course, we are trying to avoid or step around them. Fortunately, the hidden compositions and patterns in these quiet iron circles are noticed and transformed into works of art by David Gamble of Indianapolis, Indiana.

Looking Down

When David looks at manhole covers and grates, he sees pattern, line and low-relief opportunities his terra-cotta wall pieces. He enjoys capturing the interesting shapes, textures, images and text of manhole covers in a clay relief. He's not just trying to document or get a record of the manhole; he's looking for an interesting composition or combination of elements already existing on its surface. Most relief prints are just small specific sections of the manhole cover and the original source of the relief is not obvious.

The process of lifting/pulling a relief from a textured surface is an image transfer technique. It's very similar to making a charcoal rubbing except you substitute clay for paper. Print making techniques and ceramics have been combined throughout history, and exciting work has been created pairing these two media.

David uses Amaco's Terra-Cotta Clay No. 77, a heavily grogged clay. The grog opens up the clay body and promotes even drying, which keeps his wall pieces flat during the drying and firing process. He also enjoys the rich, dark-red color of the terra cotta after it is fired to cone 03, and the contrast it provides for his gold luster glazes.

Process

David starts by rolling slabs that are about ½ inch thick. This allows him to get a deeper impression

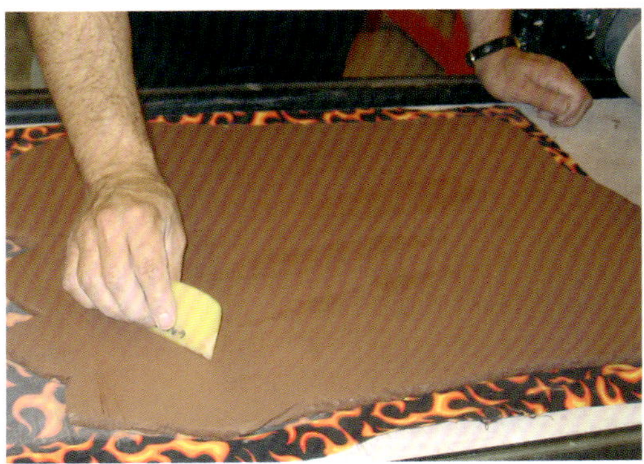
1. Prepare a slab and smooth the surface.

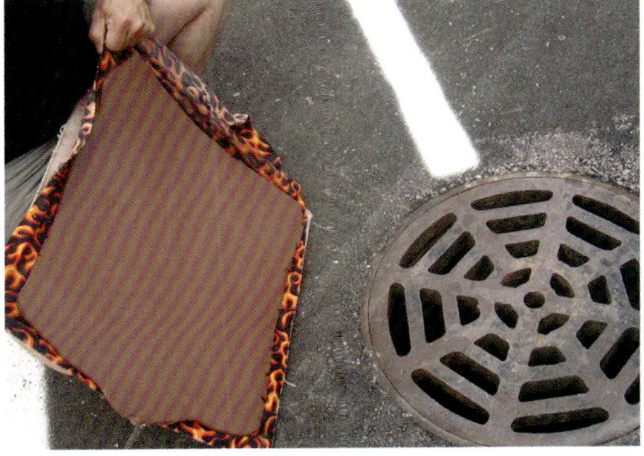
2. Position slab in front of manhole or drain cover.

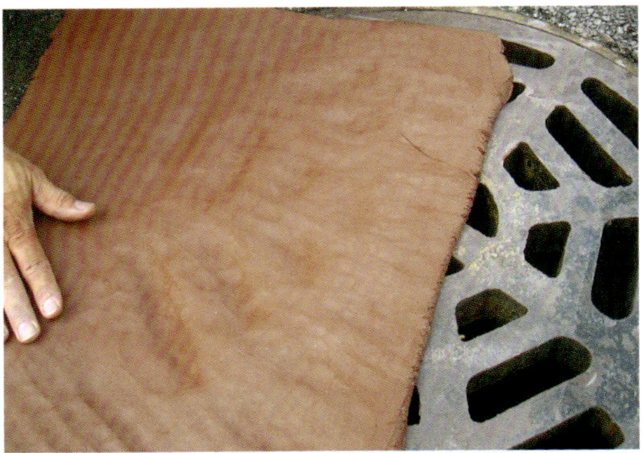
3. Rub slab with mild pressure to create deep relief.

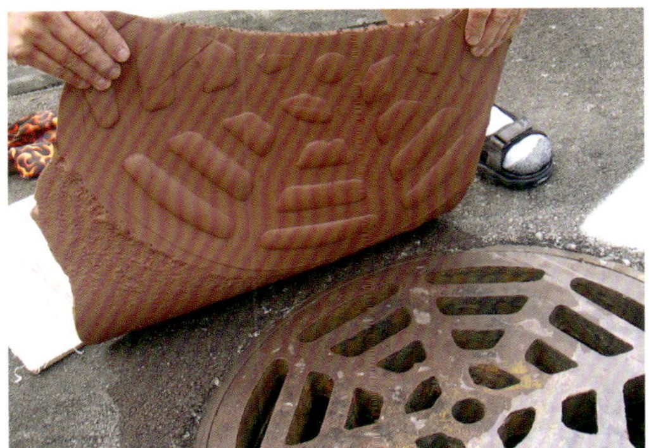
4. Gently but quickly pull slab from the grate.

and still maintain an adequate thickness in the recessed areas to prevent cracking. If the slab is too thin, it merely conforms to the surface and doesn't actually receive an impression. If you use canvas while rolling the slab, smooth the surface with a soft rib so it is clean, clear and ready to receive the image (figure 1). Roll out a few extra slabs for test prints and for constructing walls later in the process.

Place the canvas-backed clay slab on a large wooden board and carry it to a manhole or storm-drain cover. Take a brush in case any debris needs to be removed from the cover or grate. Stand the board on edge and position in front of the area of interest (figure 2), flop the slab down onto the grate, and rub with mild pressure to create a deeper relief (figure 3). Extra pressure works especially well when pulling a complex texture from the asphalt surrounding a grate.

Gently but quickly pull the slab from the grate (figure 4) and lay it back onto the board (figure 5). Take a look at the image you just pulled to see if it has the detail and depth that you need for your wall piece. As is the case with most new endeavors, your first transfer may not meet your expectations. Make a test print or two to practice how much pressure is needed for the relief, and how best to line up your slab to get the section you desire.

Since David's manhole reliefs are part of an ongoing series, he has a board precut to specific dimensions so they are consistent. Place the board over the relief and crop the areas of inter-

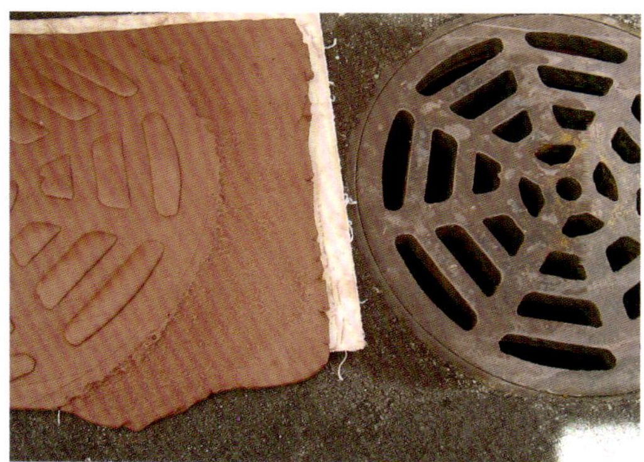
5. Lay slab back onto the board.

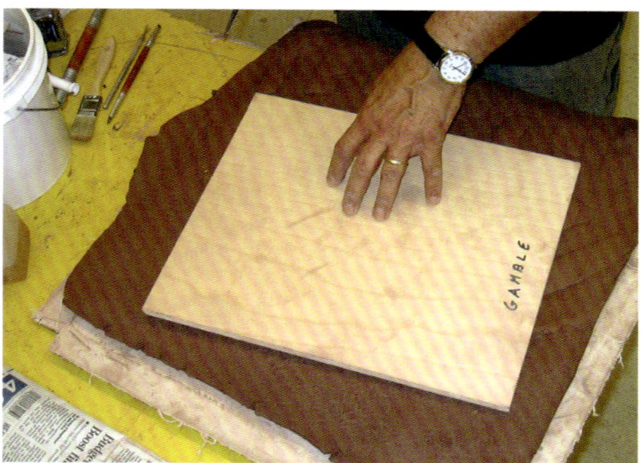

6. Determine the areas you want and crop.

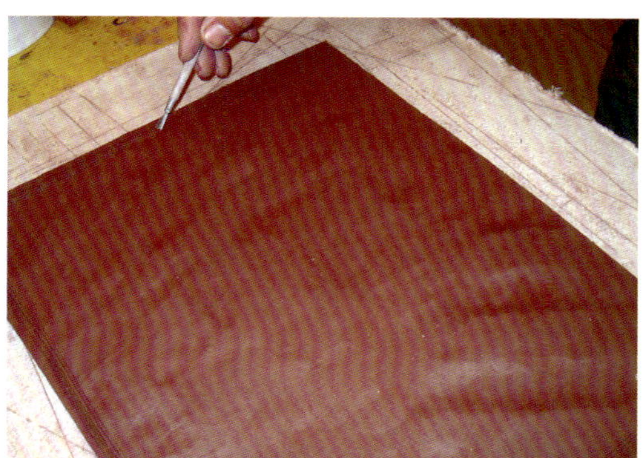
7. Score the edges with a wire tool.

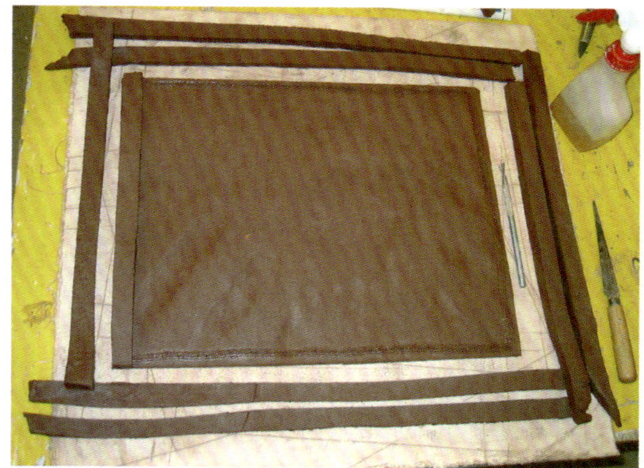
8. Cut square coils then score and spray.

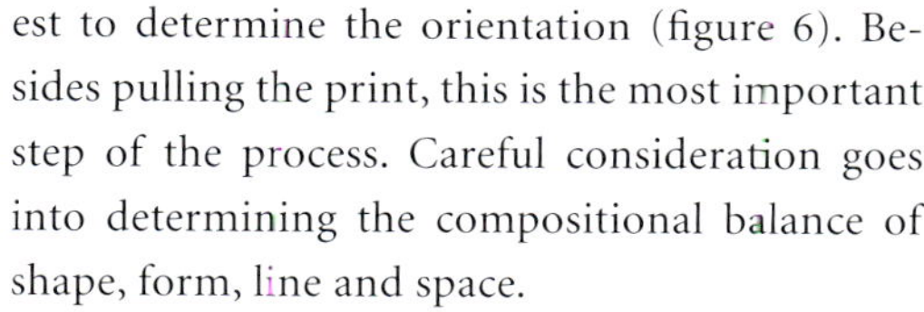

est to determine the orientation (figure 6). Besides pulling the print, this is the most important step of the process. Careful consideration goes into determining the compositional balance of shape, form, line and space.

It's important to figure out in advance how you will install or hang the piece to ensure your work can be hung easily and securely. For hanging brackets, David attaches small slabs of clay with holes punched through them. To do this, turn the trimmed relief over and score the perimeter with a wire tool (figure 7). Cut eight square coils from the remaining ½-inch slab, then score and spray them with apple cider vinegar (instead of joining slip) (figure 8). Build the walls two coils high around the perimeter, and firmly press and smooth them during the construction process.

After determining which end is the top, cut, score and spray two clay gussets to be used as hanging brackets. The gussets should be placed approximately a third of the way down from the top and trimmed to match the height of the walls (figure 9). For added strength, press and smooth a coil into all the interior seams (figure 10). Poke holes with a pointed tool through the center of the hanging brackets (figure 11) for heavy gauge wire to be strung through when ready to hang.

David finishes with stamping the date and number of the print on the back, and signs his name. The wall piece needs to stiffen to leather hard before it's turned over to avoid sagging. Once flipped, smooth the corners by hand to remove the sharp edges (figure 12). The rounded corners also help the surfaces dry more evenly and avoid unnecessary cracking or separating.

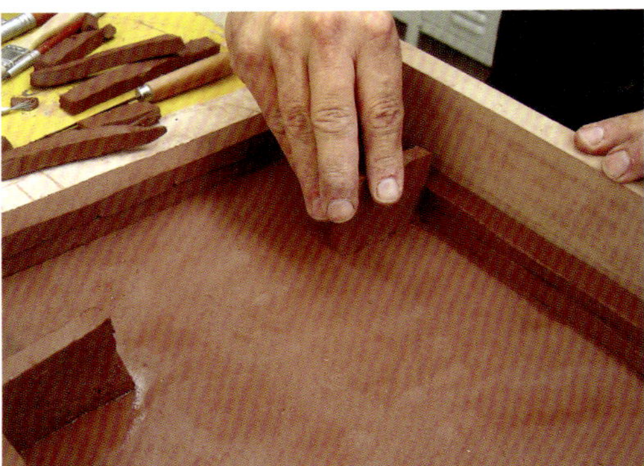

9. Place gussets a third of the way down.

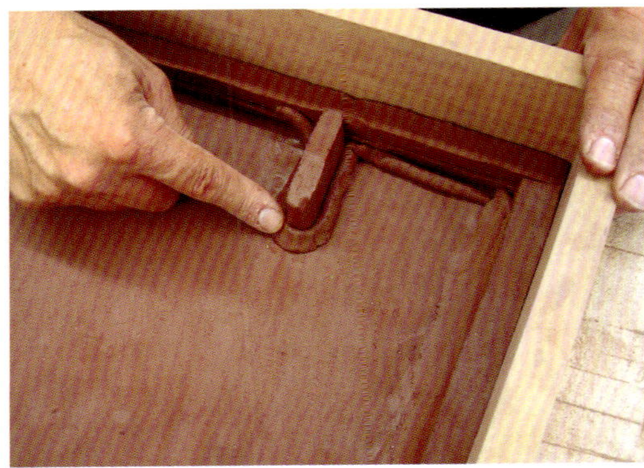

10. Press and smooth a coil into all seams.

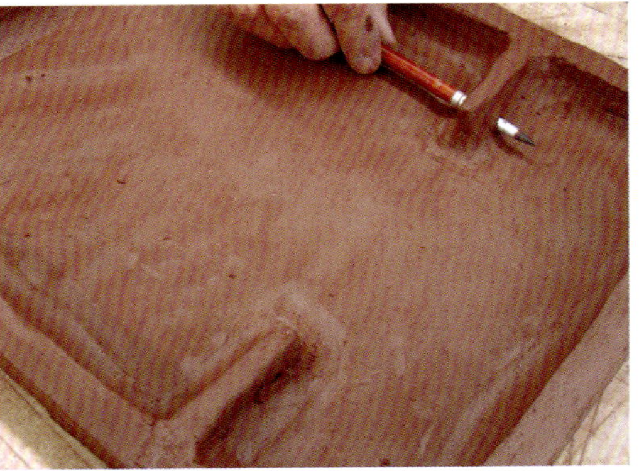

11. Poke holes in the center of the brackets.

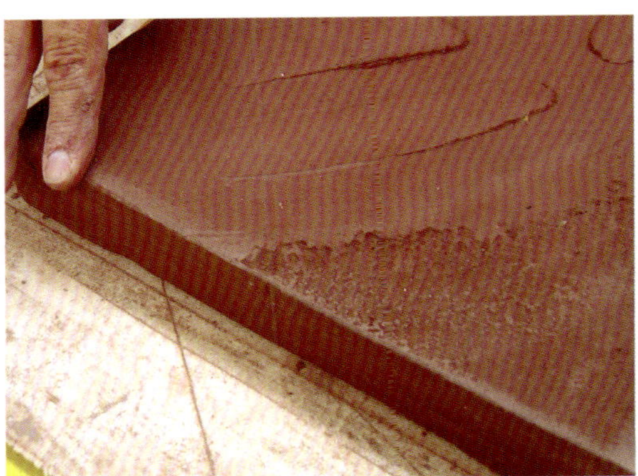

12. Smooth corners to remove sharp edges.

Finishing touches

David bisque fires to cone 03, then brushes on a black copper oxide wash into the recessed areas of the relief for added visual depth. After the wash has dried, he applies three coats of Amaco L-518 Lustre Gold, allowing the glaze to dry thoroughly between coats. After the glaze firing to cone 03, a 10- or 12-gauge solid copper wire is strung through the holes in the brackets and the piece is ready to hang.

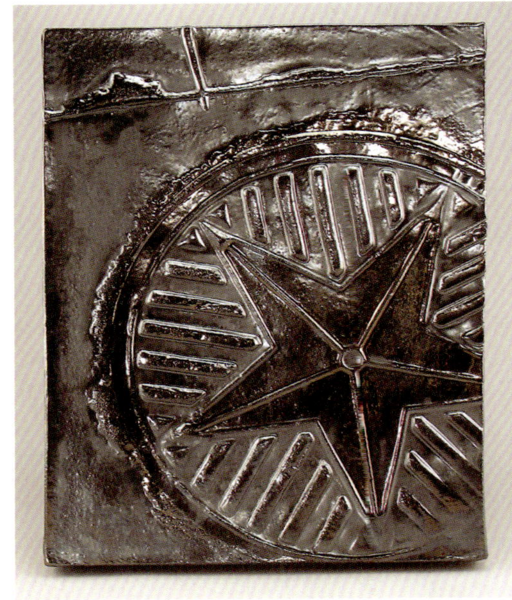

Forming & Texture

TEXTURES FROM GLASS MOLDS

by Lou Roess

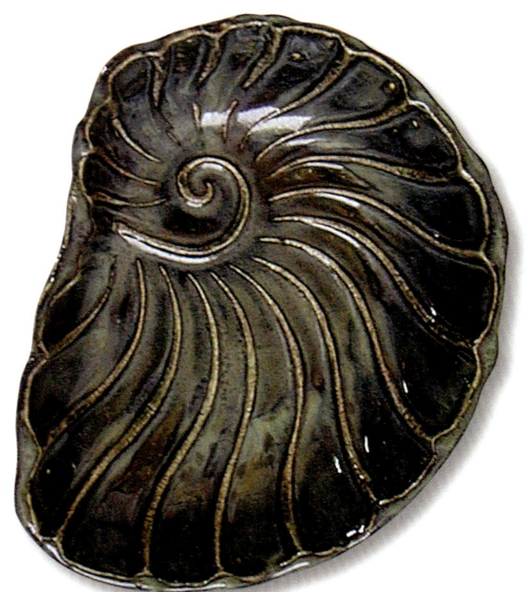

Bowl in the shape of a shell made by pressing a slab of clay onto an old glass form.

Old thrift shop glassware that has raised or impressed designs can add variety and texture to your ware. Impressing your ceramic plates and bowls with designs from the back of glassware is an interesting way to add interest to your ceramic pieces. By pressing a slab of clay on the back of the glass, you can transfer the design to the front of a plate or bowl.

You can find reasonably priced glassware with interesting designs to serve as molds at thrift shops and variety stores. Or you can pick through the pieces at antique stores. Once you start looking, you'll find many different kinds of glassware with a variety of interesting designs to use as molds.

Preparing the Slab

Once you've selected a mold, roll out a slab of clay the size and thickness needed for the plate or bowl you're making. Leave about 2–3 extra inches all around to allow for trimming. How thick you make your slab depends on how big it is—the bigger the item, the thicker your slab should be.

A couple of handling tips: First, rolling out your slab on a piece of cloth makes it easier to handle. Second, rolling a slab in just one direction can cause stress and warping, so flip your slab over several times and change the rolling direction to minimize warping.

Once your slab is the right size and thickness, place your mold on the slab and cut out the general shape, leaving a border of 2–3 inches. Allow the slab to dry until you can smooth it with a rubber rib or finish the surface the way you desire. If you want to use a slip on the clay surface, now is the time to apply it and let it stiffen. Applying it after molding the form may obscure details.

Preparing the Mold

Apply a layer of tissue paper to separate the surface of the mold and the clay. Tissue paper works well because it's thin yet strong enough to be smoothed over the damp clay surface without tearing. You also could use light plastic, like dry

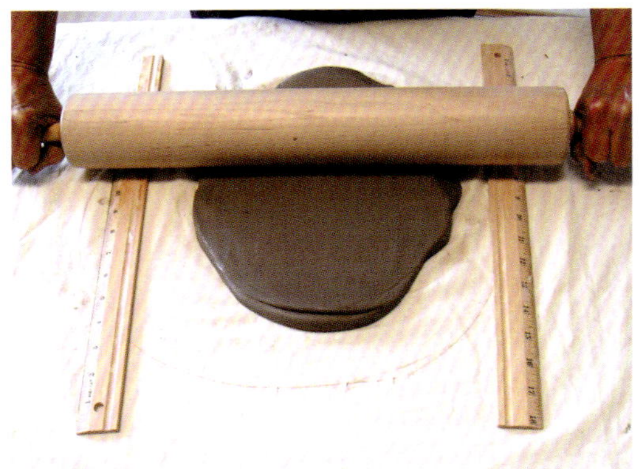
1. Roll out a slab on a piece of cloth.

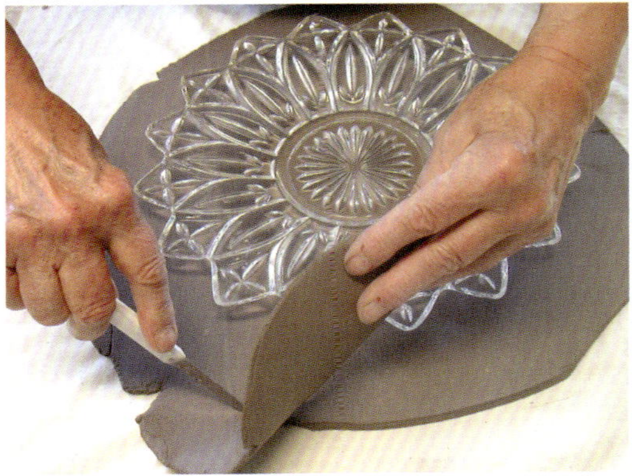
2. Place glass mold on the slab and cut out shape.

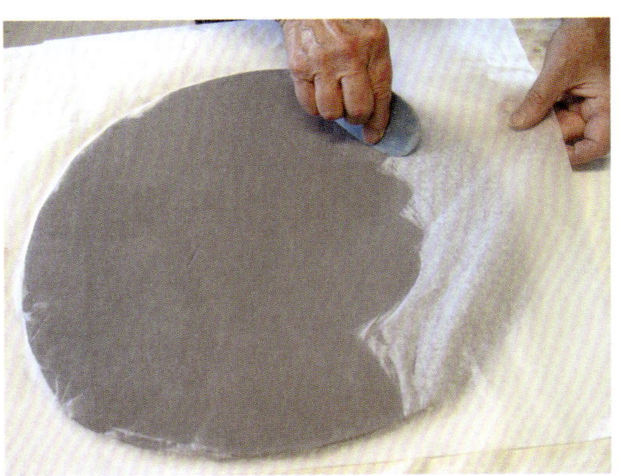
3. Smooth the slab then apply a layer of tissue paper.

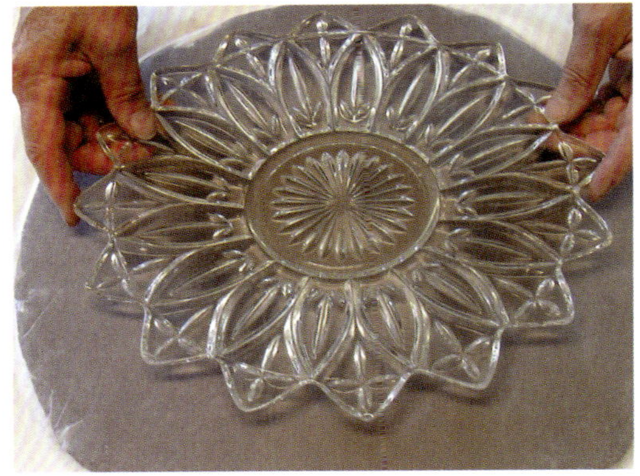
4. Place mold on top of slab.

cleaner bags, or dust the surface liberally with talc, but talc may affect the color of the clay after firing, and plastic may make it hard to trim the edge. Also, remove the plastic to allow proper even drying.

Using your fingers or a soft rubber rib, smooth the tissue outward from the center to the edge. If ridges form, lift and re-smooth. Work quickly so the paper doesn't become saturated and tear.

Molding

Place your glass mold on top of the clay slab with the patterned surface against the tissue paper, then quickly and smoothly invert the mold and clay. This method keeps the paper attached to the clay better than picking it up and inverting it onto the mold.

For the next step, the cloth should be uniformly damp. If dry, dampen it with a little water from a spray bottle. Use a soft rubber rib to wipe the surface gently but firmly to get a smooth surface on the back of the piece while pressing in the design. Wipe in different directions around the slab as well as from its edges to the center. Be sure you cover the whole surface. (If you mark a starting point on the cloth and work systematically, you're less apt to miss a spot.)

Remove the cloth and press the clay down around the edge to conform to the shape. Be careful not to press too hard or you'll create a thin area around the edge.

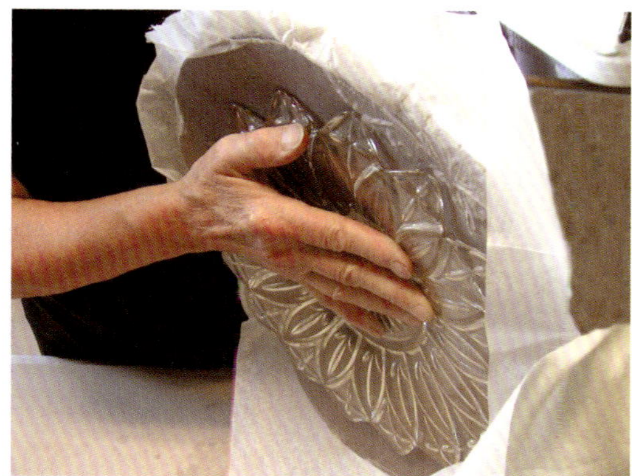
5. Turn mold and clay over quickly and smoothly.

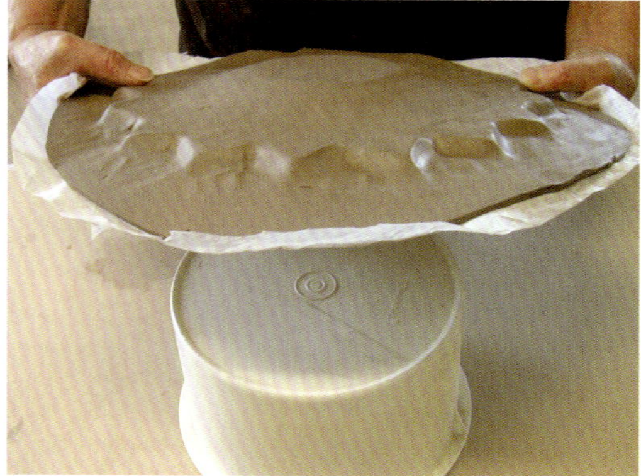
6. Place mold in a chuck to elevate it.

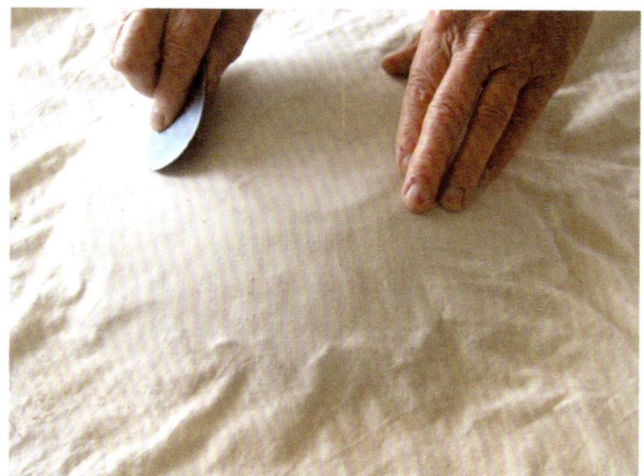
7. Press clay gently but firmly into the mold.

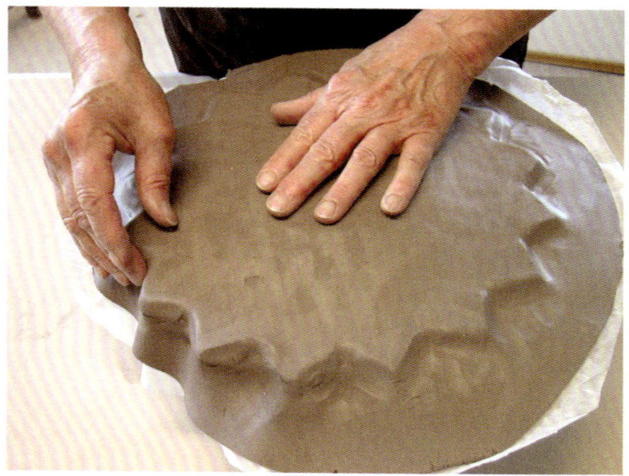
8. Carefully press edges to conform to mold.

Curing and Trimming

Allow the clay to dry until it's soft leather hard. Use a thin knife to trim the excess clay. Press on the clay just in front of your blade so the cutting action doesn't pull on the clay edge and tear it apart.

Be careful not to trim the rim too thin. With experience, you'll be able to judge just how much clay to leave around the edge of the plate.

When the clay has stiffened enough to hold its shape, but not so much that the rim starts to crack from the shrinkage, turn the mold over and, using your thumbs, gently separate the edges of the clay from the mold. Work all the way around the rim before removing the mold.

Next, smooth the edges. When the clay is leather hard, use a little water to smooth the rim between your thumb and forefinger. If you used slip on the clay earlier, use the same slip instead of water for smoothing the edges.

Firing and Glazing

Allow to dry completely, then bisque. After firing, you may find some ash from the paper left on the fired piece. Simply wipe it off with a damp sponge before glazing. As far as glaze is concerned, I like to use one that breaks all over the molded surface to accentuate the design.

The Process

Roll out a slab of clay on a piece of cloth (figure 1) then place the glass mold on the slab and cut out the general shape, leaving a border of 2–3 inches for trimming (figure 2).

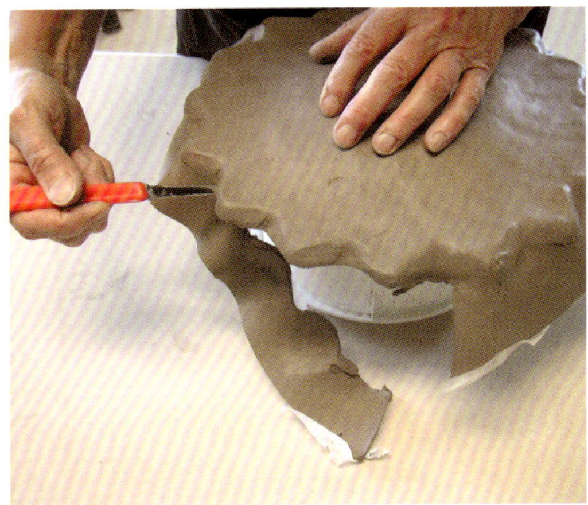
9. Trim excess clay.

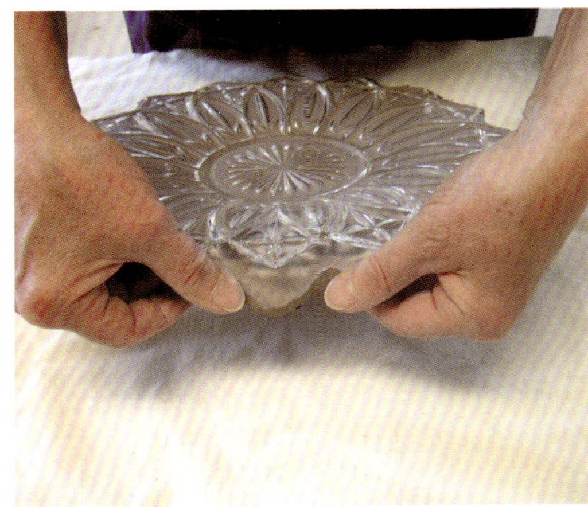
10. When leather hard, flip and remove clay.

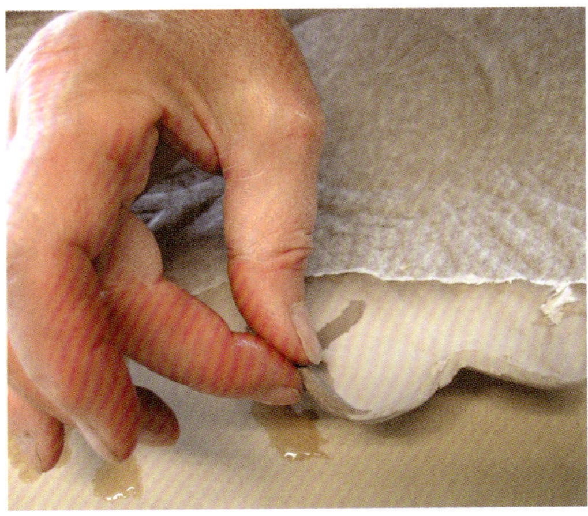
11. Smooth rim using a little water.

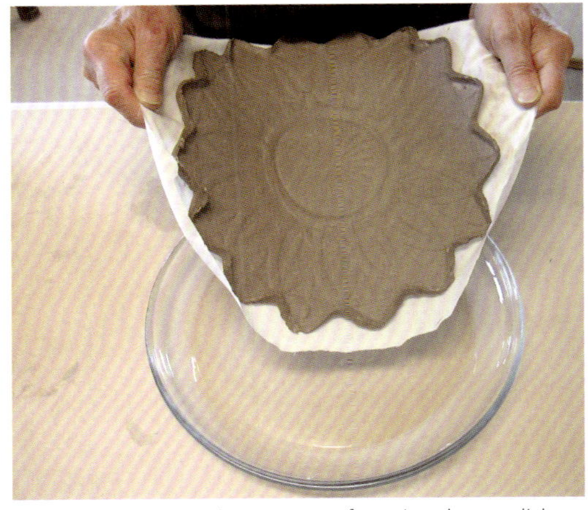
12. To prevent sagging, support form in a larger dish.

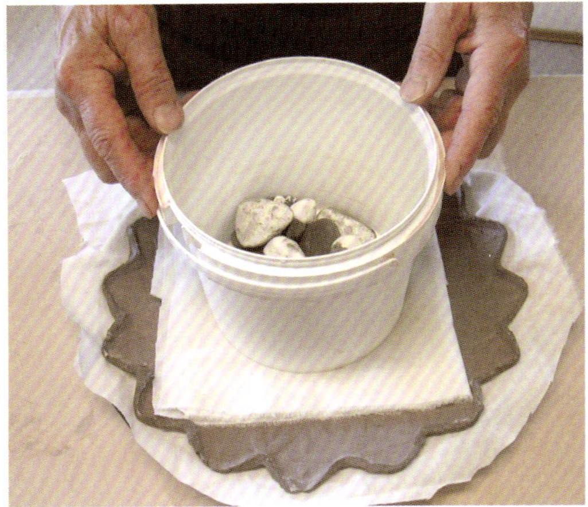
13. Add weight on a piece of foam to prevent warping.

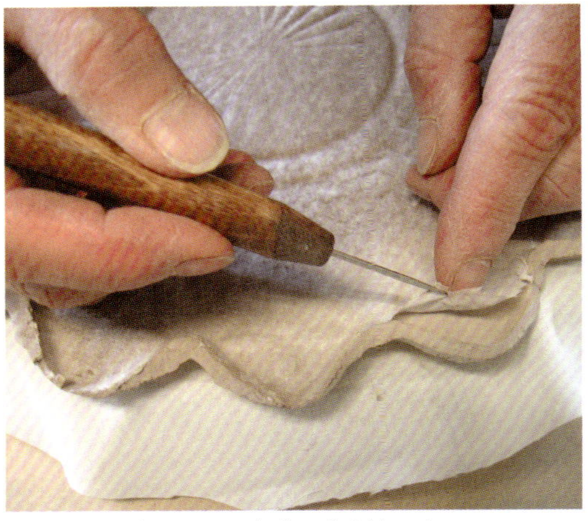
14. Remove tissue paper before finishing rim.

Let the slab dry until you can smooth it with a rubber rib and apply a layer of tissue paper to separate the mold and the clay (figure 3). Place the mold on top of the slab with the patterned surface against the tissue paper (figure 4). Quickly and smoothly invert the mold and clay, (figure 5) and place the mold on a chuck in order to raise it off the table (figure 6).

Use a rubber rib over a uniformly damp, but not soggy cloth, to press the entire surface gently but firmly (figure 7) then carefully press the edges of the slab to conform to the mold (figure 8). When leather hard, trim the excess clay (figure 9). Hold the blade parallel to the table, and cut carefully so it doesn't tear the clay. When it's dry enough to hold its shape, flip and remove it from the mold (figure 10). Smooth the rim by using a little water between your thumb and forefinger (figure 11).

Troubleshooting Tips

After molding, prevent sagging by placing the piece back inside a pie plate or another, slightly larger mold to give it support (figure 12).

To prevent warping, set a weight on a padded surface like foam rubber so you don't mar the molded surface (figure 13). Before finishing the rim, rub or pull off the tissue paper at the rim to prevent it from bunching up and leaving ridges in the clay while finishing the edge (figure 14). The rest will burn off during bisque firing.

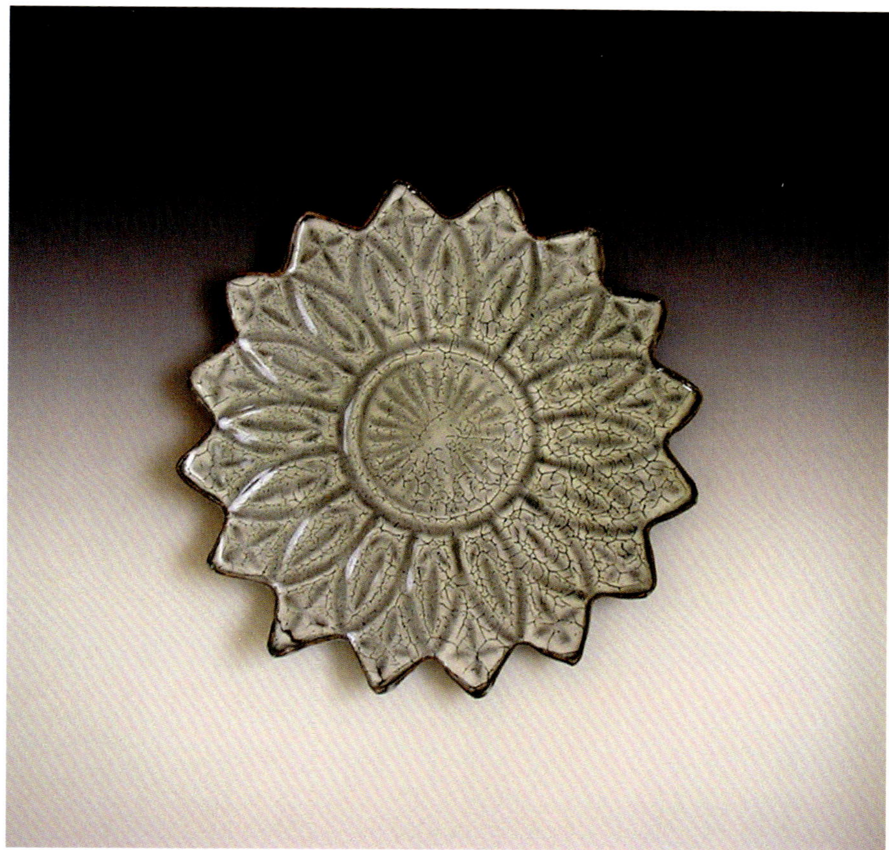

Example of a plate produced from a glassware mold, fired to cone 6, oxidation.

Forming & Texture

LANA WILSON'S TEXTURED SURFACES

by Annie Chrietzberg

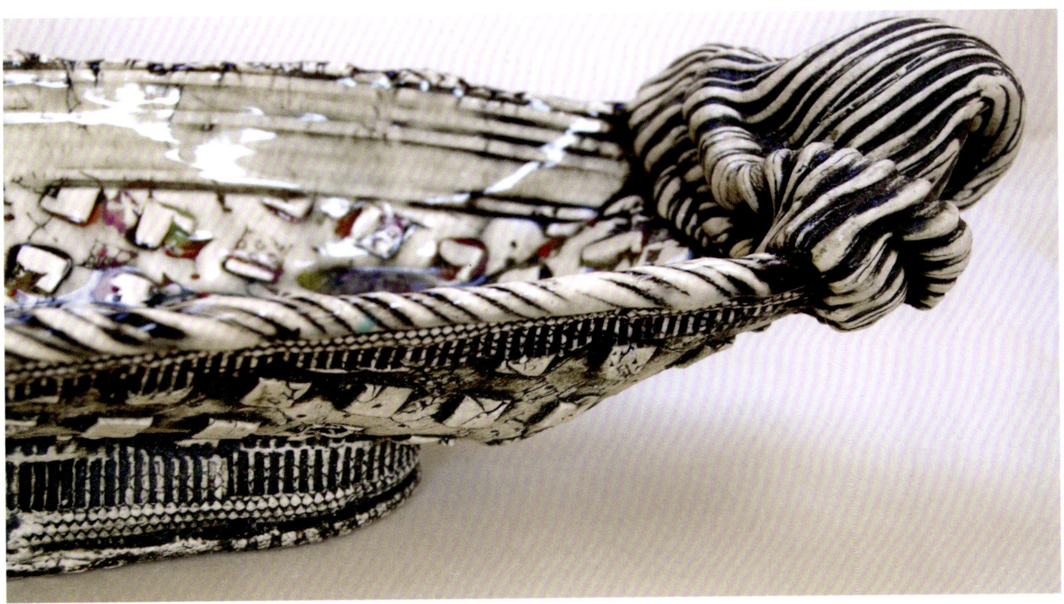

Detail of one of Lana Wilson's richly textured platters.

Lana Wilson's career spans more than 40 years and includes a vast repertoire of form and surface considerations, which she regularly shares with students.

Lana worked with functional stoneware for the first seventeen years of her life in ceramics. And then a job at a community college caught her eye, so, at age 43, she went back to school to get her master's degree. For Lana, graduate school completely changed the course of her work. "Number one, it opened up the way to lots of exploring and experimenting, which has never ended," she said. "Number two, I started making non-functional work and using the electric kiln exclusively, neither of which I'd ever done before." Now, Lana's focus has returned to functional pieces. She told me one reason: "I want my grandchildren to eat off of things that I made."

Texture Throughout

Lana applies texture in layers, and does so throughout her making process. During my visit, she made a serving platter to demonstrate how she works.

After using a slab roller to make a large slab, she lays out some fruit netting on the table, and sets the slab on top of it. This netting forms the basis of the texture composition on the back of the piece, though Lana will embellish it more at later stages. After smoothing the front of the slab with a small squeegee, Lana uses a wooden rolling pin from a pastry store to lay down some waffle texture, which created impressed squares, then in an adjacent area, she lay down and rolled over plastic sink mats that left larger, high-relief squares (figure 1). I watched her then target and go after some of the high relief squares with her small hand-held

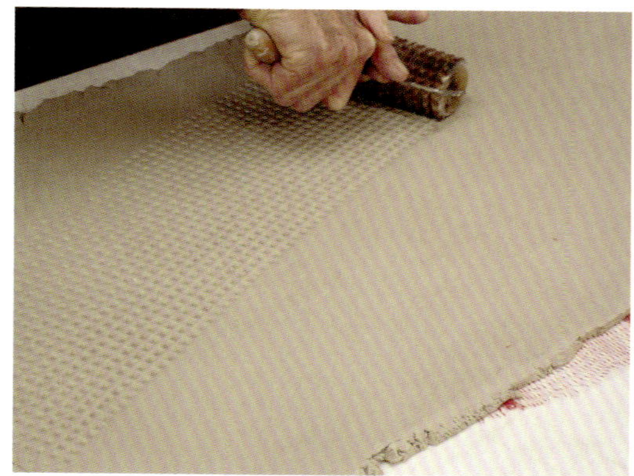

1. Smooth out a slab, layer, and press in objects then texture the surface.

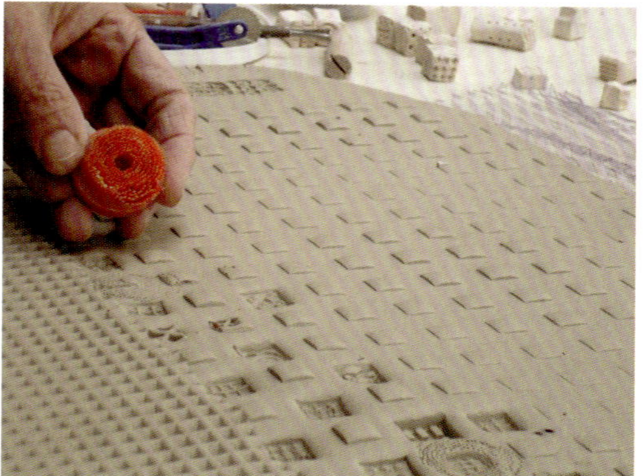

2. Use hand tools, stamps, and found objects to embellish the slab.

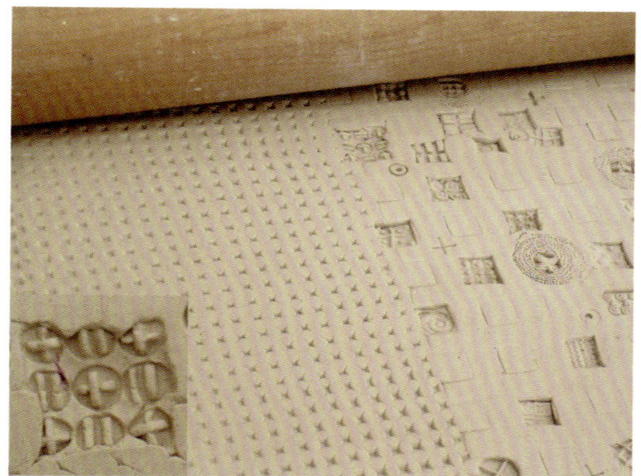

3. Roll over the texture with a rolling pin, to soften and tuck in the marks (detail shown in inset).

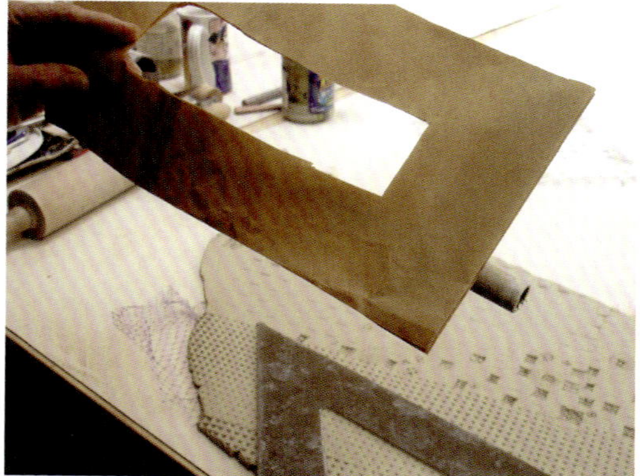

4. Use a handmade viewfinder to select the best part of the textured surface.

stamps, and some found objects, inverting them with embellishment (figure 2).

I was surprised when she picked up her rolling pin and rolled over the work she had just done (figure 3), but she explained to me, "You see, this softens it and makes it more interesting. I don't want it to look like plastic surgery. I don't like the whole Southern California glitzy sequin scene, I like old, worn friends. I like layers; I walk regularly in the Torrey Pines State Reserve when I'm home in San Diego. I love those layers of information around me."

I looked, and the effect she had created by rolling over existing texture was to "tuck in" all the little marks she had made, like treasures in lockets. After tucking in her preliminary and secondary texture with a rolling pin, Lana embellished further with one of her new favorite items, the red scrubby applicator from a Shout bottle, and an old favorite, a seamstress' marking tool.

Forming the Platter

Lana had created a slab much larger than what she actually needed for the piece she had in mind. She cut a framing device out of a piece of paper roughly the proportions of her intended serving dish (figure 4). She used this viewfinder to locate the best part of her texture drawing, marked the boundaries cut out the shape by using a straightedge.

Lana needed to take two darts out of each end to have the flat shape rise up into the form she wanted. She took the triangular piece of clay she

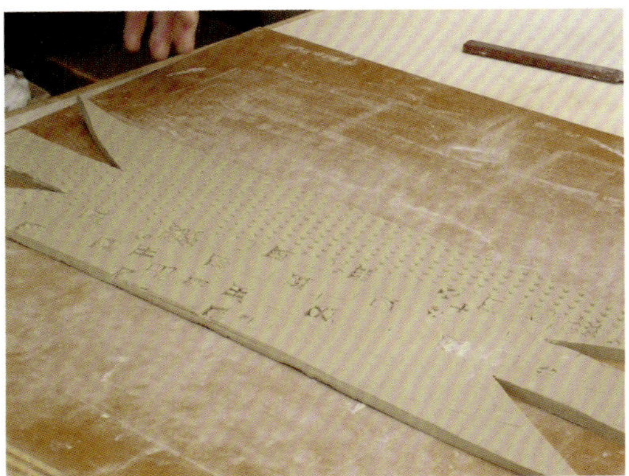

5. Cut out a dart then use it as a pattern to cut the remaining darts.

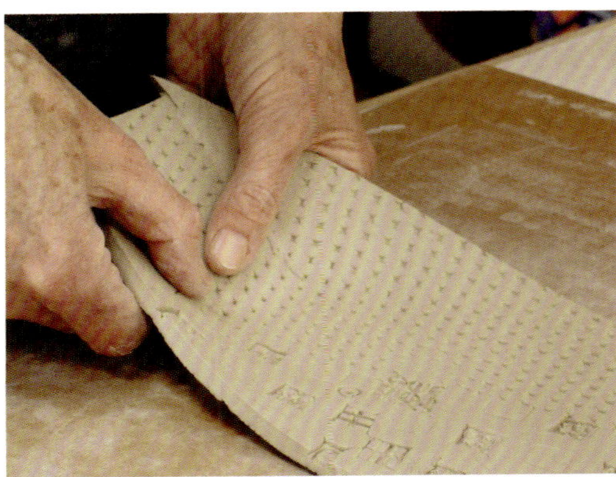

6. Lift and connect the edges where the darts have been removed.

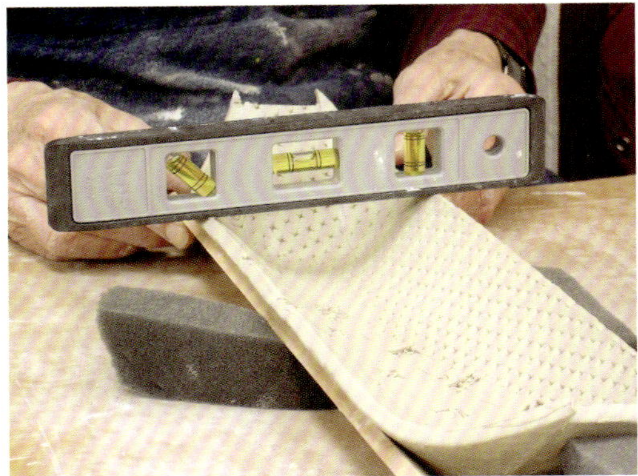

7. Prop the piece up, level the sides with a spirit level, and adjust as needed.

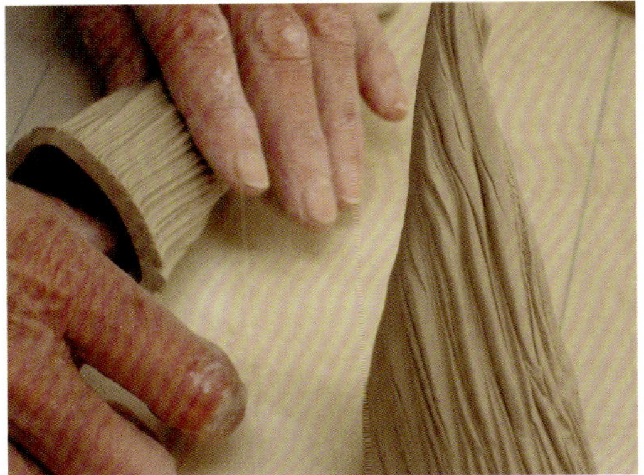

8. For handles, shape cones from large triangles cut from a textured slab.

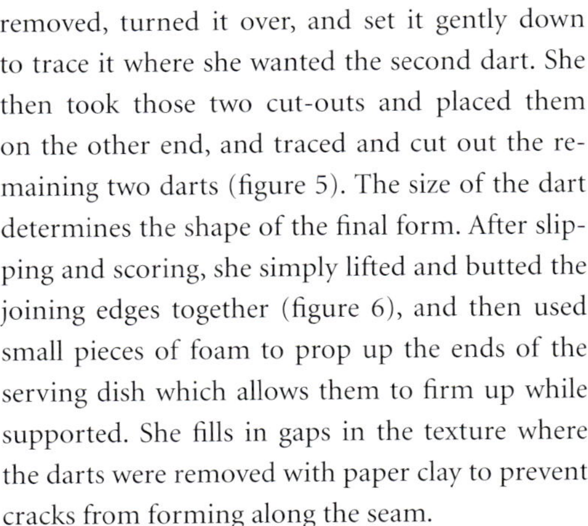

removed, turned it over, and set it gently down to trace it where she wanted the second dart. She then took those two cut-outs and placed them on the other end, and traced and cut out the remaining two darts (figure 5). The size of the dart determines the shape of the final form. After slipping and scoring, she simply lifted and butted the joining edges together (figure 6), and then used small pieces of foam to prop up the ends of the serving dish which allows them to firm up while supported. She fills in gaps in the texture where the darts were removed with paper clay to prevent cracks from forming along the seam.

To address the sides, Lana grabbed a couple of paint stirring sticks, which she used to lift the sides and then shoved pieces of foam beneath to hold them in place. She filled in gaps that had been made by cutting through existing texture on the edges, and then compressed and beveled those edges with a pony roller. Then, she used a spirit level to make sure the edges, were, um, level (figure 7). "I don't know a gallery who would take a piece that's not level," she murmured as she made slight adjustments. "There we go!"

Making Handles

The next task was to make the handles. First, she textures a slab and cuts out large triangles, then she rolls them into a cone (figure 8), seals them using a pony roller, and drops them on her workbench (figure 9). They magically gain character with each *whump*. Once she is satisfied with the result, she

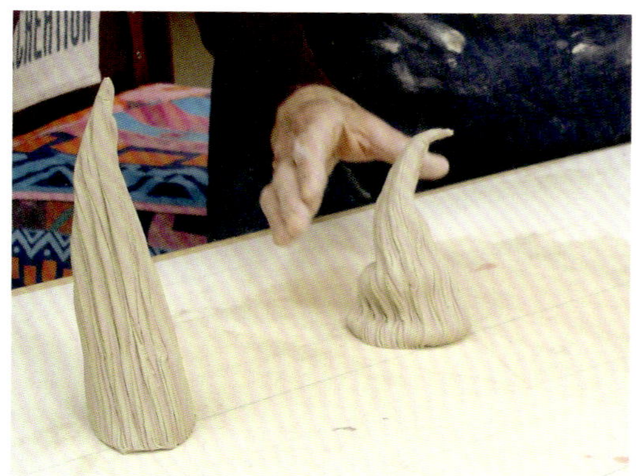

9. Lift and drop the cone two or three times to get an organic shape.

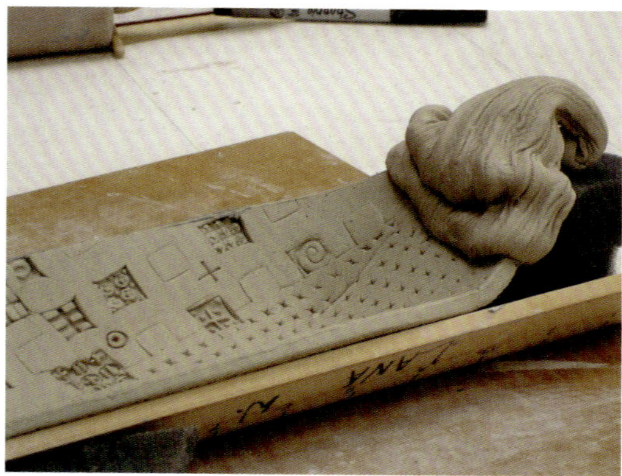

10. Slip and score the handle in place, then support it with foam.

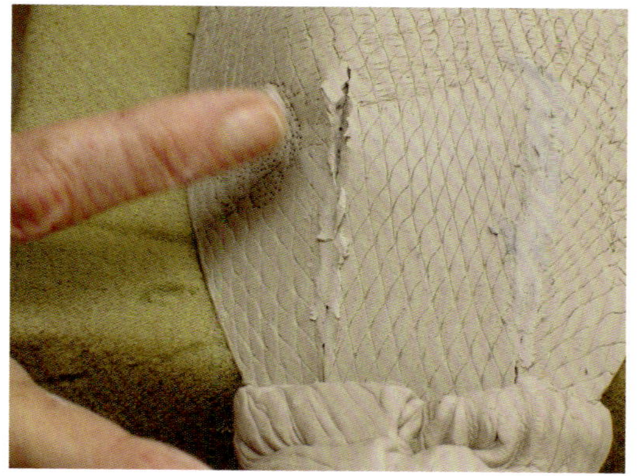

11. Turn piece over on foam supports, fill seams and adorn the repair.

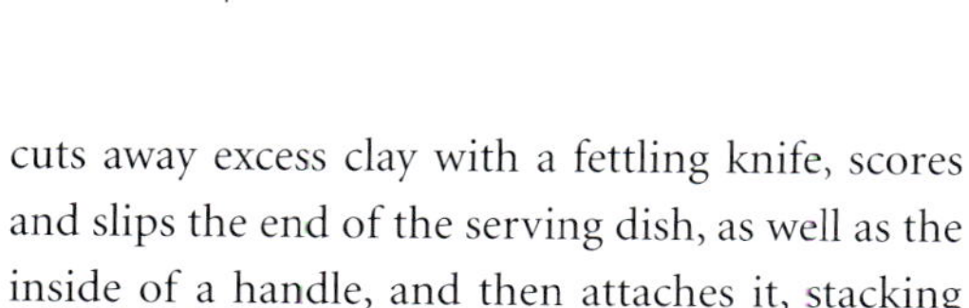

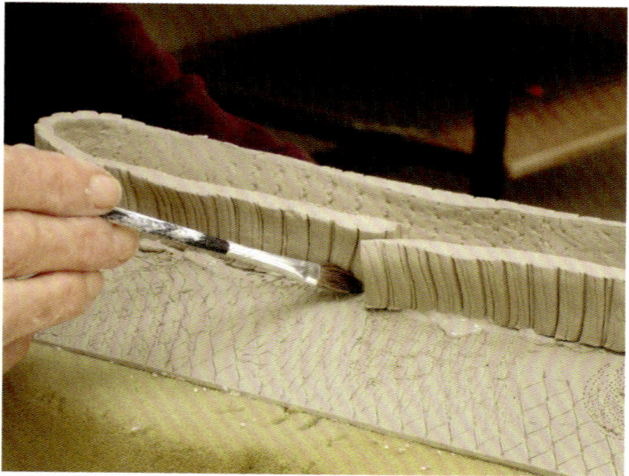

12. Make a foot from a long, thin piece cut from a textured slab.

cuts away excess clay with a fettling knife, scores and slips the end of the serving dish, as well as the inside of a handle, and then attaches it, stacking foam beneath it for support (figure 10).

Lana constantly manipulates the surface of her pieces as she is making, adding texture as she goes. After attaching the handles, she grabbed a wooden dowel with sharpened ends (a pencil would work, too) to both re-draw and enhance existing lines. After the piece had dried to leather hard, she removed the bolsters and turned it over on a large piece of foam to access the bottom. She filled the gaps in the seams with paper clay, again to strengthen them and prevent cracking (figure 11). When she makes a repair like this, she adorns it. "I could teach a whole course on cheating," she joked, while rolling a seamstress' marking tool over the filled-in seam.

Adding a Foot

The last part of the serving dish project was to make and attach a foot. Before she had turned the piece over, she had taken an approximate measurement with a seamstress' measuring tape, and had created a long slab to texture. She played around a bit with some scrap clay to determine the appropriate height, textured the slab, and used a straightedge to cut a long strip of clay for the foot. She picked up the long strip in loose folds and dropped it a few times on the table. "This makes an undulating line I just love," she told me as she worked.

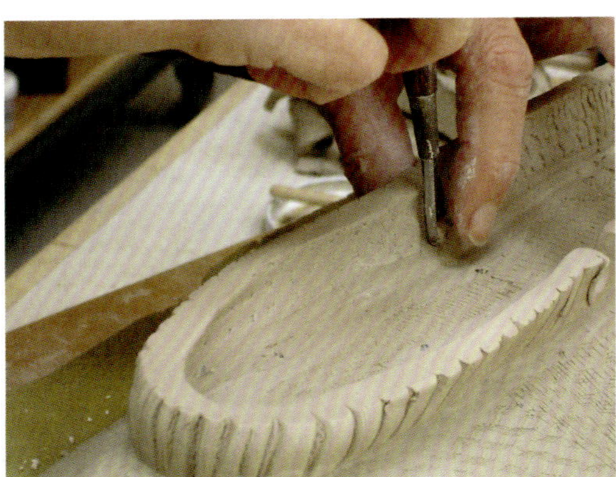

13. Smooth the foot with a roller and cut decorative arches through it.

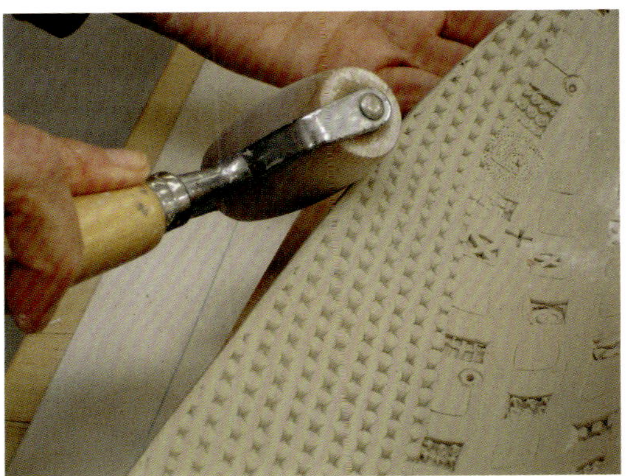

14. Use a pony roller to bevel and finish both sides of the platter's edge

She placed the foot on the bottom of the pot, shaped it how she wanted it, and cut the excess away, then joined the foot into a ring. After scoring and slipping the areas that need joined, she attached the foot ring to the bottom of the serving dish and used a dry soft brush to remove excess slip and blend the seam (figure 12). She then used a common loop tool to create a little looped arch on each side of the foot (figure 13). She rolled the edge with a pony roller (figure 14), used a ware board to flip the piece right side up, and used the spirit level again to make adjustments.

Lana has a delightfully free, direct, and easy way of making, but don't let that fool you into thinking she doesn't take her time in the studio seriously. "I've changed my style of work about six times through out my career, and each time it takes me about six months to a year to figure it out," she told me. "People don't realize that being an artist is really about daily discipline; when I'm working, I want my time to work. I'm not one of those ladies who does lunch. Ceramics is far too expansive for that."

Finishing

Lana Wilson's work is mostly black and white with bits of vibrant color splashed about. She says, "I have a background in painting, and this technique really appeals to the painter in me." She gleaned this current surface treatment from two artists, Denise Smith of Ann Arbor, Michigan, and Claudia Reese, a potter from Texas.

Simple Slip

To prepare the slip, Lana takes 100 grams of small pieces of bone dry clay and adds 10–50 grams of a stain. The percentages of stains varies according to the intensity of color she is trying to achieve.

The clay Lana uses is Half & Half from Laguna, formulated for firing at cone 5, though she fires it to cone 6. This clay body is half porcelain and half white stoneware. It's not as white as porcelain, but it does fire white rather than yellow in oxidation, isn't as finicky as porcelain, and works well with Lana's making methods. If you're buying clay from the East Coast, she suggests a clay body called Little Loafers from Highwater Clays.

Easy Application

The technique is simple. On a piece of bisqueware, first brush on black slip or one of the base colors (figure 15) then sponge it off, leaving slip in the crevices (figure 16). Then, using colored slips dab on bits of color here and there (figure 17). Remove some of that with steel wool (figure 18). "I can't use water for this step or it will muddy the colors," Lana explains. After the piece has dried, Lana uses a clear glaze to seal the surface.

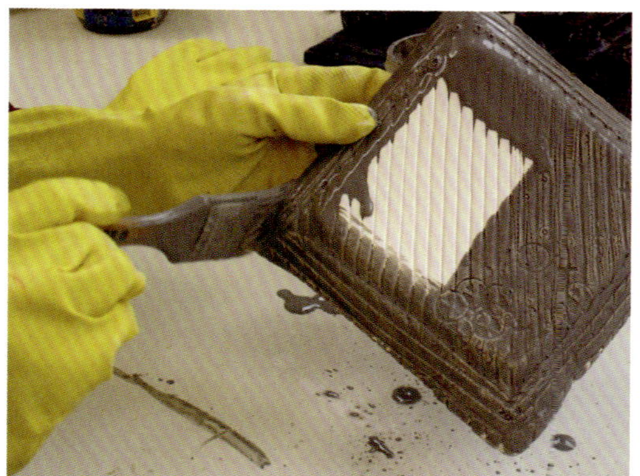
15. First brush on black slip or one of the other dark base colors below.

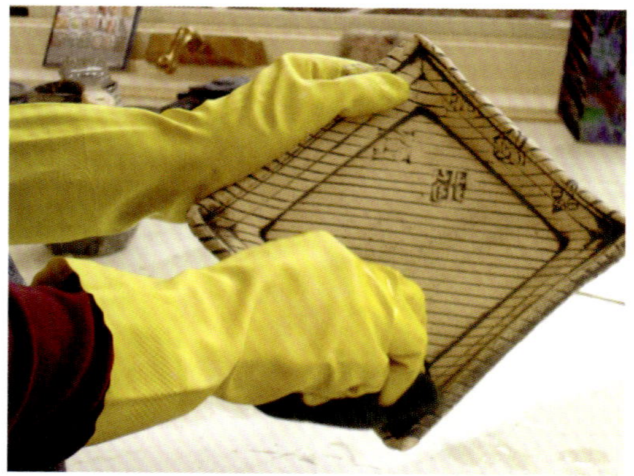
16. Sponge it off, leaving slip in the crevices.

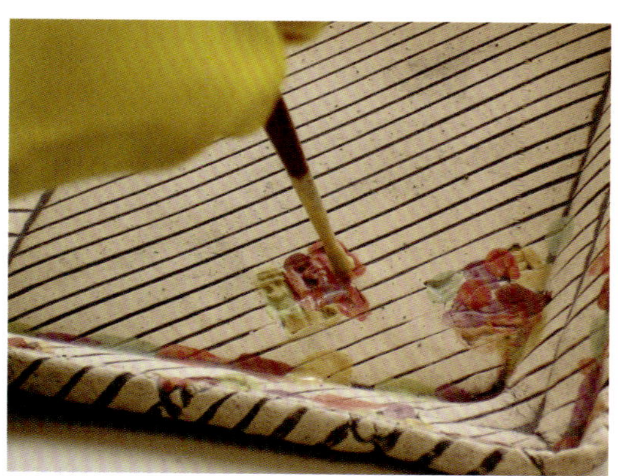
17. Using colored slips, dab on bits of color here and there, particularly in the deeper texture.

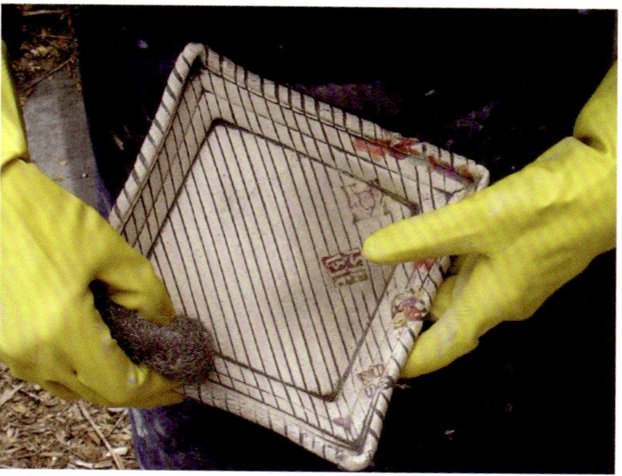
18. Remove some of the colored slip with steel wool in order to bring the clay surface through again.

Recipes

There are two groups of colored slips. The first group Lana uses for the base coat that she washes off, leaving color in all the recesses. The accent slips are more intense and removed with steel wool. All stains are Mason stains except for 27496 Persimmon Red, which is from Cerdec. Add the stains and bone dry clay to water and allow to sit for 30–60 minutes so it will mix easier.

BASE COAT OR WASH COLORS

6600 Best Black	10 %
6339 Royal Blue	5-10%
6069 Dark Coral	35 %

ACCENT SLIPS

6129 Golden Ambrosia	30 %
6485 Titanium Yellow	20 %
6024 Orange	30 %
6236 Chartreuse	50 %
6027 Tangerine	15 %
6211 Pea Green	50 %
6288 Turquoise	50 %
6242 Bermuda	10 %
6069 Dark Coral	35 %
6122 Cedar	25 %
6304 Violet	60 %
K5997 Cherry Red*	30 %
27496 Persimmon Red (Cerdec)*	30 %

* Inclusion pigments

Forming & Texture

HOW TO CREATE AGATEWARE

by Michelle Erickson and Robert Hunter

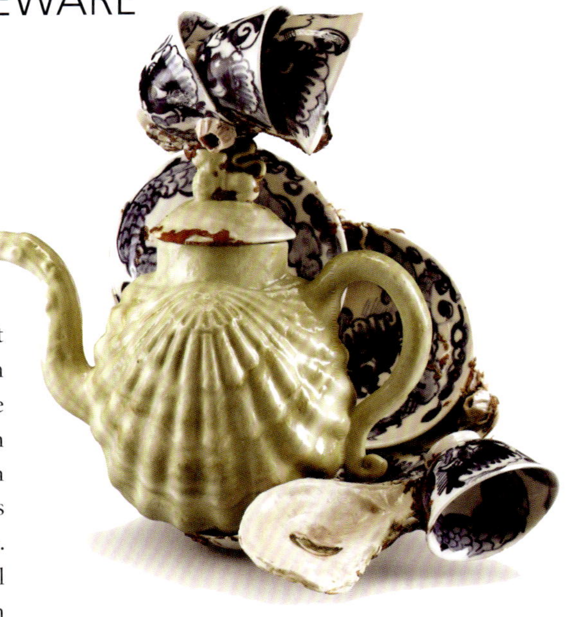

Dragon Junk, by Michelle Erickson, 12 inches in height, press molded and wheel thrown, colored porcelains, indigenous clays, cobalt underglaze decoration. The title of this piece, which is in the collection of the Yale University Art Gallery, refers to the artifacts excavated from the Chinese junk ships that sank in the process of exporting 'China' to the Western world. Conceptually, it speaks to objects changed by time through their environment. The jade-like agated copper porcelain here also speaks to a geological phenomenon of precious stone associated with the east to further the reference of crossing time and culture. The double entendre of the pecten shell form for the teapot mirrors its environment on the ocean floor. —Michelle Erickson

Semiprecious stones such as agate were prevalent as design elements in Chinese, Greek, and Roman societies and often associated with nobility. The use of multiple colored clays to imitate agate can be traced to antiquity. Beginning in the late 17th century, this technique was used to fashion a class of English ceramics generally known as agateware.

English agateware has been made for useful and ornamental purposes, collected, and written about for centuries. However, only limited discussions of production methods have been published. Our approach to decoding and recreating English agateware began with the examination of antique specimens and archaeological fragments.

Agateware can be divided into two broad categories: thrown agate and laid agate. Thrown agate describes a vessel formed on a wheel using a prepared mixture of various colored clays. We'll be focusing on laid agate, which refers to an object created from a thin sheet or slab made of agate clay. This thin sheet is draped or laid in the mold and pressed into shape—hence our use of the term laid.

While we'll examine how two or more colors of clay are used to make a variegated ceramic body generally known as agateware, a similar appearance created with slips (liquid clays) is usually referred to as marbled decoration. Although these two terms are sometimes confused, marbled decoration implies a surface treatment whereas agateware refers to a solid clay fabric.

A Brief History of Laid Agate

Laid agateware is inherently different from thrown agateware in that the pattern must first be prepared before the shape is made. In other words, the decoration is made before the pot. The second quarter of the 18th century saw many innovations in the Staffordshire potteries. One of these was the use of molds for creating forms either by slip casting or pressing. Press molding permitted new possibilities for developing agate bodies.

Thomas Whieldon of Fenton Low (1719–1795) is most often recognized for his improvements in agateware undertaken in the 1740s, including the use of white clays stained with metallic oxides. Still, a firm date for the beginning of laid agate in Staffordshire has yet to be established. Beyond the date of its introduction, however, the source of the laid agate pattern is perhaps the more important inquiry. For us, it is clear that 8th-century Tang dynasty Chinese wares inspired many 18th century Staffordshire laid agatewares. The relationship is most obviously visible in the form of globular censers, or incense burners, which are of the same size and shape as the Staffordshire teapots.

The imitation of 8th-century Chinese ceramics by Staffordshire potters is not as improbable as it may seem at first. It is known that contemporary Chinese porcelains and Yixing stonewares served as direct prototypes for many 18th-century Staffordshire tea wares. It is likely that older Chinese wares resided in European and English antiquarian collections. Such antique wares were sought for the "cabinets of curiosities" of the English cognoscenti. Intriguingly, the cabinets belonging to these scientifically minded collectors often included "agates, onyxes, and intaglios."

In 1754, Whieldon entered into a partnership with young Josiah Wedgwood. Excavations at Whieldon's manufactory at Fenton Vivian revealed a number of laid agate wasters, which appeared to have been manufactured during the period of the partnership. One of the most often cited agateware references comes from Josiah Wedgwood's experiment book on March 23, 1759: "I had already made an imitation of Agat which was esteem'd very beautiful, and a considerable improvement…" Just how much he improved the agateware process and whether he had a direct hand in copying Chinese prototypes is undocumented.

Detective Work

Deciphering the technique of 'laid agate' used by the Staffordshire potters in the 18th century was done over the course of four years. It's important to note that most of these insights were gained through direct physical interaction with the artifacts and photographs and not through any written descriptions or formulas. The material published here was not available at the time; and though published material exists, speculative theories on early production methods rarely bear results in practice.

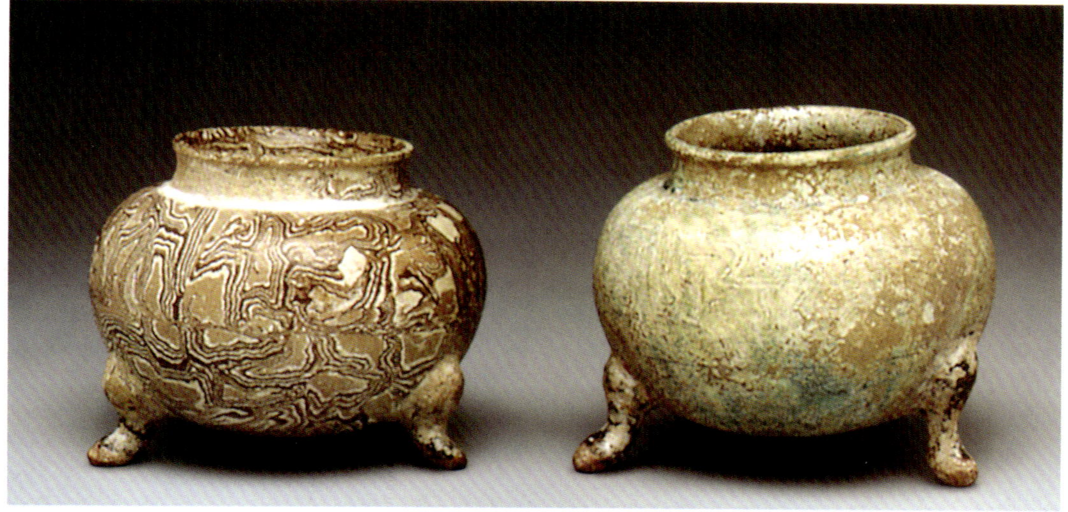

Footed censers, agateware, 3 inches (8 cm) in height, China, Tang Dynasty.
Photos courtesy Bonhams & Butterfields Auctioneers.

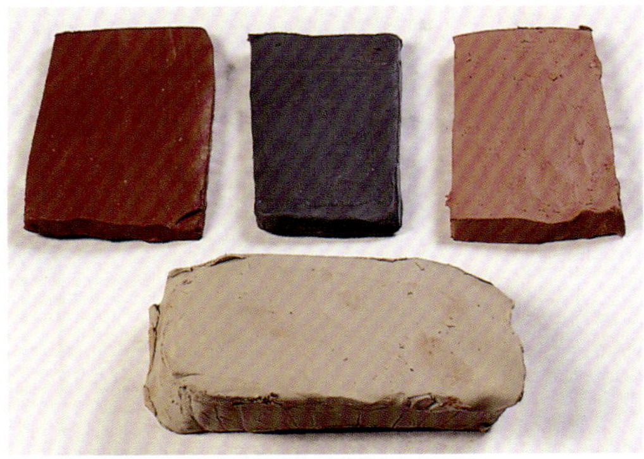

1. Colored clays: (front) uncolored white earthenware; (back) iron oxide, manganese oxide, cobalt carbonate.

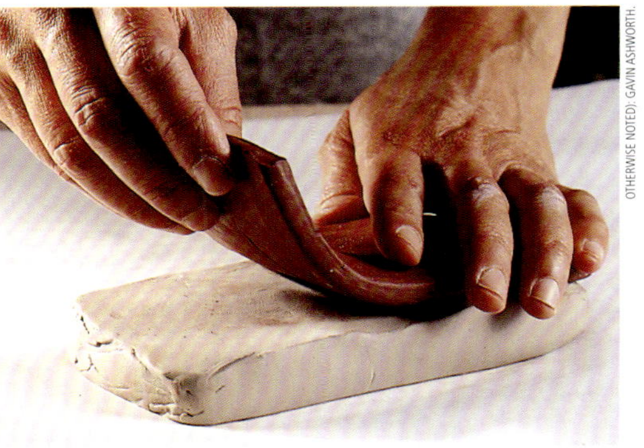

2. Lay a slab of iron enriched red clay onto a base white clay of the same dimensions but three times as thick.

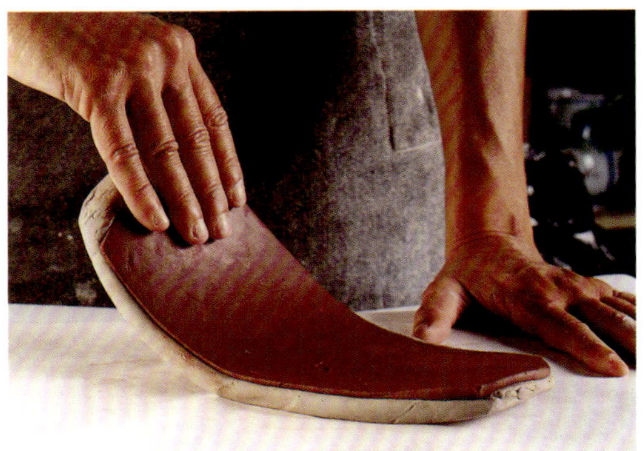

3. Throw the combined slabs down onto a hard table surface to stretch and thin the layers.

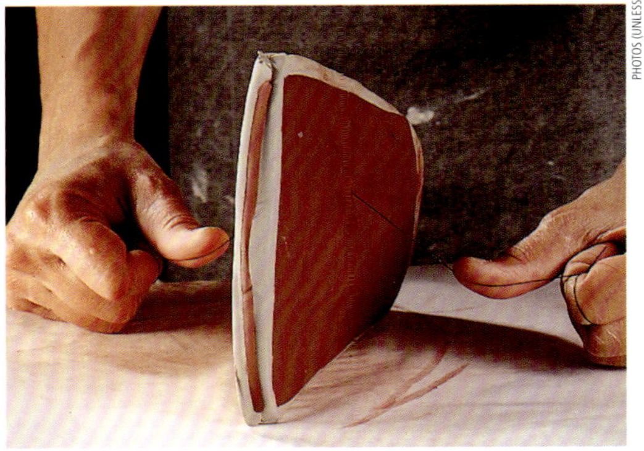

4. Cut the clay slab in half and restack the two pieces. Repeat this process of adding and thinning the layers.

PHOTOS (UNLESS OTHERWISE NOTED): GAVIN ASHWORTH.

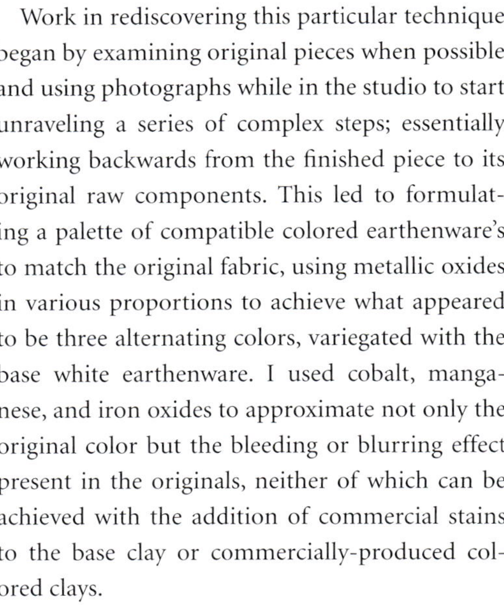

Work in rediscovering this particular technique began by examining original pieces when possible and using photographs while in the studio to start unraveling a series of complex steps; essentially working backwards from the finished piece to its original raw components. This led to formulating a palette of compatible colored earthenware's to match the original fabric, using metallic oxides in various proportions to achieve what appeared to be three alternating colors, variegated with the base white earthenware. I used cobalt, manganese, and iron oxides to approximate not only the original color but the bleeding or blurring effect present in the originals, neither of which can be achieved with the addition of commercial stains to the base clay or commercially-produced colored clays.

I created a "creamware" glaze that would give me the fit, translucency, and hue of the original wares, which took time to achieve. Simultaneously, I began measuring and studying the proportion and design of the specific antique pecten shell teapot example illustrated. In order to proceed, I modeled the original artwork for the teapot and each component in clay accounting for shrinkage and cast separate two-part plaster molds for the teapot, spout, lid and finial. The idea that these wares were molded was generally accepted but the way in which press molding preserved the integrity of the pattern became key to the eventual success of the whole process.

Beyond the molded components was the complex composition of the agate itself, I could achieve random agate patterns relatively easily but it was

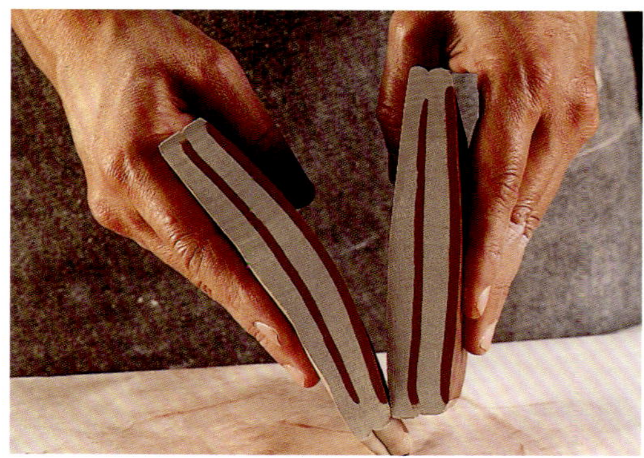

5. The combined clay slab after cutting it the second time reveals the alternating layers.

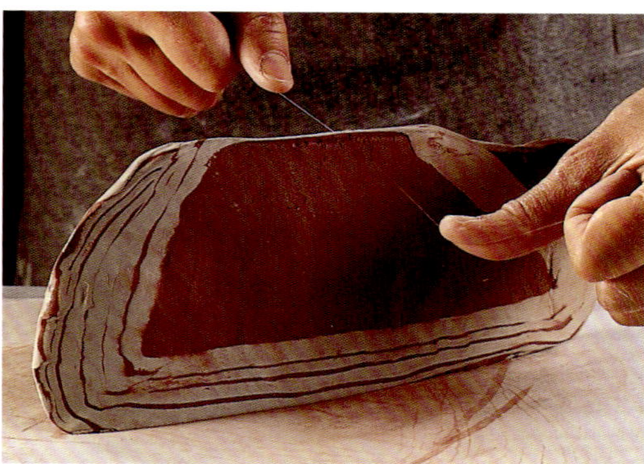

6. Cut the slab in half after repeating the stacking and thinning steps shown in figures 3–5 several times.

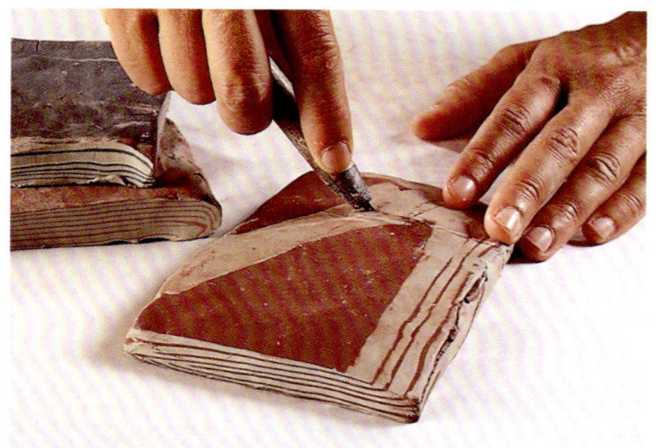

7. Trim the layered slabs to equal rectangular sizes.

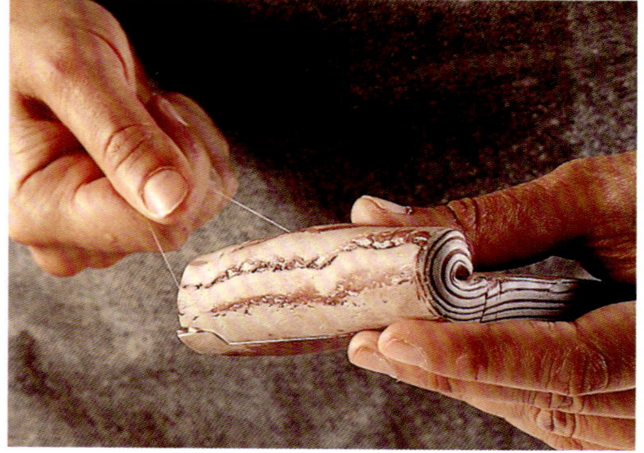

8. Roll one end of each slab into a coil, and cut from the slab.

the challenge of defining a method for this specific agate that allowed for my insight into a technique that has proven to elude many scholars and practicing ceramic artists. Each stage revealed a breakthrough only through trial and error experimentation and gradually the elegant solutions, though labor intensive, began to emerge.

Preparing the Clay

Making agateware is a complicated process; the marbling, instead of being produced on the surface, goes through the body and it requires a different set of skills other than just competent throwing. The initial preparation of clay is the key for creating laid agateware (figure 1). If using naturally colored clays, do tests first to be sure the clays are compatible. The shrinkage rates and firing temperatures need to be the same. Additional considerations include the density, plasticity, elasticity, and strength. The clay slabs are first stacked in a selected sequence (figure 2). Rather than wedging, the stacks are slammed onto a hard surface to elongate and consequently thin the slabs (figure 3). The process continues with cutting and restacking the slabs, thinning and increasing the numbers of layers (figures 4, 5, and 6). The ultimate success of the agate patterning lies in the care taken at this initial stage. If you want more colors in your agate pattern, the three color clay slabs can be prepared in the same way. Once the layered slabs are made, they are trimmed to equal rectangular sizes (figure 7).

Piecing Together a Pattern

After these slabs of thinly layered clays are prepared, they are rolled into tight coils (figure 8).

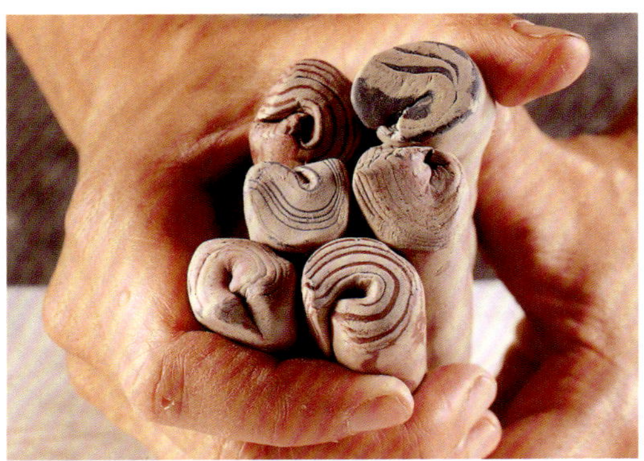

9. Arrange the rolled coils by alternating the colors.

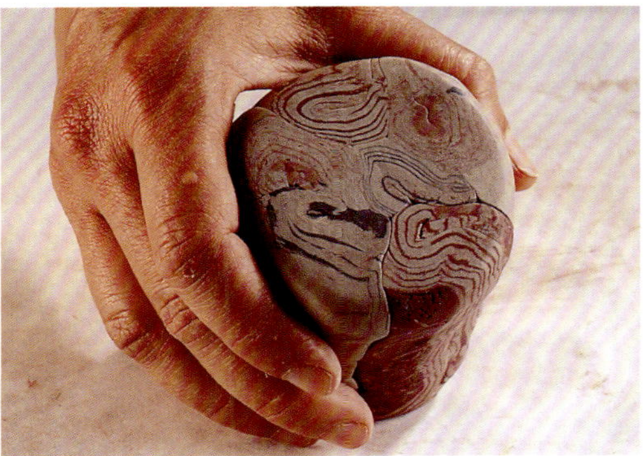

10. Press the rolled and alternating coils into a solid cylindrical mass approximately 3 inches in diameter.

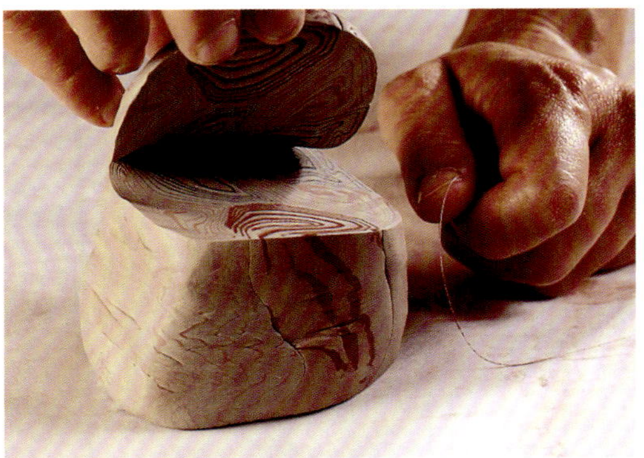

11. Square off the mass and cut thin layers from the stack, revealing the beginnings of the agate pattern.

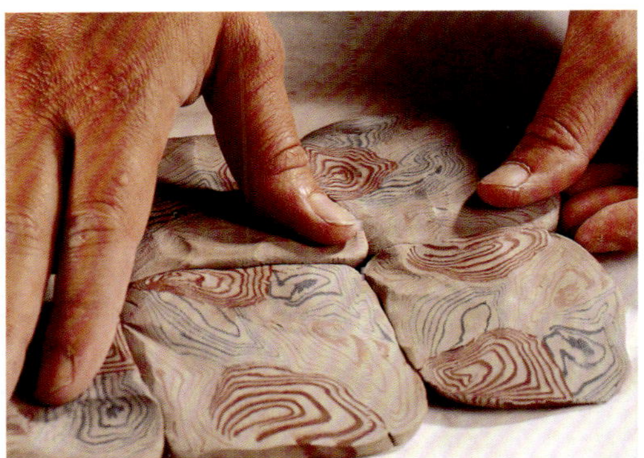

12. Arrange and carefully push the layers together on a flat surface, alternating the patterns.

These coils are then arranged, sometimes by alternating colors (figure 9), and carefully pressed into a single mass (figure 10). From this amalgamated mass, thin slabs are then cut and arranged on a flat surface to begin forming a sheet (figures 11 and 12). At this point, the outcome of the agate striations can be controlled by the placement of the slabs. Once a reconstituted clay sheet is made (figure 13), it is cut into strips and reassembled to emulate the arbitrary nature of the agate pattern (figure 14). Examination of antique pots suggests that such strips were cut and rearranged several times on both a horizontal and vertical plane or orientation. In working through this technique, it is clear that a number of variations are possible through the deliberate arrangement of the agate pattern.

For the demonstration, the patterning of the agate has been left moderately coarse so that is it easily observable in the photographs (figure 15). The slab is now usable.

Creating the Forms

Once a suitable agate pattern is created, the thin sheet of clay is ready for molding. In most cases, it appears that all elements of laid agateware were created by press molding (figures 16 and 17).

This process requires a separate plaster or clay mold for each component of a pot. This would include the body, foot rim or feet, lid, finial, spout, and handles. As with the thrown agate, joins may show smearing, or distortion.

The teapot shown here uses two-piece molds for the pecten shell body, spout, handle, and Fo Lion finial (figure 18). These molds were taken

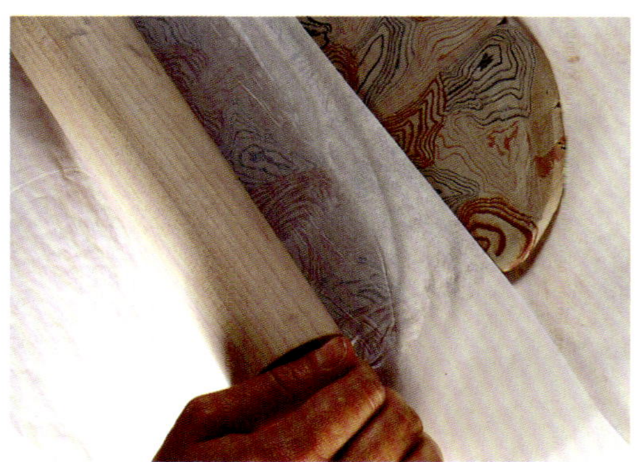

13. Join and flatten the layers using a rolling pin. Use a sheet of paper to keep the pattern crisp and intact.

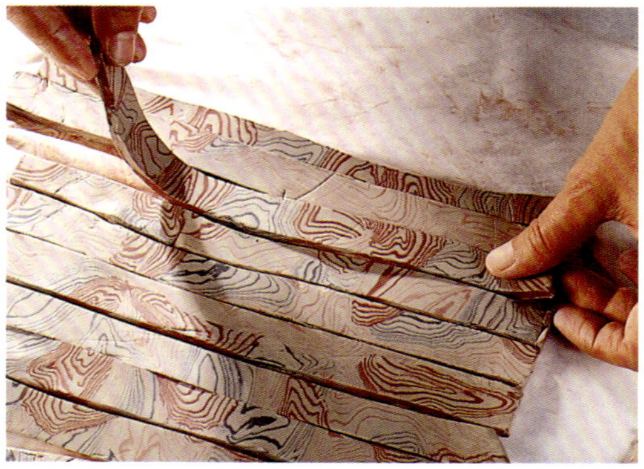

14. Cut horizontal strips from the flat slab, rearrange them to accentuate the pattern, and roll out to rejoin.

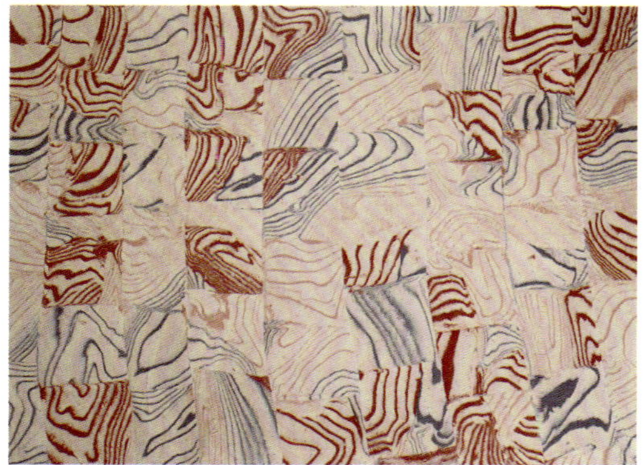

15. Cut vertical strips and roll out again to rejoin to create the agate slab checkerboard pattern.

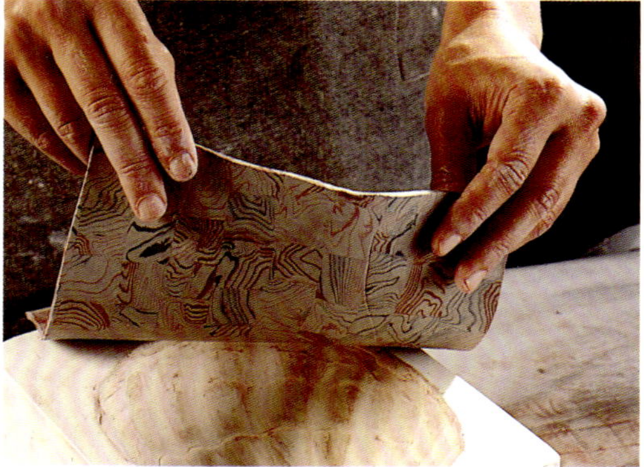

16. Lay the thin agate slab into the plaster press mold.

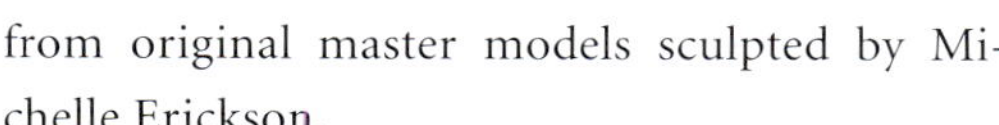

from original master models sculpted by Michelle Erickson.

Once the two halves of each part of the teapot are pressed in separate molds, they are ready to be joined. The edges are lightly scored and moistened. The two molds are aligned, and the seam is closed by working from the inside through the opening in the neck (figure 19). The exterior seam is cleaned up, then the spout, handle, and any other added elements are attached to the body (figure 20). For lidded forms, keep the lid on during the drying process. If necessary, line the rim or gallery of the pot or lid with a sheet of paper to keep the two from sticking together. Once dried, it is possible to enhance the agate surface with a light scrubbing using the equivalent of a fine steel wool; however, any heavy smudging or distortion cannot be altered. Once dry, the pot is bisque fired, glazed, and fired again.

For laid agate, although the patterning is often described as random, we have concluded that it is very deliberate. This deliberateness can be seen in a variety of other agate patterns that have yet to be fully classified.

Without question, agateware can generate a kaleidoscopic effect that some may find dizzying. A fierce competition for antique examples exists among a small cadre of collectors. Perhaps this fact alone substantiates the often heard claim that agateware is considered "the ultimate refinement of the potter's art." We hope this demonstration has provided some insight into the mysteries of the potter's art and that new research on the history of agateware can be conducted with fresh eyes.

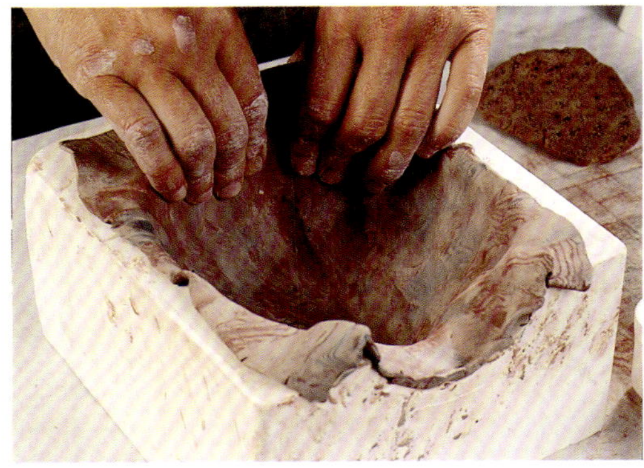

17. Press the slab firmly into the recesses and corners of the mold.

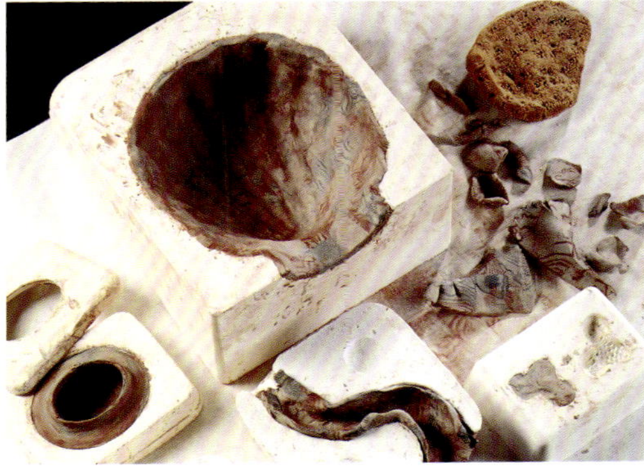

18. Several two piece molds are necessary for producing a form like a teapot.

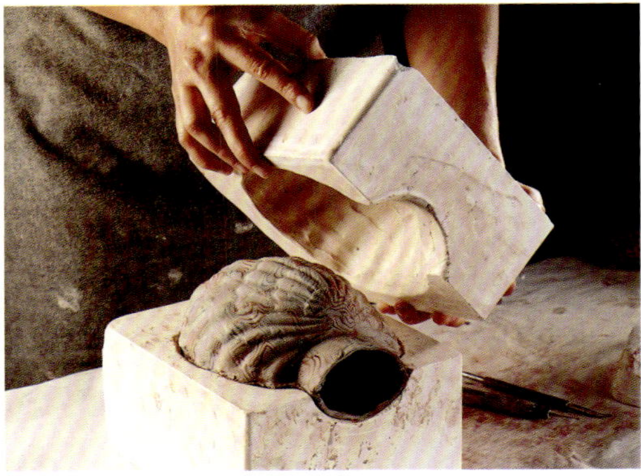

19. Score and moisten the edges, align the mold, press halves together, and close the seam from the inside.

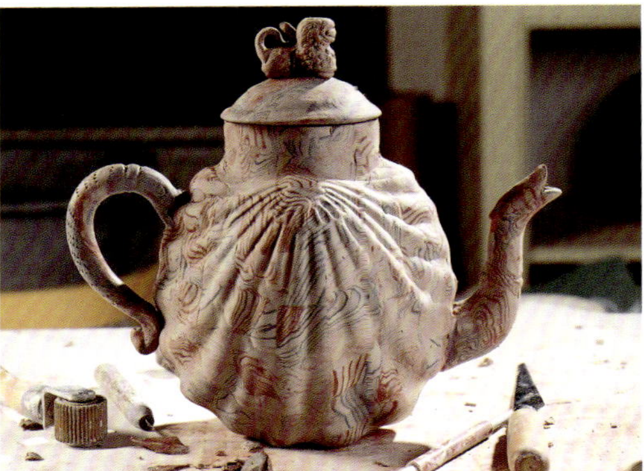

20. After removing the forms from the molds, clean the seams, assemble the parts, and allow the piece to dry.

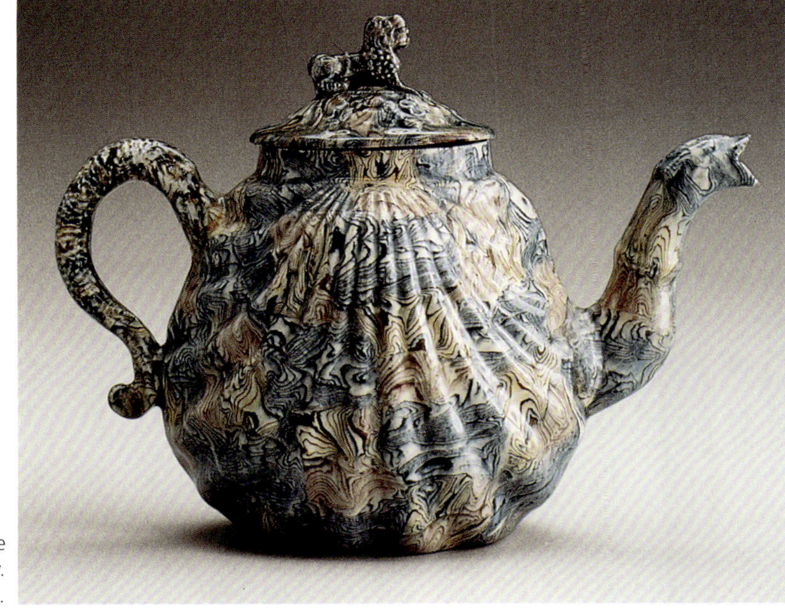

Teapot, Staffordshire, 51/8 inches (13 cm) in height, lead-glazed agateware, 1745–1755. An example of a press-molded pecten shaped teapot serves as the prototype for the demonstration of the laid agate techniques. Note the seemingly naturalistic patterning of the laid agate which exhibits alternate squares of cobalt colored clay. *Photo: Chipstone Foundation.*

Forming & Texture

ORNAMENT BENEATH THE SURFACE

by A. Blair Clemo

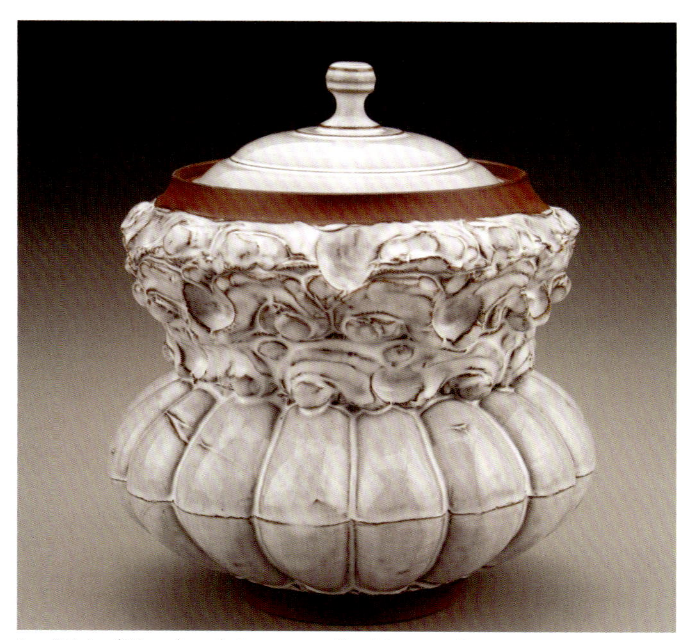

Jar, 8½ in. (22 cm), red stoneware, fired to cone 6.

There are only a few moments I can pinpoint in my life as a maker that have made me take pause, look at my work, and question it all the way down to its core. One such moment came by way of a simple mental exercise put forth by James Trilling in his book *Ornament, A Modern Prospective.*

Trilling states ". . . ornament is separable from the functional shape of the object. If you want to know whether a particular feature of an object is ornament, try imagining it away. If the object remains structurally intact, and recognizable, and can still perform its function, the feature is decoration, and may well be ornament . . ."

When I applied this exercise to my work, I noticed right away that so much of the labor I invested could be defined as such. My studio practice, and in fact the education system that I learned from, followed one simple mode of operation; ornamentation comes after generating a form, it is a secondary process.

This identification of ornamentation as a subsequent process itself does not trouble me, until Trilling continues, "Under the laws of modernist aesthetics, ornament bears damning witness against itself. If we take it away, physically or in imagination, the shape and function of the object are intact. Ornament is unnecessary."

My studio practice, at that time, centered on wheel throwing as a way of generating forms. I would sit down with a ball of clay and manipulate that clay into a utilitarian form, something that could be generically described as a vessel. This object would be clean, precise, and unadorned. By the laws of Modernist aesthetic that Trilling mentions, I could be finished at that point. I had made an object that, once glazed, would perform a utilitarian task just fine, perhaps even better than if it were ornate. From that vantage point, there was no actual need to invest more time and energy in my work.

But as a maker, I felt my work was far from over. As the clay reached leather hard it would be altered by adding layers of subsequent labor. The result is what I think of as visual interest. Whatever the process of altering or decoration one may choose, it seems important to me that

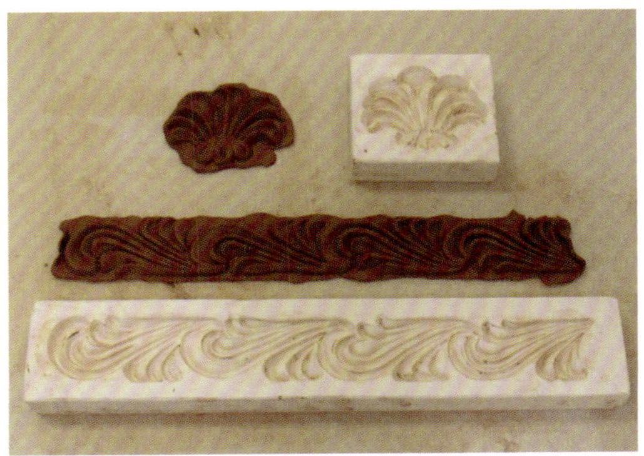

1. Decorative molds and examples of ornamental patties and strips.

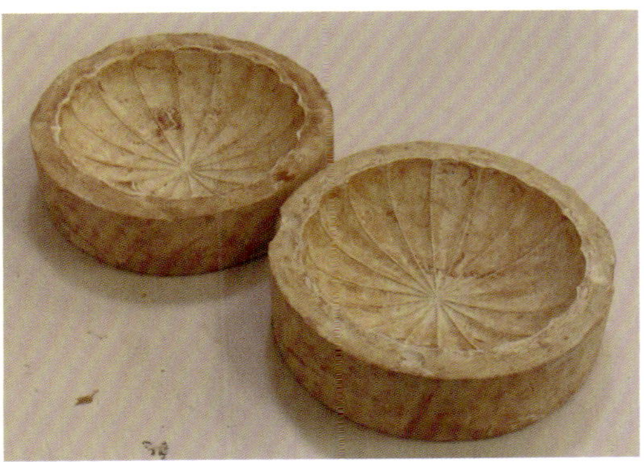

2. A form mold can be used to make an open or closed form.

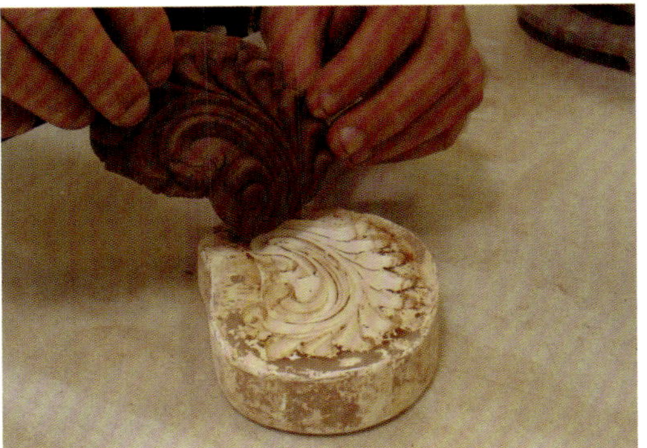

3. Clay pressed into a decorative mold.

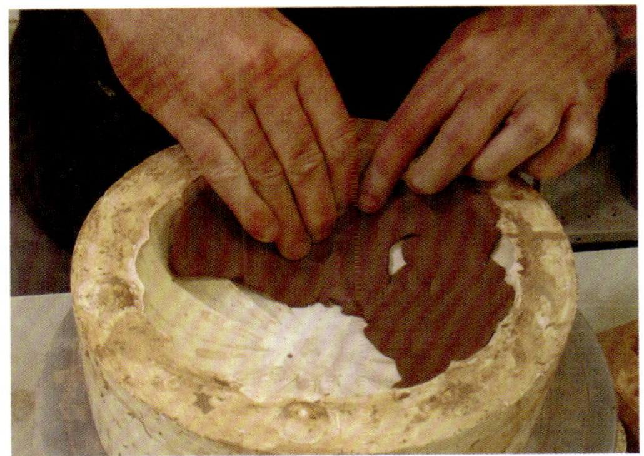

4. Decorative pressings laid into the form mold. Intentional gaps are filled from behind to create depth.

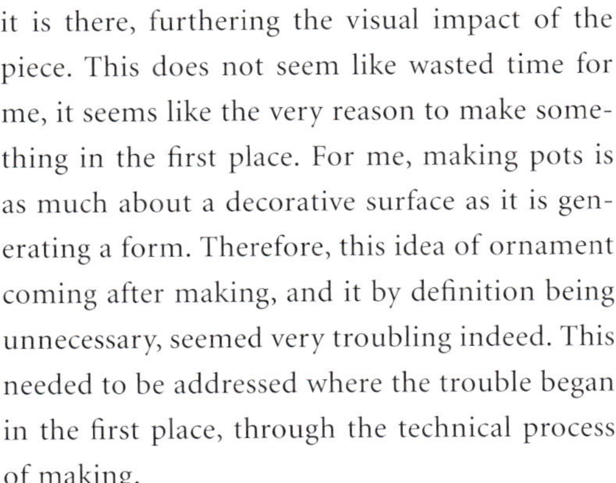

it is there, furthering the visual impact of the piece. This does not seem like wasted time for me, it seems like the very reason to make something in the first place. For me, making pots is as much about a decorative surface as it is generating a form. Therefore, this idea of ornament coming after making, and it by definition being unnecessary, seemed very troubling indeed. This needed to be addressed where the trouble began in the first place, through the technical process of making.

The system of making that I developed from this question starts with ornamental pieces, generated from press molds, that become not only the skin of the work, but also its structure and form. Ornament is the primary building block in my work, integral and inseparable from the form. It provides a different answer to Trilling's challenge. What would remain if the ornament were removed from my work? Nothing, that is, at least from a more conceptual viewpoint.

Molds

The building blocks of my work are two different types of press molds, first a decorative mold that yields an ornamental patty or coil of clay to build from (figure 1) and the other is a form mold that can be pressed into to make the actual volume of the pots (figure 2). This form mold is cast in a circular shape and, after clay is pressed into it, it is centered on the wheel and used to throw the upper portion of the jar.

To make the decorative molds, clay or plasticine is hand formed flat on the table, typically out of small elements such as coils or cones ar-

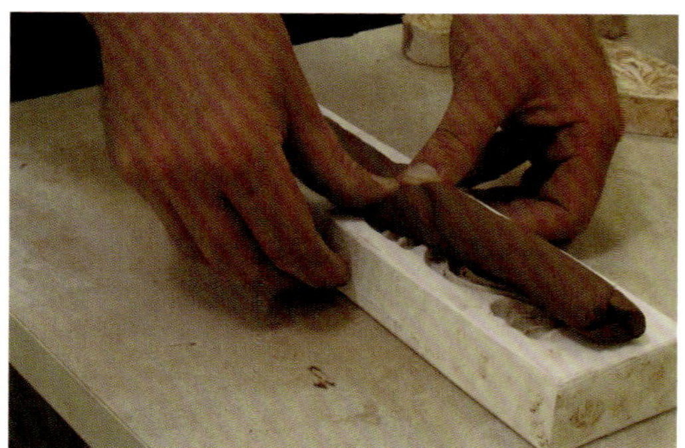
5. A coil is pressed into the decorative mold providing an ornamental strip to coil build with.

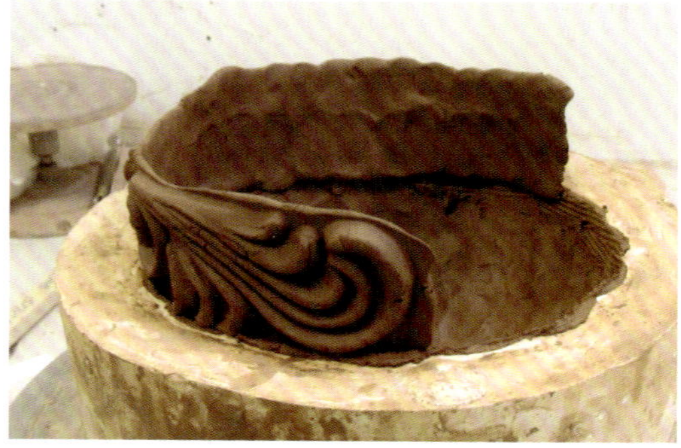
6. Decorative pressed strips are added along the rim of the pressed form mold base to form the wall of the jar.

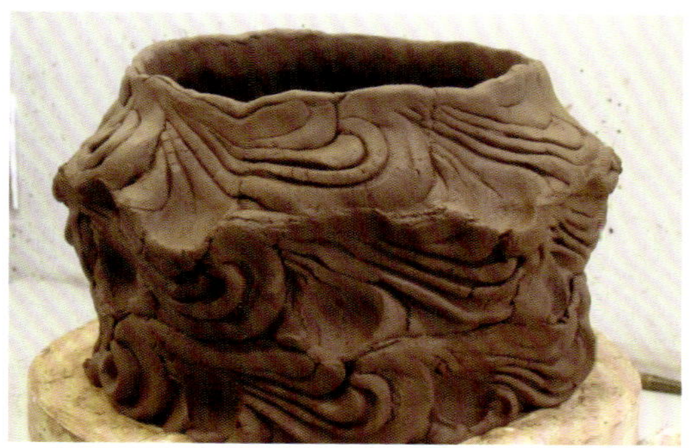
7. Angle a top strip to form the shoulder. Create another patterned layer with deep thumbprints.

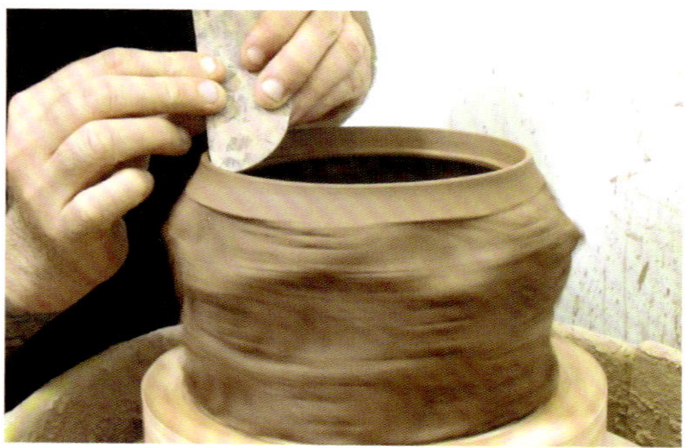
8. A coil is added to the shoulder and thrown to make the flange.

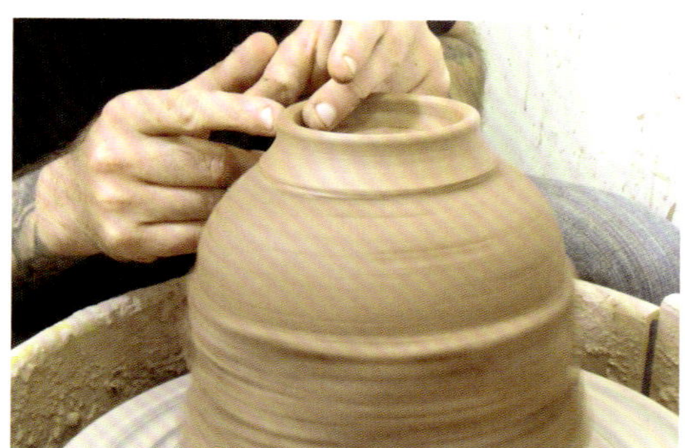
9. After the rim has set to leather hard, throw a footring on the bottom.

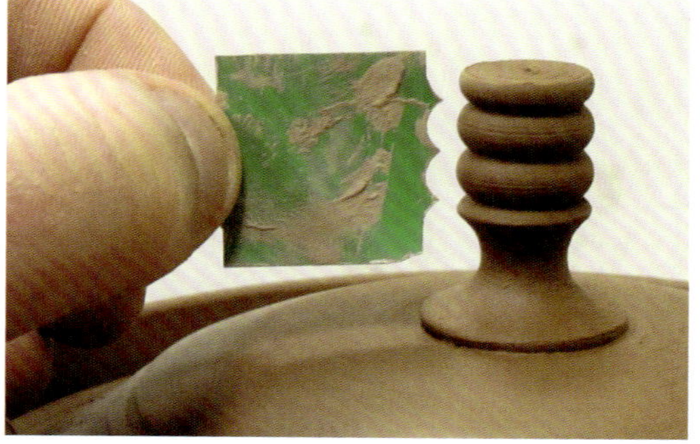
10. A metal profile tool is used to make a clean and consistent knob on the lid.

ranged in whatever shape I need. Cottle boards are set up around the object and plaster is poured in a simple, one-part-mold fashion.

The form molds begin as objects thrown on the wheel, carved when leather hard, and typically cast in two-part molds. No pour spout is needed, as these molds are made for pressing, not slip casting.

Clay

After pressing clay into the decorative molds (figure 3), I then set them into the form mold (figure 4) ornament side down. I can vary the clarity of the ornament with the pressure I use to push them into the mold—the harder I push the clay against the mold wall, the less ornament will remain. I try to be strategic in placing the ornamental parts, as the composition of the pot's surface will depend on how the ornament is set in the mold (figure 4)

Once the form mold is filled, creating a half sphere, I trim the edge flush with the mold. This will be the bottom of my jar. I press a coil into a longer decorative mold (figure 5) yielding an ornamental strip to build with. This is scored and slipped onto the press-molded base (figure 6). This jar is made with two layers of ornamental strips, one on top of the other, making up the wall of the jar. The last strip is scored and slipped in place at a 45° angle, slanting inward (figure 7). This will give me a nice shoulder on which to throw a flange for the lid to rest on.

The jar is allowed to set up to a soft leather hard, just firm enough to support the pressure of adding and throwing a coil to make the flange. I center the jar (with the base still in the form mold) on the wheel and use a needle tool to cut the rim level. I score and slip a coil into place on the rim and throw a flange for the lid (figure 8). This is one of the most dynamic parts of the finished jar; a strong horizontal line that conspicuously shows the different touch between the squishy, press-molded body and the precise thrown rim. I usually leave this rim unglazed to increase focal attention. I throw the lid immediately after the rim so that they will both shrink at the same rate. I have noticed that, even though the rim is freshly thrown, the body of the jar has already begun to shrink. This can throw off the precision of the lid fit. To compensate, I usually throw the lid slightly larger (⅛ of an inch or so) than the flange. When both the lid and the lip are leather hard, I trim the lid to fit the jar.

Once the rim is leather hard, I remove the jar from the form mold and flip it over. Because the plaster form mold absorbs moisture, the bottom is usually a soft leather hard and ready for the thrown foot. I center the jar on the wheel upside down (resting on the rim), and mark with a needle tool where the foot-ring will go. This area is scored and slipped and a coil is added and thrown into a foot for the jar (figure 9).

Finally, after trimming the leather-hard lid to fit the jar, I throw the knob. I use a profile tool made from a piece of sheet metal to give me a precise, decorative finial (figure 10). Additional profile tools are also used to make decorative marks on the inside of the lid and the bottom of the jar.

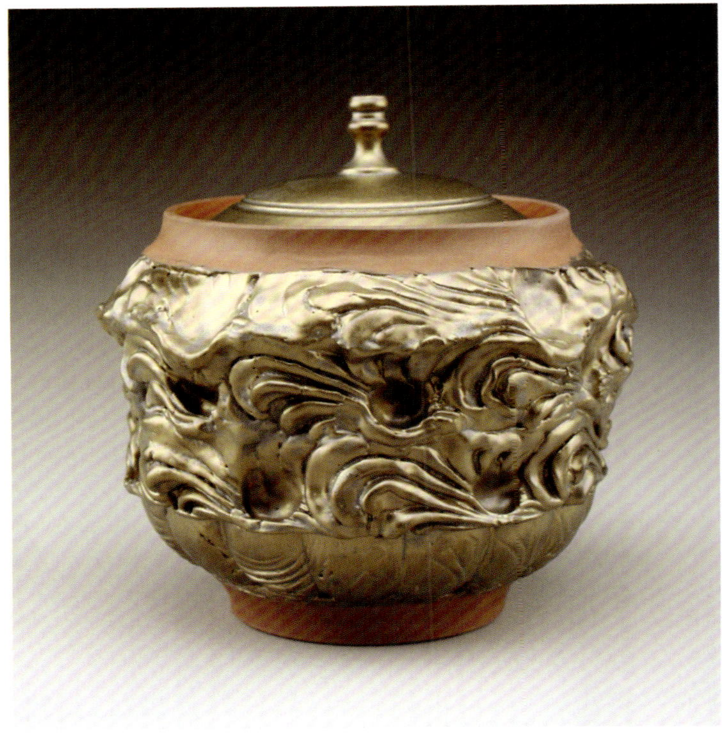

Jar, 8 in. (20 cm), red stoneware, fired in oxidation to cone 6..

Forming & Texture

PUSHING THE LIMITS OF SURFACE

by Eric Serritella

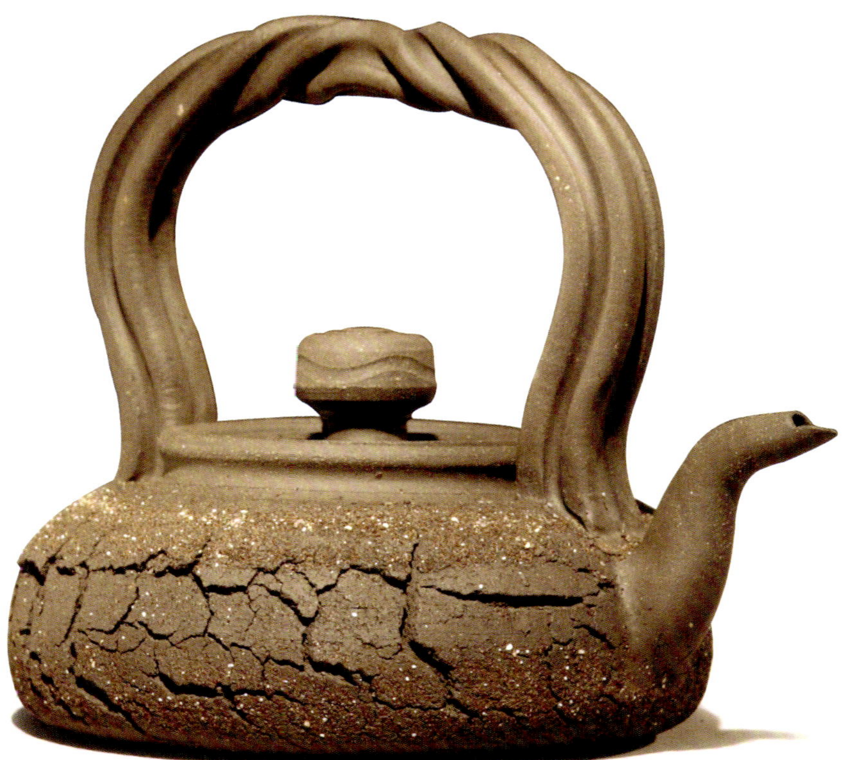

Teapot, 6½ inches in height, fired unglazed to cone 6 in oxidation. The natural canyons reveal the beautiful hidden texture of clay.

Heating clay and stretching it to create texture is a technique used by potters for ages. I was immediately drawn to the technique during an artist residency in Taiwan a few years ago. Since then, I've experimented and developed a body of work I call "opened earth," in which I try to show the inner beauty, texture and earthiness of clay.

I prefer to gently influence the outcome and let natural interactions between variables proceed with their course. Beyond revealing the beautiful natural texture of clay, I'm also drawn to the challenge of spontaneous form development. After first heating the surface of the clay, variables such as clay type, level of moisture and wheel speed effect development of the fissures as the clay is stretched. The challenge is to spontaneously make a strong form as the clay is expanded. Unplanned caverns and canyons appear as the piece expands, and these in turn influence the form.

The "opened earth" technique utilizes sand or dried clay for natural fissures and tools from around the studio for creating patterns. I work with slabs and on the wheel, adding color with glazes, slips and oxides, and using heat on the surface. With many variables involved, this is not an exacting process, but serves as a starting point.

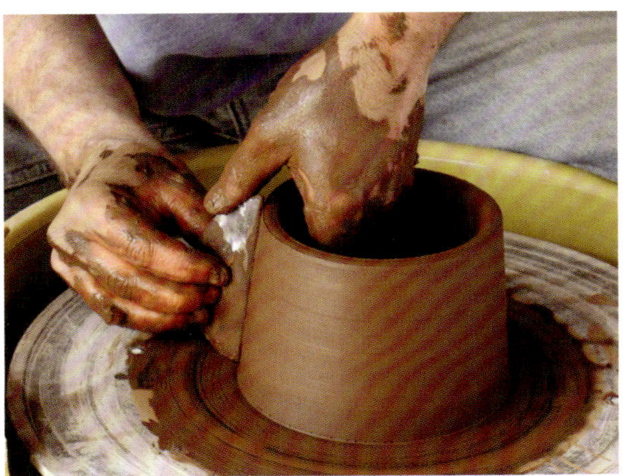

1. Straighten and even out the wall with a rib.

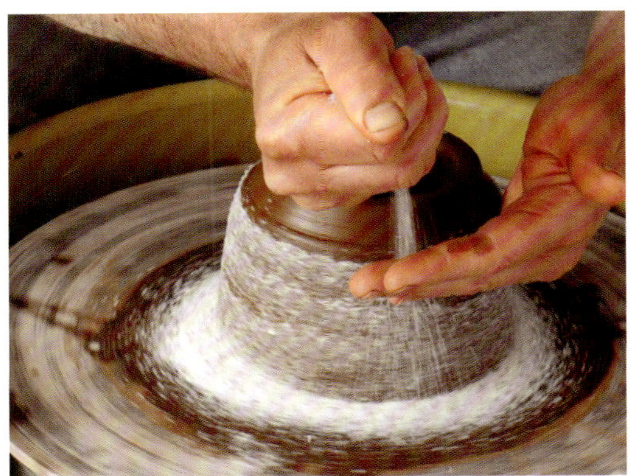

2. Apply silica sand or dry clay "powder" to the outside.

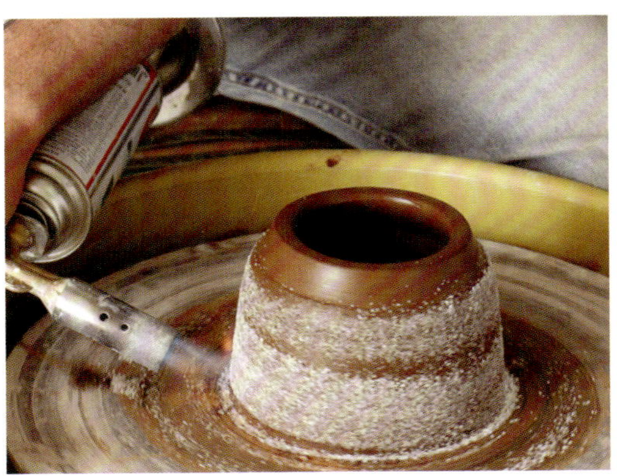

3. With the wheel turning very slowly, apply heat to dry the outside.

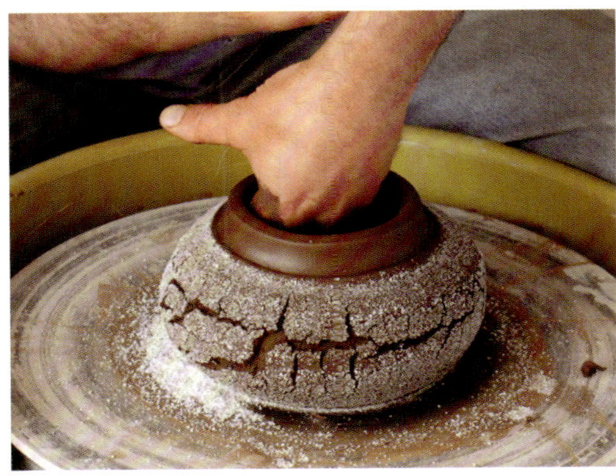

4. Begin to push out the wall and shape the pot.

Technique

Center a piece of clay 10–40% larger than you'd typically use for a piece to accommodate a thicker wall (the thicker the wall, the deeper the crevice). My walls are usually between ½–1 inch thick. Throw to the desired height using as little water as possible—the drier the better. Straighten and even out the wall with a rib (figure 1). Apply silica sand or dry clay "powder" to the outside (figure 2). While sand and clay are not necessary, they help dry the outside and provide contrasting color and texture. Leave clay uncovered at the top for the lid gallery. Tip: Apply sand with clean dry hands.

With the wheel turning very slowly, apply heat to dry the outside (figure 3). I use a hand-held butane torch, although a heat gun or hair dryer works if you have patience. CAUTION: Always work in a well-ventilated area when heating the clay, preferably with an exhaust or fan pulling the heated clay and torch fumes away from you. Also, exercise caution with an open flame. Remember that the tip of the torch will be very hot even after you turn off the flame.

Be sure to dry the surface evenly from top to bottom. The drying time depends on the output of the heat source, size of the piece, moisture level of the clay, wall thickness, distance of the heat to the clay and wheel speed. It's very difficult to quantify the level of dryness needed to get a certain type of fissure with so many variables involved. If the surface is not dry enough, then the clay won't create fissures when expanded. If it's too dry, then the wall will crack all the way through. Once the outside surface starts to become matt and is no longer

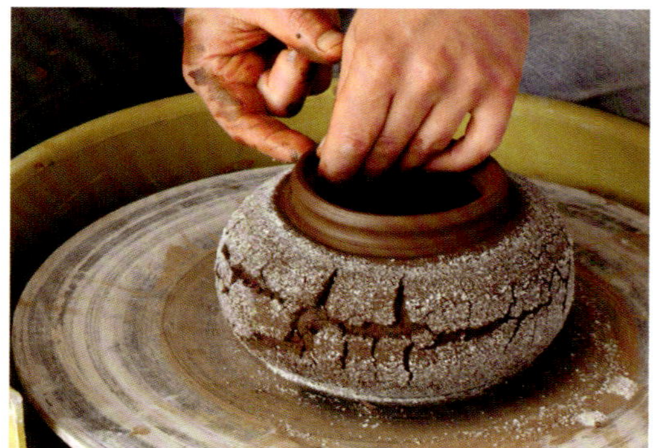
5. Finish the top rim with both hands.

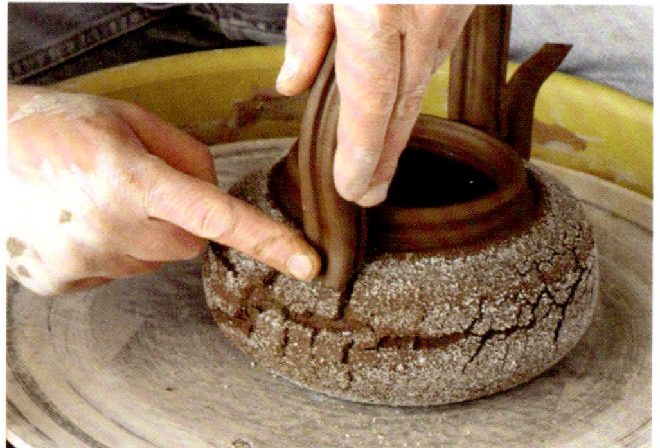
6. Trim the bottom, if desired, and add a spout and handle if desired.

tacky to the touch, it's time to start expanding the form. Some steam will usually release from the inside of the pot.

Begin to push out the wall and shape the pot (figure 4). This is one of the fun challenges, as it's necessary to create the form one-handed. Touching the outside wall ruins the texture. If you find that the crevices are not starting to open as you expand the form, apply additional heat. It's much easier to further dry a pot than to take make a dry pot evenly moist again.

Finish the top rim with both hands (figure 5) and add a gallery for the lid.

Once the pot is leather hard, trim the bottom, if desired, and add a spout and handle (figure 6). Dry the pot slowly to avoid unwanted cracking of the attachments due to the uneven wall thickness and clay moisture levels. If you're firing pieces with sand on them along with other pots in your kiln, be sure the pieces with sand are on the bot-

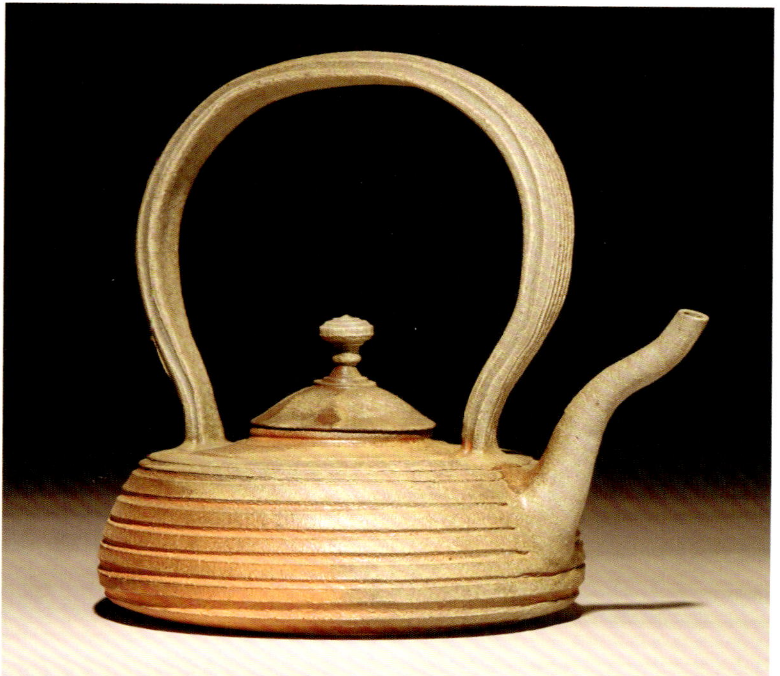
Stoneware teapot, 9 inches in height. The natural colorants from wood firing complements the surface textures.

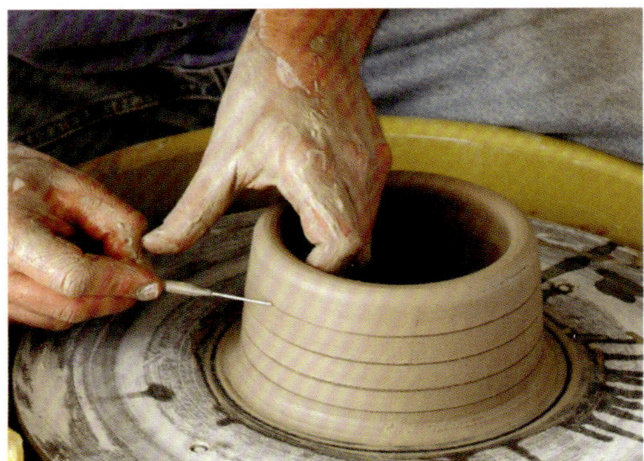
7. After throwing the form, score the pot vertically or horizontally with a needle tool.

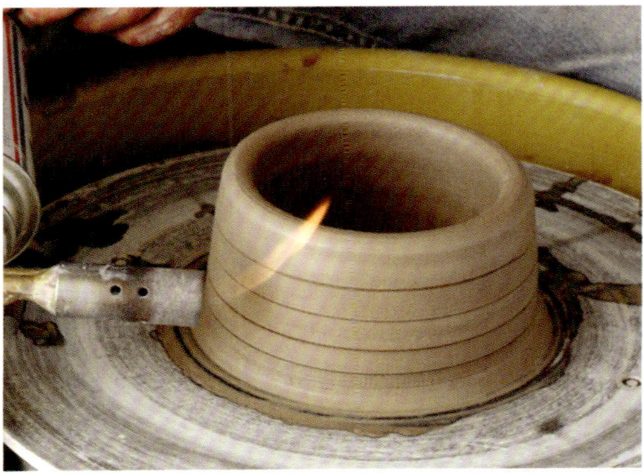
8. Heat the outside..

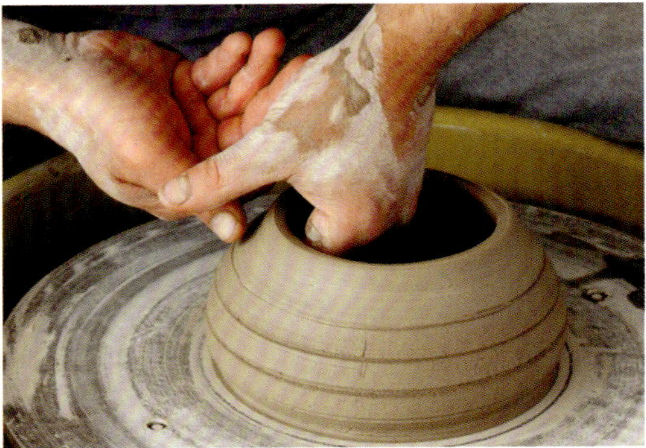
9. Expand the wall and finish the top.

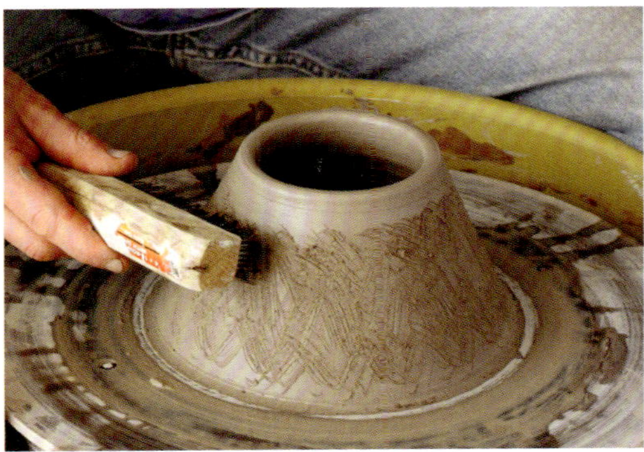
10. Another variation is to use a stiff wire brush to create shallow crevices and thinner walls.

tom. Sand pops off during firing and can stick to glazed pieces below or beside them. Vacuum out the kiln after each firing. Sand the fired piece with 200-grit silicon carbide sandpaper. This removes any surface sand that's soft and unstable, and removes that tacky feel of the unglazed clay.

Variations

After throwing your form, score the pot vertically or horizontally with a needle tool or other sharp tool (figure 7). (Note: I've omitted sand on this piece for a softer texture.) Heat the outside (figure 8), then expand the wall and finish the top (figure 9).

One of my favorite texture tools is a stiff wire brush for tight patterns that are great for many firing processes (figure 10). This tool creates shallower crevices and thinner walls. I usually use this tool without added sand.

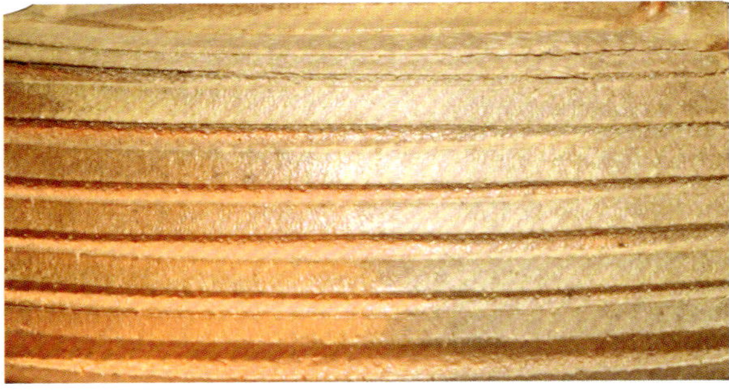

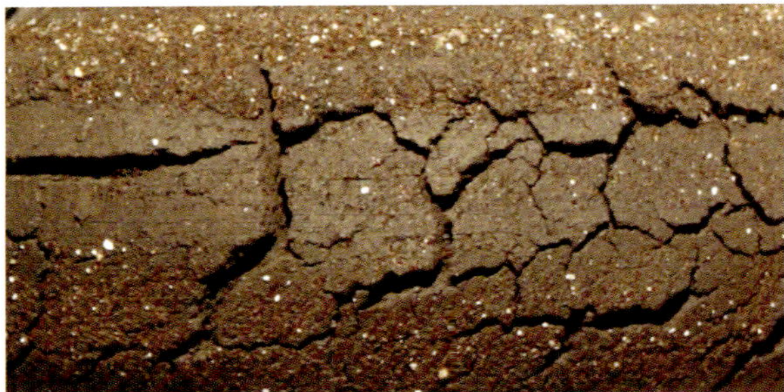

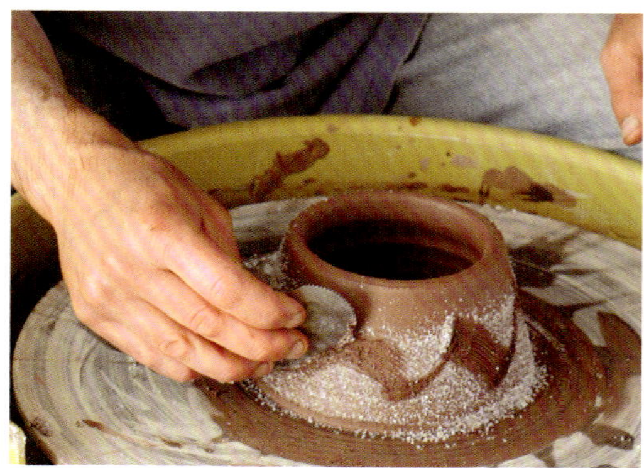
11. Another patterning technique uses a combination of shallow surface texture and deep canyons.

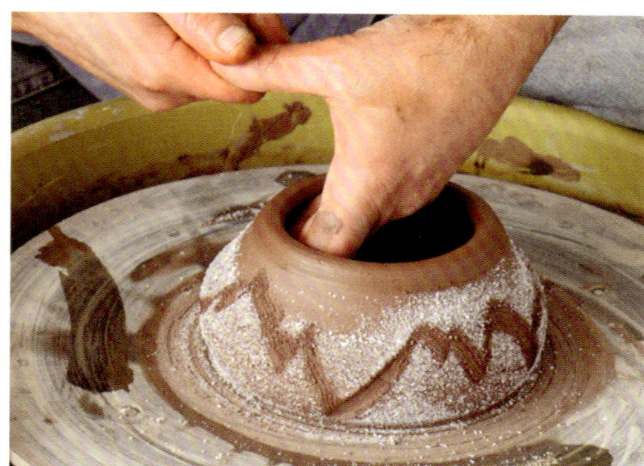
12. Soft, wide stroke create a combed pattern while deep sharp strokes becomes a canyon.

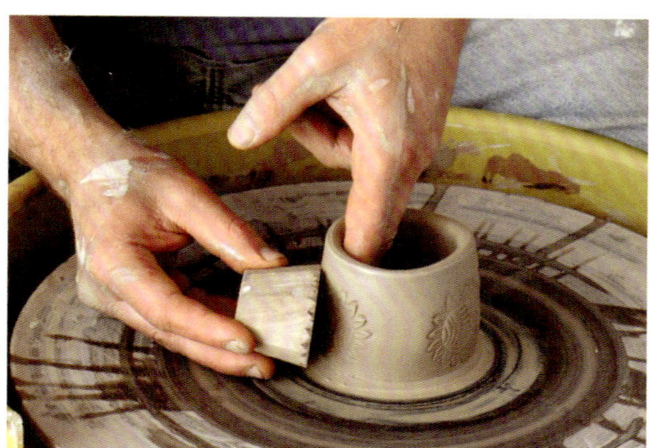
13. Stretching the clay exaggerates the pattern created by a texture stamp.

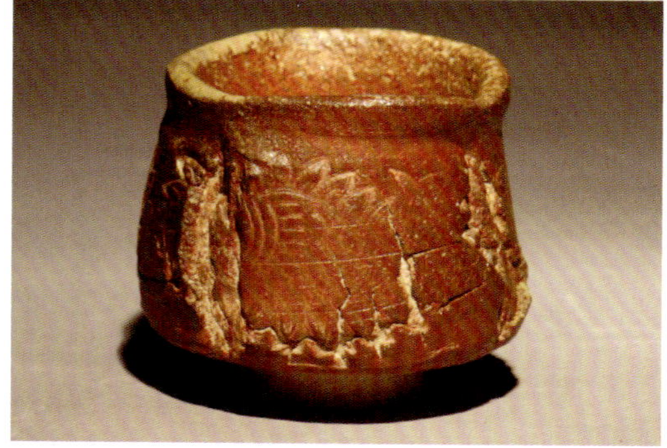
Stoneware tea bowl, 3 inches in height, with impressed patterns, wood fired.

Another patterning technique is to apply a random flowing design with a combination of shallow surface texture and deep canyons (figure 11). Rib the outside and apply sand, then score with a combing tool or rib as the wheel turns slowly. Change the angle of the tool as you make strokes. A soft, wide stroke creates a combed pattern yielding a series of shallow fissures, while a deep sharp stroke becomes a canyon that opens large and wide (figure 12).

Many different tools, materials and household items can be used to impress patterns on Opened Earth pots (figure 13). I like two discarded wooden blocks I got from a Middle Eastern textile operation. The stretching of the clay exaggerates the pattern they create on the surface. Press the pattern into the wall, supporting from the inside. Tip: If your clay is too wet from centering and opening, use a torch to dry the surface slightly and stiffen up the wall before impressing the pattern. This also helps keep the pattern-making tool from sticking in the clay.

Slab Work

For a sushi plate or tray, pound out a slab 1–3 inches thick. Impress a pattern into the clay (figure 14). Heat the top and sides, but not the underneath or bottom surfaces (figure 15). Don't dry thick slabs as much as wheel-thrown cylinders because some elasticity should be left in the slab for stretching.

Stretch the clay by throwing it down on a solid surface. Throw the slab at an angle instead of straight down (figure 16). This causes the clay to pull and stretch. Rotate the piece to stretch it into the desired shape—in this case, a rectangle (figure 17).

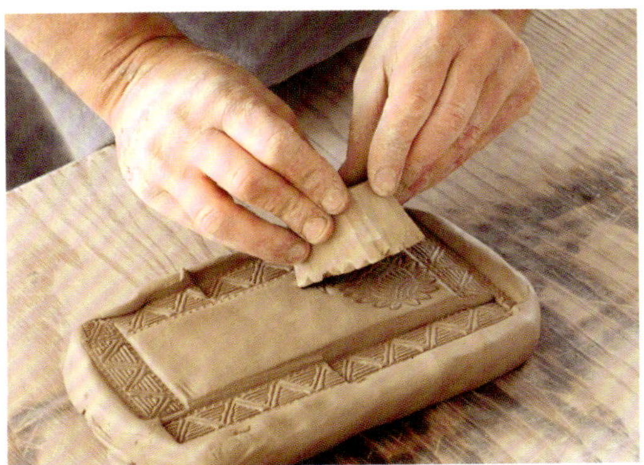

14. Pound out a slab 1–3 inches thick. Impress a pattern into the clay.

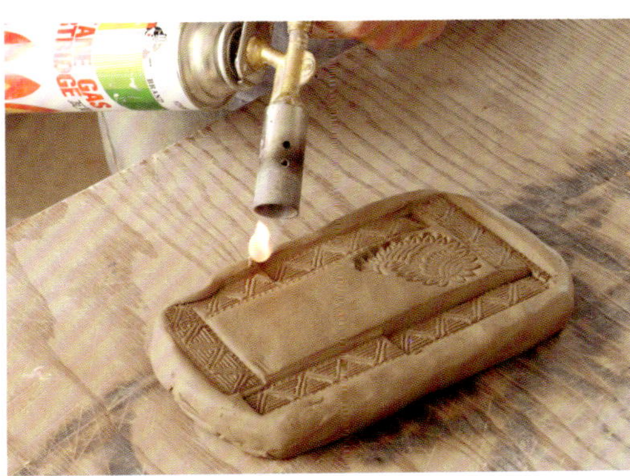

15. Heat the top and sides, but not the underneath or bottom surfaces.

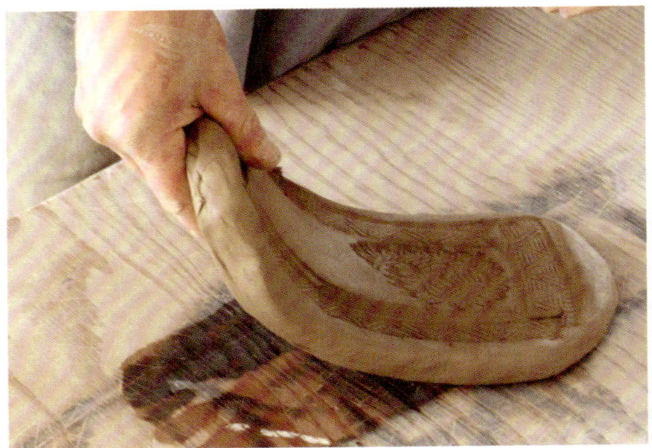

16. Throw the slab at an angle instead of straight down.

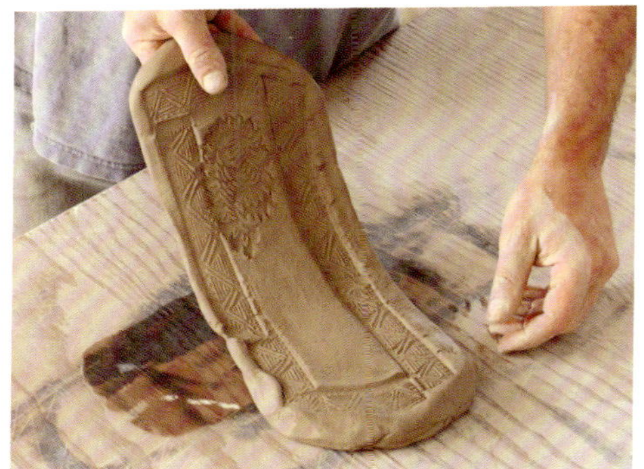

17. Rotate the piece to stretch it into the desired shape—in this case, a rectangle.

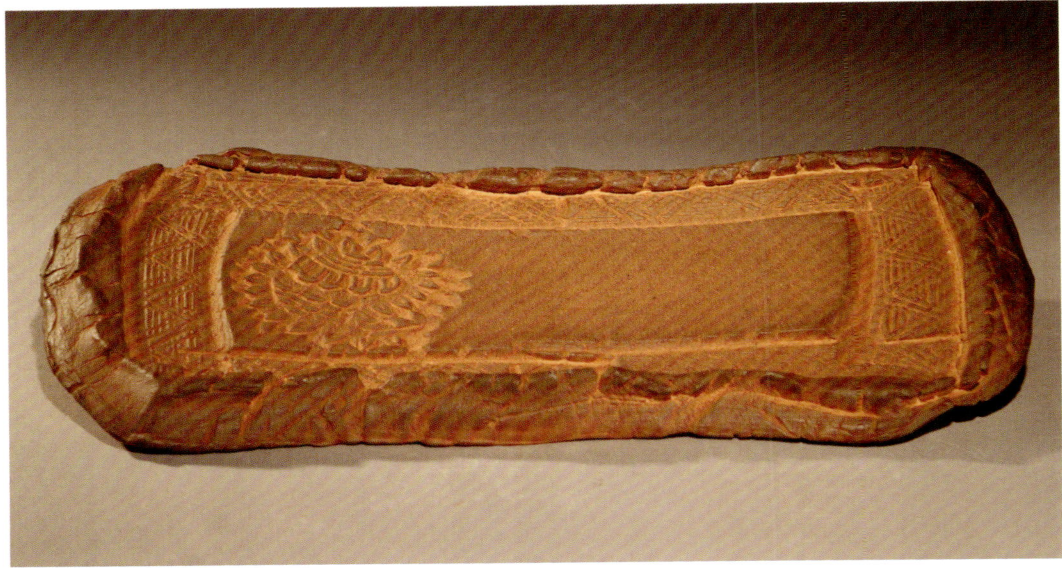

Stoneware tray, 13 inches in length, unglazed and wood fired.

Forming & Texture

CARVING A DOUBLE-WALLED VASE

by T. Dubis and Pam Luke

Constructing a double-walled vase requires little more skill than throwing a conventional vase. It is simply an amalgamation of several different parts—most of which are easy to throw. However, like any discipline, whether playing a guitar, shooting pool or throwing pots, the more skilled the maker, the more refined the final product. This process involves assembling four parts in order to create a vase. The interior vase body (figure 1a) and the upper part of the exterior vase (figure 1b) are created first then attached to one another (figure 1c), next, the lower part of the exterior vase (figure 1d) and a neck (shown at the top of figure 1e) are thrown and assembled (figure 1e).

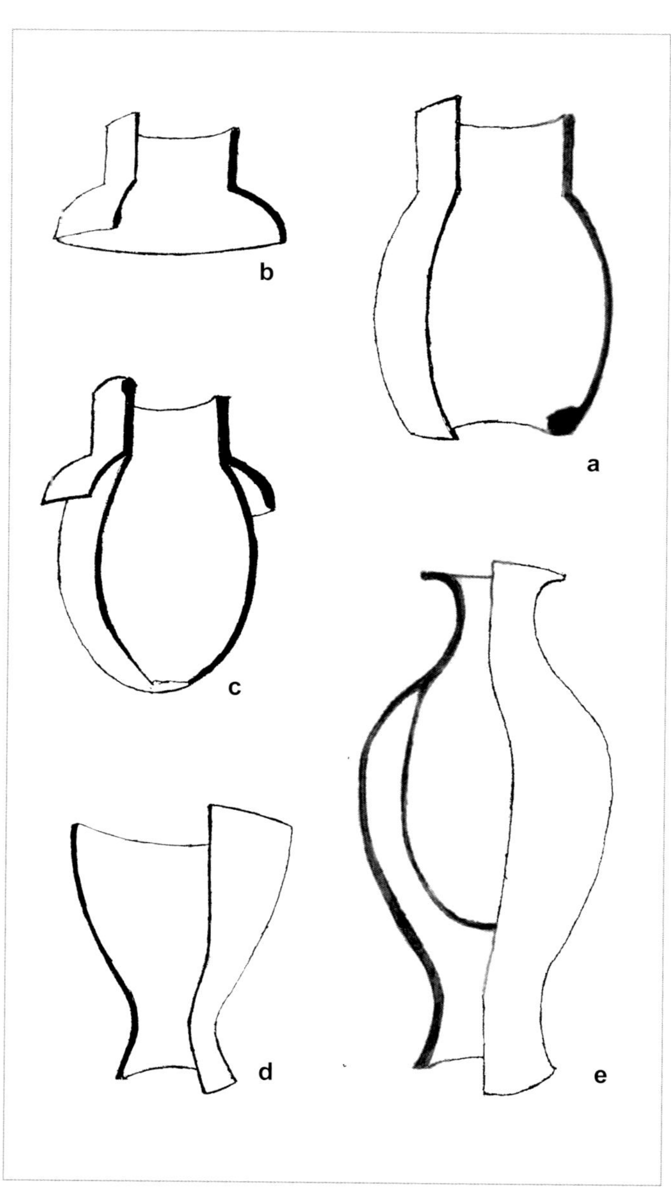

1. Illustrations showing the four main parts of the double walled vase, along with their assembly.

Getting Started

First, measure out four balls of clay using a ratio of 1:2:3:6. This is an elastic ratio, although you may want to stick to it until you are more comfortable with the process. The neck requires the least amount of clay; therefore, its weight should be the basis for the rest of the pieces. If, for example,

PHOTOS: KAY BERNIER

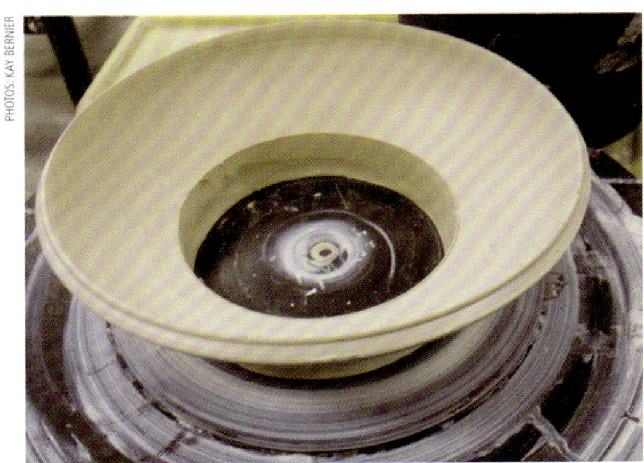

2. Center the second smallest ball of clay and create an open bottomed bowl form for the shoulder of the vase.

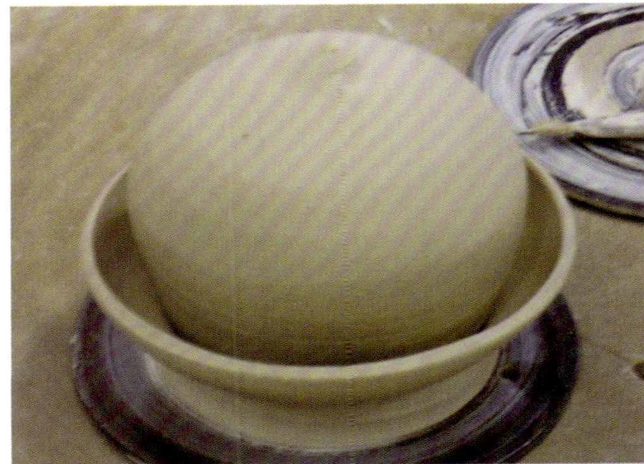

3. With the bulb inside the bowl, score and slip to connect the bulb's rim to the inside of the bowl's bottom edge.

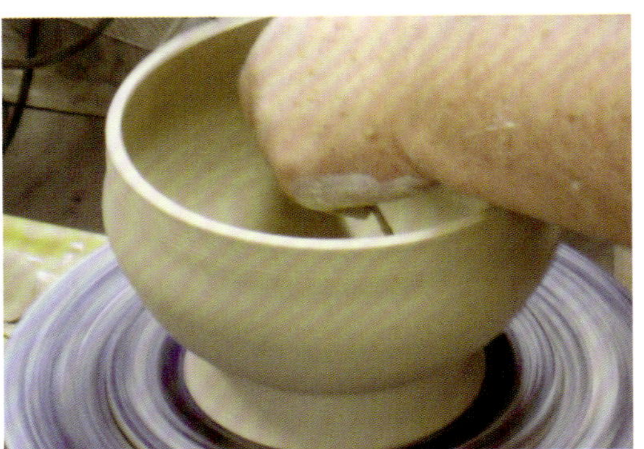

4. Throw the bottom of the outer wall, starting with a bottomless cylinder that opens to a curved bowl shape.

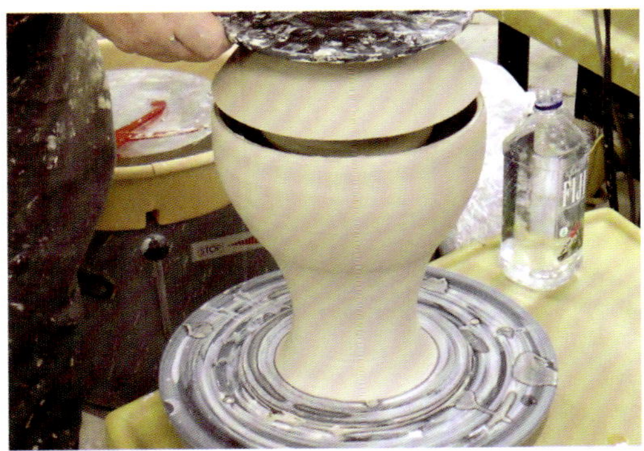

5. Flip the shoulder and bulb form over, and attach to the base.

your smallest piece of clay weighs ¼ pound, the other three balls of clay would be ½, ¾, and 1½ pounds, respectively.

Timing the throwing and combining of the forms is the most challenging aspect. The dryness of the clay is very crucial. The components should be a soft leather-hard for assembly in order to accept the stresses placed on them, and yet, should have some flexibility and be wet enough to ensure a strong joint or seam. When possible, do the throwing and assembling at the same time. This method allows for adjustments, which ensure a better fit between the component parts.

Throw Exterior Neck and Shoulder

To create the neck and shoulder of the vase, which is basically a bowl form (figure 2), take the second ball of clay, center it, and open it to the wheel head. Remember to keep the clay thick at the top of your pull. This element supports the most weight in the final product and needs to be robust. Expand the opening so that the exterior is as wide as you want the neck of your piece to be. The first pull should be done with moderate pressure. Heavily compress the rim after this pull.

Once the first pull is complete, begin the second pull. This should start about half an inch to an inch above the wheel head. Pull the clay out at approximately a 45° angle. Leave this section on the bat, remove the bat from the wheel head and set it aside.

Interior Vase Body

Using a set of calipers, measure the opening on the interior of the open-bottomed bowl just thrown. Take the third ratio piece of clay and center it,

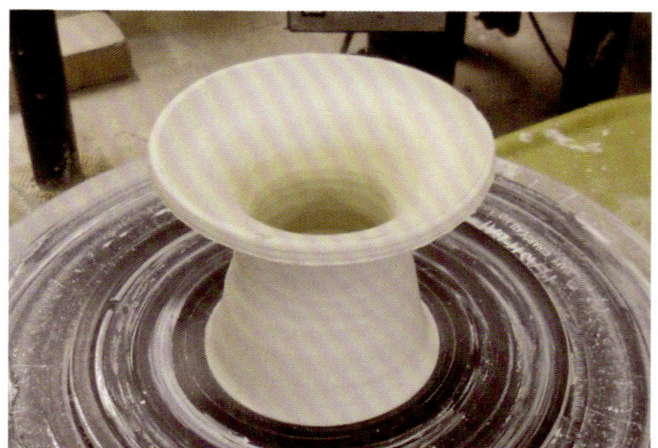
6. Throw an open bottomed form to create the neck and rim of the vase.

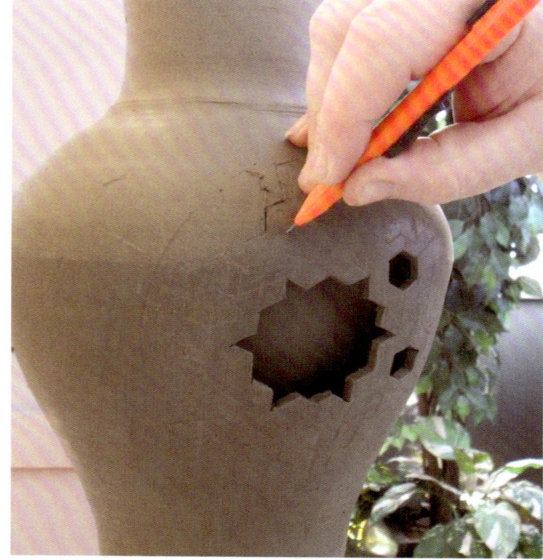
7. When the vase is leather hard, carve and pierce a pattern through the outer wall.

making it slightly narrower than the caliper measurement. Open the ball to the wheel head and expand the interior opening as much as possible without changing the exterior width of the base.

Begin throwing this form. As with the first form, leave a lot of clay at the top of this element. Enclosing it will be done later. Once this piece is to the desired height, begin shaping the form. The shaping should begin approximately 1 to 2 inches above the bat or wheel head. Since the throwing process generates a good deal of torque, it can be productive to use a heat gun or torch to dry out the bottom of this section before shaping begins.

Once you have the desired shape, enclose the form. The best method is to throw the extra clay at the top as if throwing a long neck. With the wheel slowly turning, collar in the neck element until the piece is fully enclosed (see figure 3). Once the form is enclosed, the trapped air will actually support the work. Cut the piece off the bat or wheel head and set it aside to firm up to leather hard.

Combine First Two Sections

Place the bowl form back onto the wheel head. Lightly score and slip the interior of this piece. (Tip: A few ounces of vinegar added to the slurry bucket can make a good slip.) Place the second form inside of the first (figure 3). If it is too large, you can use a scraping tool to shave a little bit of clay off of the interior of the first form. If it is too small, then it is best to try to collar in the outside clay so that they can be pushed together. A difference of more than $^1/_8$ inch in the alteration will cause the bowl form to be radically off center. Take the bat off of the wheel head and set aside.

Throw the Lower Exterior Part

Take the largest ball of clay, center it on the wheel and open it to the wheel head. Open the bottom so that it is slightly larger than the opening for the neck. Begin pulling the form. Again, you will be widening the top of the form—so make sure that there is enough clay to expand it (figure 4).

Take the calipers and measure the diameter of the bowl, which is the shoulder of your vase. Begin expanding and shaping the large cylinder so that it has a rim that is the same diameter as the shoulder shape thrown in figure 2, and the curve complements and resolves the curve started by the bowl.

Assemble the Two Vase Parts

Again, timing is crucial at this point in the process. Make sure that the component parts are dry enough to handle being assembled but wet enough to create a good seam and so that either edge can be widened or closed to allow a better fit.

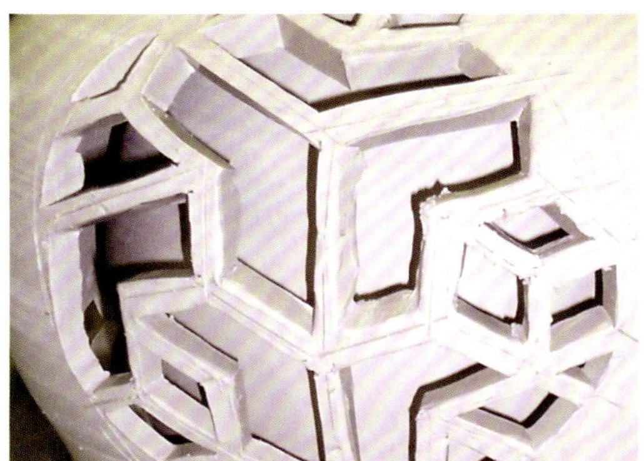
Detail showing outer carved wall of vase.

At this point, flip the interior form and hold it upside down to see how well it fits into the outer form (figure 5). After measuring the two edges to ensure they are aligned—score and slip both edges. Once the top of the piece is in place, cut it off of the bat either by using a cut-off wire or inserting the point of a needle tool between the bat and the clay while the wheel spins.

After placing the two sections together, use a needle tool to score the outside wall around the seam. Next, using a flexible rib, buff the seam to blend and smooth until it is invisible.

Throw and Attach the Neck

The neck is the last and easiest of the thrown pieces. Using the smallest ball of clay, the one that was one base unit in ratio, throw a cylinder with the bottom diameter the size of the opening on the piece. Pull up and collar in the cylinder, then finish off the rim (figure 6). Once this piece is thrown, attach it to the top of the work—using the same scoring methods used to attach other sections. Note For advanced throwers: The neck can also be thrown with the excess clay left from the forming of the interior vase and upper exterior wall. This step requires much skill as it puts a great deal of torque on the piece and requires the neck to be fairly plastic while the rest of the work is dry.

Carve the Exterior of the Vase

After assembling the vase, the exterior walls can be pierced and carved if desired (figure 7). When choosing a pattern, remember that it should leave enough intact areas to provide structural support to keep the form from warping during drying or firing. Clay becomes as soft near melting as it is when throwing.

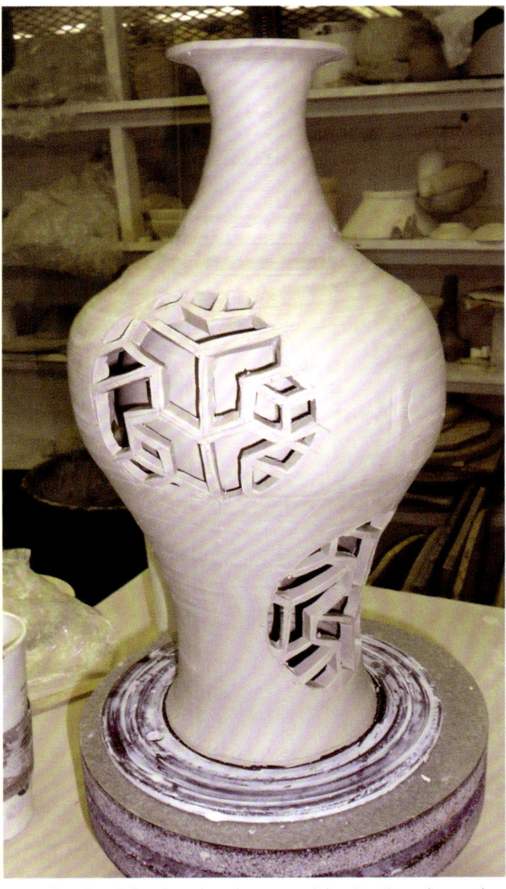
8. A finished, leather-hard vase, with piercing through the outer wall that reveals the enclosed vase, ready for drying and firing.

Carving a good deal into the exterior wall can be accomplished (figure 8), but this requires one extra form. Throw a small cylinder to act as a brace. The cylinder has to be measured to be small enough to fit inside the bottom opening on the exterior wall and be tall enough to support the interior vase. With this form helping to supporting the weight of the vase, a larger openwork design can be carved into the exterior wall.

Forming & Texture

GREAT STAMPS IN 30 MINUTES

by Virginia Cartwright

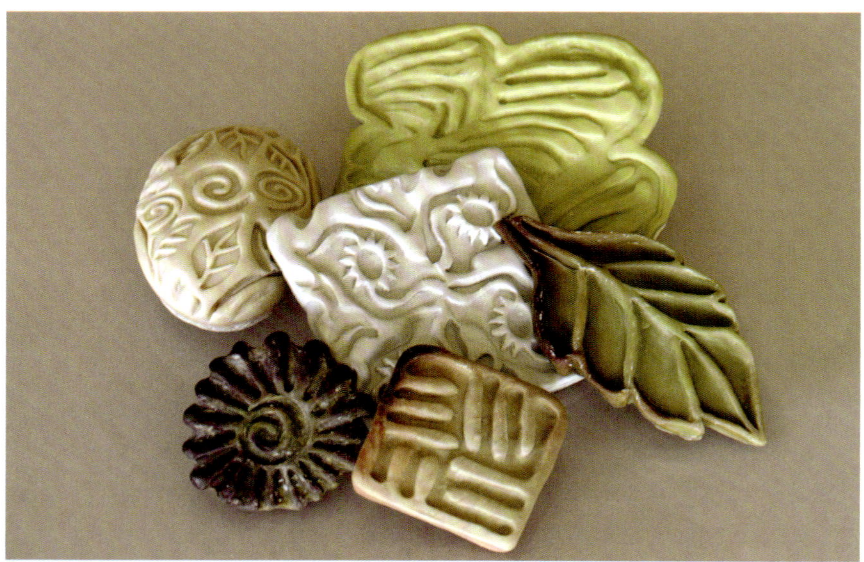

Polymer clay can be used to create a variety of clay stamps in a short period of time.

Stamps enhance your work by adding interesting textures to your pieces and depth to your glazes. For years, I carved stamps from small plaster blocks or from leather-hard clay that was then bisque fired before use. I wanted a way to make stamps more quickly so I could share them with my students and workshop participants and found that polymer clay (available at most craft stores) makes a clean, crisp impression that can be cured and ready for use in almost no time at all.

When making a stoneware stamp using regular clay, you need to let it dry then bisque fire it before you can put it to use, which could take several days to a week. Polymer stamps, by comparison, are ready for use in about 30 minutes. You can then take those stamps, press them into another piece of polymer clay, and quickly get a negative version of your designs.

Polymer clay does not crack or crumble as easily as stoneware or earthenware clays, and scraps can be easily recycled. Since it's not water based, the clay doesn't dry out. This property also makes polymer clay an ideal material for making impressions from a variety of objects, including antique furniture, kitchen tools, buttons, Indian wood blocks and tombstones.

As I began to explore the possibilities of this material further, I discovered that I could use my inlaid colored clay techniques to make the stamps beautiful as well as functional. By layering and blending colors, I can create an endless variety of intricate patterns.

Supplies

There are several brands of polymer clay available (Sculpey, Fimo or Premo), all of which are good. Sculpey has a product called "Super Sculpey" which I use because it is a strong, shatter-resistant material. Super Sculpey is only available in a tan color, so I combine it with about 25% of another color of polymer clay if I want to change the color.

You'll need a clean, non-porous surface to work on, and a Plexiglas roller made just for polymer. You can substitute this roller with an 8-inch piece of plastic pipe. You should also buy a 6-inch long cutting blade and an inexpensive pasta machine (both available at craft stores or garage sales). The pasta machine is used to soften the clay and to blend the colored clays together (figure 1).

If you're just making a few stamps, you can use your hands and roll the clay into coils until it softens. I find it helpful to attach handles to the stamps. Buy a bottle of liquid polymer clay and use this as glue to attach the polymer handle to the top of the stamp.

Polymer clay stamps are best when used on slightly firm slabs of ceramic clay. If the stamp sticks to the clay during use, baby powder or cornstarch can be used as a release agent. These embellished slabs can be used to make handbuilt vessels and sculptures, or left flat for tile work.

Process

To make polymer stamps, Condition the polymer clay by rolling it ten times through a pasta maker on the thickest setting (figure 2). If you do not have a pasta machine, manually roll the clay into coils in your hands. Your body heat will soften the clay. If you want to mix your own colors, make coils of two or three colors, roll them into one coil and twist the coil like a candy cane. Cut the twisted coil in half, join the two pieces and twist them again, repeating this process until the colors are blended.

You can make stamps using several layers of polymer clay by first rolling the clay out into a slab that is about ¼ inch thick. Thin polymer clay slabs take a deeper, clearer impression than a thick one. Put a pinch of baby powder or cornstarch on one side of the clay. Next, press the clay (powder side down) on top of a textured object. Place the polymer clay over the texture and press it with your thumbs, rather than pressing the texture down onto the polymer clay (figure 3).

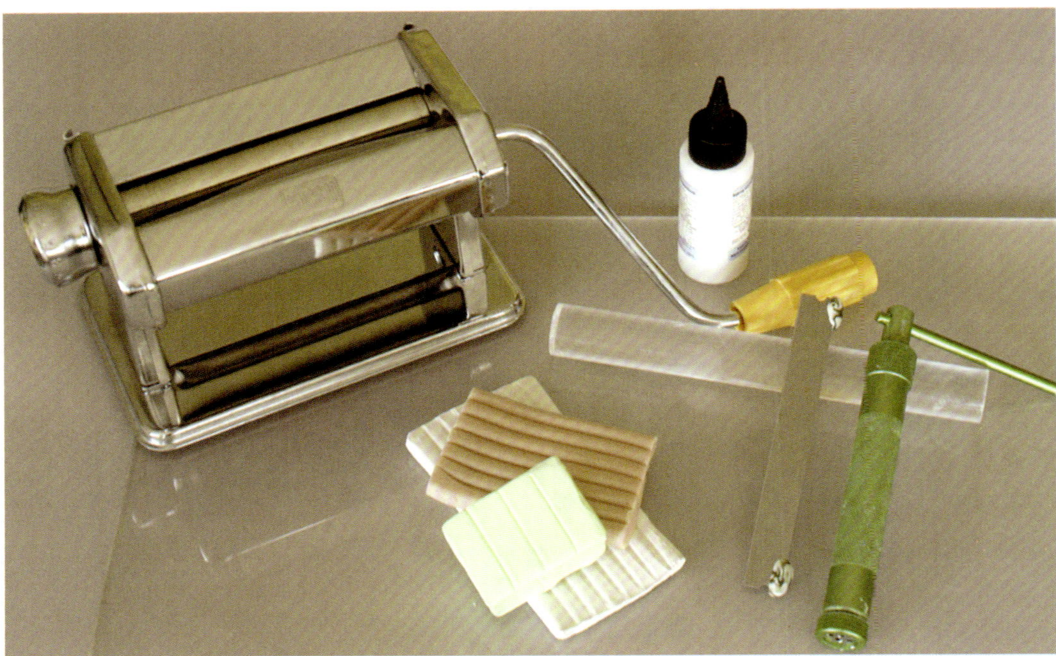

1. Supplies for making polymer stamps are readily available from craft stores.

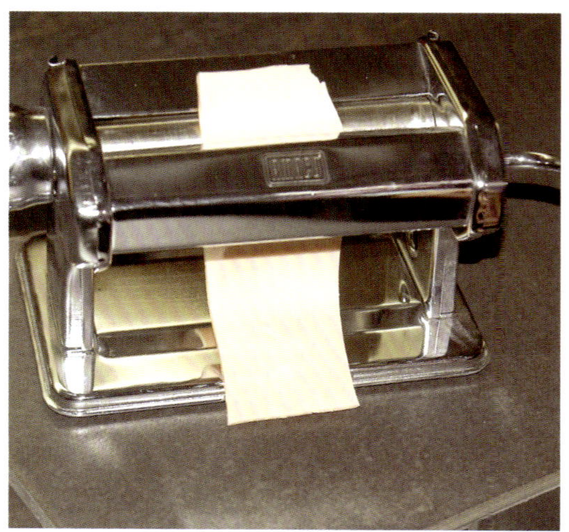
2. Condition the polymer clay with a pasta maker.

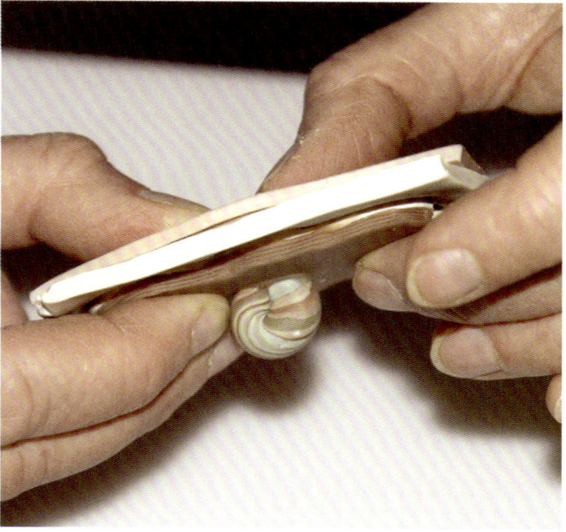
3. Place polymer clay over the texture and press it with your thumbs.

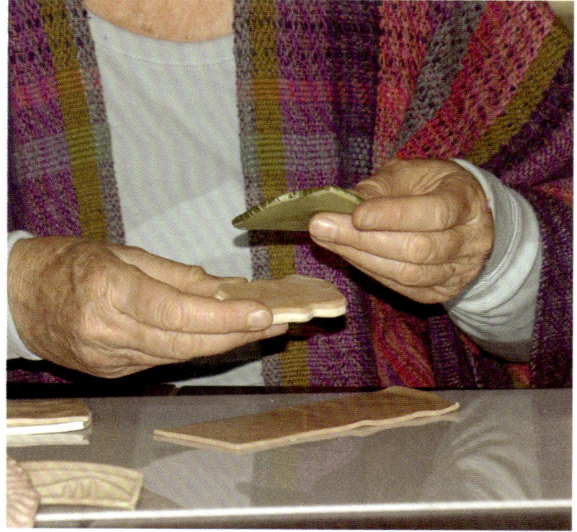
4. Add a second layer of polymer clay and press again with your thumbs.

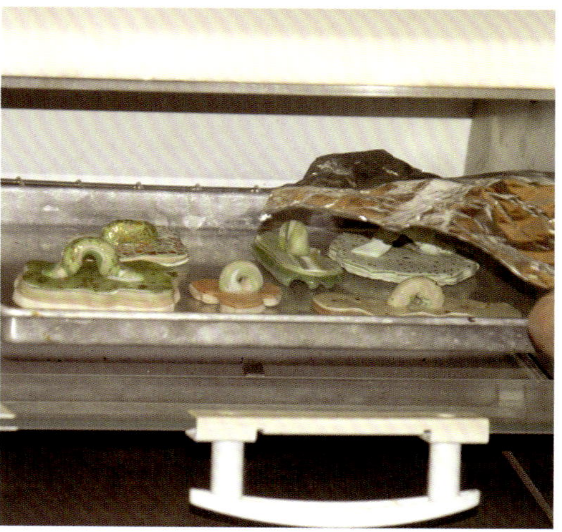
5. Bake the polymer stamps in a small toaster oven.

Leave the polymer clay on the textured surface and add a second layer of Super Sculpey clay (figure 4). Press the layers again with your thumbs. Remove the clay and trim the edges.

Bake the polymer in a small toaster oven, following the directions given on the package. Typically, it will bake at 275°F for fifteen minutes, though you may increase the time by five minutes if the stamps are very thick. Be careful not to overheat the polymer clay. You can cover your pieces with aluminum foil to prevent scorching and blistering (figure 5). If you smell a strong odor while cooking the stamps, it means that they are getting too hot. Turn off the oven, and ventilate the room. Tip: If you plan to make a lot of pieces, buy a toaster oven dedicated just to curing polymer pieces.

Finally, add a top decorative layer and a handle. I join everything together with a thin coat of liquid polymer clay and cure the piece again. The heat fuses the layers and handle together. Note: These stamps are not as strong as ceramic or wooden stamps. If you have trouble with your stamp breaking, try making the layers of the stamp thicker.

Forming & Texture

ROLLING STAMPS

by William Shinn

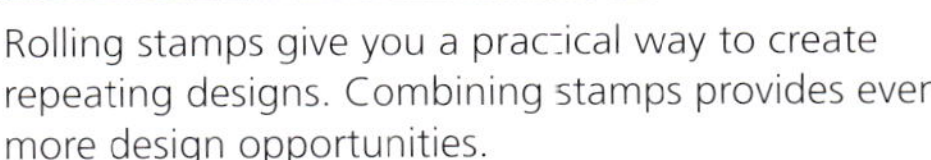

Rolling stamps give you a practical way to create repeating designs. Combining stamps provides even more design opportunities.

The early Greek potters used small rolls of clay that had been carved on the surfaces to produce repeated patterns on their freshly thrown forms. However, little more has been done with this technique by subsequent potters. This is understandable, since larger rolling stamps would, of course, distort a freshly thrown piece. With the increased interest in handbuilt, press-molded and extruded forms, the possibilities for texturing flat surfaces with rolling stamps on a larger scale can be more thoroughly explored.

The simplest method of creating rolling stamps is to roll a clay slab around a tubular shape, such as a cardboard tube, wooden dowel or plastic pipe. These produce a rigid backing when applying a texture to the slabs. A piece of newspaper placed between the form and the clay will prevent sticking when removing the support. Removal should be performed as soon as possible before any shrinkage takes place.

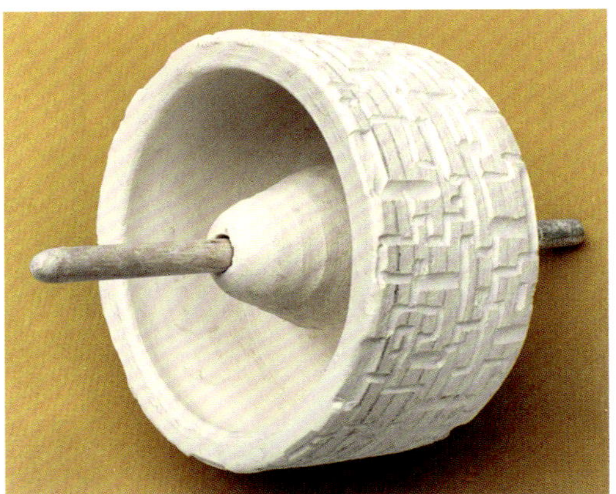

1. Stamps can be made by throwing a cylindrical or conical form.

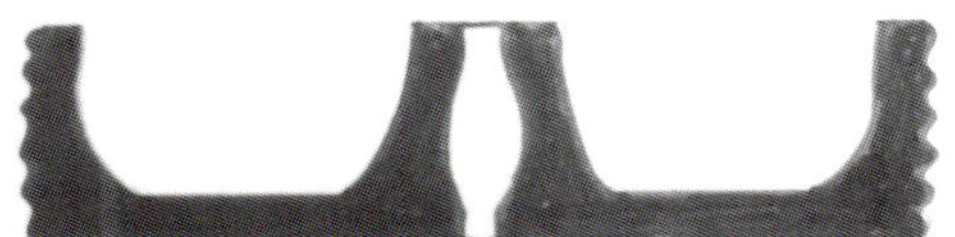

2. The outer wall forms the working surface and should be perpendicular to the wheel head.

Process

Stamps also can be made by throwing a cylindrical or conical form (figure 1). The thrown stamps are created like miniature steamer casseroles. The center spout is pulled up and compressed to an opening the size of the dowel (with allowance for shrinkage). The outer wall is then raised to form the working surface of the stamp, which will be carved at the proper stage of drying. Make sure that the outer surface is perpendicular to the wheel head (figure 2). The use of an extruder can also produce tubular shapes for

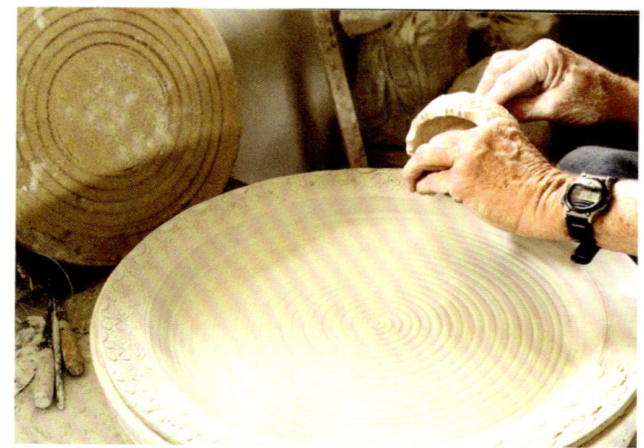

3. Hold the stamp rigidly in a fixed position then lift after exactly one revolution, which takes practice.

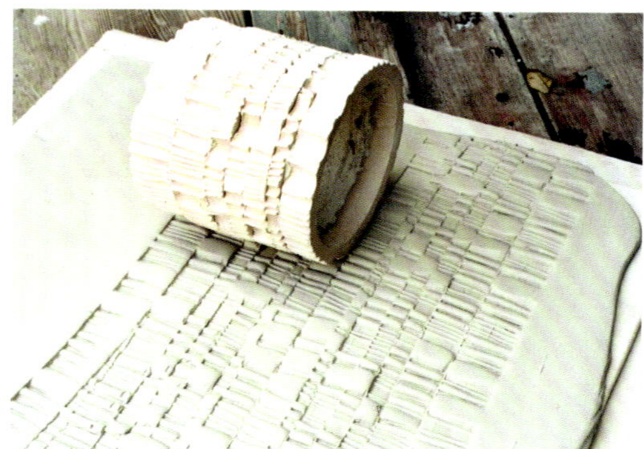

4. Cutting cylinders into sections and reassembling with glue after bisque firing produces a variety of results.

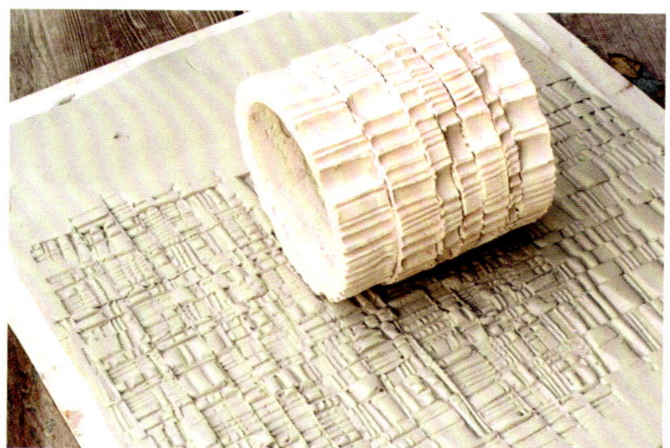

5. Rolling stamps in different directions adds even more variety to the surface.

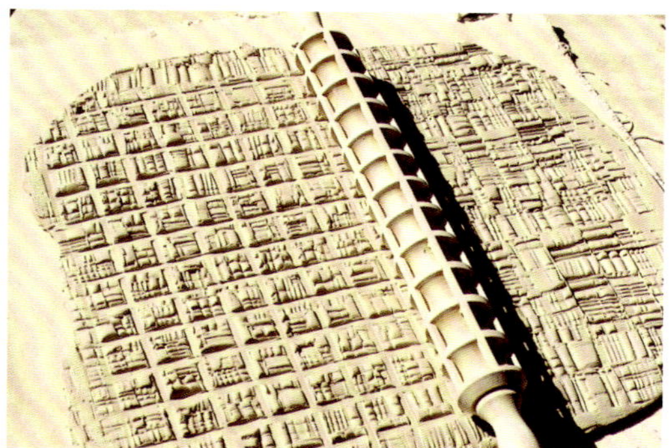

6. Other tools can add further interest to the surface.

rolling stamps. The ends can be filled in, leaving small holes in the center to allow dowels to be used as handles. Bisqued clay produces an ideal stamp with its combination of porosity, strength and permanence. Make the walls as thick as possible because a thin wall can't withstand the heavy pressure and becomes quickly saturated, losing its resistance to sticking. Use a hair dryer to solve this problem.

After creating and firing the stamps, their use is quite simple. The cylinders are rolled over the surface of the clay with the palm of the hand while varying the pressure to correspond to the width of the stamp. For small stamps, I prefer throwing the forms and using them with dowels for handles—much like rolling pins. They are more easily guided in a straight or curved line than the wider and heavier cylindrical stamps.

The rolling stamp is ideal for quickly decorating a platter rim. The stamp, held rigidly in a fixed position, quickly prints out the repeated pattern as the wheel spins. Lifting at the right moment can be tricky. A little practice is recommended when starting this project (figure 3).

Besides carving, the surface pattern can be created a variety of ways—utilizing simple stamps (repeated or varied), rolling the clay over natural or manmade surfaces, stretching the clay pattern while flat before wrapping around a cylinder, etc. The possibilities are endless. You also may notice that the impressed negative design on the clay can be quite different from the positive design of the stamp.

Very effective surfaces can be obtained by cutting the cylinders into sections and reassembling the parts into different positions. This can

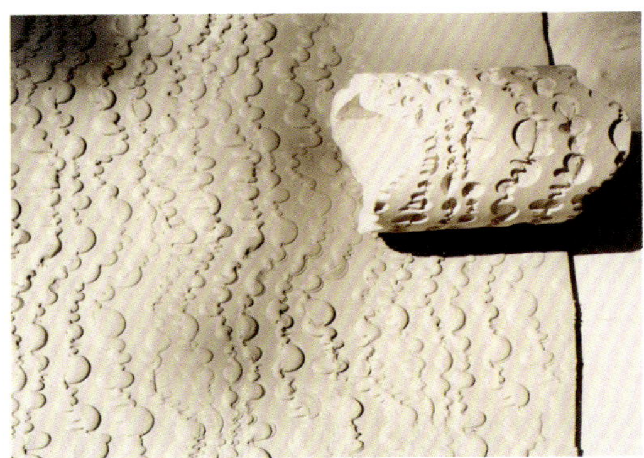

7. Design a cylinder with matched outer edges to create a repeated pattern.

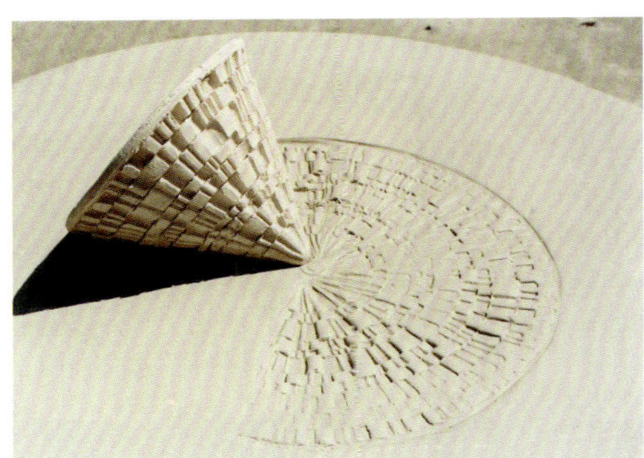

8. Use a conical thrown form to produce a round design. Combine with a handled stamp to enhance design.

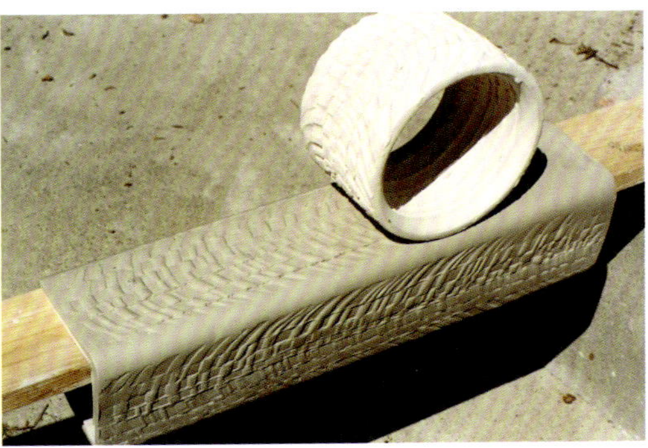

9. Support extruded shapes to with a board covered with newspaper or cloth to prevent sticking.

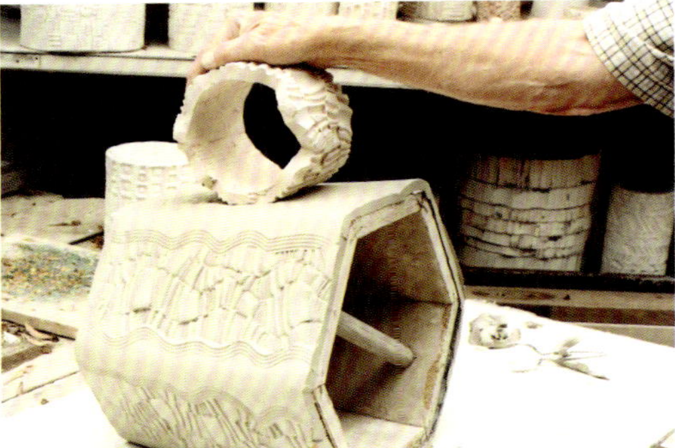

10. Unlike raised decorations, impressed designs distort very little when the decorated surface is face down.

be done when the stamps are leather hard and then glued back together after bisque firing. Such a rolling stamp can produce a variety of results (figure 4 and 5). Other tools can add further interest to the surface (figure 6).

For producing an overall surface, or for creating unconventionally shaped tiles, design a cylinder with matched outer edges. This creates a repeated pattern that fits within itself and create a continuous surface when rolled side by side (figure 7).

A conical thrown form can be used to produce a round design (figure 8). The conical stamp can be combined with the handled stamp to increase the complexity of the design.

Unlike a thrown form, an extruded shape possessing flat surfaces is an excellent form for stamping when supported from the inside. Newspaper or cloth can be used to prevent sticking (figure 9).

Simply wrapping clay around a wooden or cardboard shape presents an ideal backing for applying a stamp design. The imprinted design has an advantage over a raised pattern because you can gently rotate the work face down for support with little distortion of the design. An attached handle inside the mold helps facilitate its removal (figure 10).

When glazing the work, the imprinted design is ideal for inlaying color. After applying the first glaze, the surface is brushed off, resulting in a neatly inlaid color. Another contrasting glaze can be added over the entire surface. You can also stain the textured areas and glaze other sections of the pot. The possible variations in glazing are as numerous as the variations in stamping the ware.

Forming & Texture

USING BATIK PATTERNS

by Shana Angela Salaff

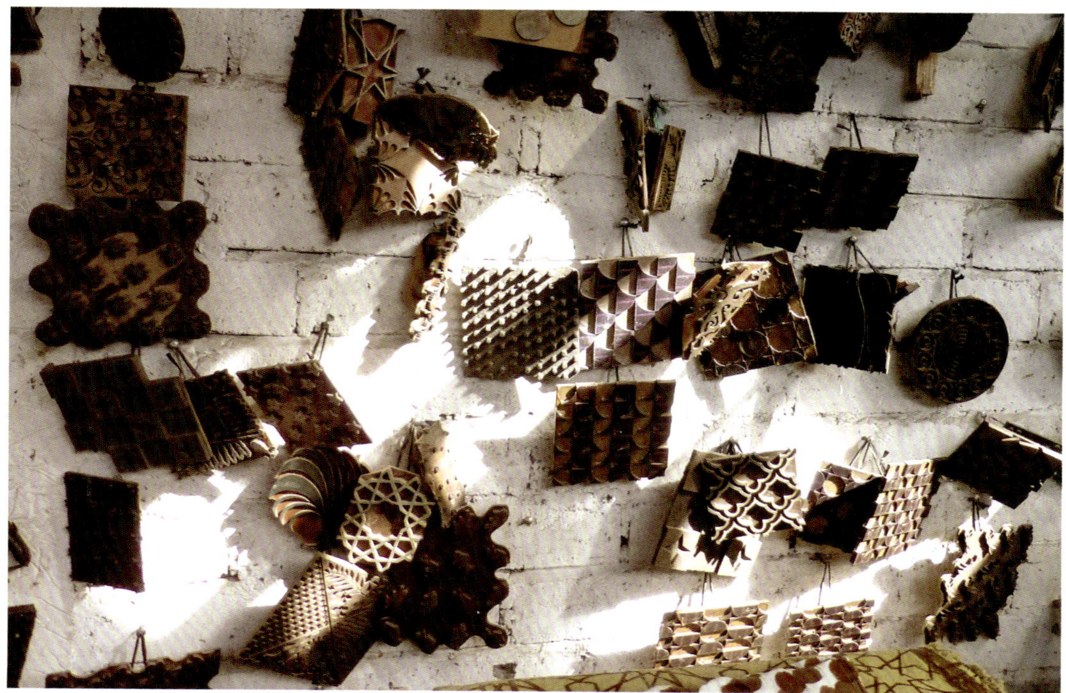

Wooden batik stamps stored on the courtyard wall at the Tjok Agung Batik workshop. These stamps also make great tools in the pottery studio.

In the summer of 2012, I travelled to Bali, Indonesia, for a residency at the Gaya Ceramic Art Center (CAC) (www.gayaceramic.com), which is located in Ubud, one of the cultural hubs of the province. Alongside my ceramic studio work, I was given many opportunities to participate in ceremonies and events. To my eyes, these seemed extraordinary and exotic, while to local Balinese they were commonplace. In fact, for the Balinese, who are Hindu, religion is completely integrated into daily life. Each day begins with the woman of the household offering blessings to the household sun shrine, and extending that blessing to the dwelling, work areas, and important tools in these areas. Our kilns were blessed daily, and larger ceremonies blessing all the tools were held every six months.

The Gaya CAC studio was a blend of Balinese and Western sensibilities. In the general workspace I found a number of texture molds and stamps available for use. One of these was a beautifully made 10-inch-square stamp with a raised pattern and wooden strap handle on the back. When I asked where it had come from, Hillary Kane, the CAC director and a ceramic artist with a textile background, explained that students from a recent Gaya workshop exploring ceramics and textiles had visited a local batik shop that used traditional batik and indigo dying techniques. The proprietor, Tjok Agung, had sold some of his handmade stamps to the students and this one was left behind for future students to use (figure 1).

Batik is a process where a pattern is painted (or stamped) onto fabric using melted wax, and the fabric is then dyed. The wax acts as a resist, so when the wax is removed with heat, the original fabric color shows in these areas (similar to the process of wax-resist glazing). This process can be repeated with layers of dye, starting with lighter colors and ending with darker ones. I used the batik stamp on slabs of clay that became the bottoms of trays for the cruets I was making.

During this visit to the Tjok Agung Indigo studio, Agung's wife (and head salesperson) showed me around the workshop, explaining through an interpreter the various techniques in use. Amazingly, in the same visit, I was able to see the stamps used to make the patterns, the process, and the finished, printed fabrics (figure 2).

Tjok Agung's Patterns

In the Indonesian tradition of batik, these stamps are made of copper, and Agung uses many of these (figure 3), but he also has quite a few made out of pressboard or Masonite. When I returned later in the summer to purchase stamps, it was

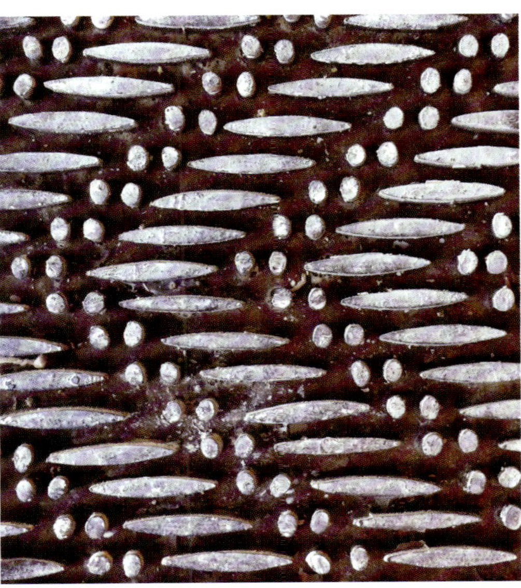

1. Wooden batik stamp that was part of the studio tool collection at Gaya CAC.

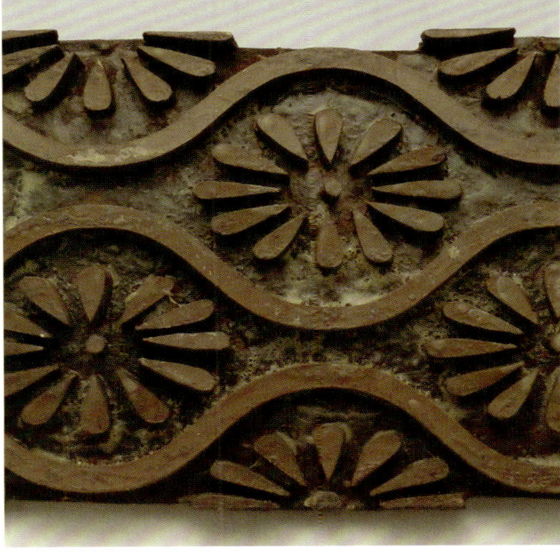

2. Wooden stamp used to create the batik pattern on fabric.

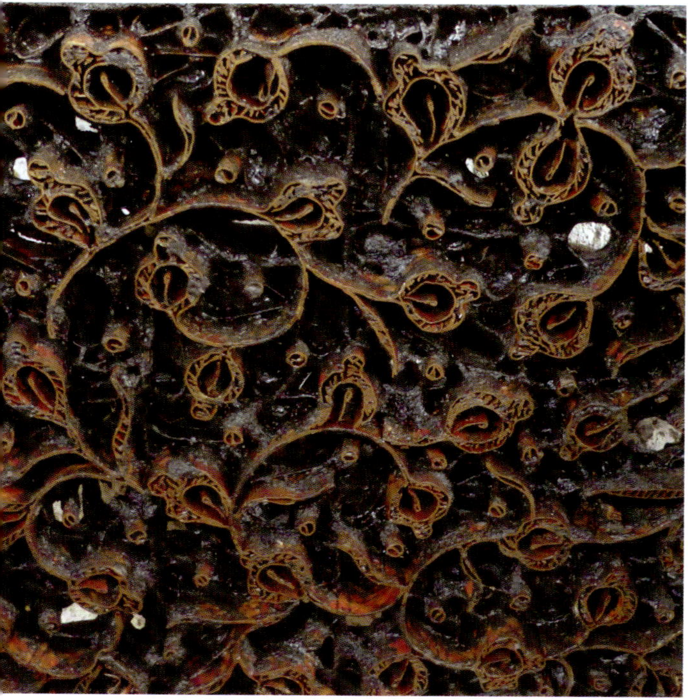

3. Wooden batik stamp that was part of the studio tool collection at Gaya CAC.

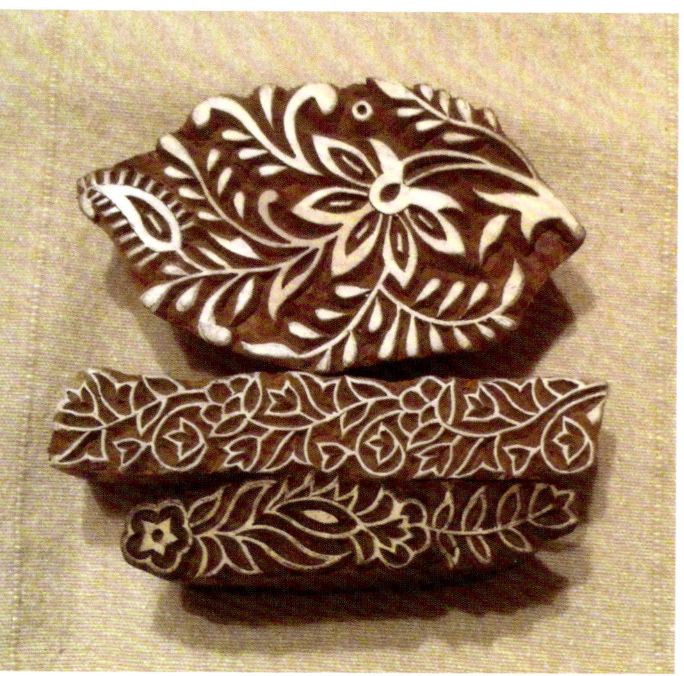

4. Wooden stamp used to create the batik pattern on fabric..

the wooden ones that Tjok Agung offered me, as these could be easily remade.

What I love about Agung's patterns is that there are such a huge variety of influences evident. Some patterns have a local Indonesian feel, while others are distinctly European in style. I was told that Agung researches pattern sources on the Internet. What a great example of contemporary artistic practice—local materials employed with regional technology, using designs sourced globally with contemporary technology!

Although I used the stamp I found in the Gaya CAC workshop many times in Bali, I have not used the ones I brought home. I find them to be beautiful artworks in their own right and enjoy having them as visual reminders of my trip.

For ceramic artists interested in patterns from Batik stamps, sources abound. Fragments or full examples of traditional Indonesian stamps are now widely available on eBay, as well as many more from other Eastern cultures such as Thailand and Cambodia. Most prevalent are the carved, wooden, textile printing stamps from India. Import shops sometimes have small wooden stamps created just for resale that are fairly inexpensive (figure 4). Larger stamps can sometimes be found in such shops, but the old ones that have actually been in use and are complete, are expensive. The stamp fragments are the cheapest, as they can't be used for their intended purpose and are smaller and easier to ship.

Using Batik Stamps on Clay

Working on soft clay slabs with batik stamps is fairly easy as long as the clay surface isn't sticky. Be sure to rub off any clay attached to the stamp each time you make an impression, as intricate stamps tend to clog up quickly. Metal stamps tend to stick more than wooden ones; either use slightly firmer clay or apply a thin layer of cornstarch to the clay first. With larger stamps, use a gentle rocking motion to release the stamp upward without tearing the slab. If the stamp is small, you can press it into the clay from above.

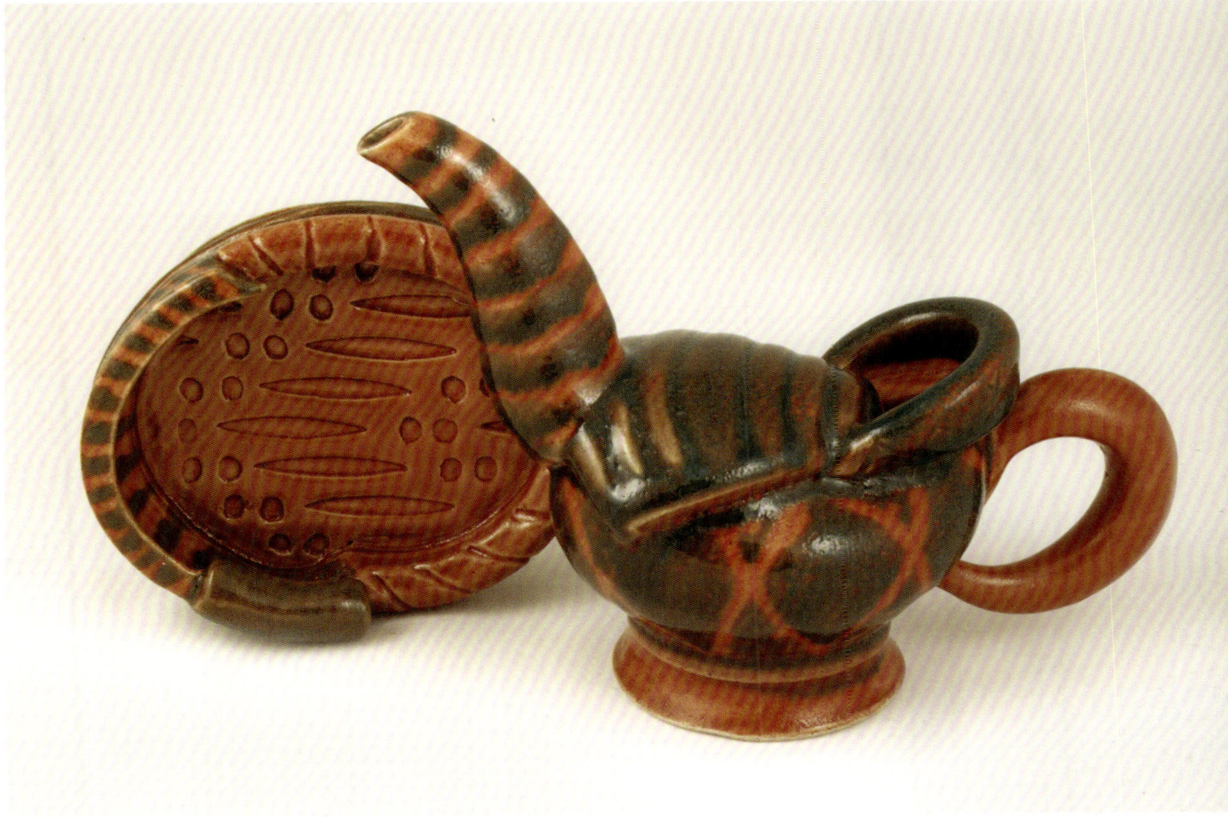

Blackie Cruet and Tray, oxidation-fired cone 10 stoneware. The inside bottom of the tray was textured using the stamp shown in figure 1. When the thrown components were still wet, the studio dog, Blackie, jumped up upon the table and got his claws into them. Instead of trying to remove the claw-marks, I continued them around the rim to create the impressed pattern. I then congratulated Blackie on his excellent suggestion!

For larger stamps, try rolling the clay over the stamp instead. Fragmented stamps can also be used on wheel-thrown work when it is still soft but not sticky. The type of mark made depends upon the thickness of the raised areas of the stamp. When not in use, keep stamps clean and protected with a soft cloth.

Other decorating techniques can be combined with the impressed patterns. Slip or underglaze can be inlaid into the pattern or can be brushed across to highlight it. After bisque firing, thin underglaze or stain can be brushed over the whole surface and then wiped away from raised areas to accentuate the patterns.

Other suggestions: use the stamps as actual stamps. Brush color over the pattern and apply it as a monoprint to flat slabs of clay. You could also try using a stamp for its original purpose: to apply wax resist.

Think of batik stamps as texture tools that have a history, a culture, and an artistic heritage attached to them. The character of the stamp will be transferred to your work, but the more you add on to it and embellish your work, the further it will get from its culture of origin. By doing a little research into the textiles made in the same area your stamp came from, you'll be sure to find some other great patterns!

Forming & Texture

SPRIGS FROM NATURE

by Judi Munn

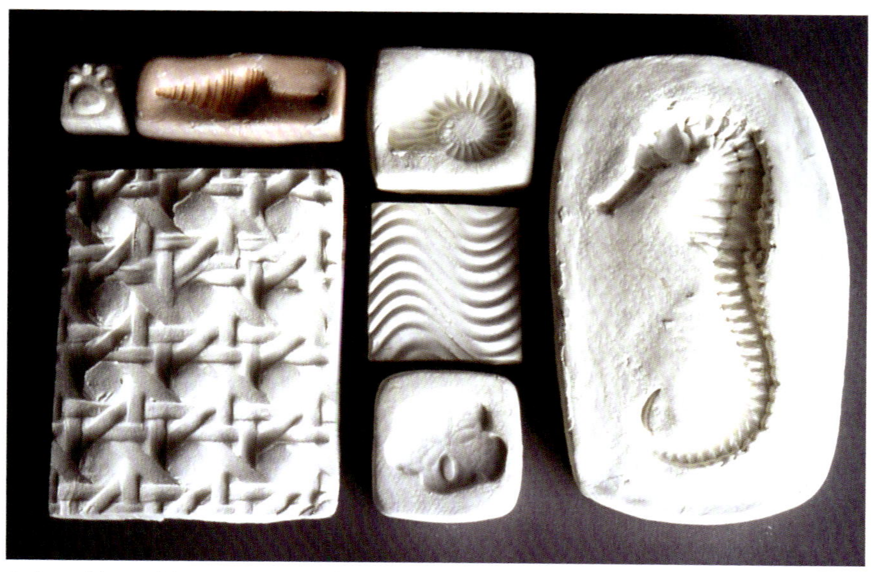

Sprig molds provide a great way to decorate your work. Made from fossils, shells, found objects, or by carving into clay, there's no limit to the variety.

When we first started firing with wood, I got really interested in texture. One of the things that I began to experiment with was creating press molds of shells that could be used to add sprigs. I had a lifetime shell collection from around the world, and I was glad to finally have a reason to use them.

Sprigs are press-molded clay pieces added to leather-hard work. They are created using small molds made of bisque-fired clay or plaster. Wedgwood Jasperware from England is a well-known example of sprig-decorated ware. While Wedgwood's patterns are very intricate, simple sprig molds can be made using almost any object or hand-modeled relief that does not have undercuts.

I use seashells as a motif even though we live in the land-locked Ozarks. On the surface, this might seem a bit out of place, but a trip to any Ozark stream proves otherwise. The creek beds are littered with fossils such as crinoids, sea fan and brachiopods. So, it's natural that I use fossils, as well as the seashells. I'm particularly fond of the beautifully spiraled ammonites.

Historically, sprigs were removed from the mold then applied to the pot. You can also press the sprig onto the pot while it is still in the mold, which can either be a gentle press or a deep one that changes the contour of the pot. Doing this requires an interesting shape for the whole sprig mold.

Process

Begin by using the finest grain clay you have. While porcelain is best, I used fine-grain white stoneware with good results. Shape the exterior of the mold by rolling or tapping on a cloth surface. To make it easier to hold on to, make the mold long or add a handle to the back. Flatten the front

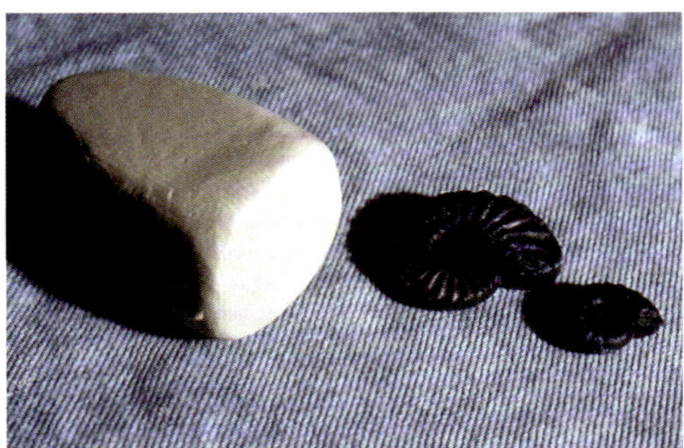
1. Add a handle to make the mold easier to hold and press on a textured cloth for added texture.

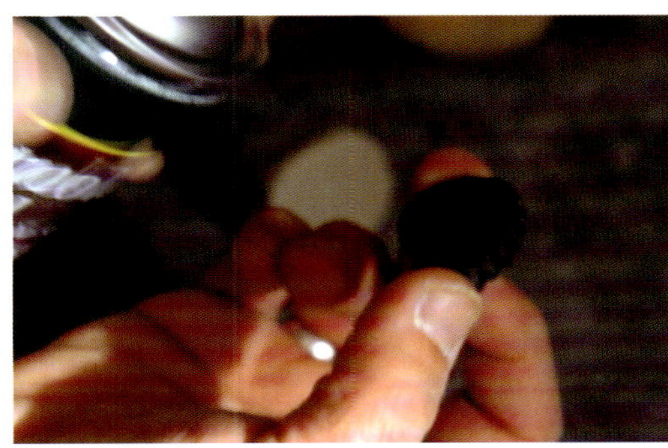
2. Use WD-40 or a cooking spray as a release agent.

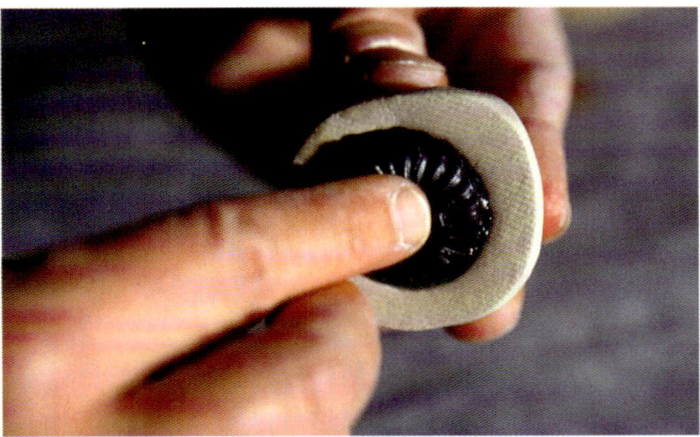
3. Center the object on the mold and press it onto the clay.

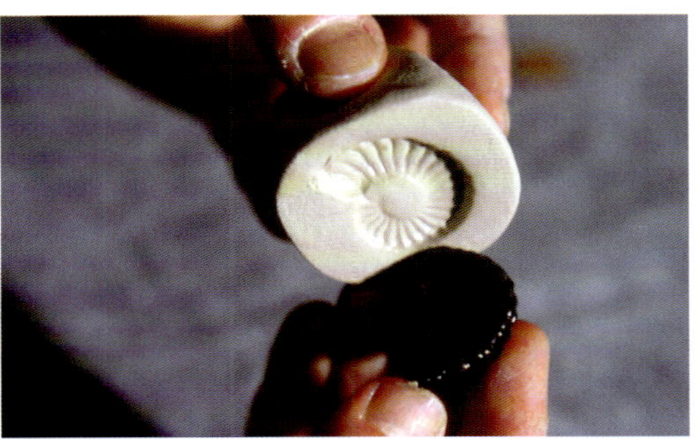
4. Carefully remove the object without disturbing the edges and allow to dry slowly.

of it. If desired, add texture by pressing the mold on a textured cloth or other surface (figure 1).

Spray the object with a releasing agent such as cooking spray or WD-40 (figure 2). Center the object on the mold and press it onto the clay (figure 3). Carefully remove the object, and don't disturb the edges. Allow the mold to dry slowly then bisque fire (figure 4).

To apply, press a small ball of clay into the deep part of the mold (figure 5). Press extra clay on the rest of the mold (figure 6). Put a small amount of water or slip on the backside of sprig. Press the sprig on the pot from the outside with one hand, using your other hand to press out toward the sprig from the inside (figure 7). If you put too much slop on the back of the sprig, it will ooze out and stick to the mold, which makes the mold stick to the pot. If this happens, just leave the mold in place until it absorbs the moisture, then it will come right off. Molds can also stick when they become wet during use, in which case you'll need to let the mold dry out before continuing.

Pressing the sprig deeply into the pot while the pot is still moist makes it less likely that it will come off in the dying process. This also gives the pot a look of spontaneity (figure 8).

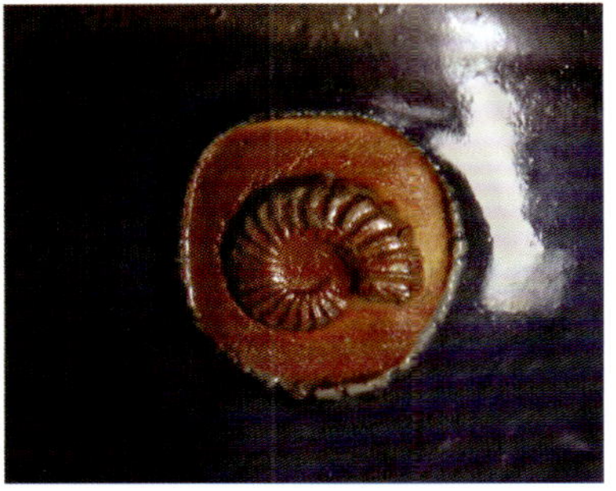
Detail of fired sprig decoration.

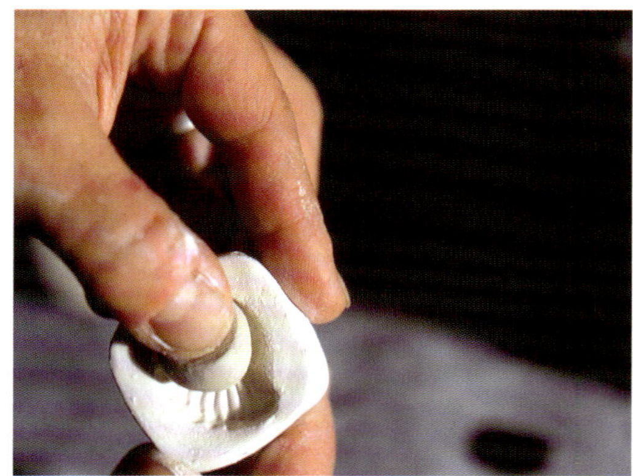

5. To apply, press a small ball of clay into the deep part of the mold.

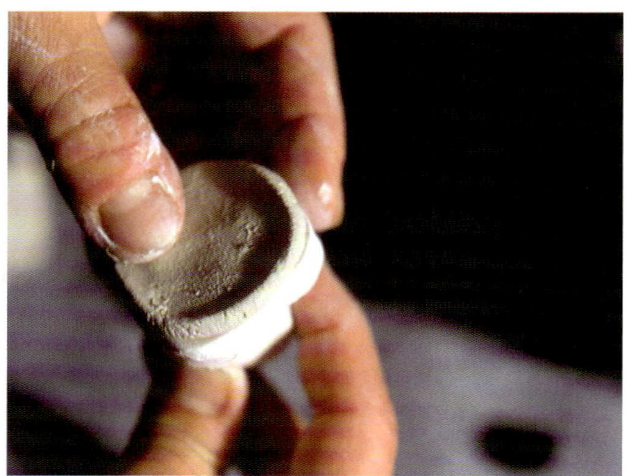

6. Press extra clay on the rest of the mold.

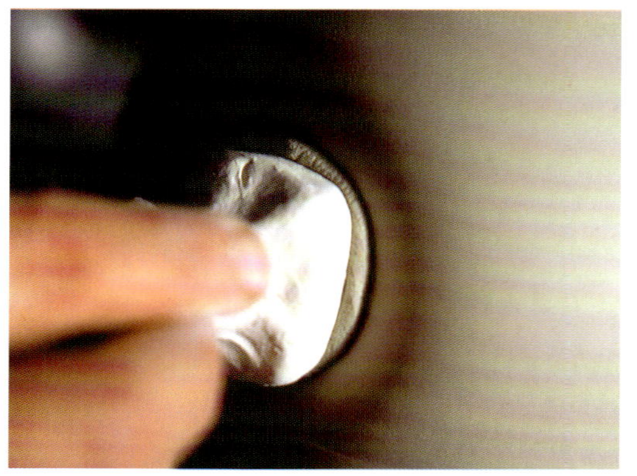

7. Put a small amount of slip, on the backside of sprig and on the pot. Apply pressure from the inside.

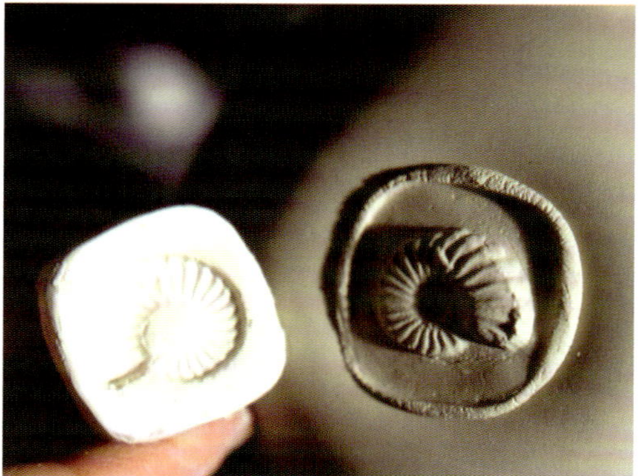

8. Press the sprig deeply into the pot while the pot is still moist to adhere it securely.

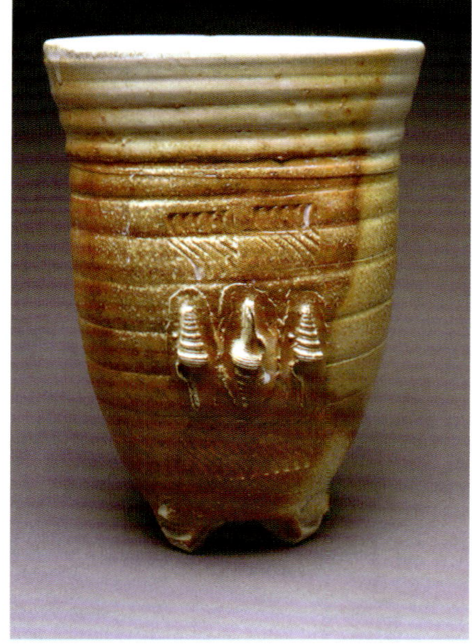

Sprigs can be used in several ways—as feet and in a surface decoration on the 7-inch vase (left). On the bottle (right), sprigs form the handles and glazing highlights a sprig decoration on the side.

Forming & Texture

CHRIS GRYDER'S SILT SURFACES

by Dori DeCamillis

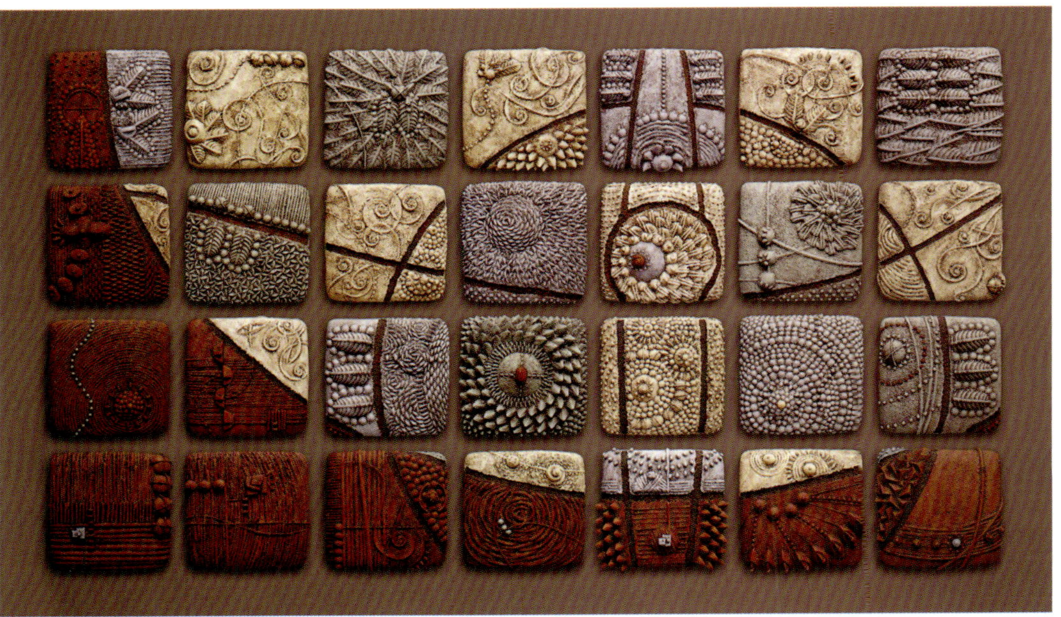

A lot of Gryder's work is comprised of special commissions like the one for the Meacham residence in Malvern, Pennsylvania. "This allows for greater freedom in developing large compositional themes," Gryder says. 7½ feet in width, silt-cast stoneware with colored terra sigillatas and dark clay wash, fired to cone 3.

Chris Gryder began exploring art by studying architecture. From the visionary designs of Antonio Gaudi and the philosophy of Louis Sullivan, to experimental work in mold making for architectural pieces, Gryder pieced together a singular aesthetic and an uncommon process of sculpture making.

For three years, Gryder worked in the field of architecture until a five-year stint in the desert of Arizona turned his head to the world of sculpture. He lived and worked on Paolo Soleri's project "Arcosanti," which had been developing prototypes for urban ideas since the 1970s in a clay studio and bronze foundry 65 miles north of Phoenix. While Gryder worked there building architectural pieces, he overwhelmingly responded to building with his hands. Working in the ceramic studio he gained rudimentary technical knowledge and started playing with the idea of making molds in the negative. With memories of Gaudi emerging, he began an interest in making organic sculptural forms.

The most striking aspect of his art making during his graduate years was the atypical process he used to create vessels. They are cast in silt and covered with neutral colors of terra sigillata. The process (see page XX) is involved and time consuming, but appealing to Gryder. He explains that in a one-off single casting the artist doesn't have to concentrate time and energy on preparing the mold for repetitive use, a process of accommodation which often informs the piece visually. More freedom of design is allowed with a mold that dis-

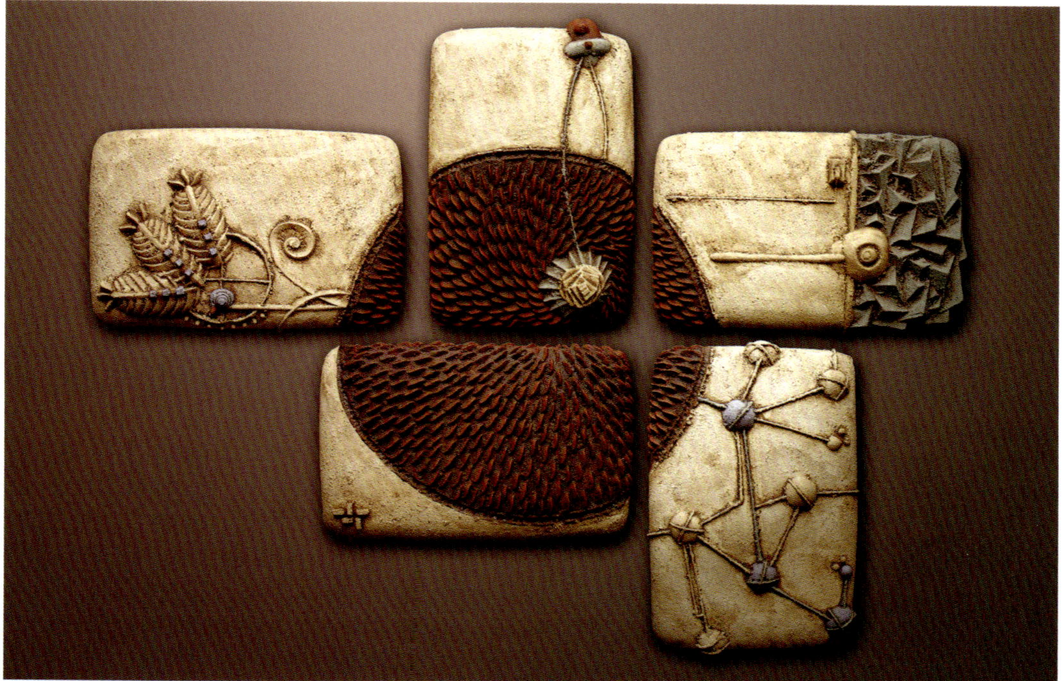

Pinwheel, 34 inches in width, fired to cone 3 One of the challenges Gryder faces with his silt-casting technique is applying the colored washes and terra sigillata without marring the silt-textured surface.

solves after each piece. The procedure also offers the opportunity for more spontaneous and unexpected results.

Covering the outside of Gryder's vessels are odd protruding forms that travel in patterns. One can imagine the act of scooping that produces the curious structure and contour. The surface is rough, like sand, with peculiar gatherings of hardened sediment tucked into the tight spaces between forms. Without knowing the process, a seasoned clay enthusiast would be hard-pressed to understand how the extraordinary surface was achieved.

Vessels were Gryder's primary focus in grad school, but he also dabbled in tiles using the same process. After graduating and finding a following for his work, tiles became more of a focus, and eventually their popularity and his interest in them pushed them into the forefront of his production. The tiles as a group manifest themselves in large wall-relief constructions, often 8–10 feet in length. Gryder starts by developing the piece linearly, focusing on overall form. The divisions of space could represent primitive ceremonial diagrams, molecular models, or planetary trajectories, conjuring associations with the metaphysical and the scientific. Like crop circles in a field of perfectly straight rows of corn, one wonders if an indecipherable map has been laid out, its function hidden behind its mysterious beauty.

Within the individual tiles are myriad abstract forms which reference, for the most part, the natural world. At first one is confident in deciphering leaf forms, but on closer examination leaves could be feathers, wings, or crystalline growth. A suggestion of insects, fruit, seeds and pods seems feasible. The eye can follow forms that insinuate ocean waves, branches on a tree, animal trails, veins on a leaf, or water ripples. And while features of the natural world are hinted at, it wouldn't be far-fetched to see the spinning cogs and mechanisms of a moving contraption. The whole impression is one of liveliness and action.

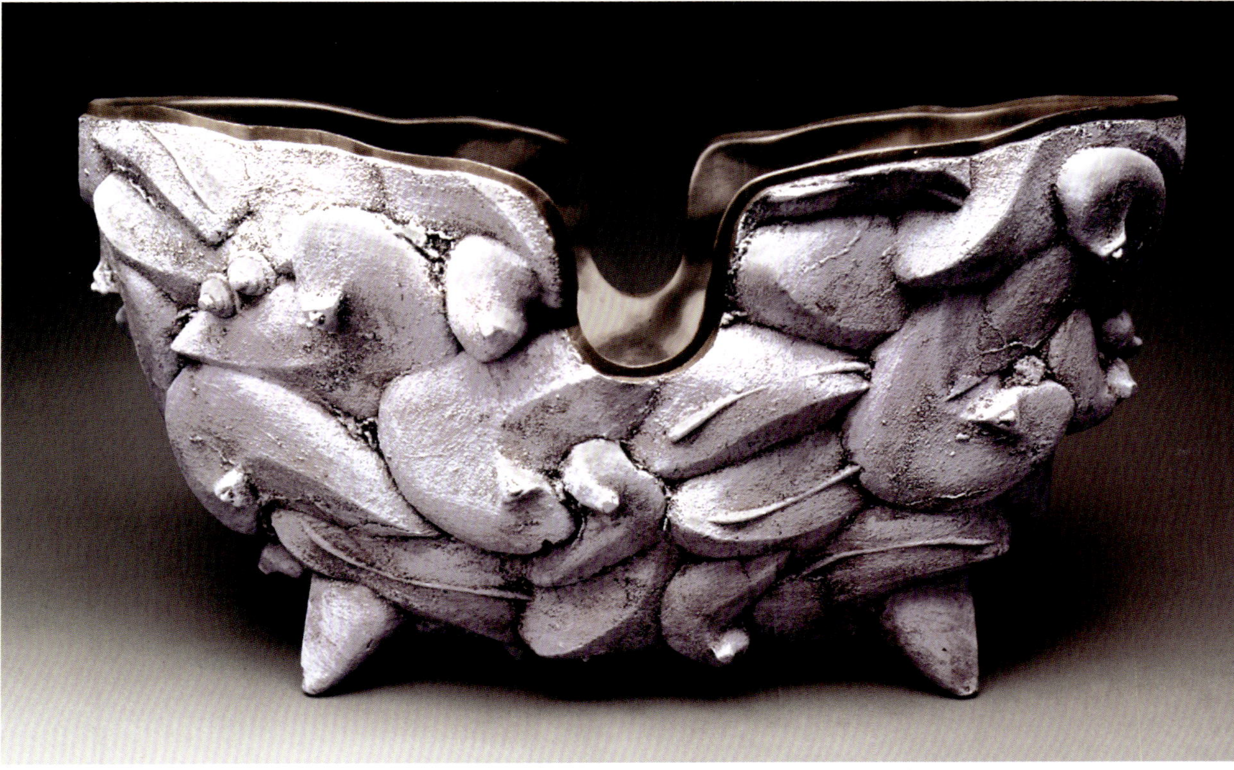

Viscus Notch, 13 inches in height, silt-cast stoneware with colored terra sigillatas, dark clay wash and manganese glaze (interior), fired to cone 3. Gryder says his forming process is "akin to drawing in the dark."

Silt Process

by Chris Gryder

My technique is akin to an actual physical process within the natural world that leads to fossils. The Latin "fossus" translates "having been dug up," and I similarly excavate my clay works from sediment. A fossil is the trace of the remains of some organic body, creature or plant, within sediment. I likewise create trace carvings in the sediment or silt. I build form with negative space. An intricate cavity is dug in the silt that ultimately acts as a dissolvable one-off mold. The material I use to cast into is silt, a very fine sediment created as a result of alluvial action. It is basically comprised of about 70% fine sand and 30% clay. The sand can be thought of as very tiny building blocks and the clay in the mix acts as a mortar to bind the particles together when wet. The porosity of the silt mold allows the basic mechanics of slip casting to operate; the water in the liquid clay migrates into the mold leaving behind slightly more solidified layer of clay at the surface.

This layer becomes thicker as the mold remains filled. Once the desired thickness is achieved, the remaining slip is removed leaving behind a clay shell. As the clay dries and reaches a leather hard state, it can be excavated from the crumbling and dissolving silt mold. This casting technique sacrifices the advantages of multiple castings in favor of rich encrusted and serendipitous surfaces that can be carved directly without concern for undercuts and seams. This is a studio mold and casting technique that approaches the immediacy of drawing rather than the precise methodical planning often associated with mold making.

Layers & Inclusions

HORROR VACUI

by Liz Smith

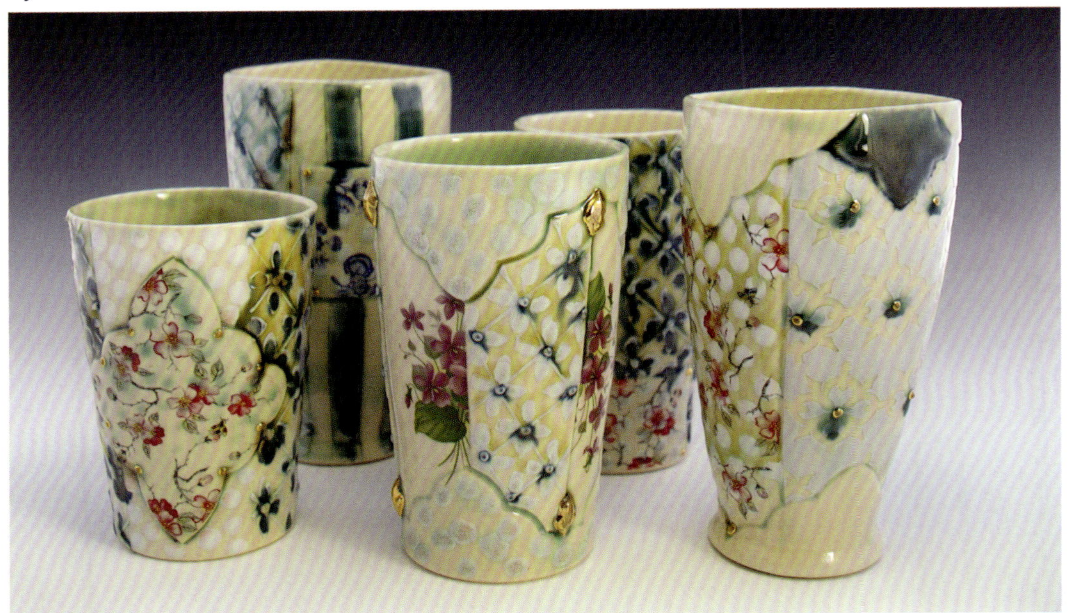

Slip-cast cups, bisque fired to cone 05, glaze fired to cone 5, decal and luster fired to cone 018.

From the moment I first saw it looking at the Lindesfarne Gospels in my freshman year art history survey course, I have loved the term *horror vacui*—the fear of empty space. I still smile when I repeat it in my mind. The Modernist phrase "less is more" has never comforted my soul. While I can appreciate visual restraint, rich ornamentation, complex pattern, and dizzying color combinations leave me feeling visually satiated. In my home I have work by artists that would fit into both categories, from the most perfectly thrown simple form to pieces so over-the-top they look like they are buckling under the weight of so much glaze! I love both, but in my studio I am drawn toward applying layered surface treatments on functional forms as I attempt to achieve the complexity I see in my mind's eye. Creating a successful three-dimensional form while maintaining the functionality of the object and applying surfaces that both reiterate the form and break it up—while considering the visual and tactile experience of the pots in use—is exciting and endlessly challenging.

Like so many makers, I have many influences. These include lectures on art, one in particular by Leopold Foulem in 2002 titled "Surface as Surface as Surface;" a thoughtful essay on the complexity of combining form and surface; European porcelains of the 19th century, from the tactility of Wedgwood to the colorful patterning of Sèvres; the textiles of Somalia; and the Egungun masquerade costumes from the Youruba people of West Africa, which I admire for their complex pattern combinations and the artists' inherent need to create beauty and meaning through function.

Of course, in my studio I don't really think about all of these things. I would never get anything made and would be paralyzed by confusion. I only think of them this literally, all at once, when

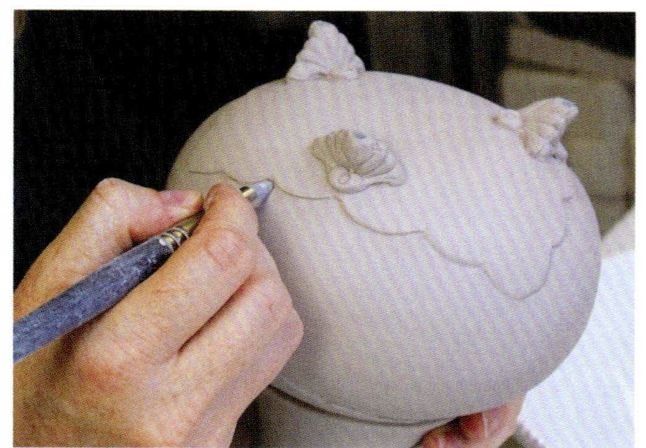
1. Trace a decorative pattern, then trim away enough surface area to create a low-relief decoration.

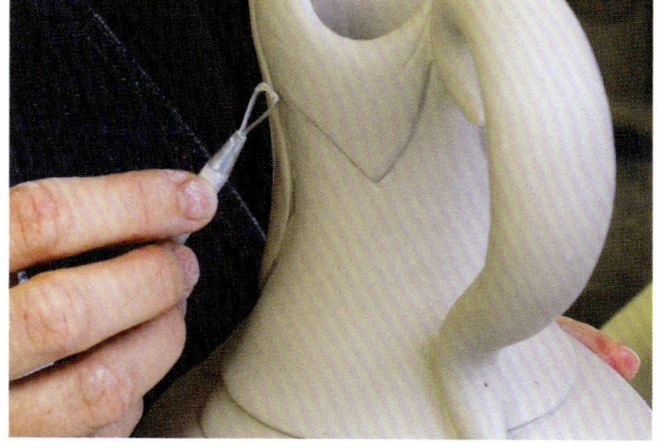
2. Use a small loop tool to carve out a low-relief shape on the neck. Cut curves into the top edge of the neck.

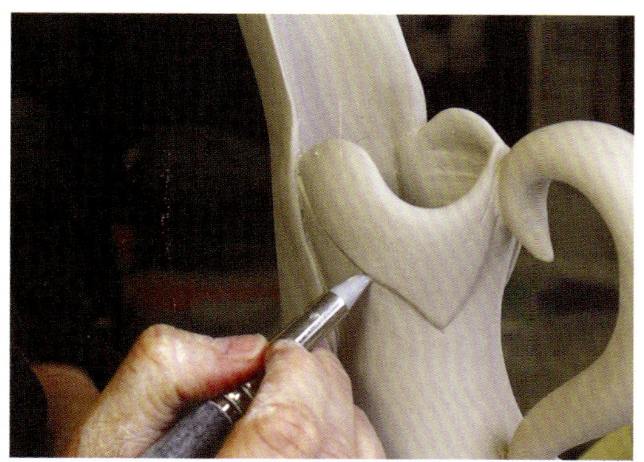
3. Use a rubber-tipped clean-up tool to refine the edge of the shape carved into the neck of the piece.

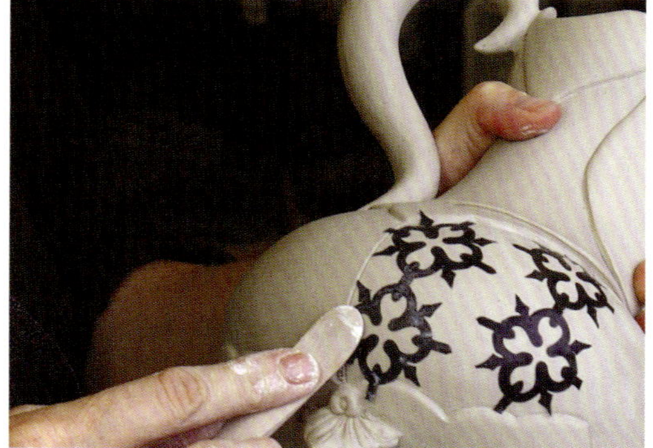
4. Burnish a vinyl template pattern into the piece with the rounded edge of a wooden tool to get a clean edge.

I am asked to write them down or give an artist's talk. However, once a piece is completed, the entirety of these influential experiences and interests are the things I check the work against to determine if it is successful.

I don't speak a second language fluently, but I assume it is an experience similar to making artwork. I have been told fluent speakers don't translate their words to their native language as they speak. Instead they are able to speak clearly because of their learned experience and practice with the language. Of course, with any language, poor choices happen and mistakes are made. In my studio I have enough successful work to keep me inspired, and enough failures to keep me feeling challenged. In the end, I love making, practicing, and experimenting more than I love perfection.

Shaping the Form, Segmenting the Surface

It's the negative spaces created by the various attachments on vessel forms that interest me. When thinking about the initial form, separate from the surface, the Chiwara headdresses created by the Bamana people of Mali are a primary influence for me. I studied African art history as an undergraduate student at Skidmore College and was fortunate enough to go to West Africa and then intern at the National Museum of African Art in Washington, D.C. To this day, the Chiwara headdresses stand out in my mind as some of the most masterfully designed objects in the world of art. I aspire to the clean and dynamic negative space and gracefully contained energy that these objects possess.

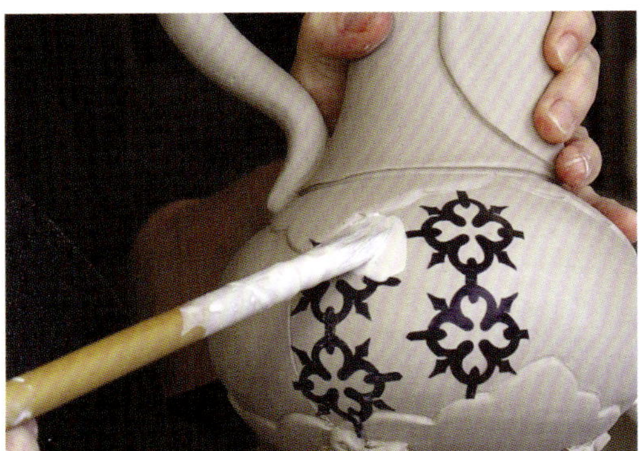

5. Brush slip over the entire vinyl template pattern.

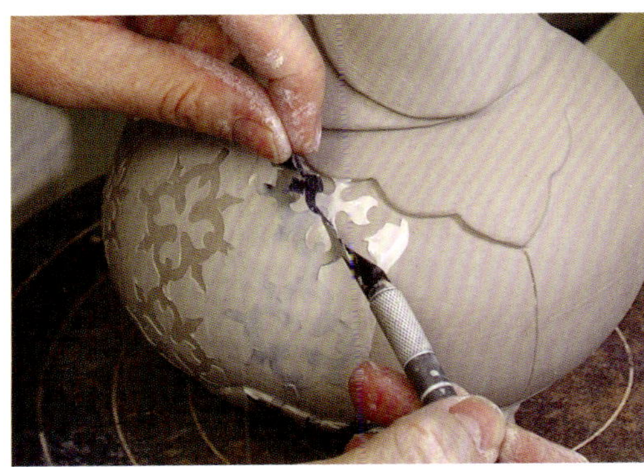

6. Peel the template off while the slip is still damp using an X-Acto knife.

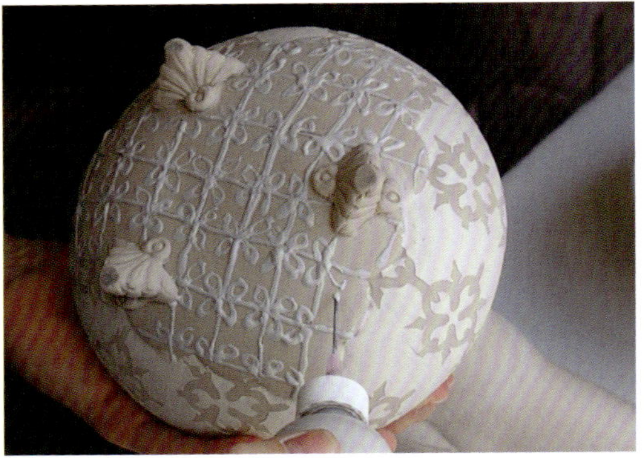

7. Apply a colored slip to the bottom of the pitcher using a small slip trailer.

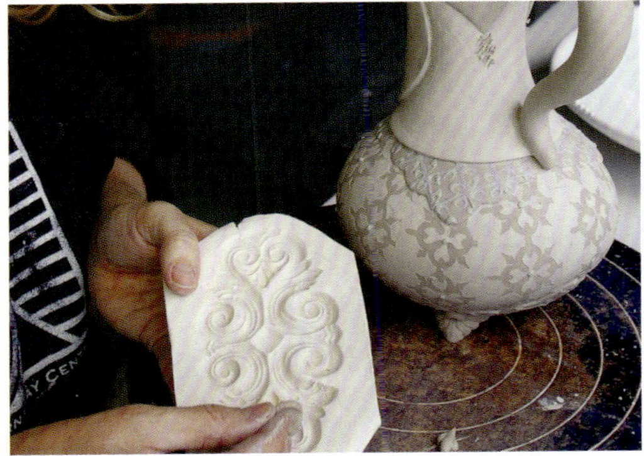

8. Make a few sprigs, then carve or refine them before applying them to the scored area on the pitcher neck.

I work in series of four to six pieces that are iterations of preliminary gestural sketches and begin each piece on the wheel. I start with the body, then the handles and spouts are cut and shaped from a slab rolled between two square dowels, and finally the feet are formed and cut from a sprig mold. After using a cut paper template to trace out a decorative pattern on the bottom, I trim away some of the surface to create the shape in low relief using a small loop tool, then refine the edges of that carved shape with a rubber-tipped tool (figure 1). The lines, echoed in a low-relief shape, are carved using a small loop tool on the neck of the pitcher (figure 2). I also cut the flat, top edge of the neck into a more curvilinear finish using an X-Acto knife and a paper template. Finally, I use a rubber-tipped clean-up tool to refine the edge of the shape carved into the neck of the piece to complete the vessel form (figure 3).

Layering on the Surface

After the form is constructed, I apply surface treatments at every stage of making. I think it may be my fear of the proverbial blank canvas. I can imagine almost nothing more daunting than looking at a table full of blank bisqueware without marking or color. To avoid having to make all of the right decisions with glaze at the end, I carve, sprig, slip trail, resist, and underglaze prior to bisque firing. I begin the decorating process by laying a vinyl-cut template onto the leather-hard pitcher, and burnish it with the rounded edge of a wooden tool (figure 4). I brush a slip over the vinyl template pattern (figure 5), then I peel the template off the surface while the slip is still damp (figure 6).

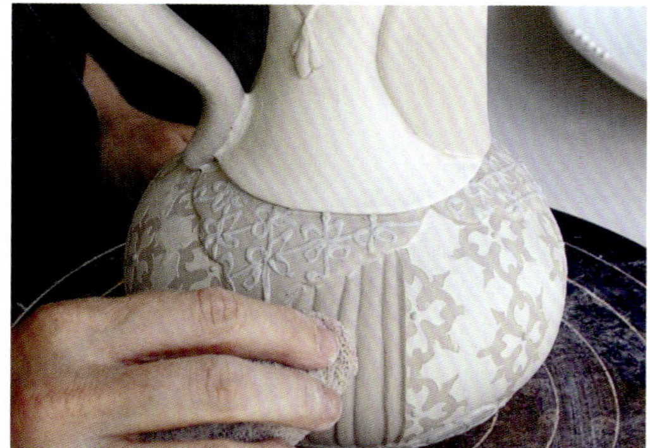

9. Carve a linear pattern through the slip decoration. Allow the piece to dry and bisque fire it.

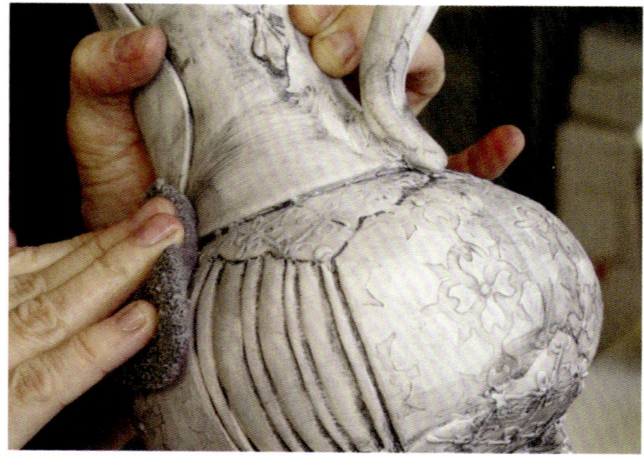

10. After bisque firing, brush a black copper oxide wash over the piece and wipe it off with a damp sponge.

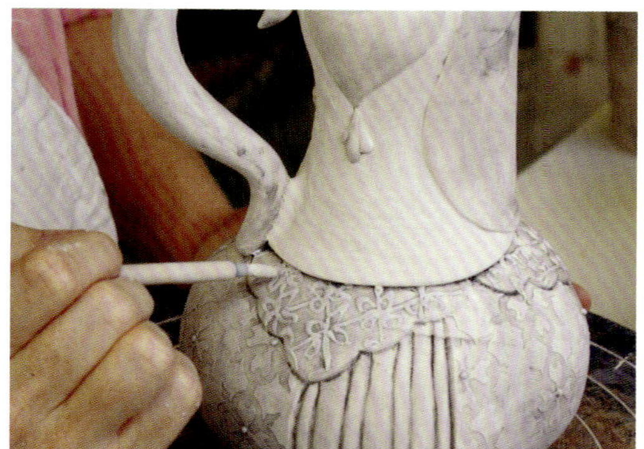

11. Brush on any and all glazes. Fire to cone 5.

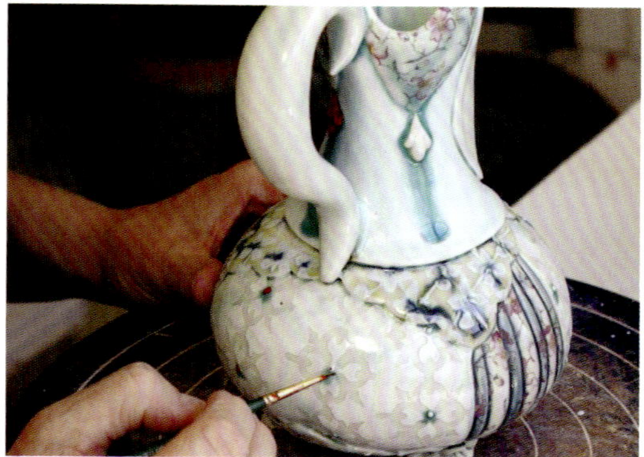

12. Apply hand-cut commercial decals and brush on lusters. Fire decals and lusters to cone 018.

I apply a colored slip to the bottom of the form using a small slip trailer (figure 7). After applying the slip trailed decoration, I make a few sprigs using press molds (figure 8), which I further carve and refine for additional detail and then apply to the neck of the pitcher. For the final pre-bisque decoration, I carve a linear pattern through sections of the slip decoration on the body (figure 9).

Post-bisque Decoration

After bisque firing to cone 05, I brush a wash mixture of black copper oxide and water over the entire piece and then wipe it off with a damp sponge. The copper accentuates the lines and textures of the surface when the piece is glaze fired (figure 10). All of my glazes are brushed on, including any intricate patterns (figure 11), clear top coats, and liner glazes. The piece is then fired to cone 5.

Adding Finishing Touches

Finally, I apply commercial and self-designed decals and also highlight details, such as sprigs, with luster (figure 12). The luster helps balance the piece and create areas of focus or a place for the eye to rest.

Toshiko Takaezu, my primary mentor, is my promoter of experimentation. When asked, as she glazed, what a piece would look like in the end she would reply, ". . . we'll see, it's all an experiment." Those were powerful words coming from an artist of her stature and longevity and I always keep them with me. When I think I have gone too far I hear Walter Ostrom—long-time professor of ceramics at the Nova Scotia College of Art and Design and who works with majolica decorating techniques—who critiqued my work only once, as a brilliant and enthusiastic proponent of decorative excess. When I choose glazes that will run across edges and break up the structure of the composition, I hear an LSU painting professor who asked me, rather pointedly, why I treat my forms like a paint-by-number project. Knowing when to stop—how to achieve balance in the work, and limit myself within this process—is what I find most difficult. My enthusiasm to experiment often overwhelms my desire for every piece to be successful. The fact that I make my living as a professor allows me this luxury as I do not rely on my work for my income and the experimentation broadens the scope of what I can share with my students.

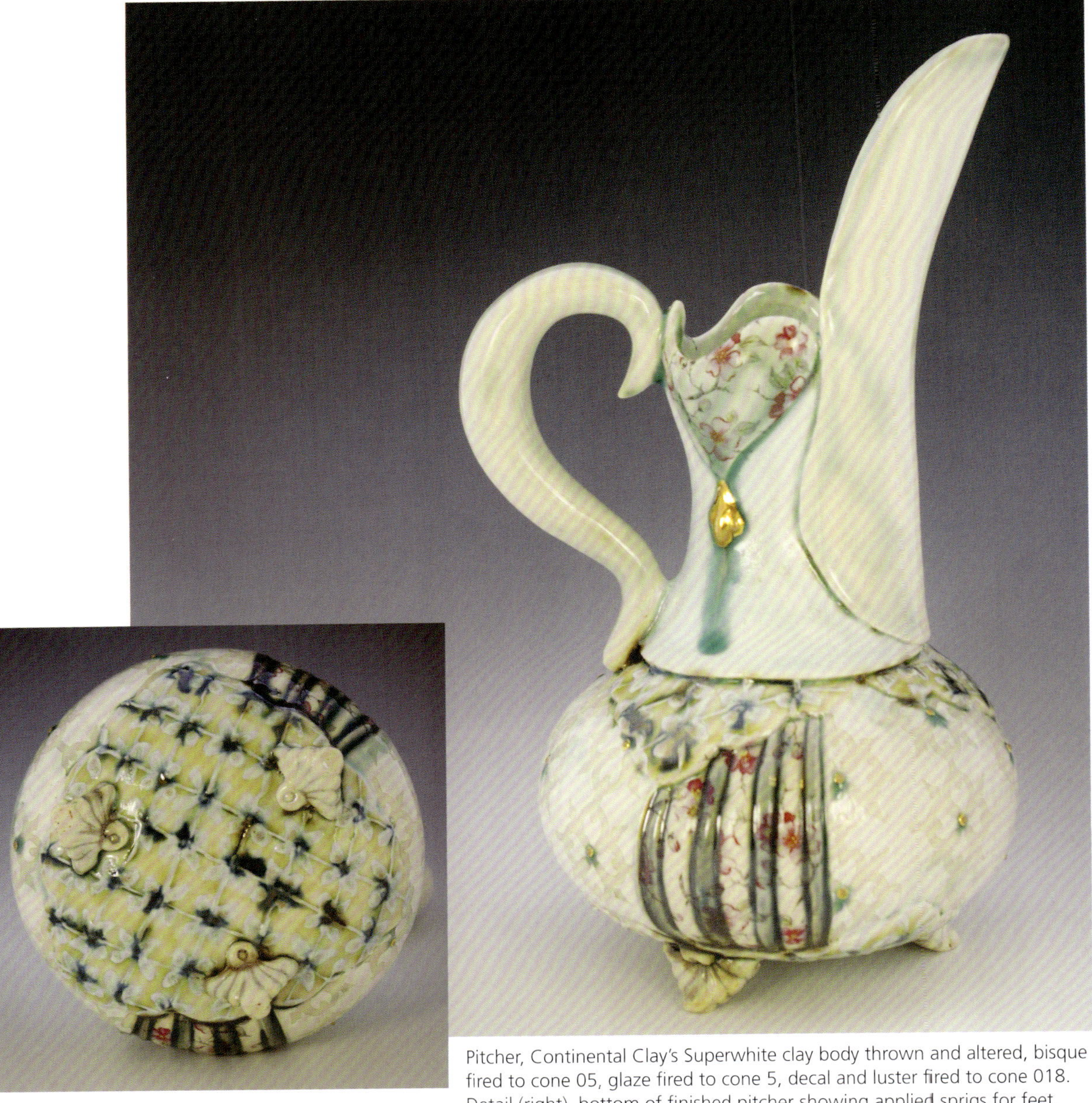

Pitcher, Continental Clay's Superwhite clay body thrown and altered, bisque fired to cone 05, glaze fired to cone 5, decal and luster fired to cone 018. Detail (right), bottom of finished pitcher showing applied sprigs for feet, slip, wash, glaze, decals, and lusters.

Layers & Inclusions

LETTERS AND LAYERS

by Connie Norman

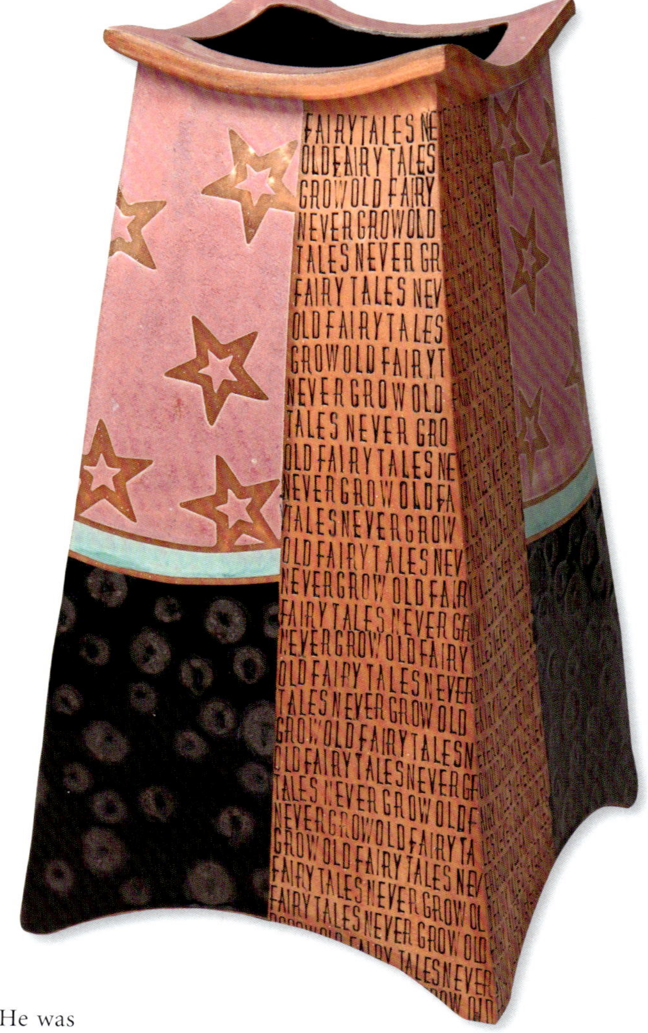

The man standing next to me at the workshop smiled and secretly showed me some hole-reinforcements labels (you know, the little white round things that go around paper for three ring binders). He was acting as if he was showing me a secret family recipe. He was using them for glaze decoration and after I saw that, I was in hot pursuit of office supplies. Texture has always been important to me, but I now use it in a subtler form. I balance text as pattern and texture, with passages of color and line. The text in my pieces acts as a path to look inward, a glimpse into my private thoughts, which at times are playful and at others are much darker in tone.

I use old letterpress type to make my texture and patterns. Rubber stamps don't work because they are not hard enough, so if possible, try to avoid them. Use a rubber tipped clay shaper to draw guide lines for the text. The clay shaper will lay down a light line without marring the surface. Decide how to divide up the vessel to

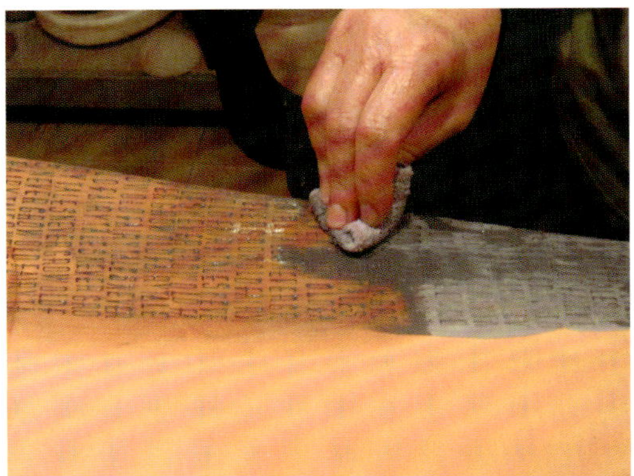

1. Wipe the extra glaze off the text with a sponge, making sure it remains in the recessed patterns.

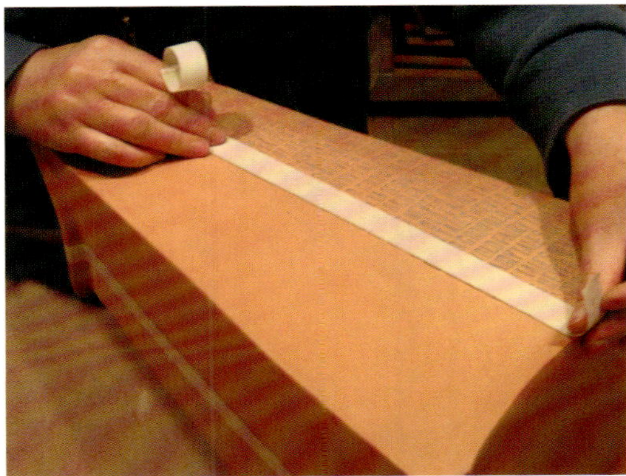

2. Tape off the dry, glazed text with masking tape. Press and seal the tape well to prevent glaze leaks.

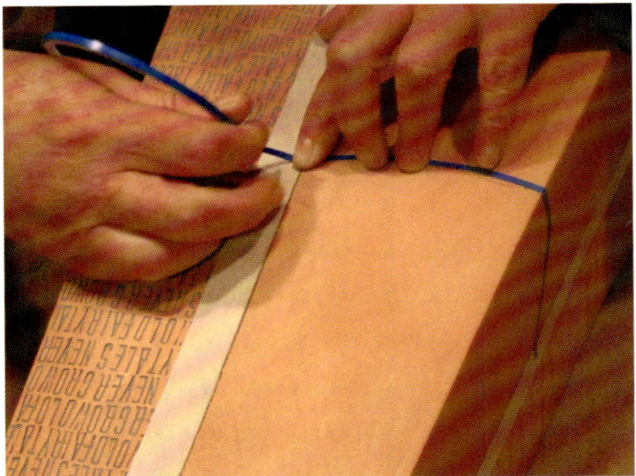
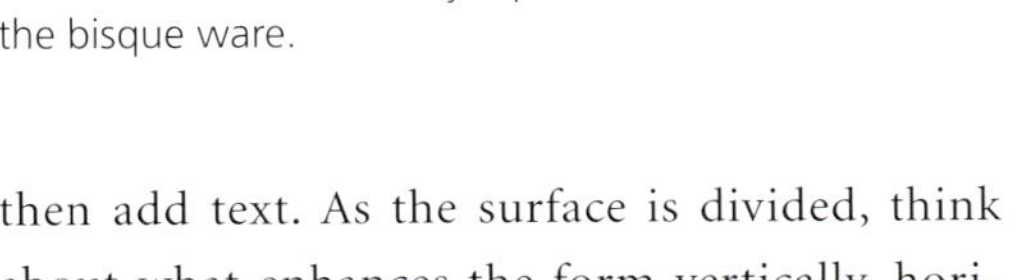

3. Use fine-line auto-body tape to make thin lines on the bisque ware.

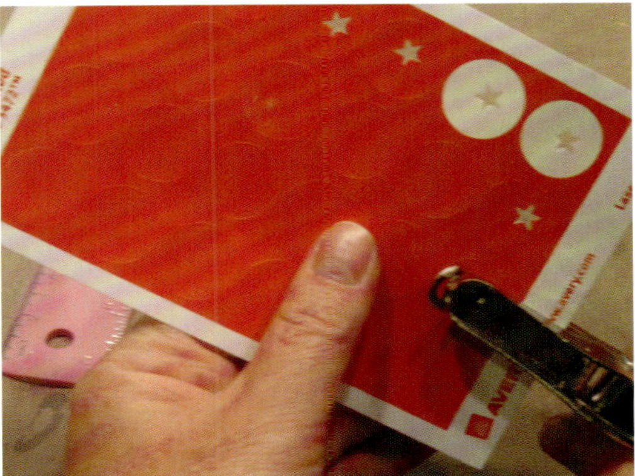

4. Punch holes into stickers to add additional decoration to your pieces.

then add text. As the surface is divided, think about what enhances the form vertically, horizontally, and three dimensionally.

I create architectural vessels using slab construction. All my forms are made with glazing in the forefront of my mind. Although every step of my process is extremely time consuming, the glazing takes the longest.

Glazing

After bisque firing, brush glaze into the text, and wipe off the excess with a sponge (figure 1). Then glaze the inside by pouring glaze in, rolling it around to cover all the sides, then pouring out the excess. Because the vessel is now saturated with water from the sponging and glazing, it needs to dry at least 24 hours before continuing. This is important because if the bisque is damp, the masking tape won't stick to it.

I love how the shiny and the matte surfaces of bare clay play off each other. Mask off the sections that will remain bare, including all the text sections that already have glaze (figure 2). The beauty of masking tape is that you can draw on the bisque because the tape is translucent enough to see the pencil marks. I find the pencil drawings helpful with making registration marks. If you don't like drawing on bisque ware you can draw on the masking tape instead. Leave the tape on the text section during the entire glazing process.

The best tape to use for thin lines of decoration is Scotch Fine Line Tape (figure 3). This

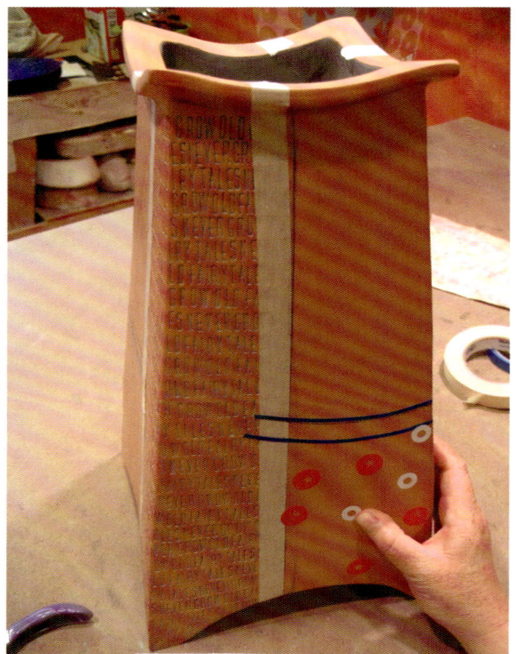

5. Apply stickers onto the bisque to create a pattern or layered design.

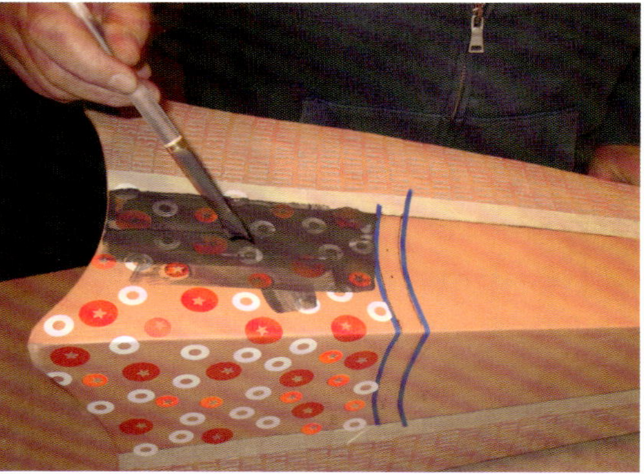

6. Brush three even coats of glaze over the applied stickers and allow the glaze to dry.

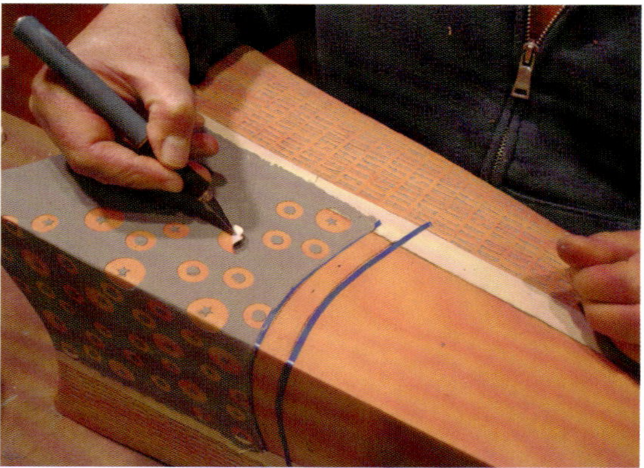

7. Use an X-Acto knife to peel off the stickers before you glaze fire.

tape is polypropylene plastic film, and it adheres well to the bisque, makes a very clean line, and also works well for curved lines. It can be found in automotive stores in the paint section.

When first creating glaze resist shapes, I started with plain office supplies—whatever my local store had available. I then started hole punching the round circles and looking for other ways to alter my office supplies (figures 4 and 5).

Once you finish applying tape and other resist shapes, brush on three coats of glaze, making sure to change directions of your brush strokes to ensure even coverage (figure 6). Peel off the tape and adhesive decorations before the glaze firing (figure 7). Make sure to remove the entire sticker and all the tape. If any adhesive from the sticker remains on the bisque, it leaves a residue and does not burn away in the kiln. Glaze fire to your clay body's temperature.

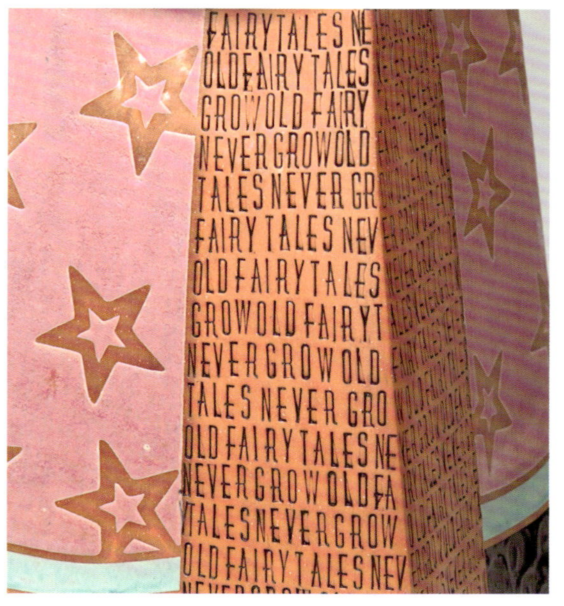

Connie Norman uses letterpress patterns as a signature design element.

Layers & Inclusions

CLAY ON CLAY STENCILS

by Hanna Lore Hombordy

When I occasionally did raku, I often yearned for more predictable results. I liked to see the accidental seeping of smoke into unexpected areas but wished for the ability to mask out specific parts of a vessel.

This led to experimentation with stencils and vessels that could be constructed together, fired together, and kept together all the way through the smoking process, greatly influencing the final result.

The best material for fired stencils was obvious—what could be more compatible with clay than more clay? Clay stencils, with their plasticity, offer useful characteristics that can't be found in other stencils. They can be custom formed and manipulated to fit the vessel. This intimate relationship works because the piece and stencil have an identical rate of shrinkage and pieces can be fired with stencils in place.

Stencils can be made with very precisely cut designs, or irregular pieces of clay can simply be rolled out and joined to form patterns. Even sturdy coils could be incorporated into a pattern. The clay stencil can be applied to a freshly made vessel and the two can be fired together. It can also be fired flat for later use on flat surfaces, making clay stencils especially useful for identical images on multiple tiles.

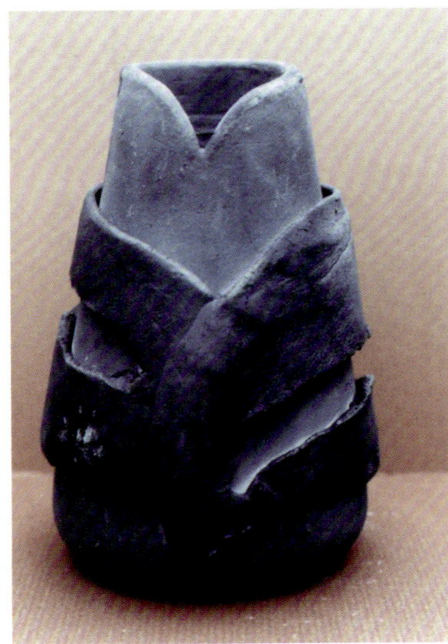

1. A clay stencil that can be slipped over the top of a vessel like a collar.

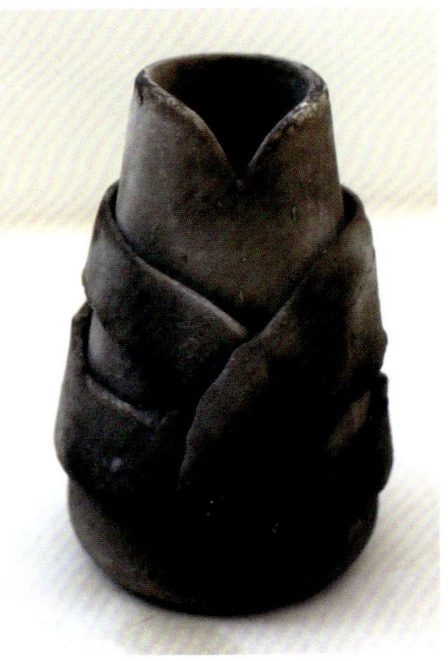

2. The stencil and pot after raku firing and post-firing reduction.

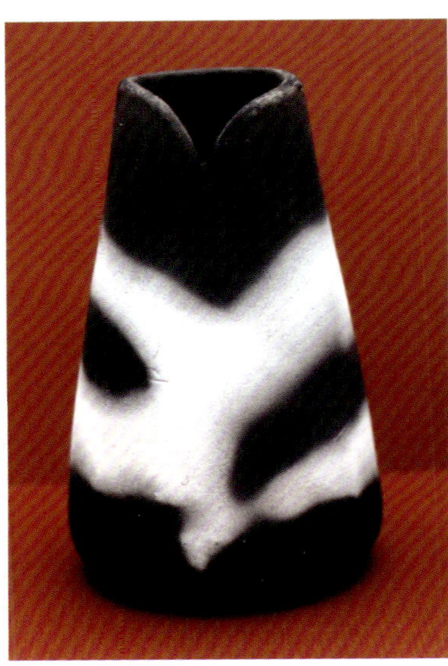

3. After cooling, slip off the stencil to admire your results.

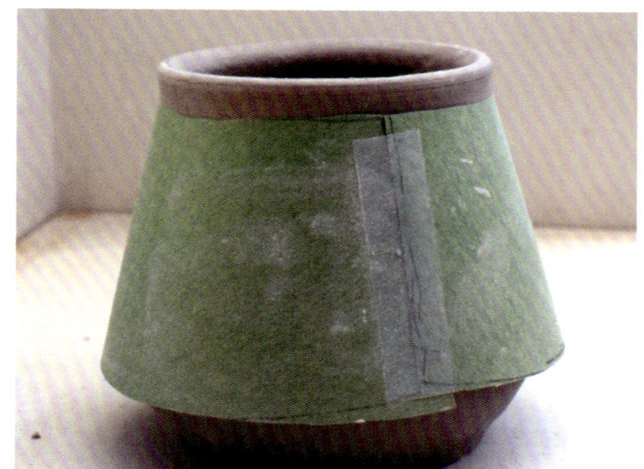

4. To make a stencil, first place a protective collar of construction paper around the jar.

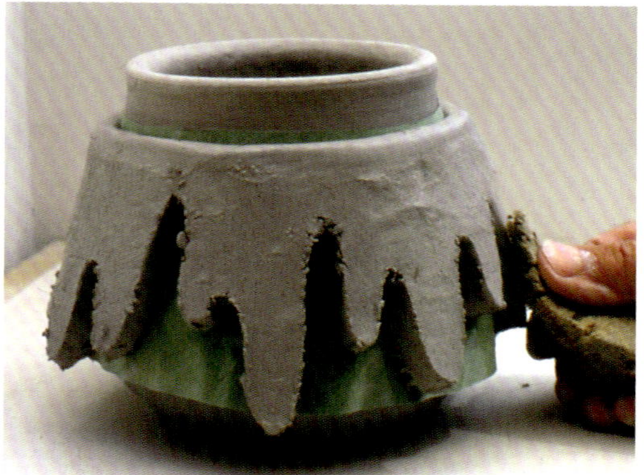

5. Remove unwanted parts of the clay collar and clean up loose bits of clay with a sponge.

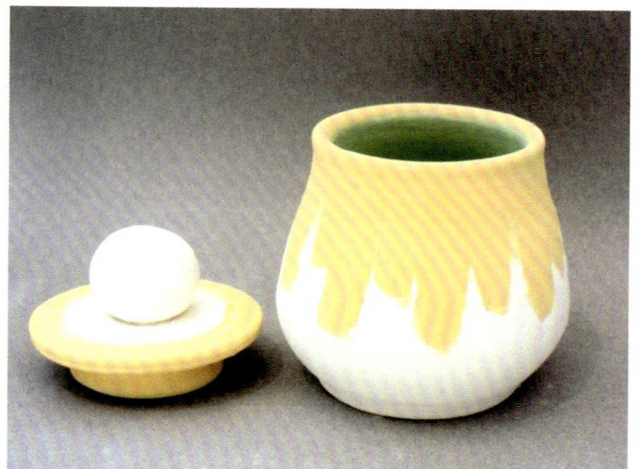

6. Brush yellow underglaze in the area to be covered by the stencil, put the stencil on and spray on other colors.

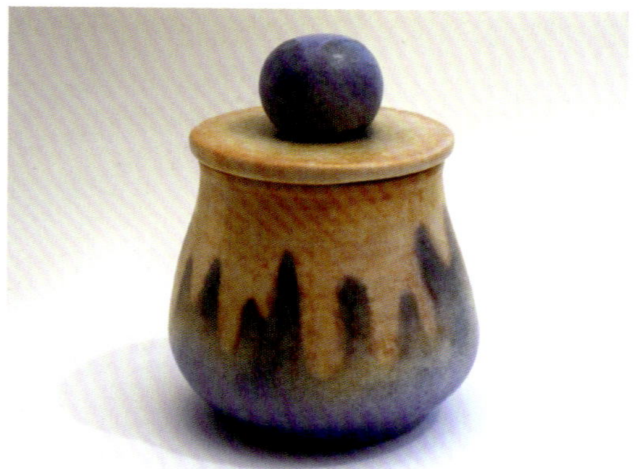

7. The finished piece has a clear glaze applied to the interior and exterior.

Creating the Clay Stencil

Work with a nearly leather hard vessel that is already trimmed, otherwise the weight of the stencil may cause distortion of the form. Place paper between the vessel and the stencil, this provides a protective shield around the vessel when carving the stencil and also prevents problems with clay sticking. Try using strips of newspaper or construction paper. Overly narrow or delicate parts of the stencil are likely to tear or crack, so keep this in mind as you design. Do not cover the whole vessel with stencils, this makes it harder to grasp without dislodging the stencil.

In addition to working with cylinder forms, try using vessels that have sloping sides to provide good support for stencils slipped over the top like a collar or shawl (figure 1). The stencil remains in place for easy transfer of the whole unit both before and after firing. This technique was originally designed for use with raku firing, so make sure there is space to grasp the piece with raku tongs. An alternative for more difficult shapes is to use fireproof gloves to transport the form from the kiln to the reduction chamber. Depending on the plasticity of your clay, you can make slabs up to ¼-inch thick that are strong, yet flexible. Roll out a shape that seems appropriate. You may need to try several sizes. The stencils need not be trimmed as meticulously as a vessel since they are serving merely as a removable mask. Work as quickly and as efficiently as you can.

Clay slabs or coil stencils can be shaped over round or irregular forms as well. A loose fitting stencil works best, especially if you're using coils, which dry quickly. The stencils on round or irregular shapes can't be as conveniently removed later, although they can be snipped apart with clippers after cooling.

Controlling Shrinkage and Sticking

If your stencil starts shrinking too much, lightly spray some water on it, or temporarily cover it with a damp cloth. Your vessel may start to dry and therefore shrink before you're able to incorporate a stencil. Although you're using the same clay for the stencil, it's softer and has a higher water content. If you simply made a collar and placed it on a drier vessel, the collar would shrink more and crack as it dried. To prevent this from happening, merely add more layers of paper strips between the stencil and the vessel, giving more separation to allow more room for shrinkage. As the collar begins to firm up enough to be handled, remove the paper and set it back into position on the vessel.

The work can now be set aside to dry slowly before firing. Occasionally check to be sure the stencils aren't getting too tight. Should there be a tight spot, the inside of the stencil can be lightly sanded to make a more comfortable fit. If the stencil fits well after both pieces are bone dry, they can safely be fired together.

Raku Firing with Stencils

When you fire your piece with the clay stencil in place, use the same bisque temperature that you normally use. Then, still leaving the stencil in place, proceed with your choice of raku, pit or barrel firing. After cooling, remove the stencil to admire your results (figures 2 and 3). If you often work with the same shape you may be able to salvage your clay stencil and use it again.

Using Stencils in Various Firings

Clay stencils can be used in regular firings, either oxidation or reduction, and at any temperature. The jar and lid illustrated here were thrown, then trimmed. A protective collar of construction paper placed around the jar serves to separate the stencil from the form and to prevent scratch marks from the needle tool (figure 4).

Roll out a collar of clay and place it over the paper and around the form. Here, a freehand wavy line was cut into the clay stencil. After making the shape you want, remove unwanted parts of the stencil and clean up loose bits of clay with a sponge (figure 5). Do not lift off the stencil until it firms up enough to move without danger of distortion.

After removing the stencil as well as the paper barrier, you might have noticed that an outline of your stencil shape was left on the pot's surface by the imprint of the needle. This can serve as a guide for applying color. If the outline is faint, wait until the clay is nearly bone dry, replace the clay stencil, and trace it with a pencil.

Guided by the outlines, brush on two thick coats of yellow underglaze (figure 6). There's no need to be precise, the next step is to replace the stencil and begin airbrushing over it with a green color. Most opaque underglazes can be layered over each other so you may prefer to ignore lines and merely layer the colors. In the example shown here, blue is airbrushed on last. Spray each color on the lid as you go along to save time in rinsing out the airbrush between colors.

Dry the piece slowly with the stencil in place. Check it now and then to be sure shrinkage isn't causing the stencil to fit too tightly. Bisque fire the stencil along with the vessel so you can reuse it.

After the bisque firing, you have three choices. First, fire the piece unglazed to a higher temperature to make it stronger. Second, glaze the inside of the piece and leave the outside as is. Finally, as in this example, the clay vessel was glazed inside and out with a cone 5 semi-clear matte glaze. This softens the colors considerably but affects greens more than any other color. If brighter and clearer colors are preferred, use a bright clear glaze (figure 7).

Layers & Inclusions

CREATING A WEATHERED PATINA

by Dennis Maust

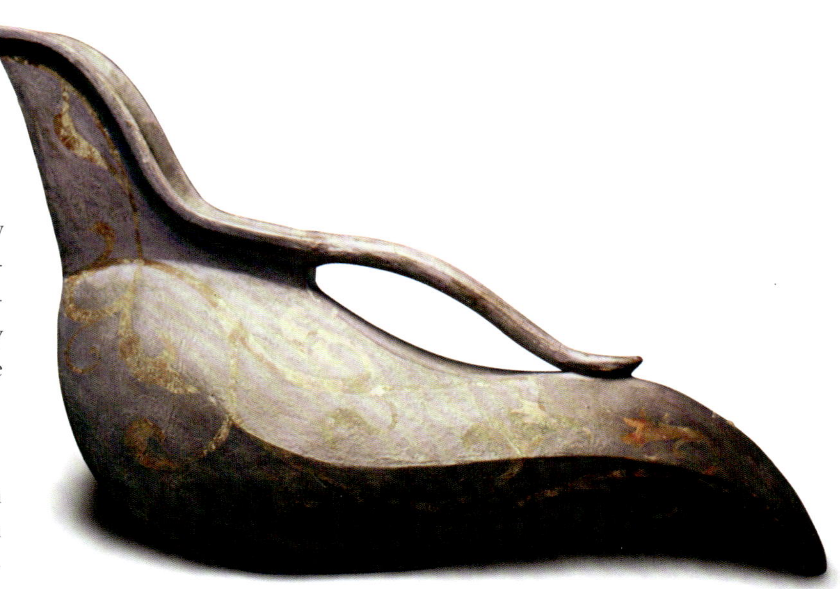

I have always been drawn to surfaces that show their weathered history and am intrigued by images that suggest, rather than spoon feed, a message. I discover new possibilities each time I try this technique and maybe that's what has kept me using these methods year after year.

Newspaper and Slip Technique

This technique involves the repeated application of different colored slips using newspaper as an application tool. Brush colored slip on newspaper to place on a leather-hard piece (figure 1). Smooth the slipped newspaper out somewhat. Leaving some wrinkles adds to the texture (figure 2). When the paper has been smoothed to your satisfaction, peel it back off (figure 3). Immediately paint a different-colored slip on the same piece of newspaper, and apply it to the piece in the same or different location (figure 4). Repeating these steps using slightly different colors of slip builds up complex, random surface design.

Press Mold and Slip Technique

I sometimes use patterned plaster press molds to vary the surface, making it more interesting (figures 5–7). Before laying the slipped newspaper on my pot, I lay it on the plaster mold and peel it off. I then paint another layer of slip over the slipped newspaper and apply it to the pot. Peeling this off again leaves an imperfect image of the pattern but leaves the impression parts were worn off over time.

Other Techniques

On some pieces, I build up many layers of this random slip decoration. Then, on the areas I find most appealing, I wax resist and spray areas of solid color slip or oxide wash to create a sense of shards having been put back together (the plain color being the part fabricated to support the "found shards"). A variation on this has been to draw a more intentional design with wax resist over an area of layered slip (after the piece has been bisqued) and then spraying a glaze or terra sigillata over it.

I have varied the thickness of the slip and at times dried the slip-covered newspaper, crumpling it before painting the subsequent layer of slip. Each variation gives a different effect, sometimes a marbleized appearance or that of peeling paint.

Slip trailing on newspaper, then painting another layer of slip over it before applying to the

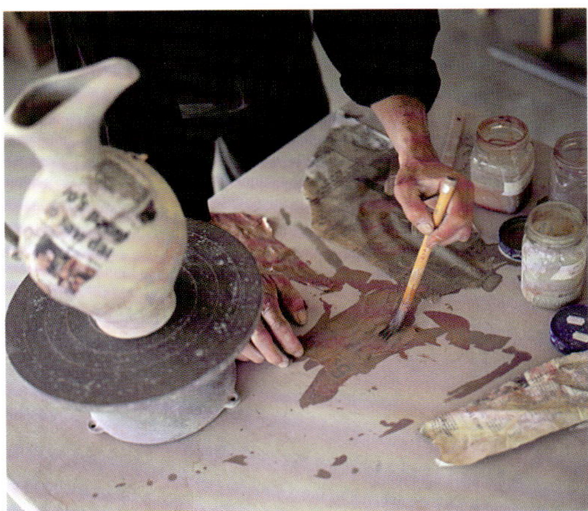

1. Brush colored slip on newspaper to place on a leather-hard piece.

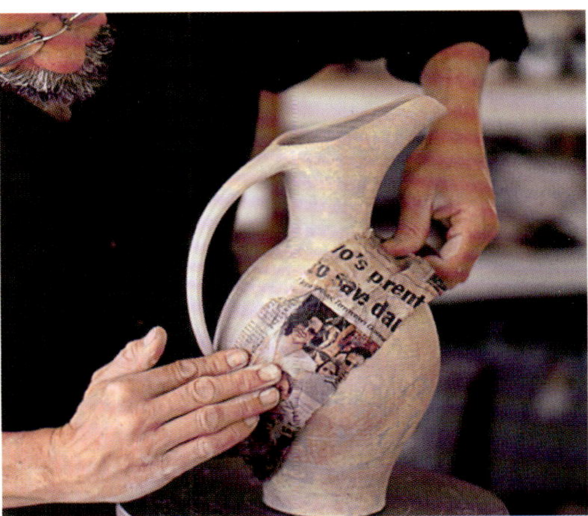

2. Smooth the slipped newspaper out somewhat, leaving some wrinkles to add to the texture.

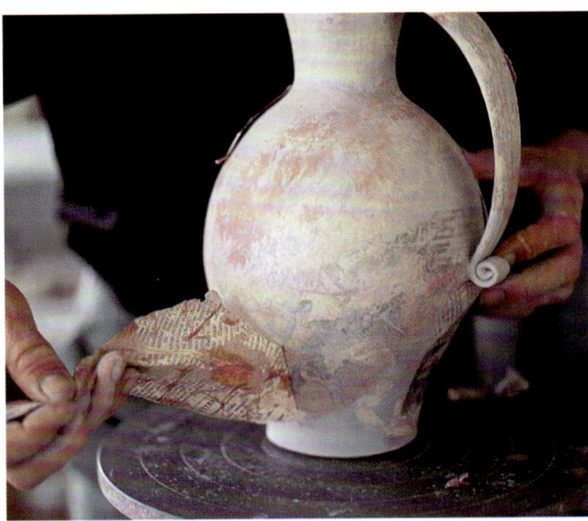

3. When the paper has been smoothed to your satisfaction, peel it back off.

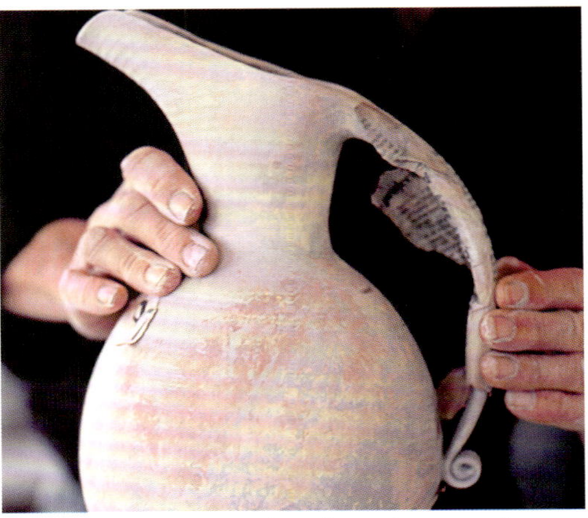

4. Immediately paint another slip on the same piece paper, and apply to the same or a different location.

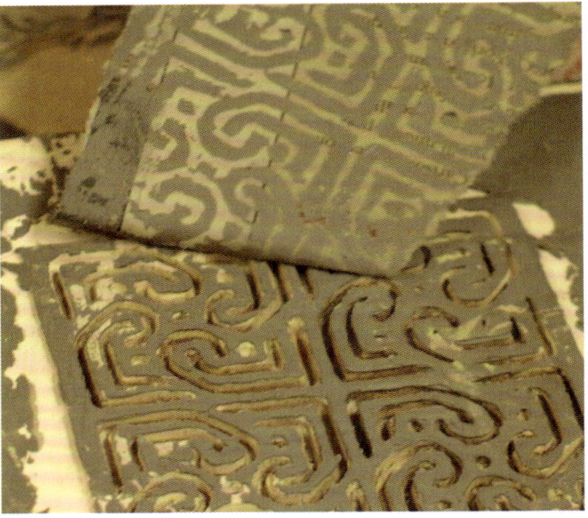

5. Lay the newspaper on a patterned mold.

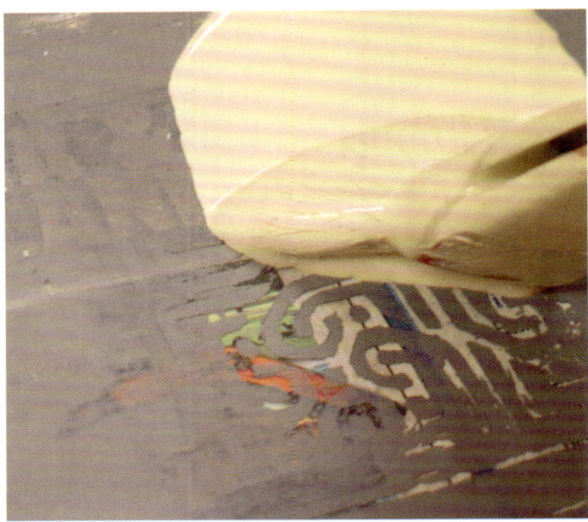

6. Paint another layer of a different slip on the paper.

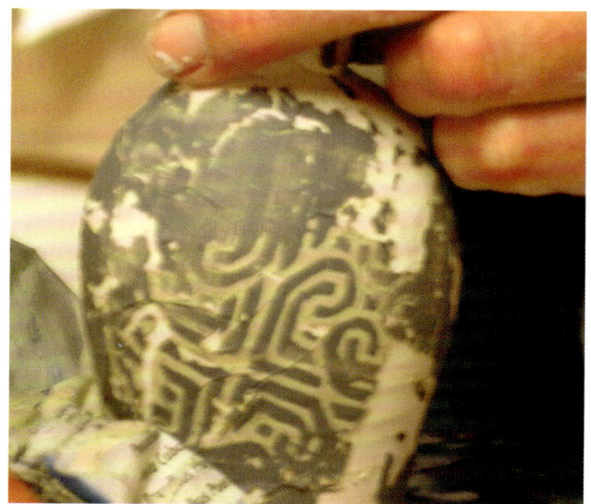

7. Apply to the pot, smooth out and peel away to reveal the pattern.

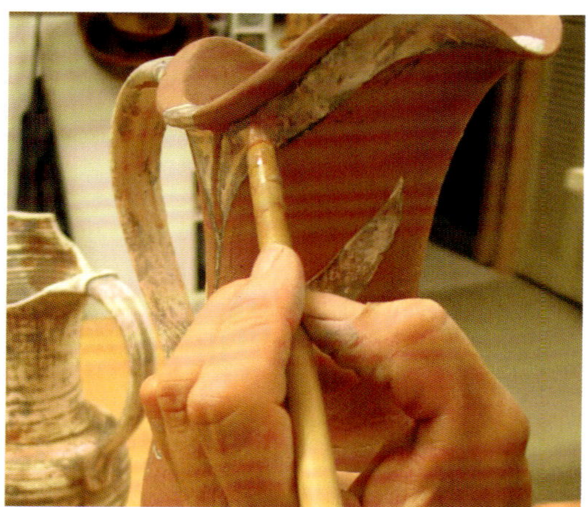

8. Applying an oxide wash to a piece that had been painted with a wax-resist pattern.

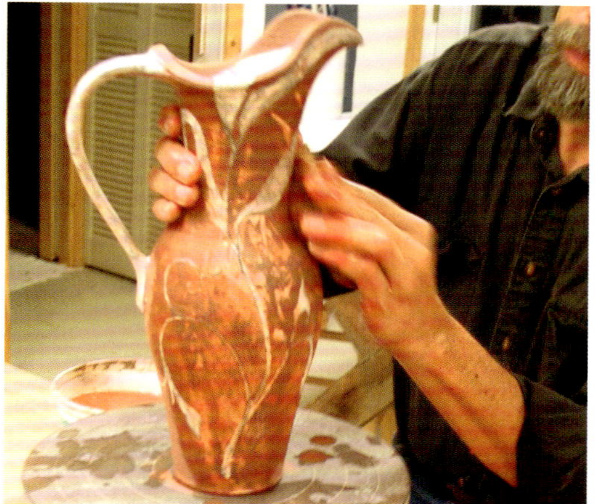

9. Wiping off the oxide. Right: Finished work created using that technique.

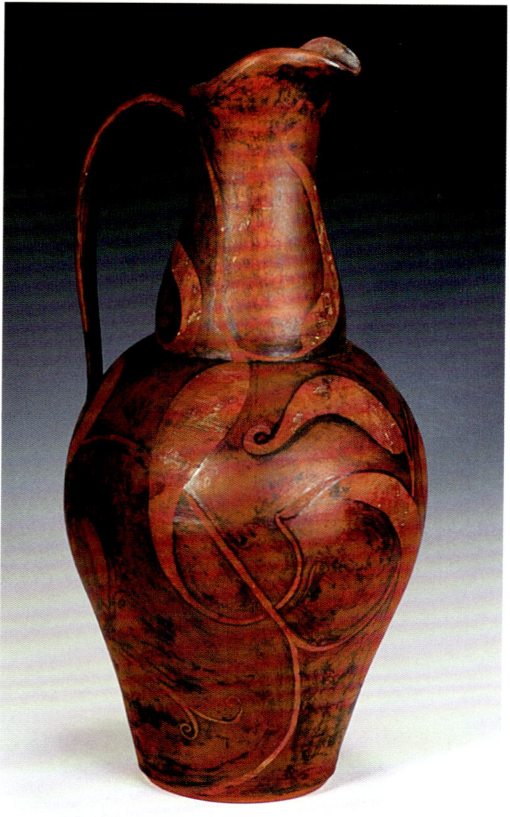

Finished work created using slip transfer technique.

pot, also enables one to work on a flat horizontal surface for gestural work that may be difficult on upright curved surfaces.

After Bisque Firing

After bisque firing I often brush oxide washes over the surface and then sponge off. The edges of the various layers of slip show up more giving the surface more depth under a glaze.

I have also used this technique with terra sigillata on bone dry burnished ware. The resulting work tends to be smoother and more convincing as something ancient.

Layers & Inclusions
A PAINTERLY APPROACH

by Tim Ludwig

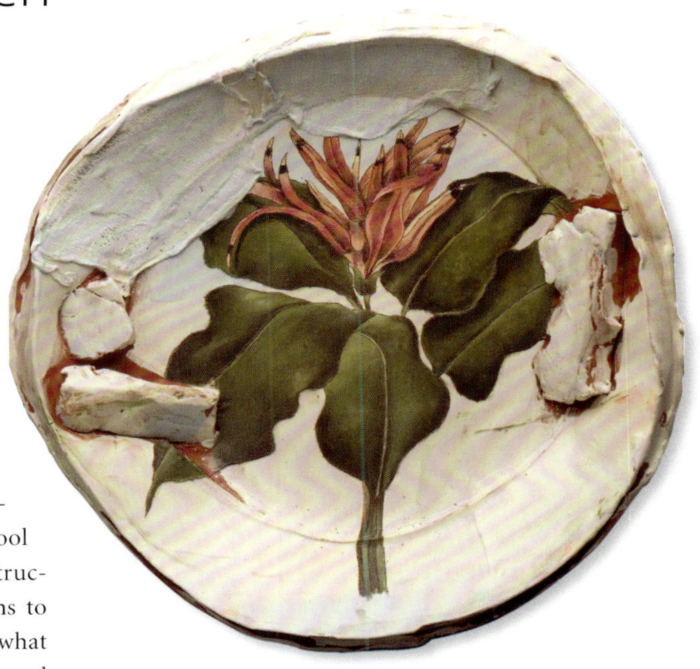

Tim Ludwig's work combines expressive forms and a layered surface of textures and images inspired by historical botanical illustrations. *Photo: Randall Smith.*

A few years ago, I started to feel that it was time to change my work, and that I wanted more control over the surface. This came after nearly 30 years of making work, and for a time finishing it in salt, wood, primitive, and saggar firings. So, I enrolled in a summer class at Arrowmont School of Crafts in Gatlinburg, Tennessee. The instructor, Bede Clarke, was using slips with stains to create a surface that was astonishing. Using what I learned about creating these surfaces, I started integrating them with the loose vessel forms I had developed over many years, forms influenced by the 1960s abstract expressionist, Peter Voulkos, and everyone else who thought it was okay to make crooked pots.

Choosing the images for the surface became the focus for about a year. I moved from animals, to figurative subjects, and then to plants. I settled on botanical illustrations from the 1700s and 1800s, from my admiration of those artists who set forth throughout the world seeking flowers to paint and illustrate and to sneak in a little artistic license.

The beauty of this process is that I did not have to change the way I was making pots. I decided on an earthenware body that I have used for fifteen plus years. The slip recipe was from Bede and has proved to be very compatible with my clay, stains, and firing. If you decide on a different firing temperature or clay color, there are clay and slip formulas that work just as well; use what you're comfortable with, or have already tested. If you're starting from the beginning and looking for compatible recipes or commercial products, remember to test, test, and test some more before you leap in and start working on finished pieces.

I learned very quickly to take good notes, measure, weigh, and test when it comes to creating the colored slips I use. The painting process can take many hours of hard work, so don't leave it to guessing. I mix 1000 gram batches of the base slip to a consistency of mayonnaise, which provides a good starting thickness to cover the surface of the piece and to begin mixing with the stains to produce a color palette. Test your colors before committing to using them on a piece.

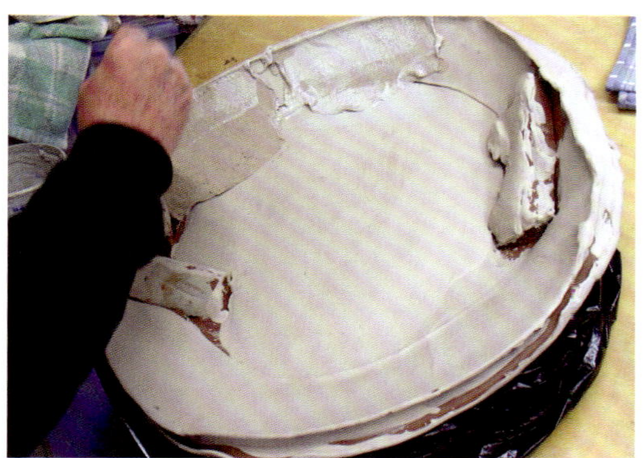

1. Add cheesecloth dipped in the slip to create an additional visual and tactile layer.

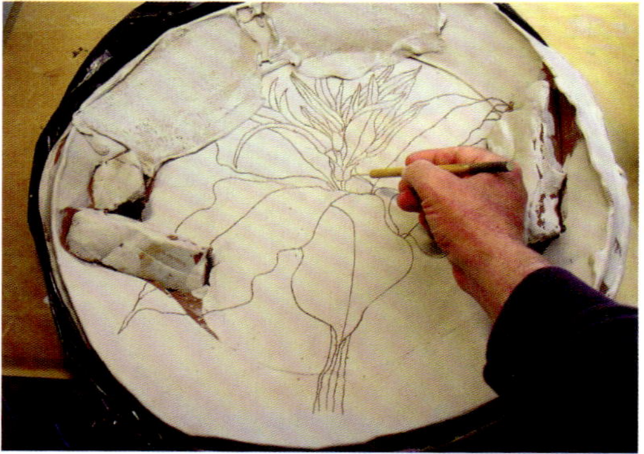

2. Begin drawing the image with a needle tool and/or a sharp pencil. Draw in details last.

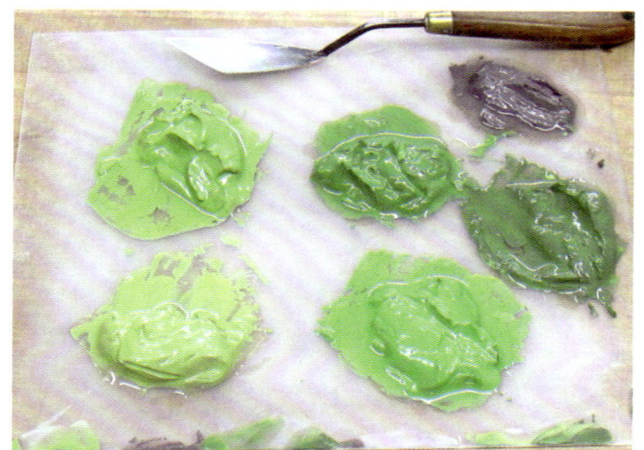

3. Work with one color family at a time. A base green is mixed with other stains creating a value scale.

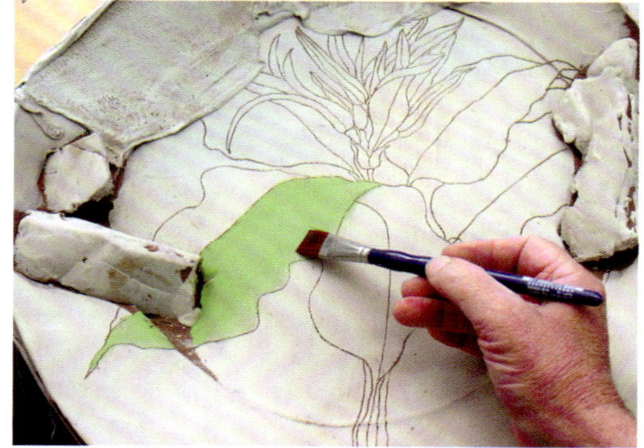

4. Painting the leaves, laying down a layer of a light green first.

Priming the Surface

Generally I throw four to five pieces at a time. When the pieces are a little shy of leather hard, I brush two coats of the base slip across the surface, leaving the red clay slightly exposed in small areas for aesthetic purposes. Then, when the slip has dried, these pieces are covered with plastic and put away in a storage cabinet or damp box to be worked on individually at an appropriate time.

On the surface of some of the pieces, I add cheesecloth dipped in the slip to create an additional visual and tactile layer. The cheesecloth burns out in the bisque and leaves behind a raised impression (figure 1).

Painting the Image

Before I start mapping out the image, I add colored slip to the certain areas (see the yellow areas of the background in figure 2). Once the slip has lost its sheen, I draw the image into the soft, leather-hard surface with a needle tool and/or a sharp pencil (figure 2).

When I'm ready to start painting, I measure out the base color, in this case green, on a piece of clean Plexiglas and create a value scale by mixing in additional stains using a palette knife (figure 3). I begin painting the image, usually the leaves first, and refine any of the drawing at this time. I use the drawn lines as a guide as I paint (figure 4). The lines define the edges and veins of the leaves and petals, and mark where the shading and highlights of the image shift or change. Blending of the slip can be achieved with a good brush; I use Kolinsky sable, and have found that a smooth transition across the given value scale is accomplished with

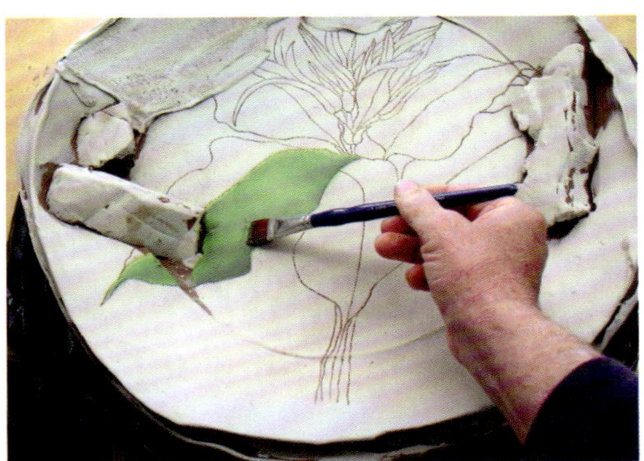

5. Create the shading using a colored slip mixture of a slightly darker value.

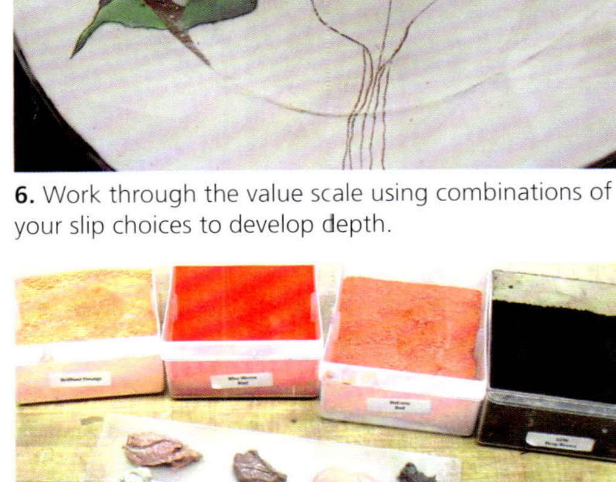

6. Work through the value scale using combinations of your slip choices to develop depth.

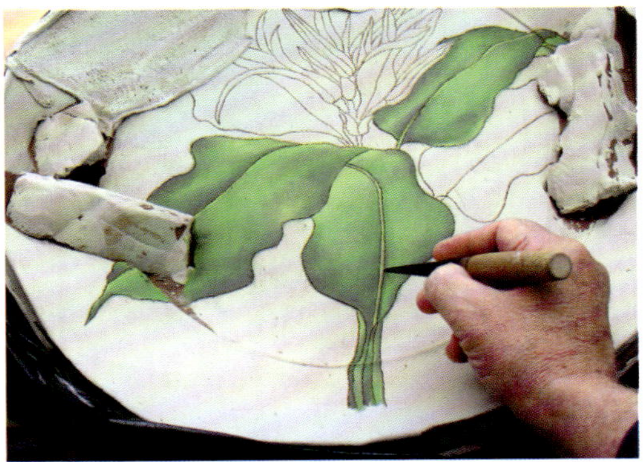

7. Clean out the incised lines occasionally during the painting process using a fettling knife.

8. Create a value scale for the flower colors on a clean piece of Plexiglas.

patience (figure 5). Start with a light to medium shade, and then add highlights and shadows. Here you can see one of the completed leaves with the shadows and dimension added using the different shades (figure 6).

As I paint, I will stop occasionally and clean out the incised lines with a thin fettling knife (figure 7). I've found that the needle tool does not work well as it leaves small clay grubbies or crumbs on the surface.

Similar to how a plant grows, after I finish with the leaves and any other darker tones, I continue on to the flower of the plant, measuring out the base color onto the Plexiglas palette and creating a value scale again (figure 8), then painting the image in the same way (figure 9). Unlike painting with glazes, the finished, unfired slip image will be close to the colors of the final, fired piece, especially if you use commercial stains as colorants (figure 10). These stains have been fired as part of the manufacturing process, and so the color you see is close to the final color that will be produced, depending on the surface you paint onto, the firing temperature, and whether or not you choose to glaze the piece. Check with the manufacturer to see what temperature individual stains can be fired to before the color starts to burn out.

After I've finished creating and cleaning up the image, the platter is fired to cone 04 for the bisque. After firing, I mix a clear, satin, commercial glaze in a 50/50 ratio with water and spray a very thin coat onto the bisque ware. The piece is refired to cone 06. This final firing allows the color to brighten and intensify in comparison to the bisque stage.

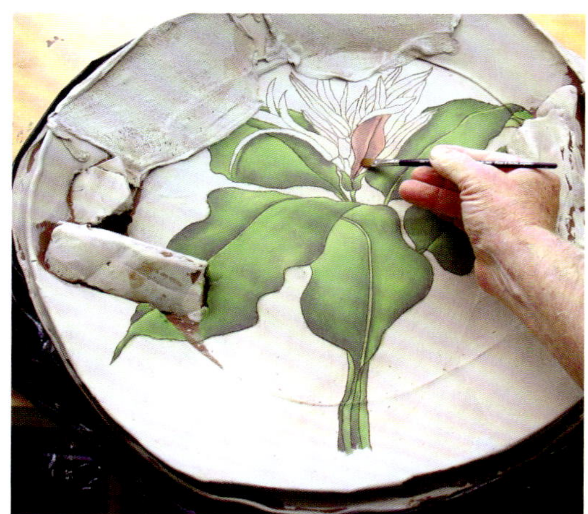

9. Apply to the pot, smooth out and peel away to reveal the pattern.

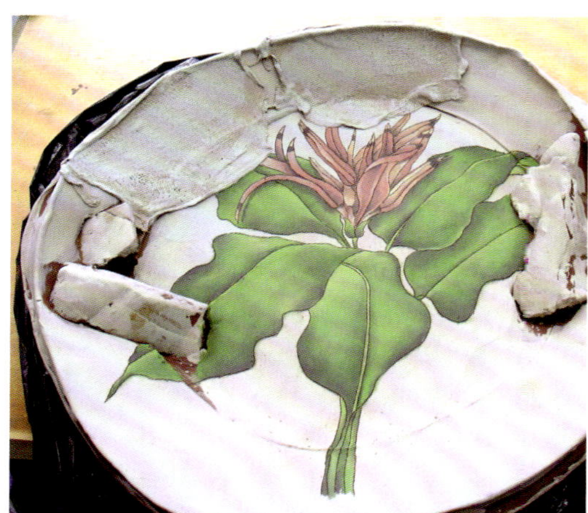

10. Applying an oxide wash to a piece that had been painted with a wax-resist pattern.

Tips for Branching Out

Take time to refine your technique and find subject matter that engages you. Using slips to paint images on clay has been around a long time; if the process interests you, look around to find examples for inspiration. Matching the image with the form is extremely important. You can't compensate for a bad form via surface decoration or firing. The image and form should respond to one another; do not just make an object to paint. I have become much more comfortable with my decision to create the work shown here. It's hard and takes a lot of time to complete a piece, so be prepared if you plan to adopt a similar method.

STEPHENSON'S SLIP

EPK Kaolin	12.5 %
Tile 6	12.5
Ball Clay	25.0
Ferro Frit 3124	20.0
Talc	5.0
Silica	20.0
Pyrotrol (pyrophyllite)	5.0
	100.0 %
Add: Zircopax	10.0 %

This slip has been very stable with the clay body I use and is quite compatible with the stains. You may want to add glycerol to the slip/stain mix on the palette to improve the viscosity for brushing.

I mix up small quantities of the colored slips in 300 gram batches, using 5–20% stain depending on the color. I store them in small resealable containers and take them out as I need to paint each piece. I keep my dry stains in a nuts and bolts cabinet. The drawers make them easy to access, and the clear plastic allows me to see the colors.

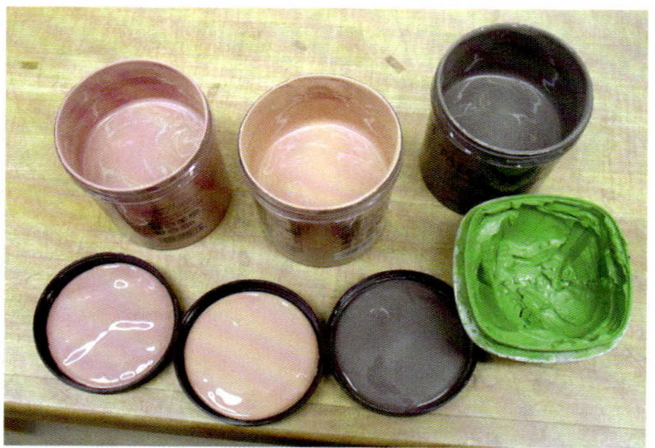

Mix small quantities of stained slips. Here 300 gram batches are prepared with 5–20% stain, based on tests of each color.

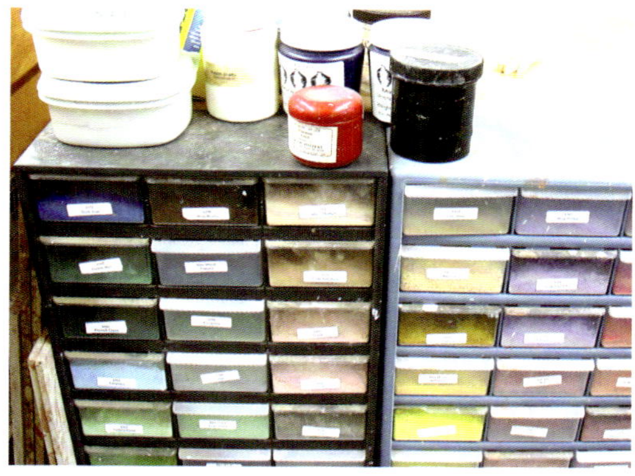

Storing dry stains in a cabinet with clear drawers allows for easy access, good visibility and organization by color family.

Layers & Inclusions

DECORATING WITH WIRES, NAILS AND TERRA SIG

by Jeremy Randall

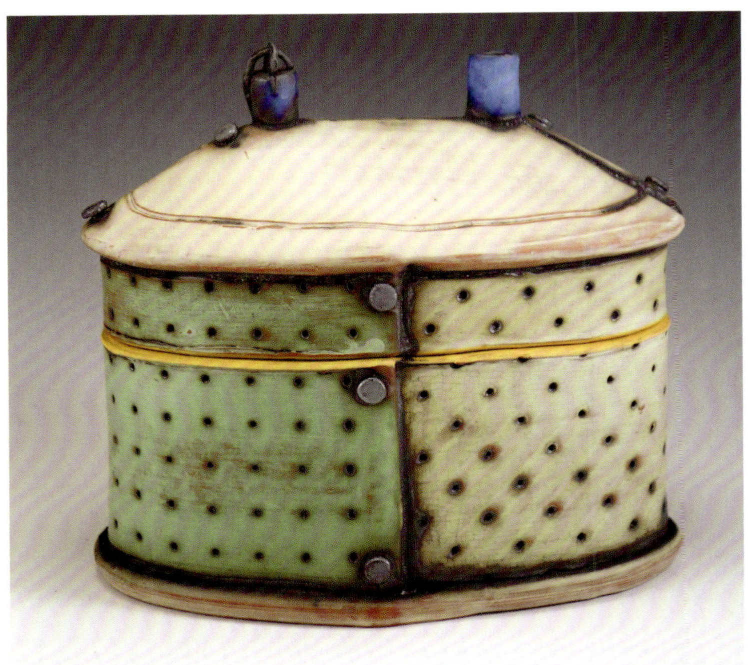

Barn Salt Cellar, earthenware with terra sigillata, crackle slip, copper oxide wash, steel carpet tacks, and nichrome wire. *All photos: Sarah Panzarella.*

I can trace my interest in the patina of use and the implications of function to the objects that surrounded me when I was a child, and can follow those objects as they have found a place in my own adult life. The iron-oxide wash on an early-American primitive pine cabinet with close to 175 years of use, the early-American, blue milk-painted blanket chest worn bare around the edges, or my grandfather's hammer, the handle smooth from years of use. These objects feel comfortable, both to hold and touch as well as to live with. This is the desire that I have for my pots. The information that can be received from using handmade objects and living with them can be rich and fruitful and at the same time quiet and contemplative.

Working with slabs allows me to create surfaces that can be primed with textural information, and then move from flat surface to form almost instantly. The soft leather-hard qualities of the clay allow for immediate construction of the piece without having to wait for things to stiffen. This sheet material is also closely related to the materials that I love to look at as inspiration. The corrugated steel walls of a grain silo, for instance, are incredibly thin in relation to the structure, but the space that is created is voluminous and beautiful. The textures that I use are derived from various found mats and commercial surfaces, collected over the years as I cross paths with them. I have even pulled over while driving in order to pick up an old dish mat that was lying in the middle of the road. I have enjoyed creating surface texture for years and have used it on countless pots.

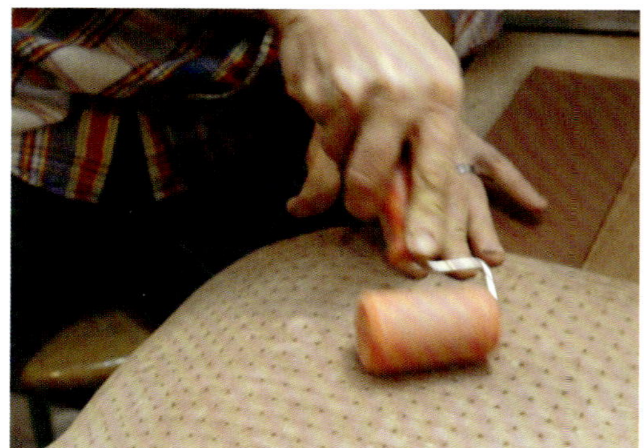
1. A plastic textured mat and a brayer are used to develop the surface of slabs.

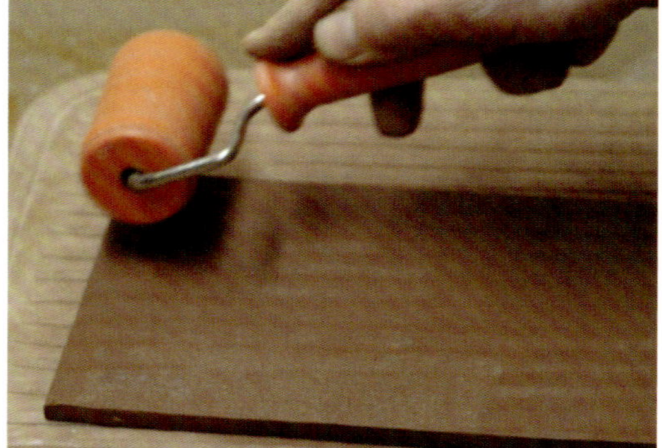
2. You can roll the mat texture into the clay or roll the clay into the texture.

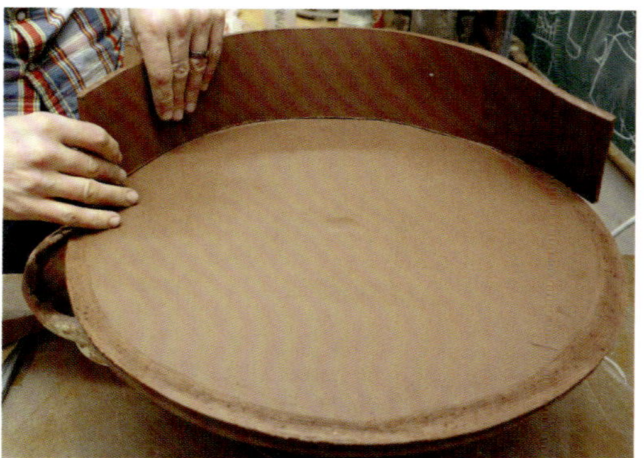
3 Slightly stiffened slabs are joined to a base slab to form the vessel.

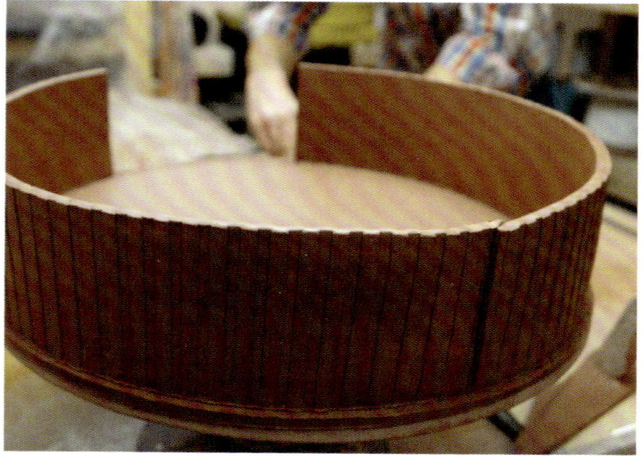
4 Seams are left rough with the slab edges exposed to reference a used object.

Forming Used Objects

When building my vessels, I start with a dialog on the surface between the front and the back of the piece. The plastic mats, made for a sink or for the floor of a car are pressed into fresh rolled and cut-to-size slabs (figures 1–2). The mats generally have a pattern on one side and some have patterns on both the front and the back. They are made out of a heavy, slightly flexible plastic and hold up very well to repeated use. For my purposes, they create a surface that shows how objects and building materials weather over time and use.

Scale is also important. When I add the textured slabs to the base slab of the vessel (figure 3), I consciously consider the vertical and horizontal planes of the piece, then determine how the texture can make the viewer's eye want to move around it (see figure 5).

As I secure the side pieces to the base and the trim pieces to finish the rim, it is important for me to make sure the seams and the edges are not straight and true (figure 4). I don't want to overwork them and risk the possibility of losing the reference to a used object that contains a sense of history (figure 6). The roughness that remains will also catch the stains that are applied after the bisque firing.

While researching industrial and construction references, I spent time in the hardware store looking for bits that could be used in my pots. Rather than adding more texture that might clutter the surface, I found that standard steel carpet tacks could be pressed into the surface and remain

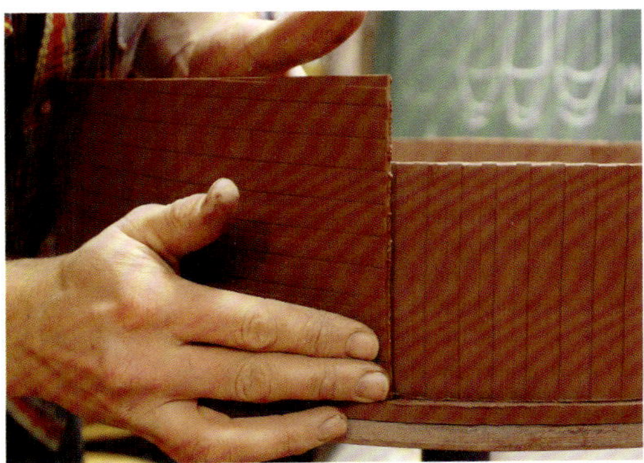

5. The texture varies from horizontal to vertical orientations adding variety.

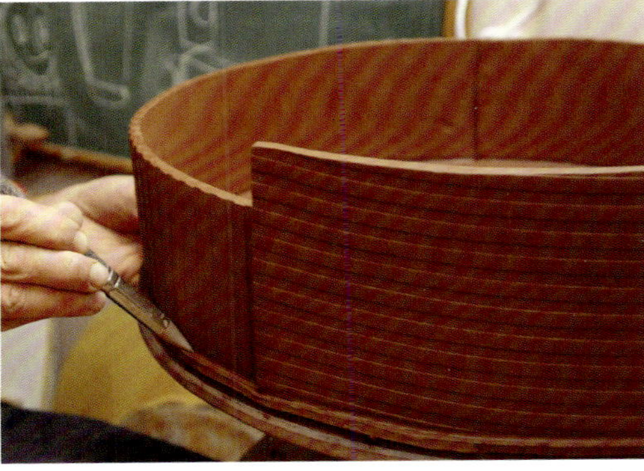

6. Seams are secured and edges are left visible rather than blended together to retain the qualities of construction.

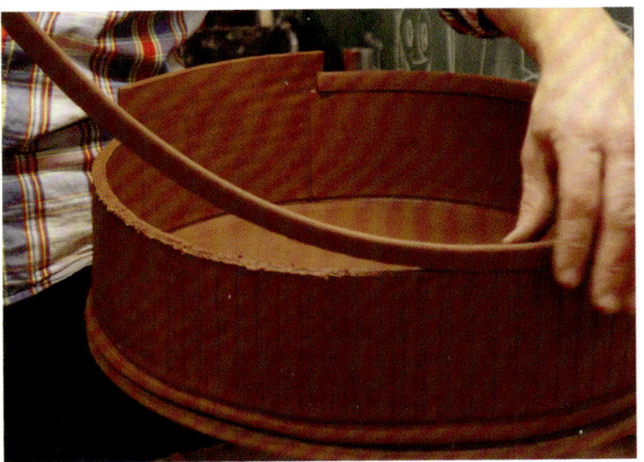

7. Extruded trim pieces are added to finish the rim.

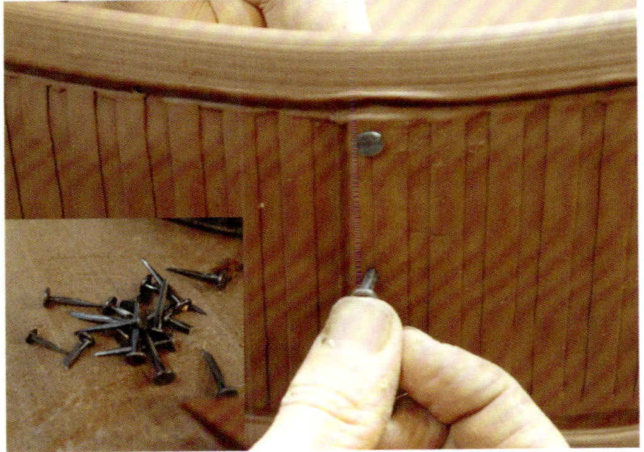

8. Steel carpet tacks (inset) are added to both secure the seams and reference construction material.

intact after the firing because I fire to a temperature that is lower than the melting point of steel. I add them to places where seams come together as they may even help to secure the construction (figure 8). The other non-clay material that I add to the pot is nichrome wire. The wire adds to the shifting scale of the pot while also adding to the reference of material like corrugated steel, roofing material, or barn wood (figures 9–10). Both of these materials also help to break the plane of the rectangles and the repeated textures.

Developing a Weathered Surface

I have always steered away from traditional glazes for my pots. I want the exteriors to allude to the layered surfaces that I reference, and a glassy shine has never really seemed right. Using terra sigillata has filled a number of my goals, and provides a new vocabulary of surface and color. Firstly, to apply it properly, I have to touch each curve and crack of the piece, becoming fondly reacquainted with every detail of all my pots. This surface material and its application are ancient, most known for their use on the surfaces of pottery from ancient Rome and Greece, and extremely simple to make, leading to a simpler studio practice.

The colors I use are Mason commercial ceramic stains, mixed into a jar of terra sigillata to the desired intensity, applied at the bone dry state with a soft brush, and burnished with a plastic bag stretched over my finger. The surface obtained is soft and waxy, much like the surface of an eggshell or semi-gloss latex paint . . . or better yet, milk paint. This surface quality remains after bisque, and because it is smooth and somewhat

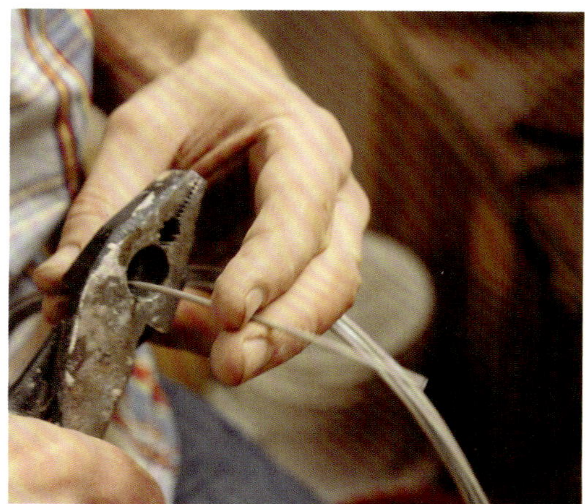
9. Cut nichrome wire to length with wire cutters.

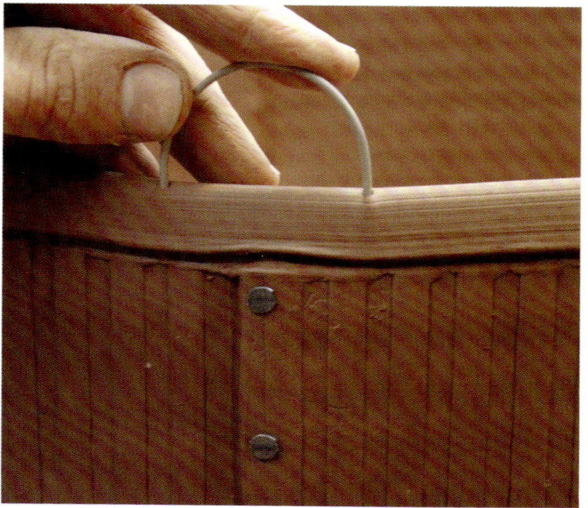
10. Nichrome wire breaks the plane of the pot's flat, level rim.

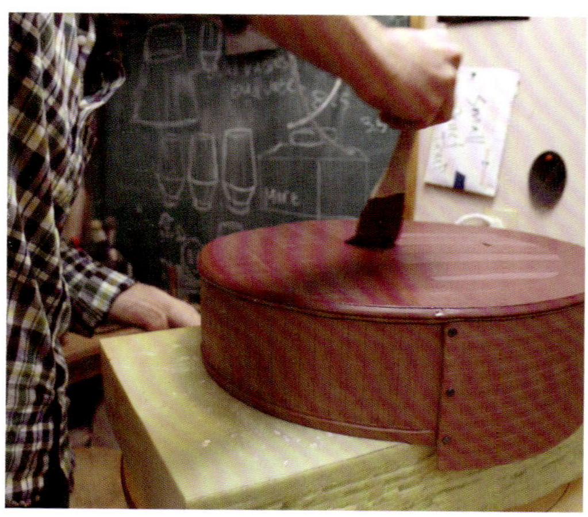
11. Broad strokes of terra sigillata are applied using a hake brush.

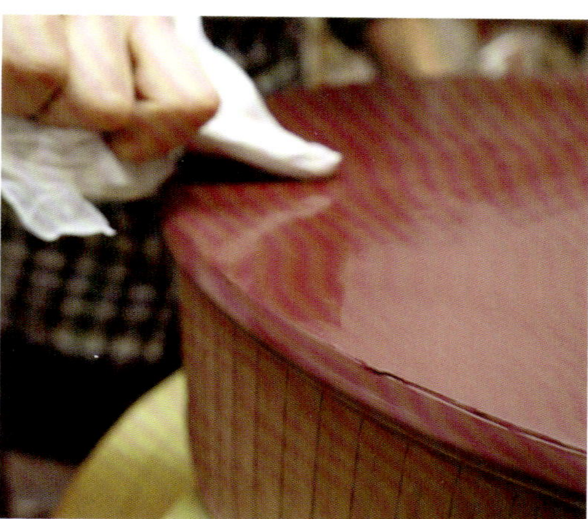
12. Just as the surface sheen has disappeared, burnish it with plastic stretched over a thumb or finger.

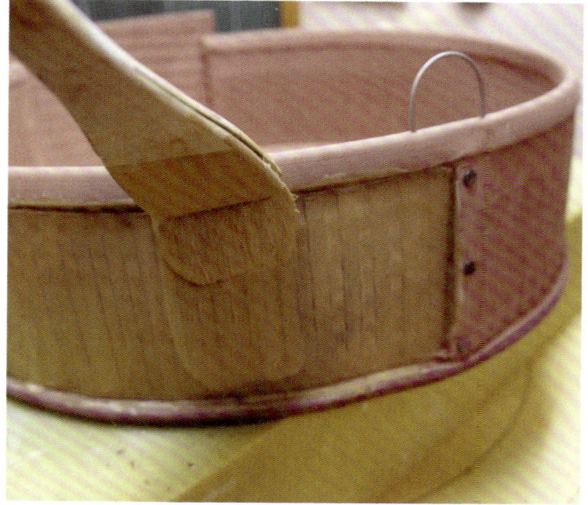
13. Contrasting colors are added for visual interest.

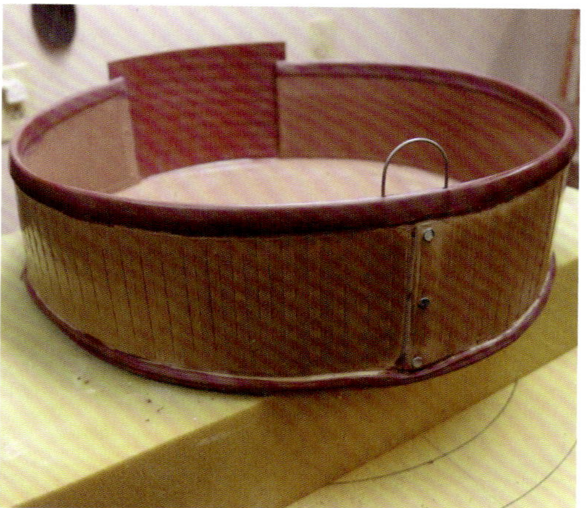
14. The finished pot. After bisque firng, add a liner glaze to the interior and apply copper oxide wash.

shiny, the copper oxide wash I use to patina the surface, when applied after bisque, wipes off the surface easily. The copper then fumes during the firing and adds halos around the texture, lending a sense of uncertainty to every firing. Finally soda ash washes and selected sculpture/texture glazes help to bring my surfaces closer to the constructed and weathered surfaces that I am referencing.

Building the Surface with Terra Sigilatta

I apply the terra sigillata to bone dry pieces. This is a great way for me to semi-seal the clay without having to use a glaze. My terra sigillata (3½ pounds of water mixed with 2 tablespoons of sodium silicate and 14 pounds of OM4 Kentucky Ball Clay) is mixed with a ratio of approximately 1 cup of sigillata to 1 tablespoon of stain and sieved if necessary. I increase the amount of stain if I desire a more intense color. The sigillata should be the consistency of thin milk. I apply it to the pot in broad strokes using a hake brush (figure 11) and burnish the freshly coated area with a plastic grocery bag stretched over my fingers just after the sheen has disappeared (figure 12).

I choose my colors based on contrasts and the ability of the combinations to add visual interest for the viewer (figure 13). I like the way it references traditional milk-paint—milk mixed with pigment and washed over wood—surfaces often used in early American furniture and having a soft satin sheen. After the surface and the pot itself, which has absorbed water from the terra sigillata, have dried, the piece is ready for the bisque firing (figure 14).

I want my pots to be used so I add a black liner glaze to the interior. For a finishing on the exterior, I apply a copper oxide wash, brushed on to cover the entire exterior then wiped off, leaving a residue of copper material within the textures and grooves. The remaining copper will fume and give an overall sense of history and wear.

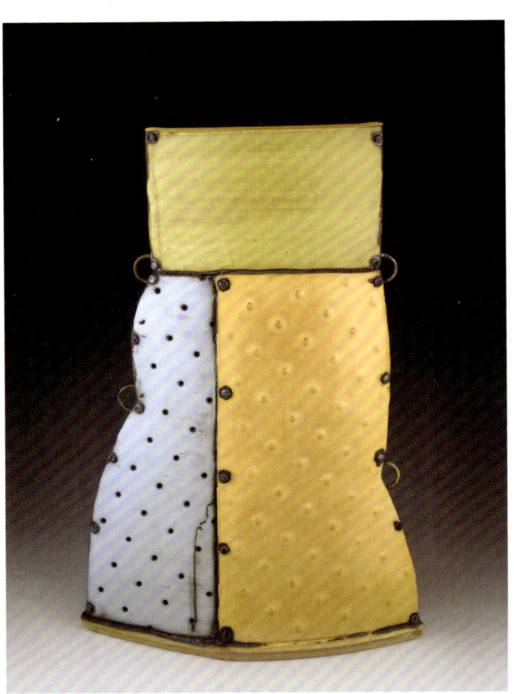

Flat Stack Vase. Upon completion, the sources of reference are embedded into the piece, quietly reminding the user of things and places that they may have seen.

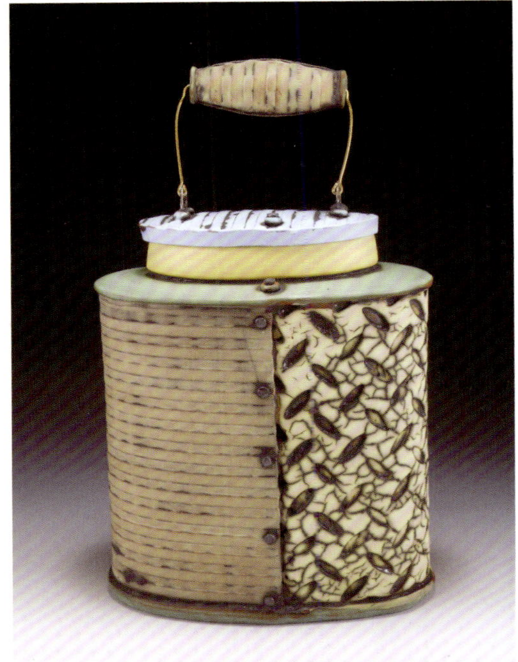

Lidded Tank. Nostalgia is a trigger. It brings a person back while at the same time allowing them to be present, in time and space, with the pot.

Layers & Inclusions
BARBECUE SMOKE FIRING

by Sumi von Dassow

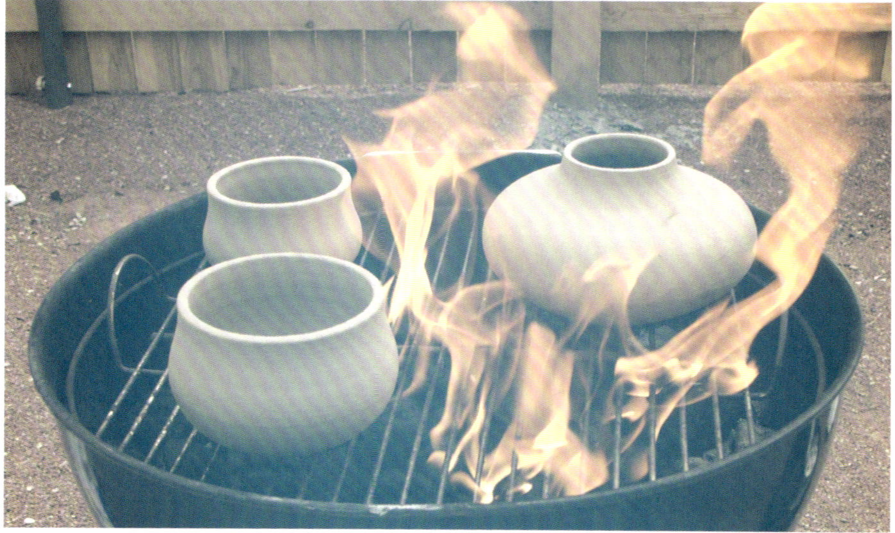
Pots on the barbie; greenware placed on top of the cooking grill while the charcoal preheats.

If you don't have a kiln but still want to fire some pots—or you have an electric kiln but you'd like to do some smoke-firing without digging a fire-pit in your yard or alarming the neighbors too much—the grill is a surprisingly versatile alternative.

I used a 22½-inch round grill, achieving a variety of effects with several kinds of clay and surface finishes. In order to replicate the look of Native American pottery fired in outdoor bonfires, I fired pinch pots and small wheel-thrown pots made from micaceous clay. This clay incorporates small particles of mica in addition to grog, which makes it beautiful as well as very resistant to heat shock. In New Mexico it's traditionally used to make flame-ware for cooking directly on a fire or on the stove-top. I also tried a variety of smoke-firing techniques on pots made from smooth stoneware clay that was burnished either with a stone or using terra sigillata. Micaceous clay is available from Coyote Clay (www.coyoteclay.com) or New Mexico Clay (www.nmclay.com). You can also buy powdered mica and add it to your own clay body. Red clay for burnishing is available from Navajo Wheel from Industrial Minerals Company (www.clayimco.com).

Grilling Greenware

To fire greenware on the grill, make pots with walls that are about ³/₈-inch thick throughout—no fat bottoms or thin rims—and dry them thoroughly before attempting to fire them. You don't need to use micaceous clay, but use a clay which is resistant to thermal shock such as raku clay, groggy stoneware, or paperclay.

Make sure the grill is clean, removing any ashes or partially burned coals in the bottom, then get it going just as you would for cooking, pouring lighter fluid over mounded charcoal and lighting it. Note: Wear gloves and protective eye wear whenever handling pots around the grill, from placing them onto the grid to taking them out of the coals after the firing. As the coals gradually begin to smolder, preheat the pots on the cooking grid above them.

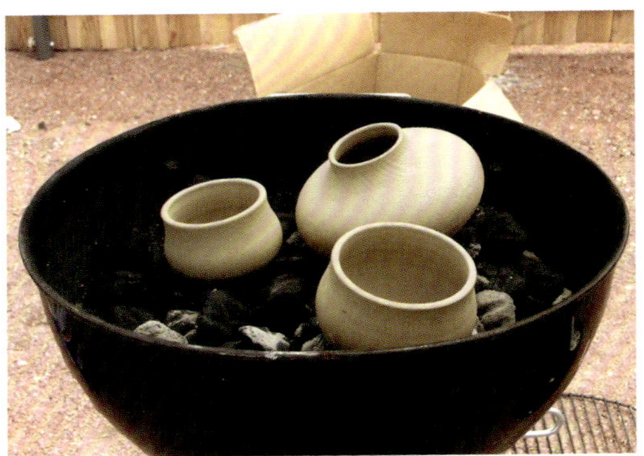

1. Lift out the cooking grid, spread out the coals and put the preheated pots on the coals.

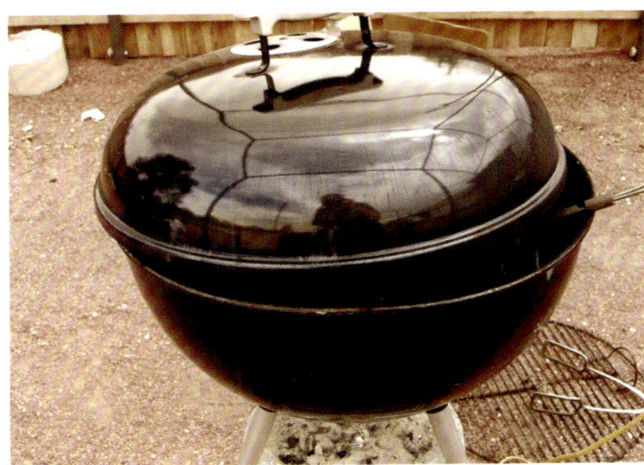

2. Cover the grill but leave the cover cocked to allow for air flow.

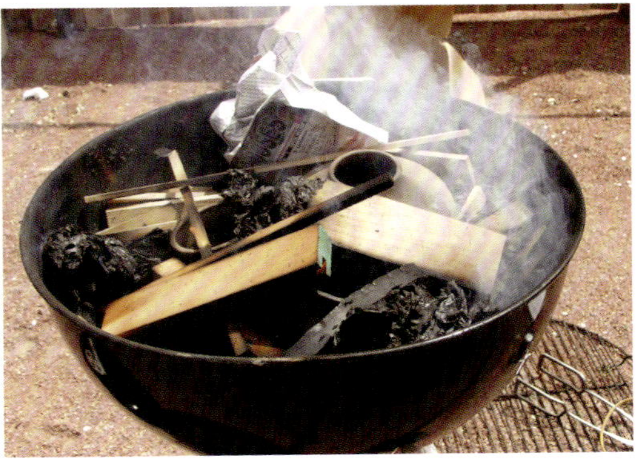

3. Surround taller pots with wood scraps. Use newspaper to encourage the wood to burn.

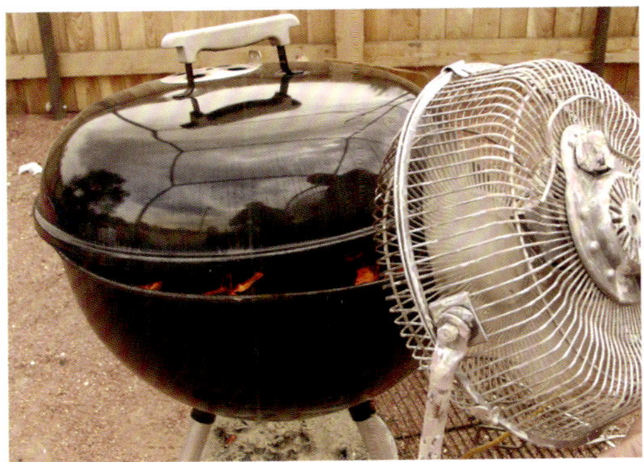

4. To raise the temperature, use a metal fan to blow air into the partially opened lid.

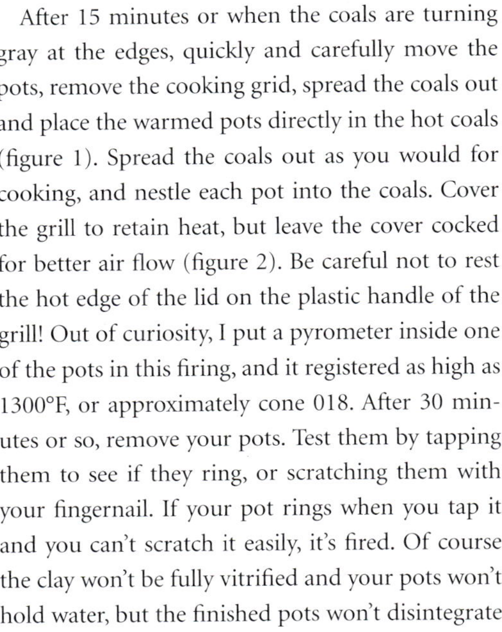

After 15 minutes or when the coals are turning gray at the edges, quickly and carefully move the pots, remove the cooking grid, spread the coals out and place the warmed pots directly in the hot coals (figure 1). Spread the coals out as you would for cooking, and nestle each pot into the coals. Cover the grill to retain heat, but leave the cover cocked for better air flow (figure 2). Be careful not to rest the hot edge of the lid on the plastic handle of the grill! Out of curiosity, I put a pyrometer inside one of the pots in this firing, and it registered as high as 1300°F, or approximately cone 018. After 30 minutes or so, remove your pots. Test them by tapping them to see if they ring, or scratching them with your fingernail. If your pot rings when you tap it and you can't scratch it easily, it's fired. Of course the clay won't be fully vitrified and your pots won't hold water, but the finished pots won't disintegrate in water as greenware would. Coals alone reach a temperature of at least 1100°F, and will be enough to fire small pots. For pots above two or three inches tall, or to increase the firing temperature, you might want to pile wood scraps around them to ensure an even firing temperature from the top to the bottom of the piece (figure 3). To increase the heat even more, try blowing air into the grill with a fan (figure 4), though it's possible that doing this repeatedly may shorten the life of the grill, particularly of the charcoal grate. Adding wood to the fire makes it smoke more and consequently the pots come out with more smoke markings.

Alternative Surfaces

For a beautiful decorative effect, place horse hairs on the pot immediately after removing it from the fire (figure 5). When working with this technique,

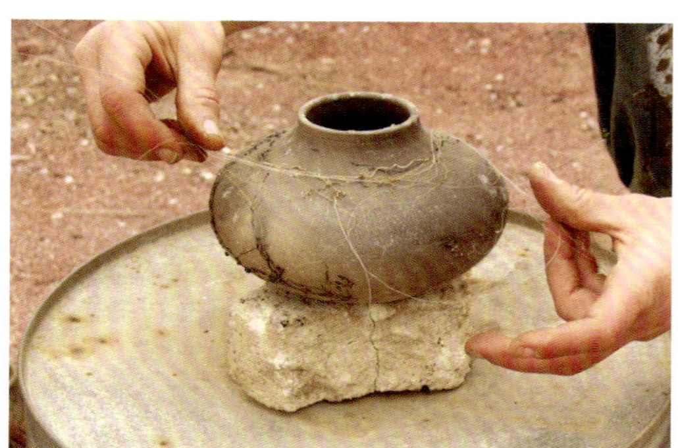

5. Remove the hot pot from the kiln and place horse hairs on it to create squiggly black lines.

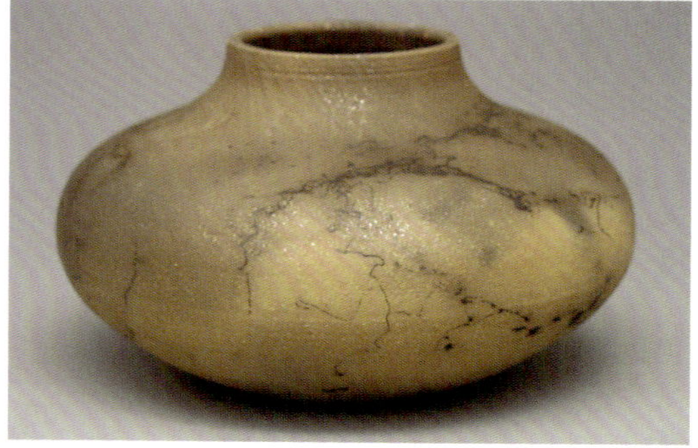

6. Wheel-thrown micaceous clay, fired green in horse-hair decoration.

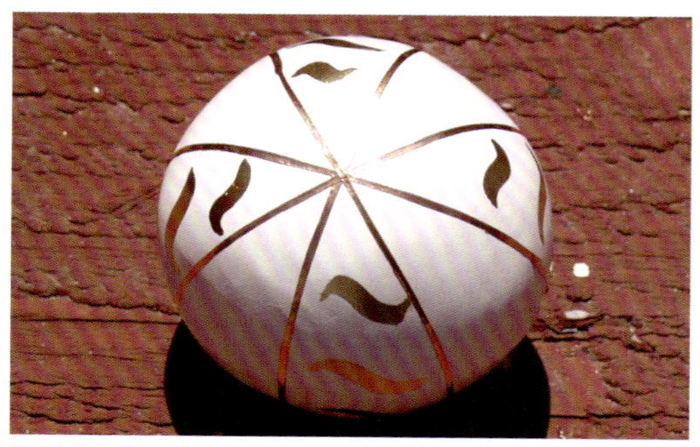

7. This sphere has designs drawn with a gold leaf pen and lines made using copper foil tape.

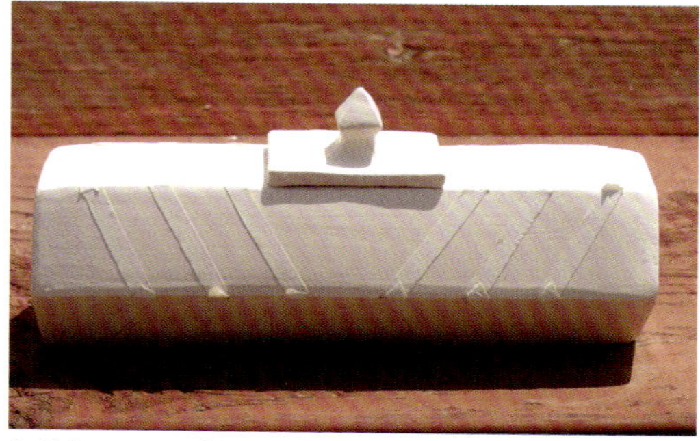

8. This pot was bisque-fired to cone 010, masked with tape, and brushed with terra sigilatta.

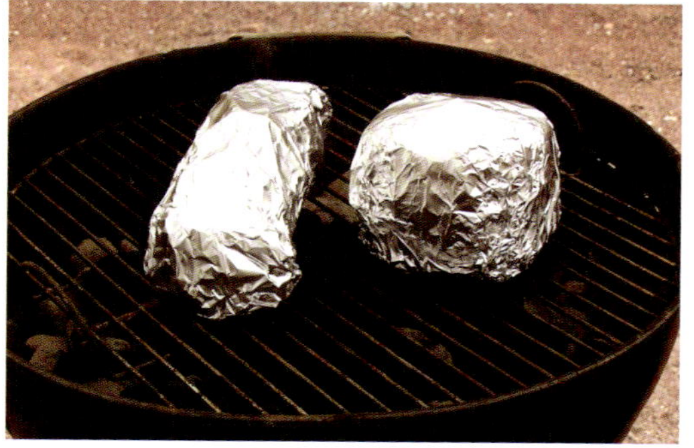

9. Place foil-wrapped pots on the cooking grid rather than on the coals as foil disintegrates in high heat.

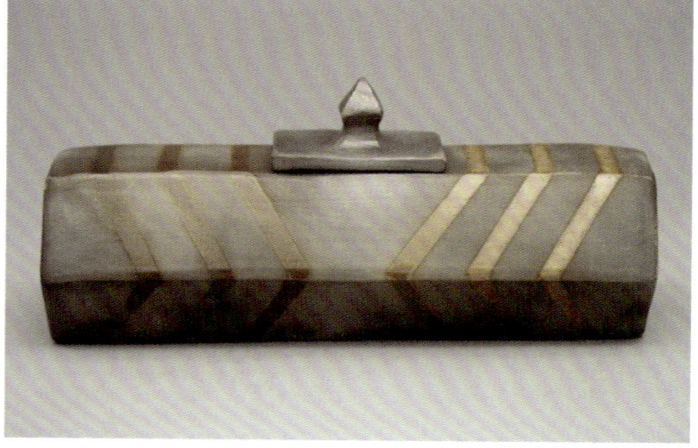

10. A white stoneware lidded box with masking tape resist decoration after a smoke firing in a Weber grill.

remove the pot using tongs, and place it on a piece of warmed soft brick to avoid cracks from thermal shock. The hairs will burn and leave squiggly black marks on the pot (figure 6). Have the hairs ready and work fast—you only have a few seconds before the pot cools down too much.

For other effects, try burnishing your pots with a stone or applying terra sigillata. Depending on the type of clay you are using, you might want to bisque fire them in an electric kiln and use the grill for decorative effects. I create patterns on pots with copper foil tape (intended for stained glass work), gold leaf pens (figure 7), or masking tape (figure 8). Decorated pots can then be wrapped with a double layer of aluminum foil and placed either directly on the hot coals or on the cooking

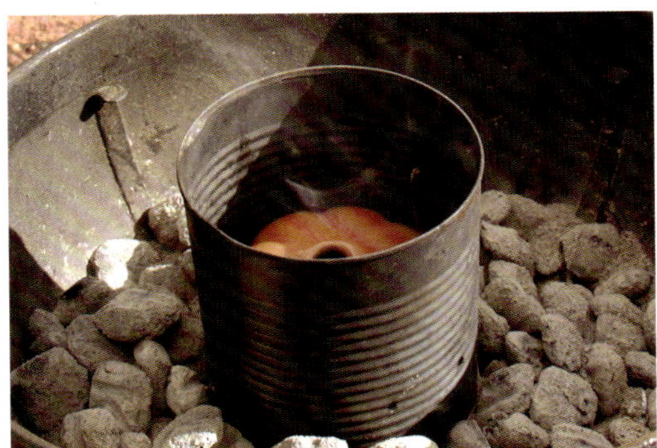

11. Place burnished pot inside a perforated coffee can prior to firing to create an even, glossy black surface.

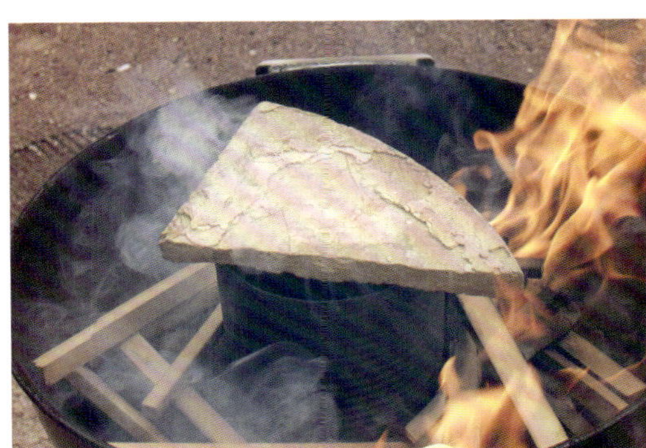

12. Surround tin can with wood scraps to create more heat and smoke. Cover opening with piece of kiln shelf.

grid for 30 minutes (figure 9). I placed these tape decorated pieces on the cooking grid instead of in the coals because aluminum foil disintegrates when placed directly on the coals, which can allow smoke to blacken the pot too much. Since the grill can't produce enough heat to burn off the adhesive on the copper foil tape, this needs to be scraped off after the firing.

Different brands of masking tape can have very different effects—some burn quite quickly and may leave your pot completely black if left on the grill for the full 30 minutes, while other brands have a great deal of sticking power, provide a strong resist and need to be scraped off after firing. The white stoneware piece (figure 10) was brushed with terra sigillata, bisque fired to cone 010, decorated with masking tape, wrapped in a double layer of aluminum foil and fired in the grill.

One more beautiful effect you can achieve firing in your grill is the rich glossy black of burnished and smoke-fired Pueblo Indian pottery. For best results, burnish a smooth red stoneware clay with a stone. If you want to bisque-fire it in an electric kiln first, fire it only to cone 018 to retain the burnish. To blacken it in the grill, wrap it in newspaper and then aluminum foil and place it in the coals. For a deeper black, place it directly in the coals and surround it with wood scraps.

When the wood is burning merrily, cover the grill, shut the air vent on the grill cover and close the damper on the underside. To protect the burnished surface from getting scratched or marked by the fuel, follow the same general steps but start by placing the pot in a coffee can or cookie tin that has holes pierced in the sides. Nestle it into some wood shavings at the bottom of the can, place the can into the coals (figure 11), and cover the can with aluminum foil or a piece of kiln shelf (figure 12). This way, smoke can surround the pot but the pot won't be in direct contact with burning wood or coals. After 30 to 45 minutes, when the grill has stopped smoking, the pot can be removed. If the pot wasn't bisque-fired beforehand in an electric kiln, you'll need to carefully preheat it and fire it directly in the coals to get it hot enough to vitrify—but you'll probably get the richest black color this way.

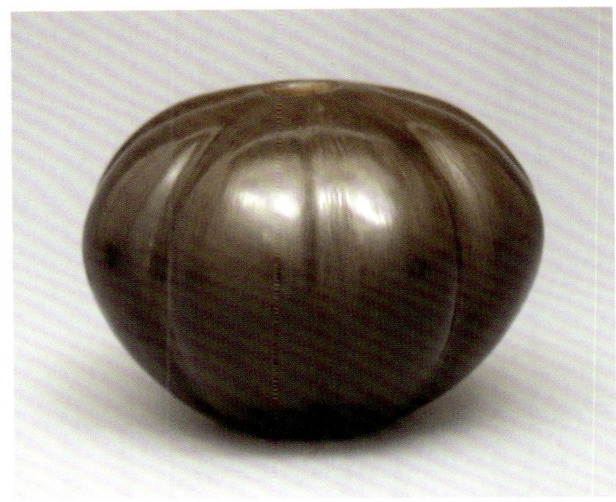

A red stoneware, stone burnished pot, bisque-fired to cone 018, placed inside a perforated coffee can and fired in a Weber grill.

Layers & Inclusions

ADDING CRUSHED CLAY FOR COLOR AND TEXTURE

by Hanna Lore Hombordy

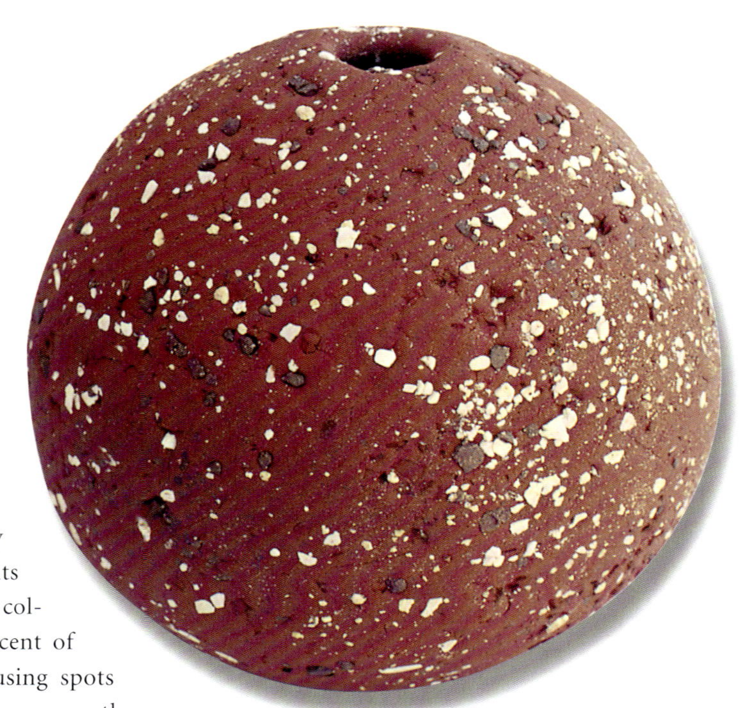

Bits and pieces of crushed clay of different colors can be embedded in the surface to create an unusual surface.

Color and texture have intrigued me since I first began working with clay. I wanted to take advantage of clay's versatility and emphasize some of the unique characteristics that couldn't be produced by any other material. Combining bits and pieces of several kinds of colored clay in a manner reminiscent of impressionistic painting, and using spots of color in an abstract pattern, were worth exploring, plus the specks of clay also provide a subtle texture.

Sources

There are several ways to acquire bits and pieces of clay. You can collect scraps that accumulate from previous projects; check for leftovers and colors others have available; color your own clay by mixing in oxides or stains; or ask your ceramics supplier if they offer sample packs containing several different kinds of clay formulated for your firing temperature. Your ceramics supply house may have a selection of ready-made coarse or medium-sized grog available in various colors. They are also a good source for small amounts of ilmenite, silica sand, granular magnetite, vermiculite and silicon carbide. I've found that clays that mature at differing temperatures can be compatible when combined.

Preparation

It's easiest to begin with small leather-hard scraps. Spread your scraps out on paper or cloth and break up the larger chunks (figure 1). As the pieces get smaller, tap them more lightly. If the clay is already dry, wear a mask and place a cloth over the clay before proceeding to reduce dust. Another option is to begin with rolling damp clay into a thin slab. After this stiffens and is fairly dry, break it into pieces by going over it with a rolling pin.

With either method, you'll end up with an assortment of bits and pieces. Pour your crumbs through a sieve suspended over a water-filled container to get rid of powdery residue and absorb the dust (figure 2).

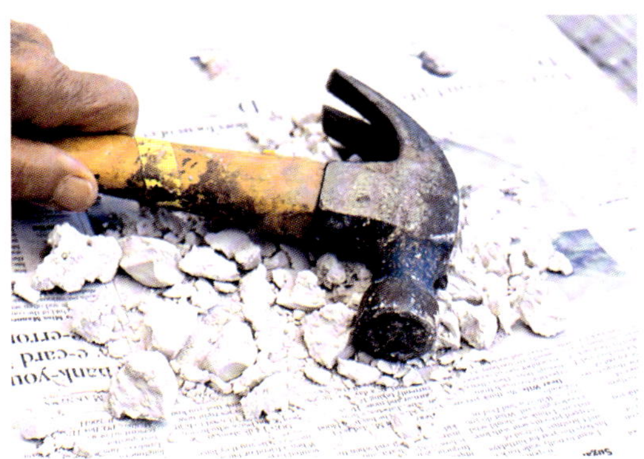

1. Spread your scraps out on paper or cloth and break up the larger chunks.

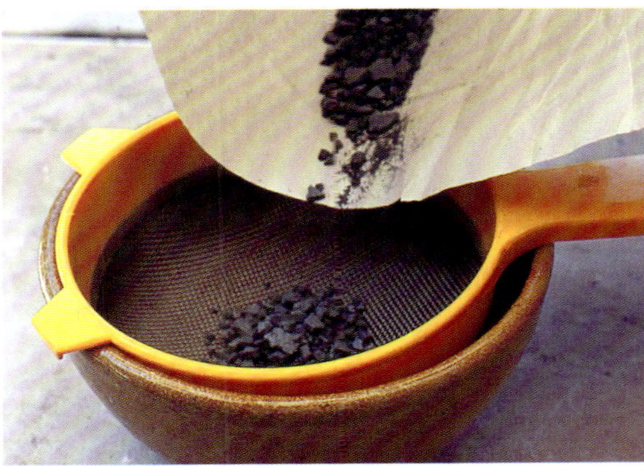

2. Pour crumbs through a sieve suspended over a water-filled container.

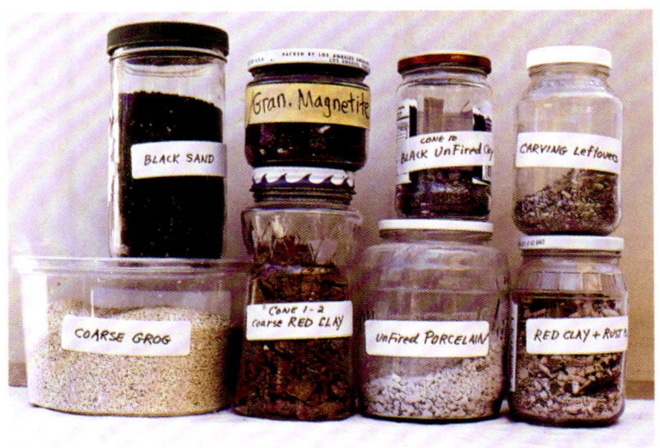

3. Store your collection in transparent, clearly labeled containers for easy access.

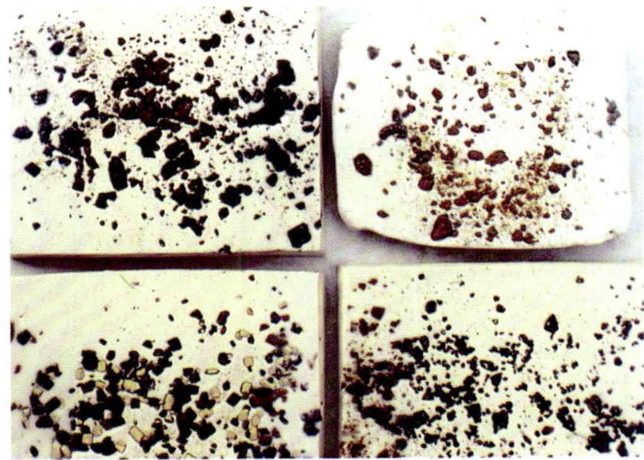

4. Sprinkle your selections onto damp slabs of clay and press them in with a rolling pin or paddle.

Grog (already-fired crumbs of clay) also works well. You can work fairly damp and the assorted colored clay pieces will not blend together. Make your own ceramic grog by putting ground clay into a bowl and firing it to bisque temp or higher.

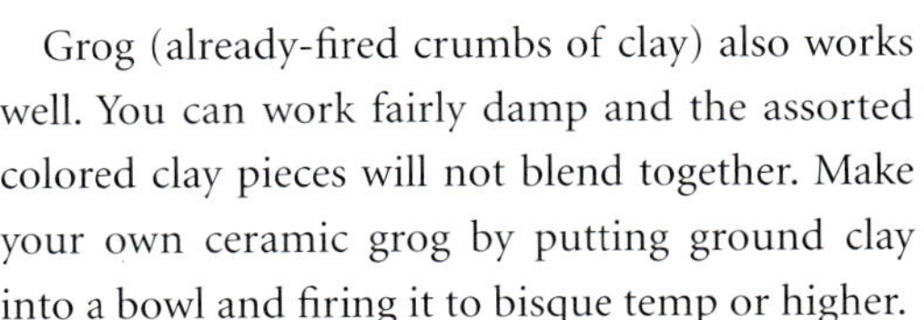

Store your collection in transparent, clearly labeled containers for easy access (figure 3). I've tried many of the ingredients above but have been most satisfied by just using pieces of actual clay or grog incorporated into my work.

Testing

Fire a few test samples using different clay combinations. This helps you figure out how to best distribute your bits and pieces, and helps you decide what size you'd like them to be. Sprinkle your selections onto damp slabs of clay and press them in with a rolling pin or paddle (figure 4). Put a clear glaze on part of your tests to see if you prefer the glazed look. Identify all the materials used on the back of the tests (figure 5).

Picking up the Pieces

While you could merely sprinkle the clay crumbs on the surface of a damp vessel, you'll discover that a majority will fall off while drying or after firing. My favorite method for encouraging pieces to stick is to work with a closed form. I throw a cylinder, round it out and gently shape the top inward until the sides join together in the center (figure 6). This traps air inside the vessel and provides a firm working surface. The clay is too soft to handle immediately after throwing, so wait a while, then wheel trim the bottom as far as possible. Next, cut the piece off the bat and set it aside to firm up. Use a rib for further hand trim-

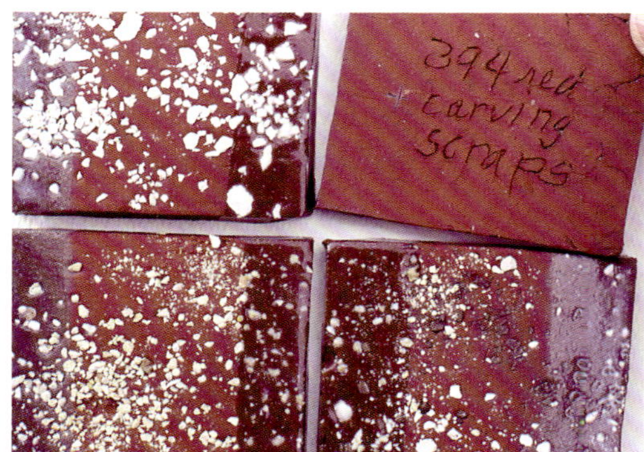

5. Identify all the materials used on the back of the tests.

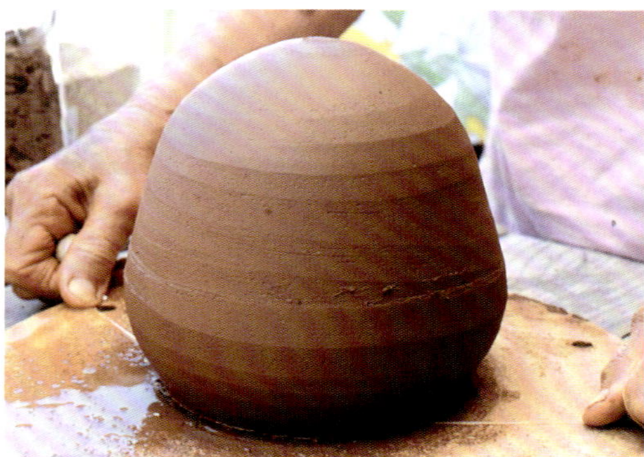

6. A thrown closed cylinder with trapped air provides a firm surface to imbed clay bits.

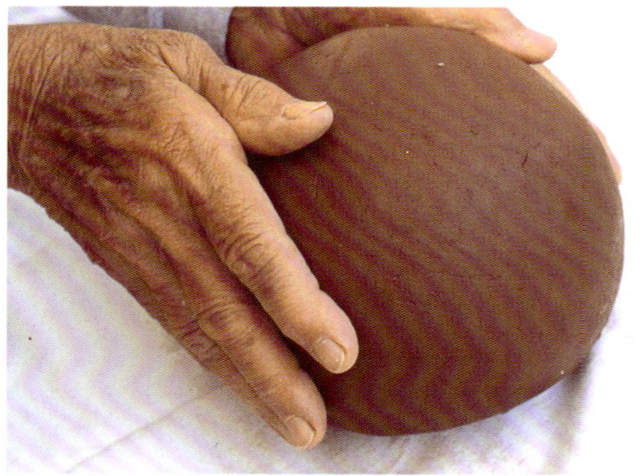

7. Rolling on a padded surface evens out the shape and prevents unwanted marks.

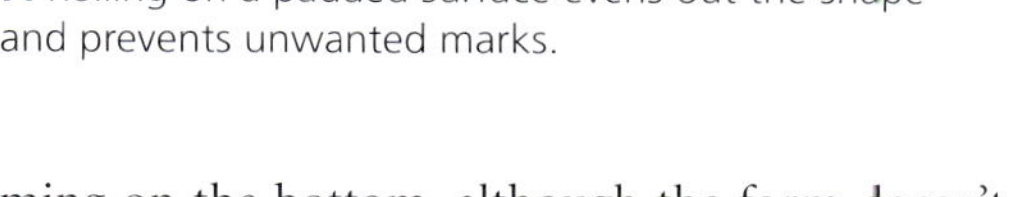

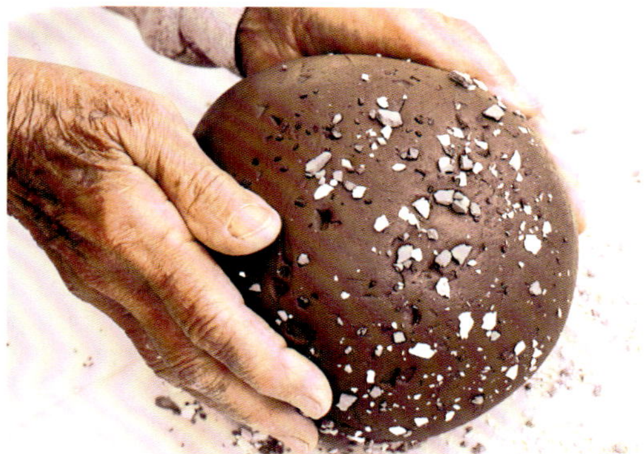

8. Roll the piece over the clay bits to help press them into the vessel.

ming on the bottom, although the form doesn't need to be perfectly smooth.

When your form is firm enough to withstand handling, but not so stiff that it cannot change shape, place on a smooth flat surface. Pad with a few sheets of newspaper and cover with a soft cloth. Rolling evens out the shape and prevents unwanted marks (figure 7). Uneven rolling alters the shape of a vessel while even rolling in all directions results in an almost perfectly spherical shape.

Once you've attained the shape you want, randomly sprinkle pieces on the dry cloth. Roll the piece over the clay bits to help press them into the vessel (figure 8). The clay should be soft enough so that most of the crumbs stick. To further imbed the clay crumbs into the vessel, (figure 9). Persistent gentle paddling results in maintaining a smooth and elegant shape. At this point, you should be aware of two possible problems: First, paddling may cause the form to become too dry to accept additional crumbs and the surface may begin to crack. If this happens, evenly spray the form with a small amount of water. Wait a while for this to sink in because the moisture needs to penetrate gradually. Don't keep adding water or you'll get puddles on your surface, and the several colors of clay will soften and fuse. Should this happen, you can still save the work later by letting it dry totally and giving it a very light sanding. Second, make sure your paddle doesn't become dirty. Wipe off traces of clay with a damp cloth and let the paddle dry before you proceed.

You may treat the clay with a bit of reckless abandon, revealing all the marks of the paddle and the construction process (figure 10), but don't overdo it!

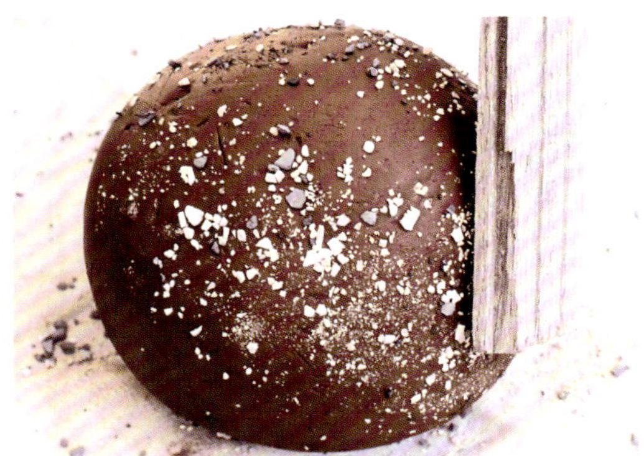

9. Use a paddle with a gentle rhythmic touch, aiming in a different direction with each stroke.

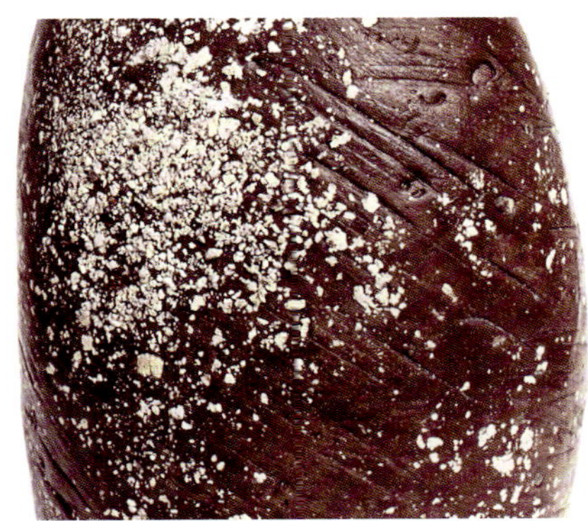

10. Use the paddle to create additional texture, but don't overdo it!

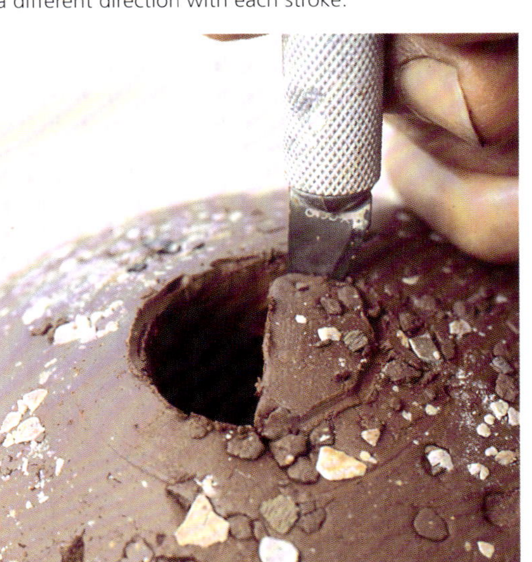

11. When firm leather hard, use an X-Acto blade to cut a neck hole.

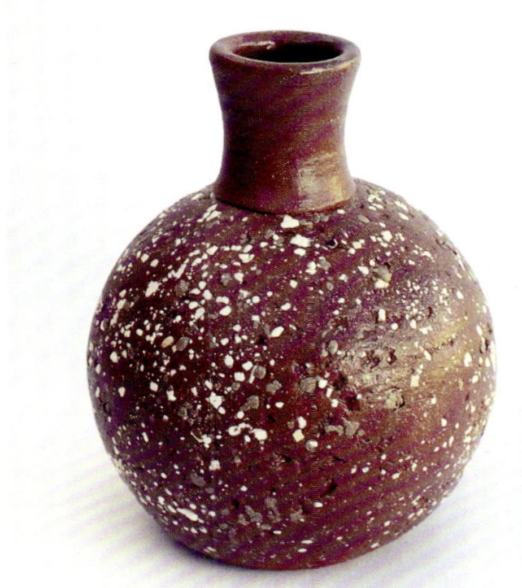

12. Add a thrown or handbuilt spout, rim or neck.

Finishing

If working with an enclosed shape, set it aside for a while but be careful not to let it shrink and get too dry. There is air trapped inside that can't shrink so you must help it escape with a needle prick. You can finish the piece by cutting a hole into the form with a hole cutter or fettling knife (figure 11). Tip: When using a knife, make a straight cut, then cut out the circle. This way, should part or all of the cutout fall into the form, it will be in two smaller sections that can be retrieved through the hole. Finally, add a thrown or handbuilt spout, rim or neck (figure 12).

There are invariably some little indentations or craters in the surface where a few bits and pieces have fallen off. These are not objectionable from a design standpoint for they are little shadowy spots that add to the texture. They are negative spaces that contrast with the positive areas provided by the bits and pieces, and firing this work should not present a problem.

Bisque and glaze fire as you normally would for the clay you are using. Occasionally, I spray a light coating of clear glaze over the outside of a piece, but I really prefer the unglazed look.

Layers & Inclusions
ORGANIC BURNOUT MATERIAL

by Richard Burkett

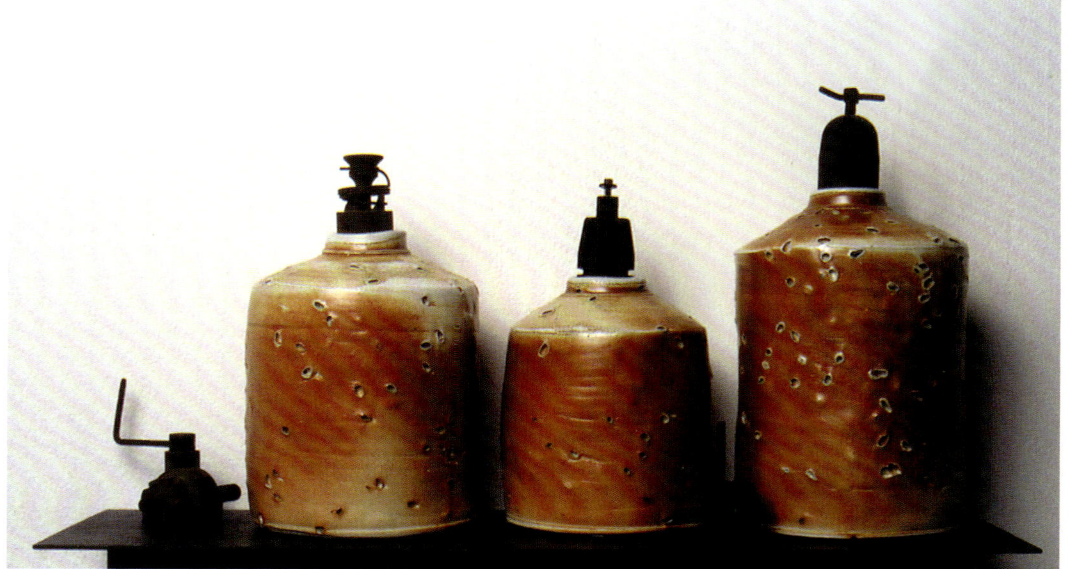

Pressure Vessel series. Soda-fired porcelain with soybean burnout texture and found object lids and steel shelf.

In *Pressure Vessels*, a series of ceramic works, I've tried to include visual references to both science and industry, as well as Midwestern life of the past century. Through the use of soda or wood firing and organic (carbon-based) materials included in the clay that burn out during firing, these vessels take on a corroded appearance. They represent failed vessels in their porosity, no longer being able to hold liquids or pressurization—castoff relics of another time. Many of the forms find resonance in memories of my frequent childhood visits to my father's chemistry laboratory, and my fascination with the many shapes of flasks, beakers, and other chemical glassware. Other works, more threatening in their references to weapons of war, address darker issues of the connections between science, industry, and the military industrial complex.

Although the porosity left by the burnout materials is appropriate to the *Pressure Vessel* series, I have worked out ways to use these textures in other more functional forms that must hold liquids. I find that the burnout-material textures offer surfaces evocative of landscape and geological formations for an ongoing series of oval dishes that reference the Western U.S. landscape, especially mesas and buttes.

Firing Burnout Materials

Clay with burnout texture materials requires a special bisque firing. The bisque firing must be slow enough to allow the organic materials to burn out slowly. Especially important are both a longer-than-normal preheat soak of the kiln below the boiling point of water to remove extra moisture in the organic material used, and a prolonged temperature hold at about 400–420°F, just below the ignition point of carbon-based materials. Obviously, good ventilation is critical, both to burn out the texture materials completely and to safely remove gasses from the kiln (burning organic materials will produce carbon dioxide, or, without enough oxygen in the kiln, carbon monoxide). Gas kilns are preferred for bisque firing burnout materials, but bisque firing can be done in electric kilns with good ventilation equipment installed.

The following is a suggested firing schedule for burning out texture materials. Thicker sections of clay, or larger amounts of burnout materials, may require slower firing. (Thanks to Louis Katz for his suggestions on firing rates when I first started firing these pieces.)

1. Soak the kiln at 180°F for 4–12 hours, depending on clay thickness and the amount and size of texture materials, to remove moisture from the clay.
2. Heat the kiln slowly (20–50°F per hour) to about 420°F, and soak at this temperature for another 4–12 hours (or more if the work is quite thick) to allow the organic materials to carbonize and release as many gasses as possible. This is a very critical phase in the firing.
3. Continue the firing, with a similarly slow heating rate (20–100°F per hour, depending on clay thickness) to at least 600–700°F to allow the gradual burnout of the rest of the carbon-based materials. For thicker sections of clay, a soak for an hour or two at this temperature is recommended. Keep the kiln well ventilated until nearly red heat (1000°F) to ensure enough oxygen to burn out the organic texture materials.
4. Once the kiln has reached red heat and is past quartz inversion, the firing can proceed at fairly normal rates (100–250°F per hour), depending on the size and thickness of the work.
5. Normal cooling of the bisque is okay.

Tips for Success

- One challenge with organic texture materials in clay is to work quickly. Organic materials mold and rot quickly in the damp clay. Wedge the materials in the clay then finish working the clay within a day and let it start drying to avoid mold. (This might be a challenge in warm, humid areas!).
- Don't add scraps of organic texture material clay to your scrap barrel as it decomposes into a smelly mess.
- Burnout materials accidentally included in scrap clay that is reused for regular production can also cause blowouts in a bisque firing of normal speed.
- Chunks of wood or sawdust can also be used for other types of texture.
- Be careful not to use materials like plastics that can create extremely toxic gasses when they burn, or seeds that have been treated with antifungal chemicals.

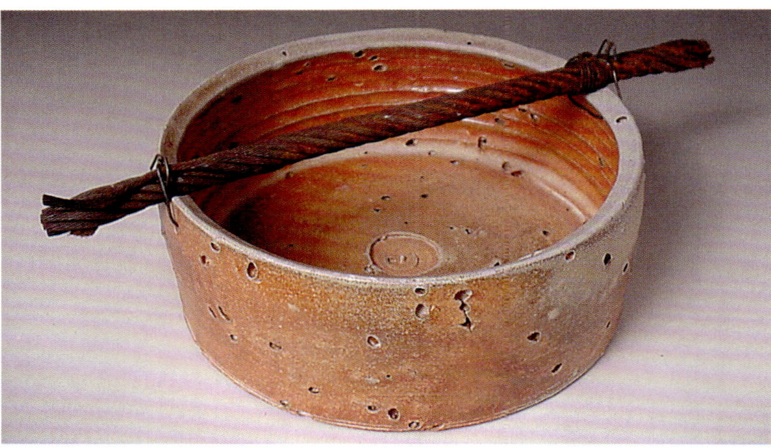

Tray, soda-fired stoneware with soybean burnout texture, with found object handle.

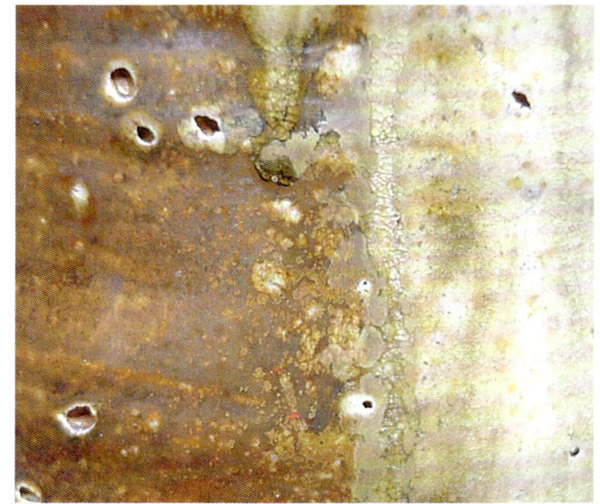
Detail of anagama-fired burnout texture, small addit on of barley along with coarse feldspar chunks.

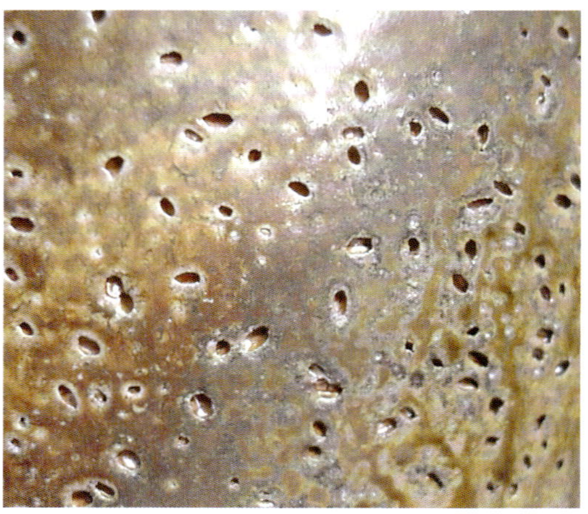
Anagama-fired burnout texture with a large amount of barley added.

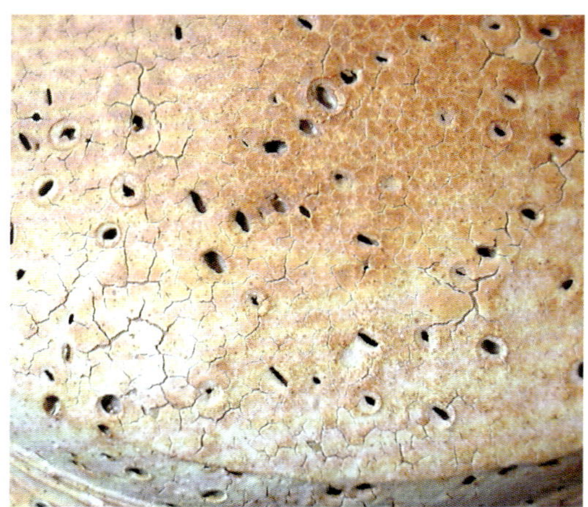
Crackle slip added over the burnout texture at the bisque stage. The form was then soda fired.

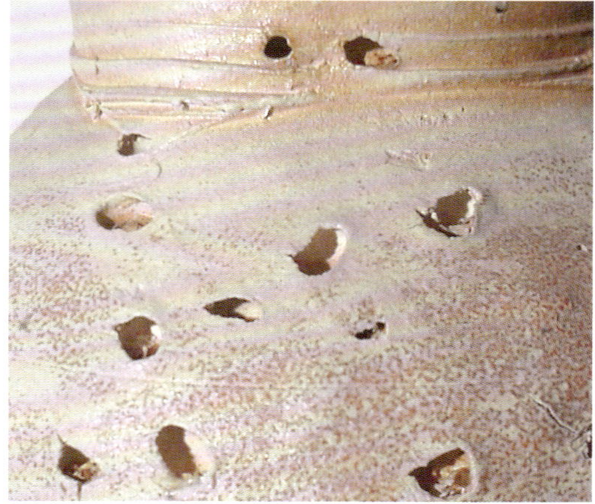
Soybeans create a much larger hole when they burn out. Soda fired after flashing slip applied to bisque.

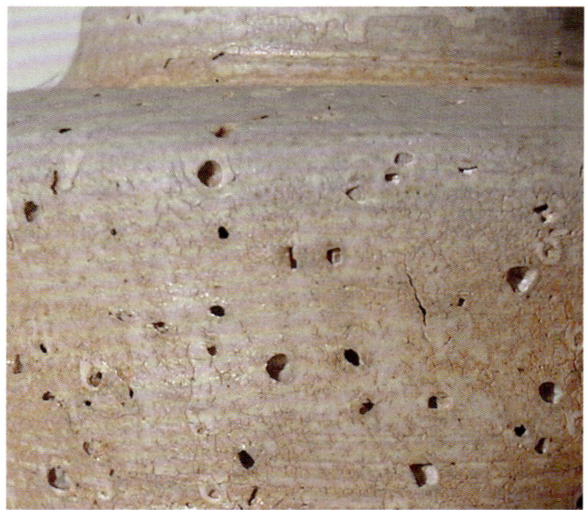
Buckwheat groats burnout texture with a very light soda vapor glaze.

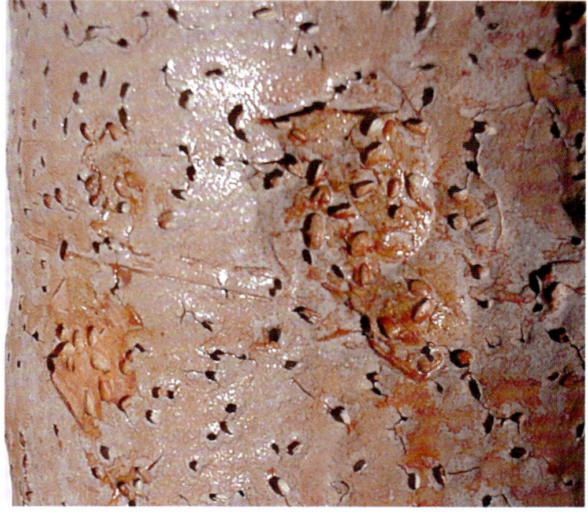
Bisque firing too quickly causes steam and burnout gasses to blow pieces out of the side of the form.

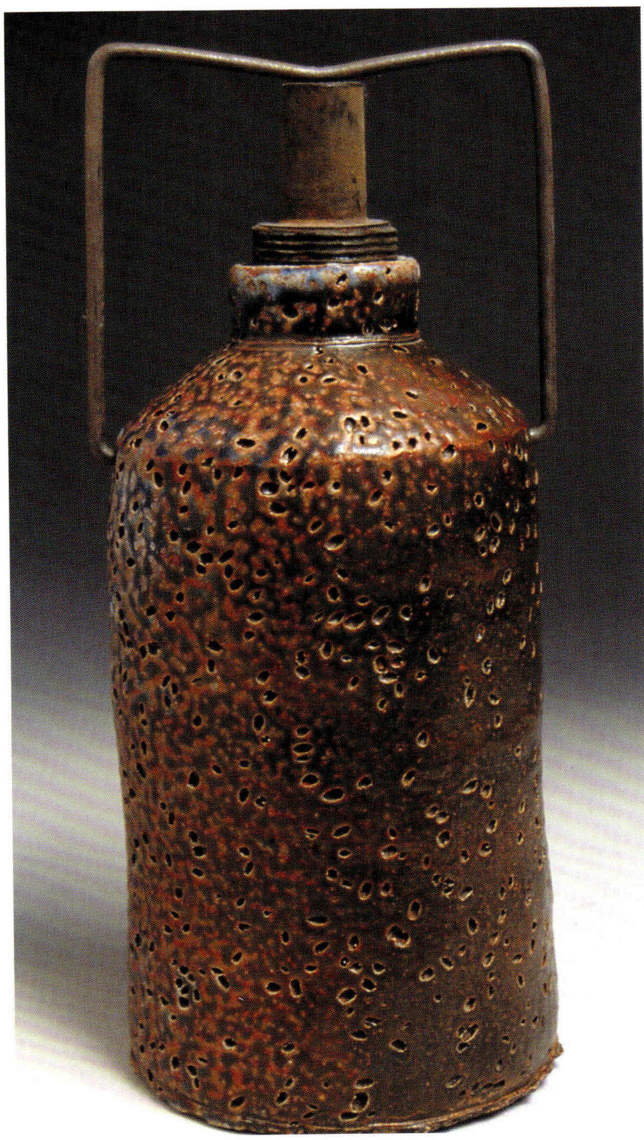

Pressure Vessel series, stoneware with soda vapor glaze, refired to cone 06 with terra sigillata, and steel lid and bale.

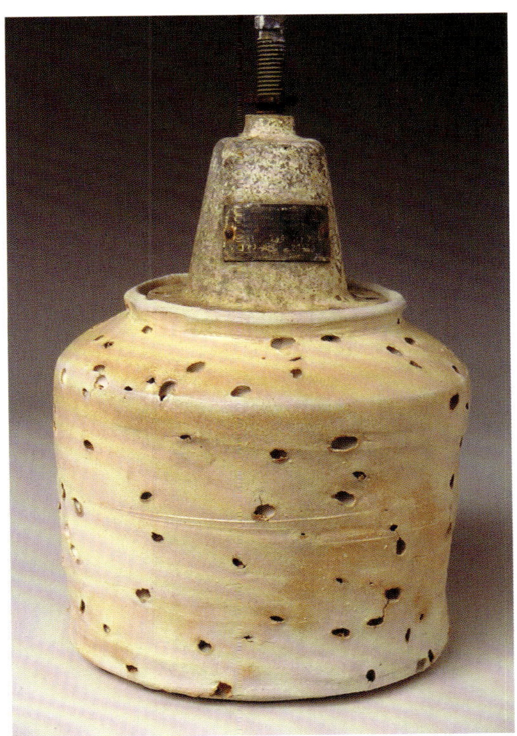

Pressure Vessel series, soda-fired stoneware with soybean burnout texture and found object lid.

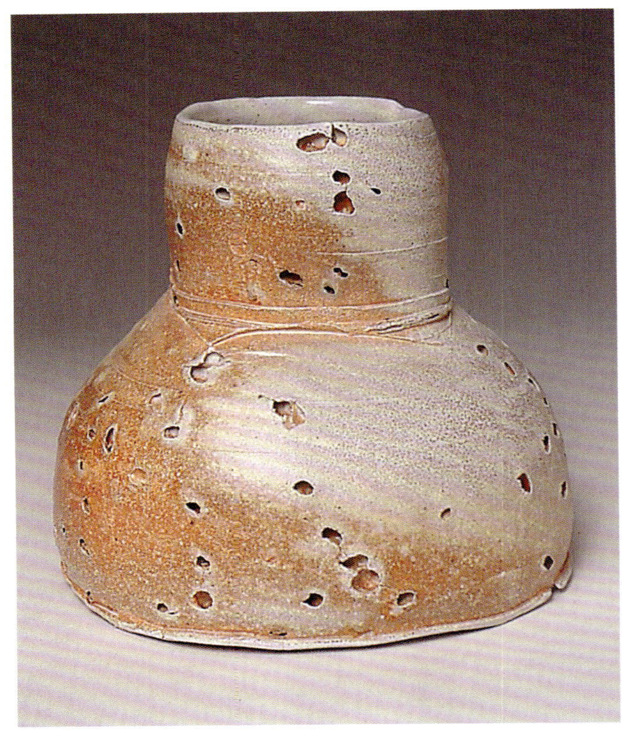

Vase, soda-fired stoneware with soybean burnout texture.

Layers & Inclusions

GILLIAN PARKE'S FELDSPAR INCLUSIONS

by Kathy Norcross Watts

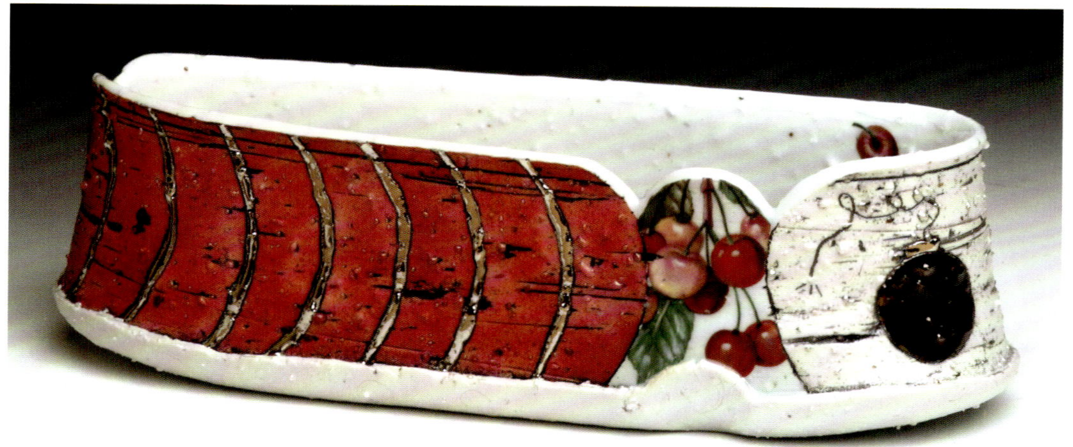

Above: *Cherry Bomb*, 12½ inches in length, wheel-thrown and assembled porcelain with feldspar/molochite inclusions, underglaze patina and inlay, celadon glaze, fired to cone 10 in gas-reduction; luster overglaze, open-stock decals, multiple firings to cone 017 electric. Below: *Orange Daisy, Blue Rose*, 8½ inches in height, wheel-thrown and assembled porcelain with feldspar/molochite inclusions, underglaze patina and inlay, celadon glaze, cone 10 gas reduction; lusters, overglazes, open-stock decals, multiple firings to cone 017 in electric.

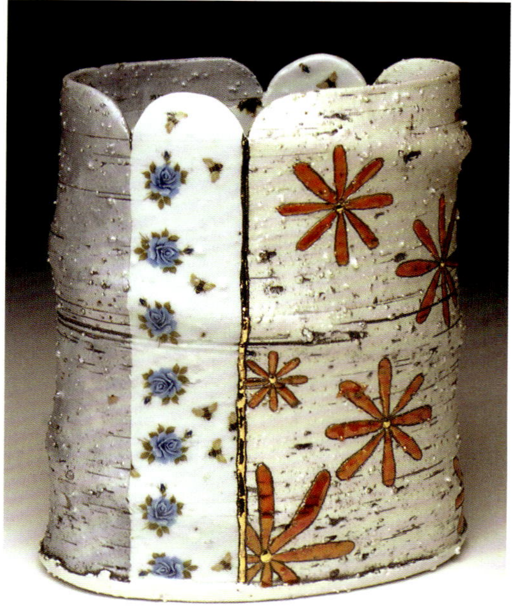

After several years being deeply involved in pottery, Gillian Parke began combining porcelain with feldspar inclusions, applied decals and lusters to create one-of-a-kind pieces. "I was trying to take the English porcelain tradition—white and feminine—

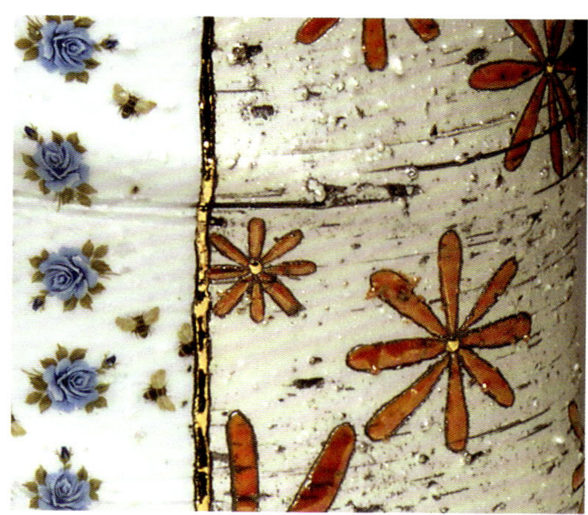

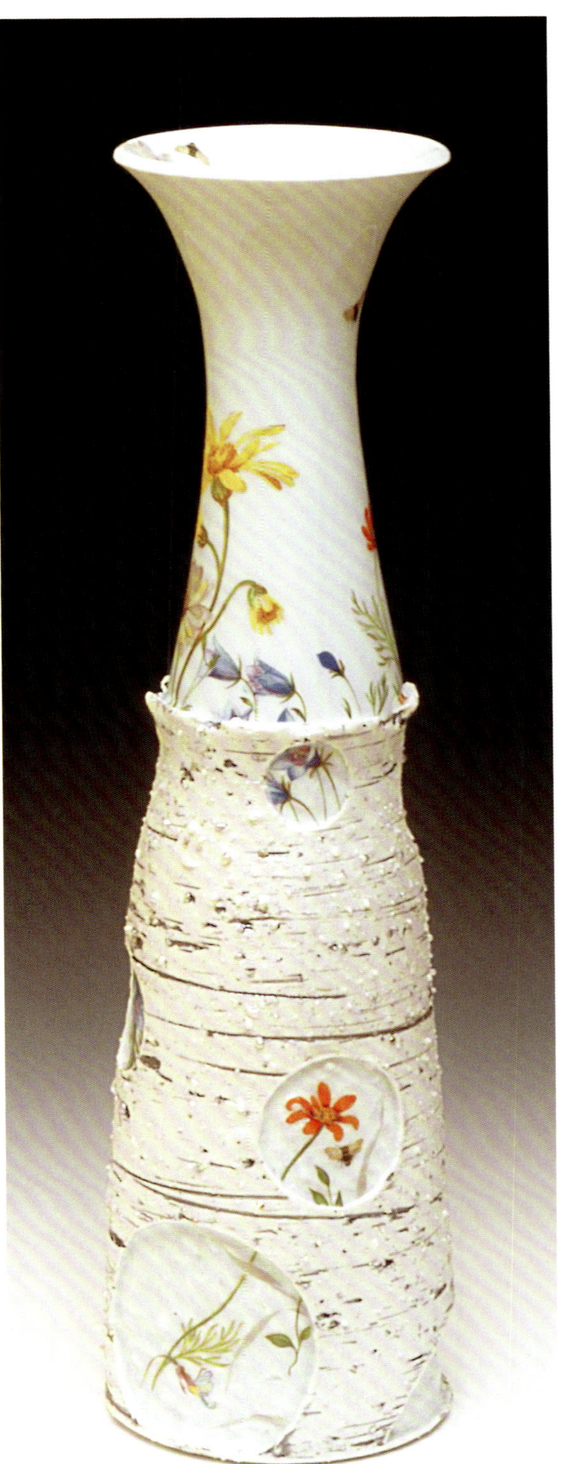

and merge it with this Japanese Shigaraki tradition; it's very masculine," she explains of the process in which organic forms are fired with wood, and the flame hits the pot leaving nature to play a vital role in the outcome. As she adds layers of glazes and decals, each piece undergoes multiple firings to achieve the effects she seeks, sometimes as many as five to ten firings per piece. She wants her work to comment on the world. "Taking manufactured images and putting them on handmade pots is fascinating to me," Parke explains, adding, "I am interested in the conflict created by kitsch images on handmade objects, and in challenging the aesthetics and values presented when using such materials unconventionally. The resulting works illustrate the contrasts in aesthetics, forms, traditions and function found between Japanese pottery and fine porcelain."

Throwing with Feldspar Inclusions

by Gillian Parke

I usually work in stages on a set of pieces using Highwater Clay's Helios porcelain with coarse Custer feldspar (1–10 mesh, Seattle Pottery Supply) and 50–80 mesh molochite wedged in. Throwing with the inclusions requires using a substantial amount of water to provide sufficient slip for lubrication.

Wildflower Portal, 13½ inches in height, wheel-thrown and assembled porcelain with feldspar inclusions, underglaze patina, celadon glaze, fired to cone 10 in reduction; luster overglaze, open-stock decals, multiple firings to cone 017 electric.

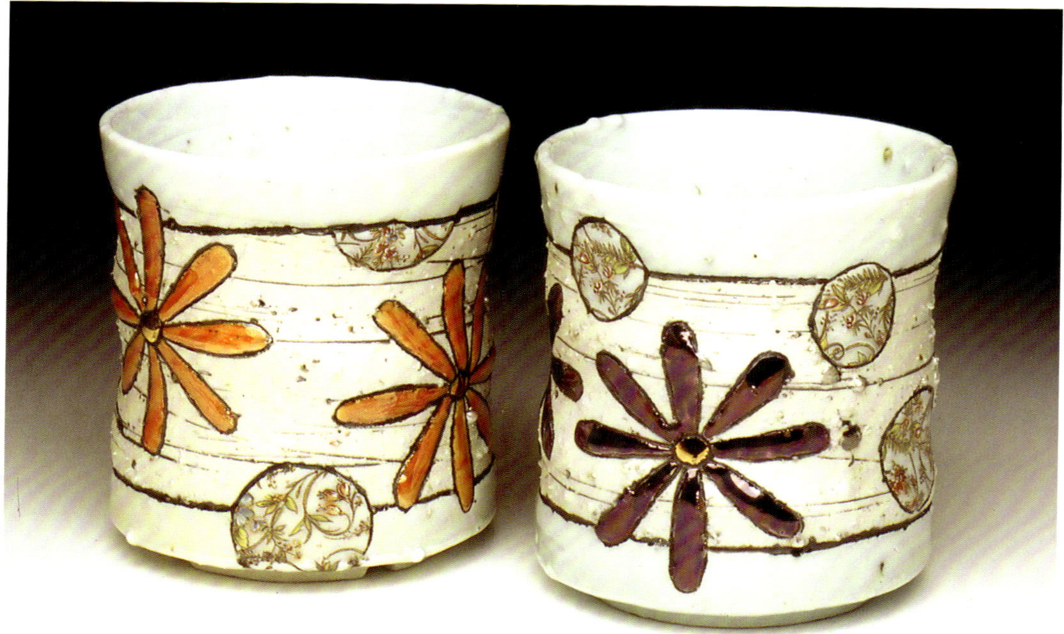

Orange & Blue Daisy Teacups, 4 inches in height, porcelain with feldspar/molochite inclusions, underglaze patina and inlay, fired to cone 10 in reduction; luster overglazes, open-stock decals, multiple firings to cone 017 electric.

This helps prevent both finger cuts and tears in the turning clay. However, the piece will lose its strength and collapse due to the low plasticity of porcelain if too much water is used.

Each stage is thrown on the wheel and allowed to dry. Before removing the piece from the wheel, the feldspar and molochite matrix is exposed with a metal rib or trimming tool. This also serves to remove the surface slip.

After assembling the piece, it is completely dried and wax resist is painted onto areas that will eventually be glazed. Underglaze is then applied to the unwaxed clay areas. The underglaze is removed from the surface with a damp sponge, leaving an underglaze patina that accentuates the feldspar and throwing lines.

Wax resist is again applied to the dry surface. Using a needle tool, lines are etched through the wax, revealing the clay below. After wiping clean with a damp sponge, black underglaze is applied to the inlaid line.

After bisque firing to cone 07, wax resist is applied to black inlay lines so that glaze will not cover the line and affect the color. Glazes are applied by pouring, dipping and/or brushing. The resulting piece is then fired in a gas kiln to cone 10 in reduction.

Feldspar inclusions result in pearl-like eruptions covering the surface of the vessel. This surface is painted with various luster overglazes and fired in an electric kiln to cone 017 multiple times per layer of surface treatment.

Layers & Inclusions

CONNECTING THE DOTS

by Elizabeth Spar

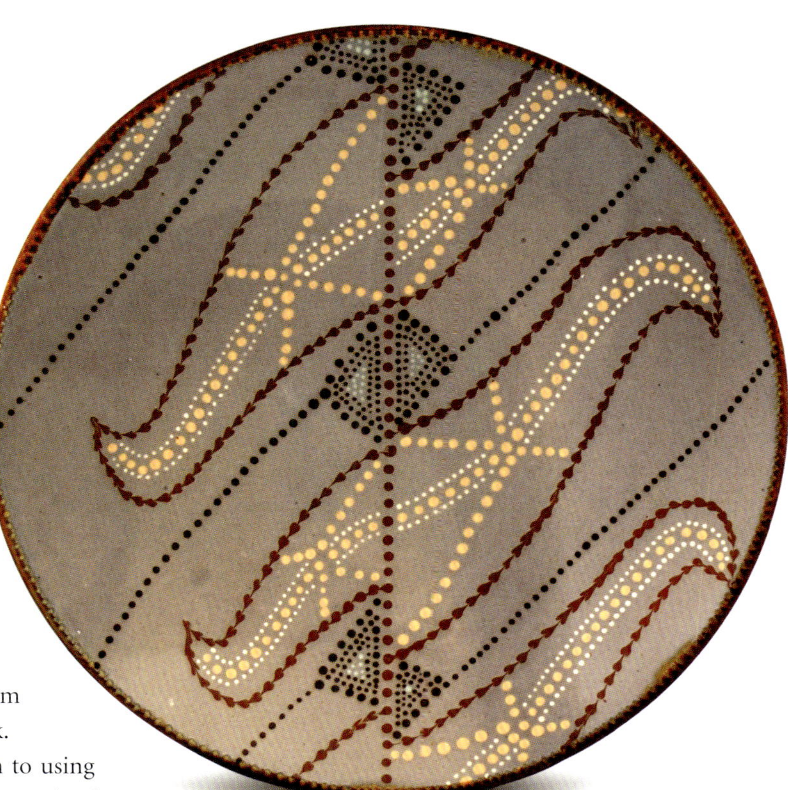

Birds, 20 inches in diameter, local Alfred clay, slips, and glazes, fired to cone 3.

I make pots from clay that I dig from the earth. I also use local clay in terra sigillatas, and use recycled glass, and locally sourced wood ash for glazes and surfaces. I enjoy my relationship with these materials, the process of experimentation, and the beauty and depth that using them gives to me and to the work.

This particular approach to using slip was born during graduate school at The New York State College of Ceramics at Alfred University, in Alfred, New York, where I was encouraged to look beyond the surface of what I like and to really understand why. I began using the local Alfred clay there, designing a new glaze palette at cone 3, and studying old slipware pots. I learned the techniques of feathering and marbling from an old magazine. I then tore through books and ceramic history while gaining an awareness of the process of inquiry, going deeper and allowing my work to come from within after digesting all the research. Creating patterns with dots came from a sense of play and discovery, and has been an exploration ever since. I have to be totally present and mindful to execute the pattern well, and the best ones come out differently than originally planned. Geometric structures and plant life are the main themes.

Base Form

For plates, I begin by pounding out enough wedged clay to make multiple slabs at once. I pound it to a circular shape about an inch larger

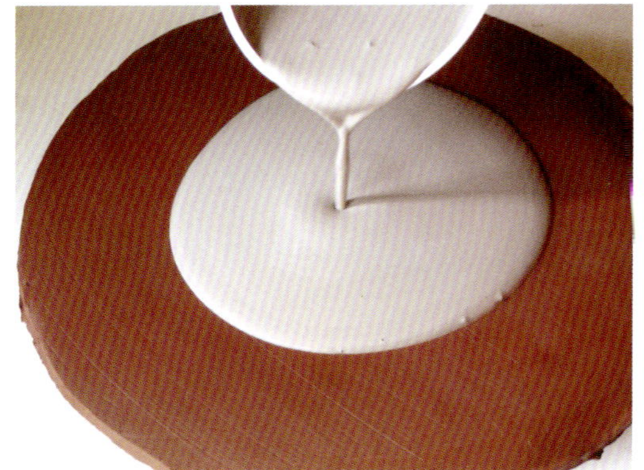

1. Pour a base coat of slip onto the slab.

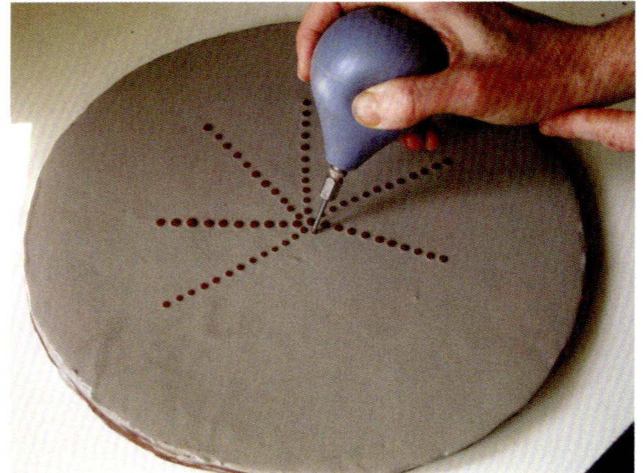

2. Begin applying the dots in different colors of slips on the base slip.

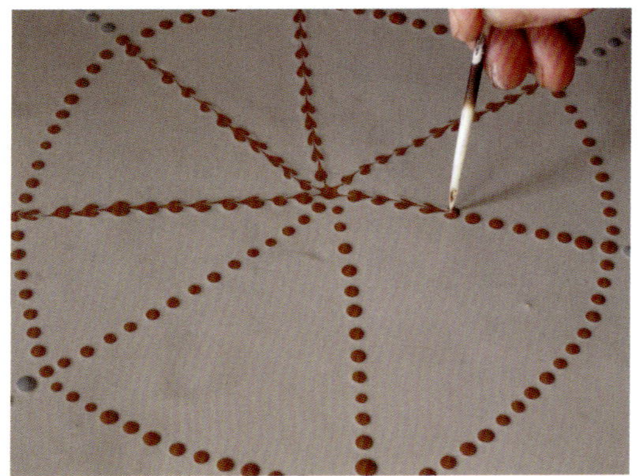

3. Feather the dots by dragging through them with the fine tip of a porcupine quill.

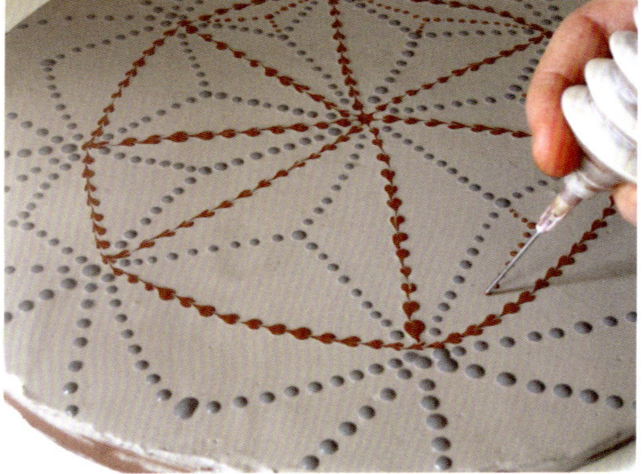

4. Fill in the pattern with dots that will not be feathered.

in diameter than the mold I will use. This allows for some shrinkage, some curvature, and a way to crop the image nicely later on. I then use slab cutters, made from notched wooden sticks and a cut-off wire to cut ⅜-inch-thick slabs.

After cutting the slabs, I compress the top surface before taking it off the pile, then flip it and compress the other side. I put each slab on a bat and trim it to the edge of the bat so it is perfectly round.

I pour a base coat of slip onto the slab (figure 1). The slip is thick enough that it stays wet while I feather the added dots or lines before they dry. I create a slip using a light clay body and a dark clay body with the same shrinkage. Alternately, you could choose a slip recipe with a high amount of silica, as this allows the slip to be thick without cracking as it dries.

Slip Trailing and Feathering

I then begin applying the dots in different colors of slips on the base slip (figure 2). I like to use a few different kinds of slip trailers in order to get a variation in the size of the dots. Metal-tipped bottles are nice, as well as simple ear syringes from the drugstore.

I then feather the dots by dragging through them with the fine tip of a porcupine quill (figure 3). I do this first, while the slip is the wettest. After completing the outline, I fill in the pattern with dots that will not be feathered (figures 4–5).

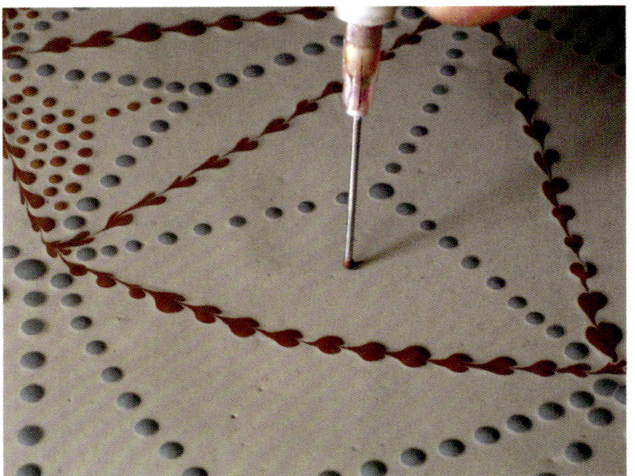
5. Add more dots according to your design.

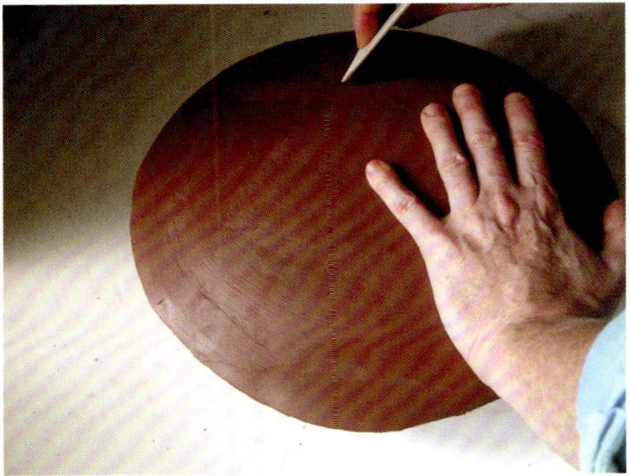
6. Compress the slab over the mold.

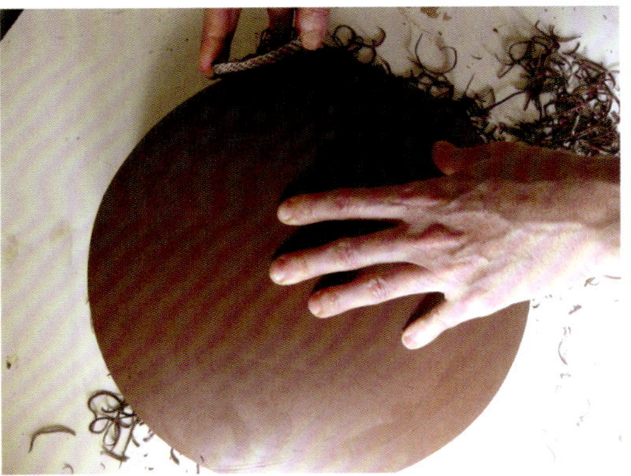
7. Once the slab is leather hard, remove it from the mold and Surform the edge.

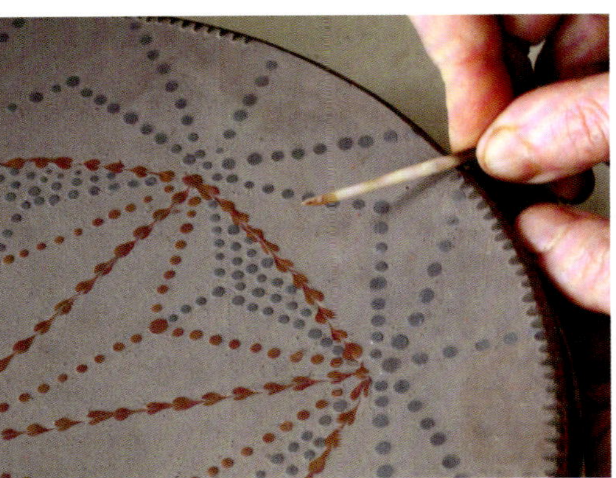
8. With the form upright, press the inside with multiple marks to refine the rim.

Shaping the Form

I let the slip dry to leather hard. I want it to be dry enough that the pattern stays clear and crisp without smudging as it is put against the mold, and the slab to be flexible enough to be compressed into shape over the mold (figure 6). I leave it on the mold until it is stiff, then shave the edge with a Surform up to the edge of the mold (figure 7). I then either shave the bottom flat, or put it on the wheel and thrown a coil for a foot. I place it upright and press the inside edge with multiple marks of my porcupine quill to refine the rim (figure 8). I then dry the form upright before glazing it.

Glazing

I use a cone 3 clear ash glaze over the decorated surface. Some slips flux more than others in the firing, and I like the way that some of the pattern is clear while other parts are slightly blurred. Still, my favorite phase of each pot is right after the slip has been applied and is still wet, showing the traces of each moment and glistening with potential.

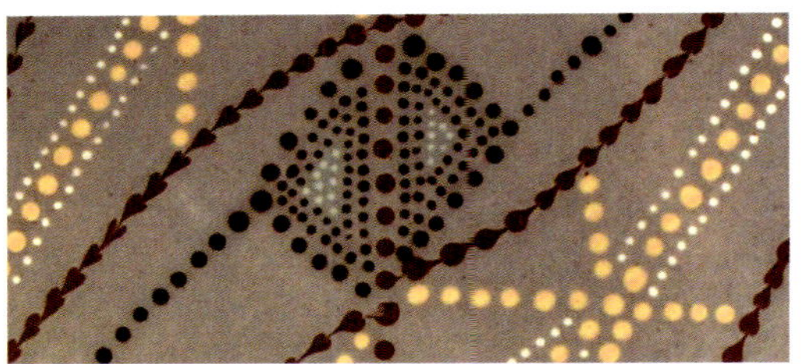

Layers & Inclusions

SLIP TRAILERS

by Bill Jones

Slip trailing conveniently adds color, accents, letters, and even texture to greenware or bisque. For years, though, this technique was limited for many potters because the most common slip trailers available were either the condiment dispenser, a recycled glue bottle or a bulb syringe, none of which are suitable for fine work.

All that has changed with the availability of precision applicators. The precision applicator features a fine hollow metal tube with an opening from 14 to 22 gauge attached to a cap or connector that fits on a flexible squeeze bottle or bulb. (Note: On gauges, the higher the number the smaller the size.) There are numerous manufacturers of precision applicators and we looked at three of them—Aardvark (makers of Falcon tools), Amaco, and Xiem. Each of these companies distributes the applicators widely through ceramic art suppliers and art supply stores.

The best part about precision applicators is that they're ideal for creating fine lines, details, and lettering. As a bonus, they can be used for applying any liquid—underglaze, glaze, stains, soluble salts, wax, etc., as well as non-ceramic materials around the house like lubricants, adhesives, or paints.

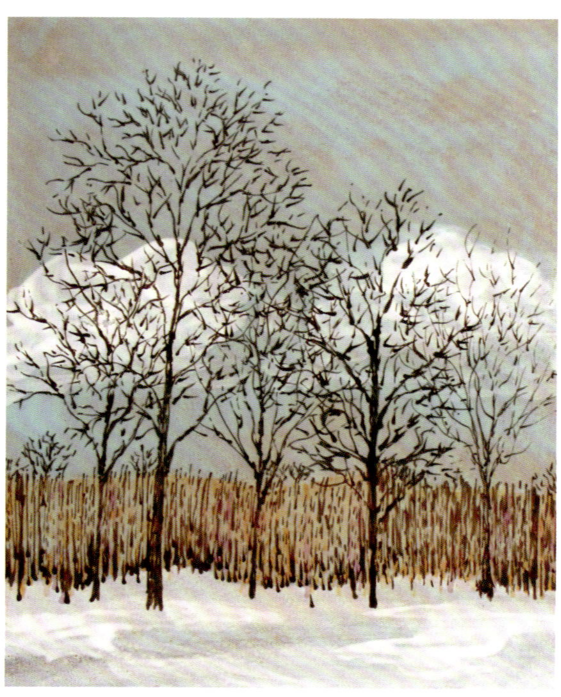

Winter Scene by David Gamble using an 18-gauge Amaco applicator for the trees and tree line. *Photo courtesy of David Gamble.*

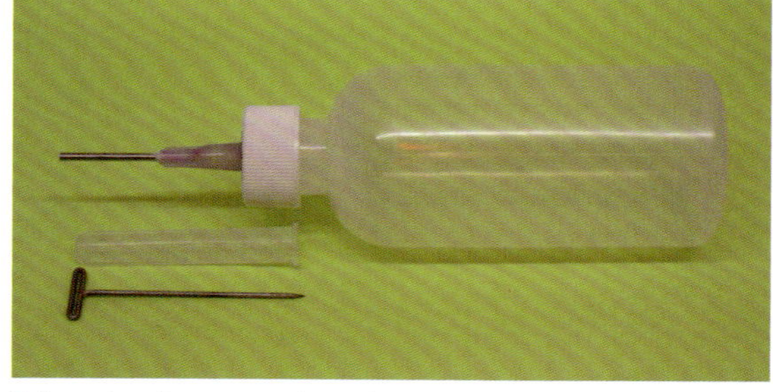

Falcon Applicator consists of a 2-ounce polyethylene bottle with 16-gauge opening, cap, and a stainless steel 1-inch-long needle for cleaning. *Photo courtesy of Aardvark Clay & Supplies.*

Tips for Use

- Always trail the slip. Moving the applicator forward can clog the tip with clay or glaze.
- Always store applicators with the lid on.
- For applicators 16 gauge and higher, screen liquids through an 80 mesh screen if the needle is plugging up.
- Clean applicators with soap and water, flush thoroughly and store in a dry place.
- Do not store applicators in water.
- Higher gauges are best suited for stains and oxides, lower gauges for slips and underglazes.
- If the applicator is blocked, do not squeeze harder! Stop and unplug the needle before proceeding.
- Always test flow on a piece of newsprint.

Sources

Aardvark Clay & Supplies — www.aardvarkclay.com
Amaco — www.amaco.com
Xiem Tools — http://store.xiemclaycenter.com

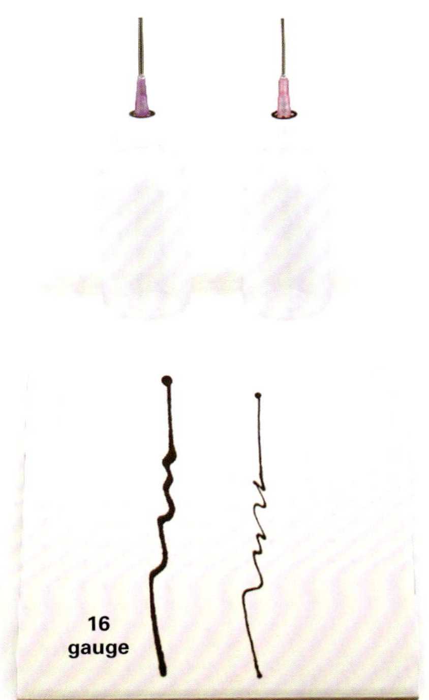

Amaco Underglaze Applicators are available in two sizes—16 and 18 gauge—the two needle sizes allow you to make medium or fine lines, dots, and letters. Sold separately. *Photo courtesy of Amaco.*

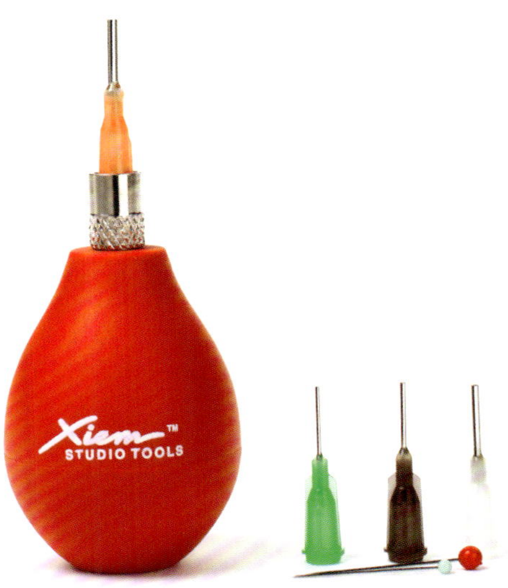

Xiem Precision Applicator. Xiem offers a choice between two soft rubber bulb sizes (1- and 3-ounce), eight tips (14 through 21 gauge), a suction adapter for filling the bulb, and a nickel-plated connector. Items are sold separately or you can purchase a set that comes with a bulb, three color-coded tips, two cleaning needles, and an adapter. *Photo courtesy of Xiem Gallery.*

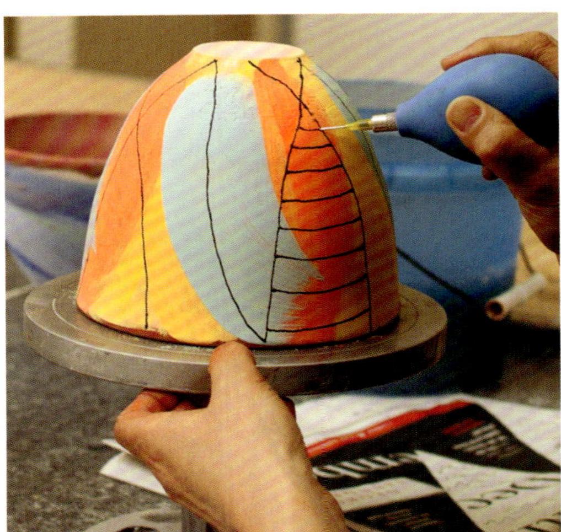

Mary Oligny applying lines using 3-ounce Xiem Precision Applicator (20-gauge tip). *Photo courtesy of Xiem Gallery.*

3

Carving & Etching

MATT REPSHER'S PERFORATED POTS

by Katey Schultz

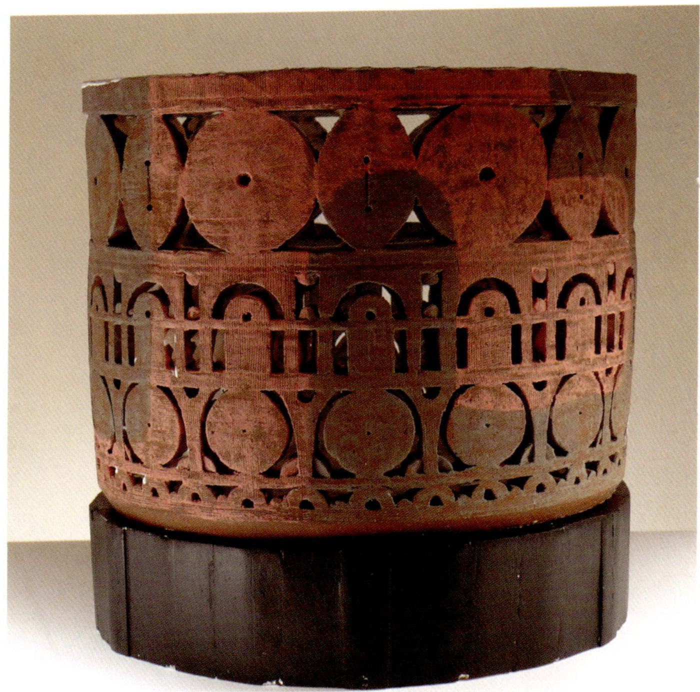

Barrel, 12¾ in. (32 cm) in height, stoneware and wood.

Known for his thematic obsessions with architecture and geometric design, Repsher's mid-range, red stoneware vessels, jars, mugs, bowls, and sculptures evoke a sense of stability, movement, and growth. That may seem contradictory at first, but spend a little time with his work and the connections start to form. Through his careful use of embedded cutouts and repeated patterns, a mug or bowl not only maintains its utilitarian function, but also challenges the edges of the form. The three-dimensional cutouts are typically shaped after some element of ancient architecture, such as arches, pillars, cantilevers, or portals. Repsher's signature surface design in colored slips adds layers to an already dynamic surface. Rather than precisely mirroring the patterns created by his cutouts, Repsher paints freely over the surface in swaths of color that often contrast the movement already established by the form.

There's a lot going on in Repsher's work. When viewed through the lens of formative influence, it's impossible to isolate a single, dominant element. I like to begin where I believe most viewers do, and that is with Repsher's attention to the visual quality of his structural lines. "My dad built the house I grew up in," Repsher says. In addition to being an architect, his father also studied pottery. "I grew up exposed to stud walls and various other unfinished elements that exposed the structure of the house. Now, I can't look at a house without imagining its underlying structure."

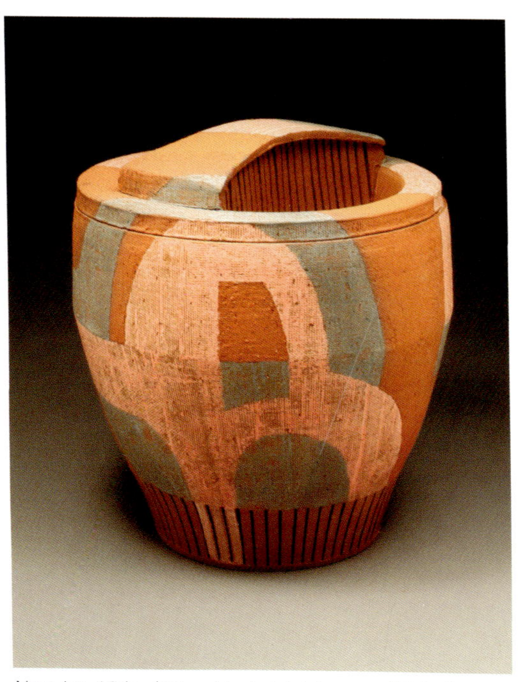
Nest Jar, 10 in. (25 cm) in height, Laguna SB Red cone 6 clay, slip.

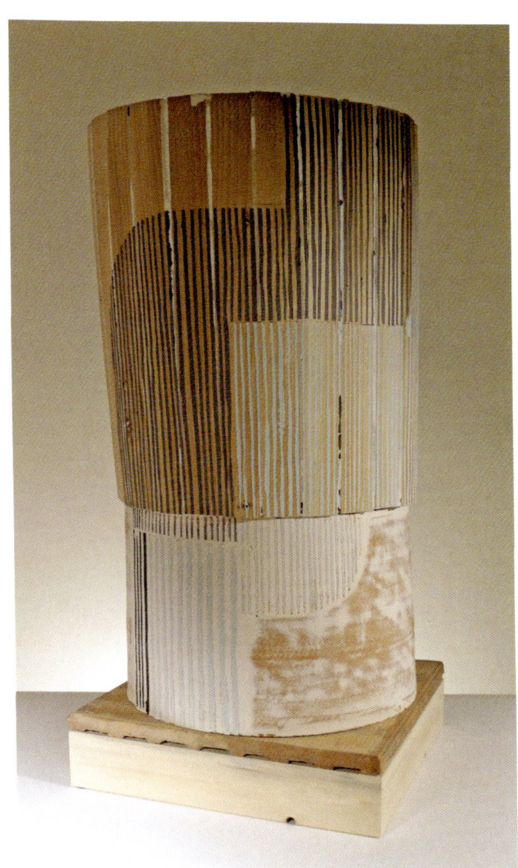
Burke, 28 in. (71 cm) in height, stoneware and wood.

Another element of Repsher's work is his use of pattern and surface design to suggest growth. While his architectural cutouts imply stability and a certain feeling of staying put, the repetition of patterns these cutouts create around the form add a sense of momentum. "I'm both camouflaging the structure of the piece and accentuating it as I move around the work," Repsher says. Arch after arch, pillar after pillar, the eye starts to move along the pattern and it builds on itself.

How does Repsher know when to stop repeating a pattern? When to add colored slips that complement the embedded cutouts, and when to paint in a way that contrasts? It's a feeling, an intangible gauge of completeness that harkens back to an amalgam of memories too layered to name, but he knows it when he experiences it. The way Repsher has synthesized all of this into his work is inspiring. But, surely, what he creates is more than the sum of his influences. One way Repsher keeps his process fresh is by refusing to stick to certain labels or categories. "I bounce around a lot between words like *sculpture*, *vessels*, *pots*, *container*, and *construction*," Repsher says. "When I am making a mug, I feel like I am sculpting the handle. By saying 'sculpting,' I feel I may be in a different mindset than if I was 'potting.'"

He applies this same intuitive openness to his surface treatment. The interior of each piece is often the only part that is glazed. Repsher adds a

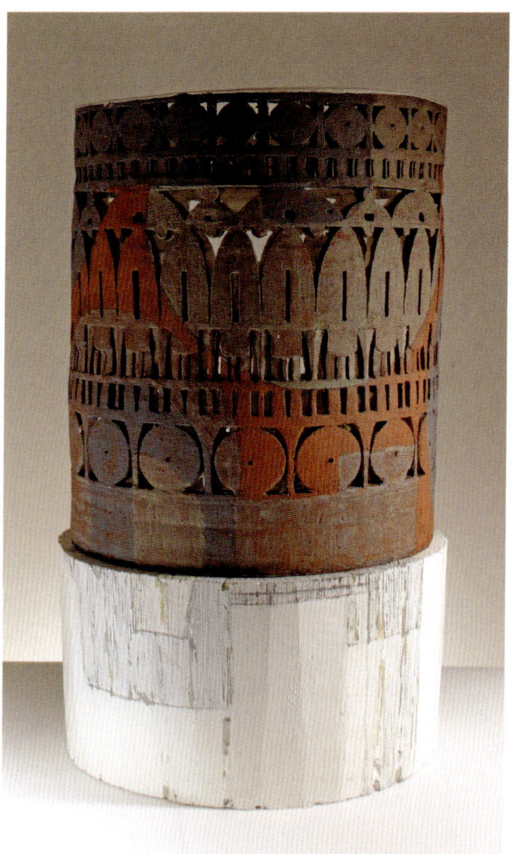

Render, 21 in. (53 cm) in height, stoneware, wood.

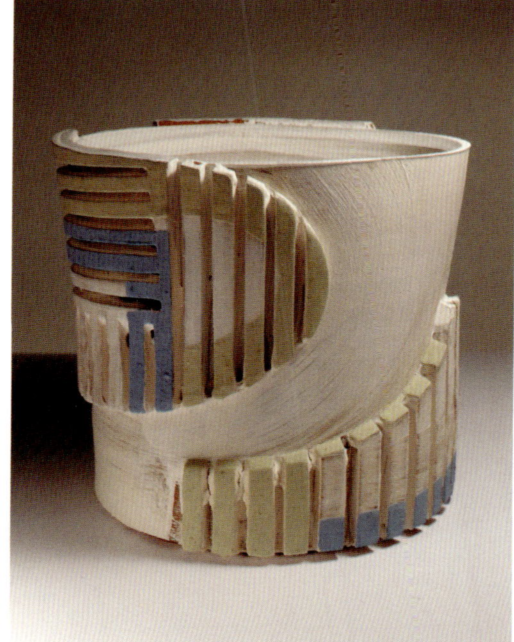

Circuit Vase, 10½ in. (27 cm) in diameter, stoneware.

clear glaze over a white slip. "I see this as a clean zone for the food to play its own visual role," Repsher says. But for the exterior, possibilities abound. He usually combs his surfaces with a toothed edge (usually a piece of a hacksaw blade). Next, Repsher adds colored slips: "The combed surface is covered with the colored slips and then the top layer of slip and clay are wet sanded and removed, inlaying the slip into the surface of the clay." For Repsher, this play between positive and negative space, between rough and smooth, actually enhances the blending of light and shadow across the surface of his pots. This technique, along with his curiosity about combining wood and clay, keeps Repsher on his toes—and that's a good thing. "I don't have a desire to make two things alike, and this is one way for me to avoid that," he says.

For his next body of work, Repsher plans to focus on his desire to return to the East Coast. He's been talking on the phone with his father more, collecting stories, and staying in tune with where he'd like to see himself a few years from now. It's just as exciting to think about where Repsher has come from, as where he's headed next.

Perforated and Slipped Surfaces

by Matt Repsher

I am very interested in layers for building up t he surface of my vessels, beginning with my choice of clay for the foundation. I work in the cone 6

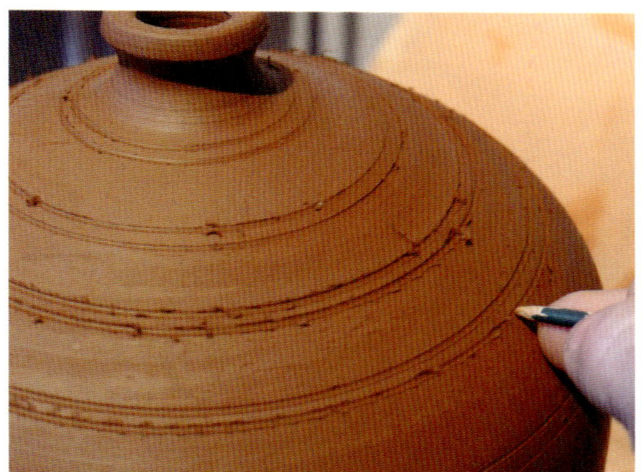

1. Incising concentric guide lines for the carved pattern on the neck of the vessel.

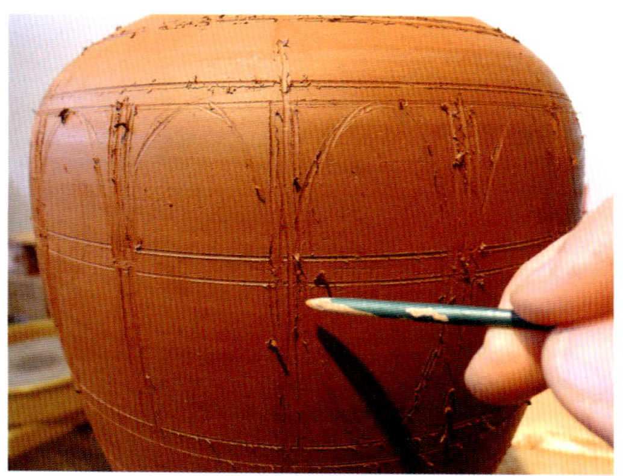

2. Incising vertical and arched lines onto the surface. The space between the curved line and the grid will be cut out to form the pattern.

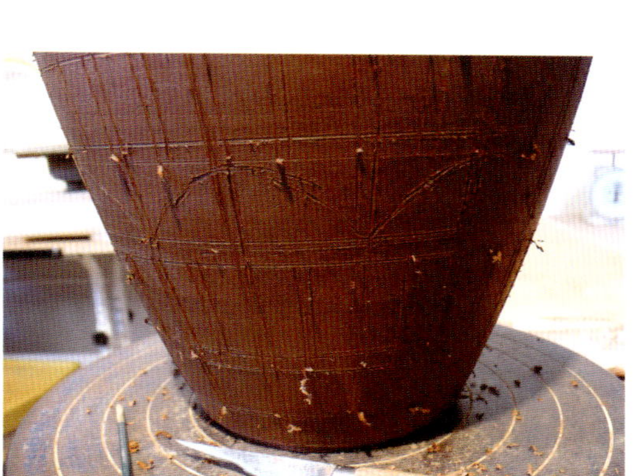

3. The grid and curved pattern continue to the bottom of the form. Next, an altered fettling knife and hacksaw blade will be used to carve and complete the pattern.

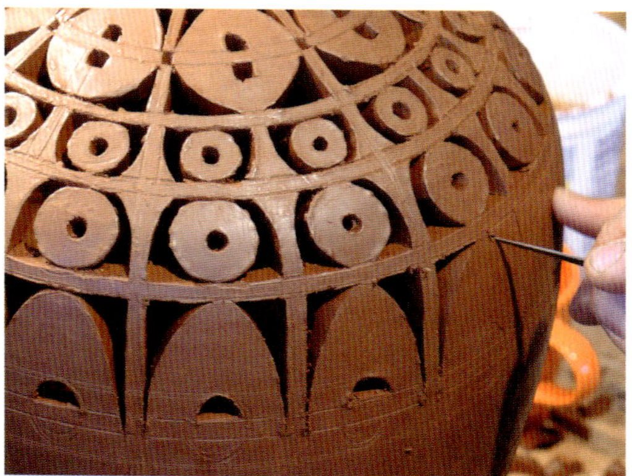

4. Working from the top of the form toward the bottom keeps the base stronger so it can support the form and resist warping.

range with red clay, preferring the contrast it has as I am working. In my eyes, light and shadow are more intense and the form and carvings are clearer. The leather-hard and fired color of the clay I use, Laguna's SB Red, are very similar, so I can envision the final surface early on. The allusion to red-brick construction materials is also something I consider to be an important bit of information the red clay offers.

I lay out the carvings by drawing on the surface, working by eye rather than measuring, preferring to keep the pattern inexact so that the forms have a veil of perfection created by the overall visual effect with little differences in the repetitions revealed on closer inspection. Carving is done with a fettling knife that has been ground down so it's very thin and short. Its thinness keeps the clay from separating too much as it is cut, and therefore prevents any clay from being pushed out of line in the finer cuts.

After carving, the surface is combed with a fine-tooth hacksaw blade. This texture is then accentuated by painting colored slip patterns over the surface. I brush on the slip with a more spontaneous action in comparison to the carved patterns. I use wide swaths of color, creating shapes that play off of the form of the vessel and the carvings. The painting is meant to flow around the vessel in a

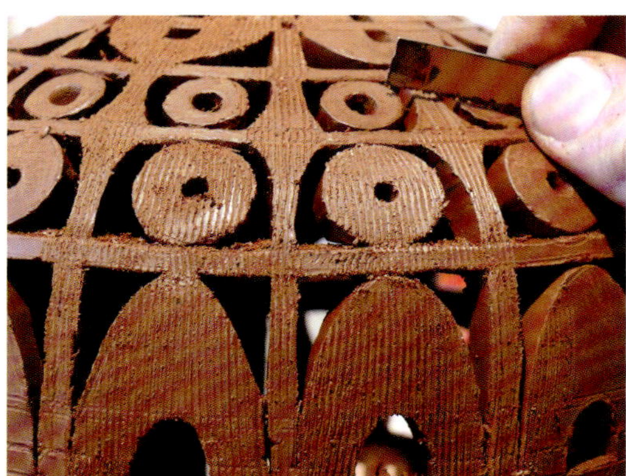

5. Running a cut-off hacksaw blade across the surface makes a roughly lined texture that creates recesses for slip application.

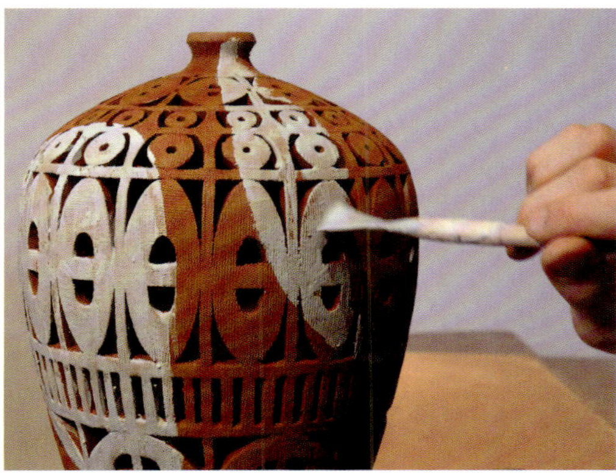

6. Additional shapes are created on the surface in response to the first, with the negative space between them being an important design element.

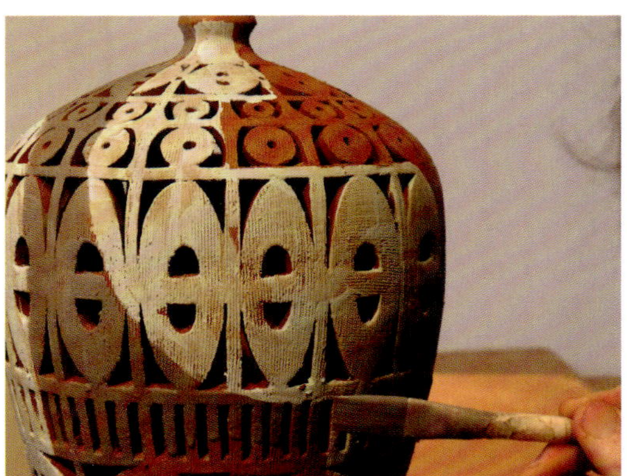

7. A contrasting slip color is applied to the negative spaces, with a thicker application being used in areas where a more intense color is desired.

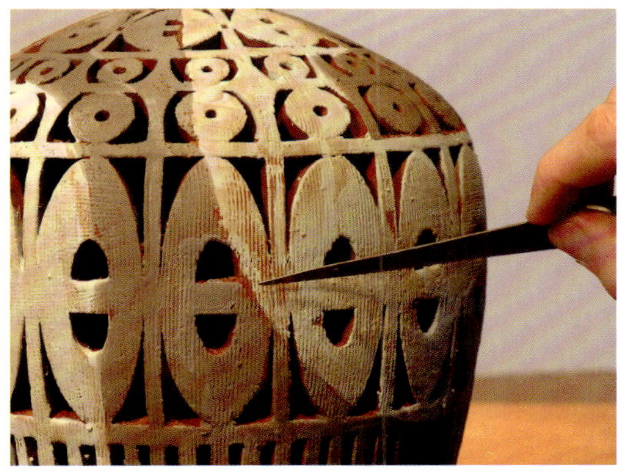

8. After the slip dries, the top layer is scraped away using a fettling knife to reveal the clay color on the raised areas.

way that can visually alter its shape as it's seen from different viewpoints, both accentuating and camouflaging the form. Once the colored slip is dry, I remove the top layer with a knife to bring back the clay color on the raised areas, but leaving it in the recessed texture, creating a striated pattern. The revealed inlay softens the surface and edges of the color shapes. I prefer the matte surface of the slip and clay, so my tendency is to keep the glazing to a minimum, confining it to the interior.

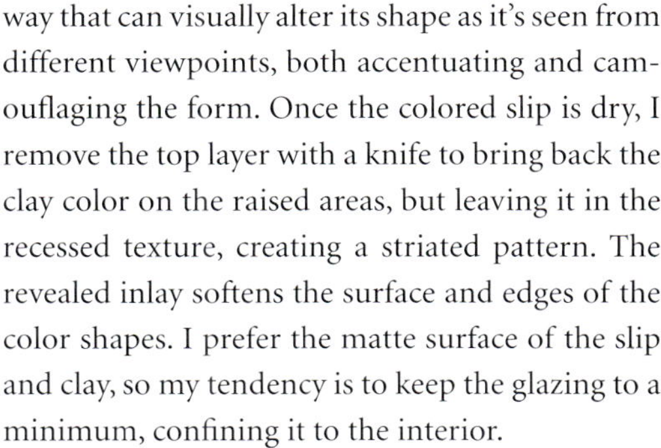

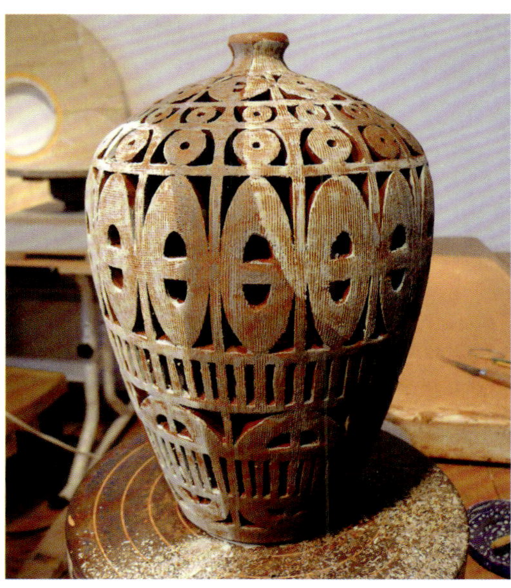

The finished, leather-hard vase after the top layer of slip has been scraped away. This provides additional contrast and depth, as well as giving the surface an aged, weathered appearance.

Carving & Etching

CARVED BLOCK PRINTING STAMPS

by Ann Ruel

My favorite pottery surface designs involve textures created by carving directly into a piece after it's been formed. I've been experimenting with carving my designs onto block printing material, a flexible eraser-like material that won't crumble, crack or break. In this way, I can test and polish my design choice before I apply it to the clay, and at the same time create a reusable design tool.

Block printing materials are readily available in arts and craft stores or online. There are several sizes and depths of blocks available from which to choose depending on your design (figure 1). In addition, you also need to purchase a carving tool and a few interchangeable gouges. These are usually found alongside the printing blocks.

Purchase three gouges of varying shapes since one will not be sufficient. Get one gouge with a tight V shape to remove a narrow section of debris, a wide U-shaped gouge for removing a wide sweeping amount of debris, and a third gouge with a shape that's in between the other two. As you begin to understand how each of these work, you'll develop preferences for gouges that fit your specific needs.

Decisions, Decisions

The first step to carving the stamp is to decide on your specific design. For the first few stamps, choose bold, blocky designs, as these require only simple carving strokes. As you begin to understand how different variations of gouges affect the overall design, you can become more creative.

There are several ways to work the design onto the surface of the block. You can draw the design directly onto the face of the material using a pencil or use designs from an ink-jet printer, laser printer or newspaper. Images from a printer may need to be traced in pencil before being transferred. Pencil marks can be erased if needed but can also smudge.

Line up your design face down on top of the block surface. Rub the back of the paper with a blunt edged object until the carbon transfers completely to the surface. Instructions on the block state that you can run a warm iron over the top of the design to transfer the image.

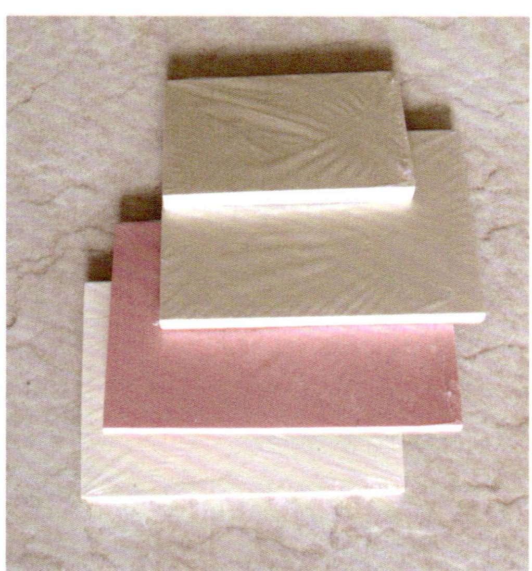

Block printing materials come in a variety of different thicknesses allowing you deep to shallow reliefs.

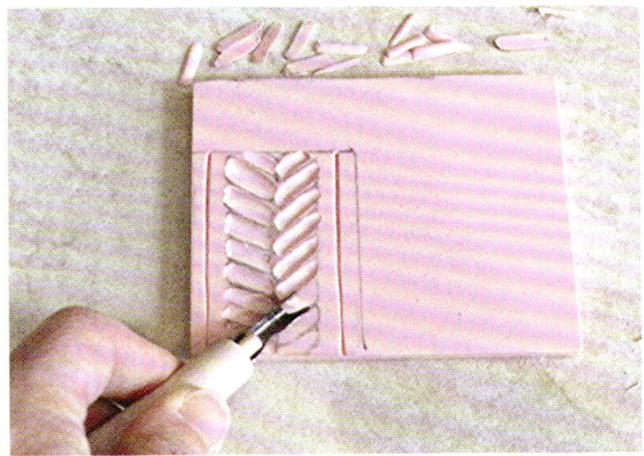

1. Use the U-shaped gouge to carve the center braid design. The tight V-shaped nib creates the border lines.

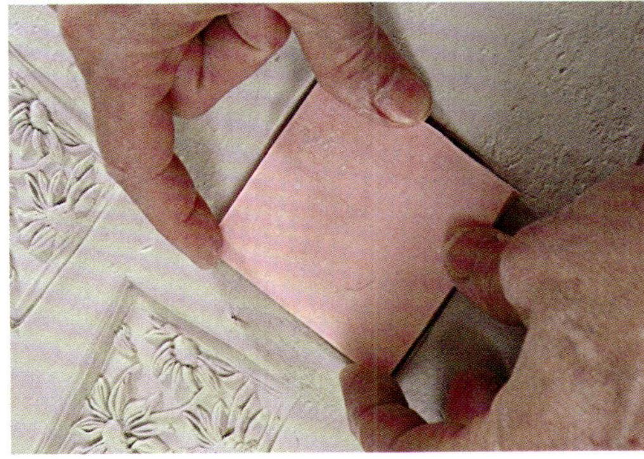

2. Stamp more images than you actually need so you will be able to choose the images with the best quality.

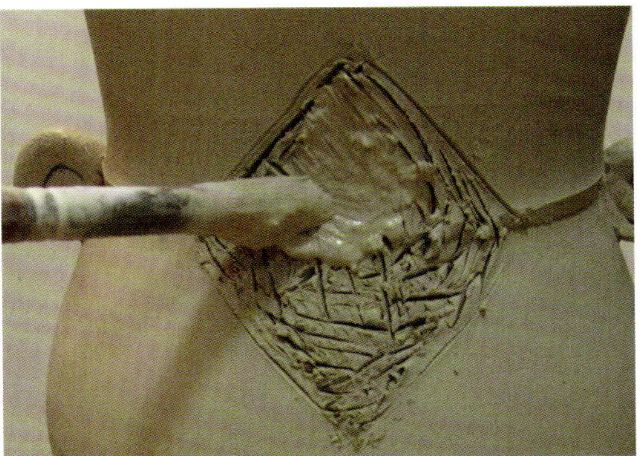

3. Score the area within the traced outline on your pot then use a wide paint brush to apply slip.

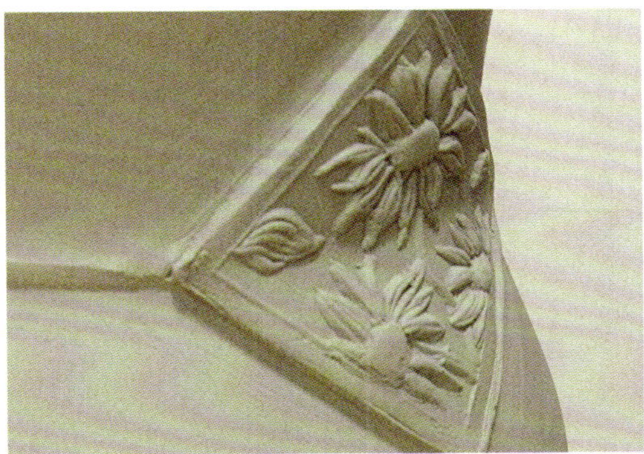

4. Adhere the stamped slab to the pot. Make sure that all areas are tightly bonded.

Carving the Block

Low-relief and high-relief carvings can be created using block printing material. Low-relief carving includes simply gouging ditches along outlines or shallow gouging away from the positive design areas (figure 1). These techniques result in one, level positive shape protruding slightly from the clay surface. High-relief carving involves a more complicated approach where areas of the stamped design sharply protrude from the base of the clay at many different levels. To achieve this look, make some cuts in to the block deeper than others, based on your design. Remember that the farther you cut into the surface of the block, the more the resulting clay will jut out once stamped.

After carving the design of the stamp, use a sharp edged blade to cut a straight line or beveled edge along the stamp edges to create a border. Before using the stamp on a prepared piece, be sure to test it out on scrap clay first (figure 2). It's easy to become confused and accidentally gouge away the positive space of your design when you should have removed the negative areas or vice-a-versa. Unfortunately if this is the case, the stamped image will result in the reverse of what you intended and you may need to start over.

Stamping Strategies

You'll find that many different looks can be achieved from one stamp. By varying the contact pressure to the stamp when applying it on the clay surface, you can control design texture. The least amount of pressure results in less definition from your carving and you get a smoother surface. When you apply more pressure, the opposite is

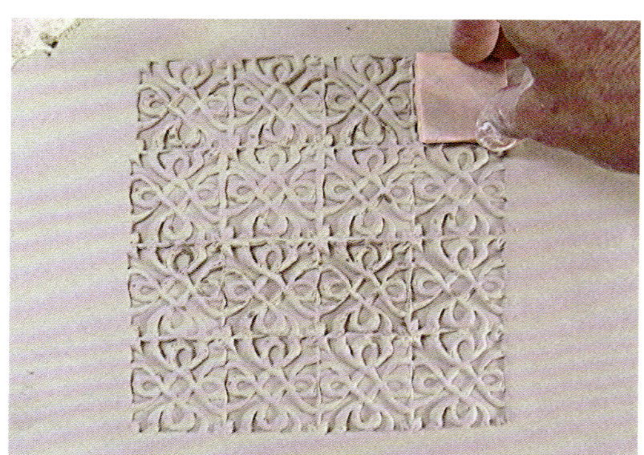

5. This design intentionally runs off the edges of the stamp so it can be used to create a repeating pattern.

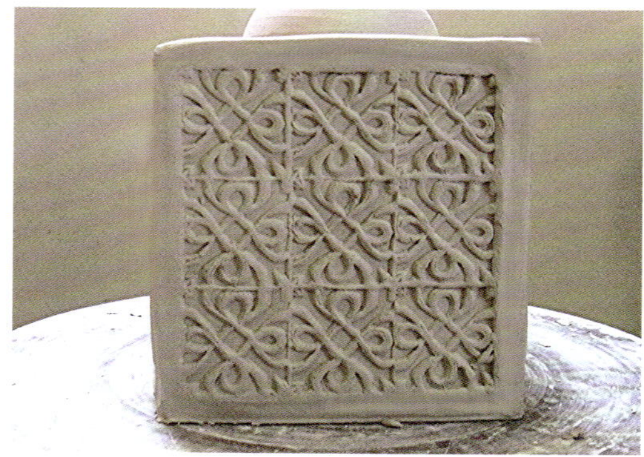

6. Stamped slabs were used to create the body of this Victorian style box.

true and more texture results. If you want to ensure consistent pressure to the entire stamp at one time, attach the stamp to an acrylic or wooden block for easier use. You can also achieve a varied look after the clay has been stamped by altering the border lines around the stamp.

Indirect Application

There are two techniques for applying the block printing stamp to pottery—indirect application and direct application. When indirectly applying the stamp, keep in mind that not all pottery is conducive to this technique. Objects that tend to flare out as they get taller, such as bowls, do not do as well. Stamps applied to the exterior of the bowls, generally fire without any problems, but sometimes the stamped area tries to flatten out when fired, thus causing the bowl to warp. Cylindrical shapes have less trouble.

To indirectly apply the stamp, roll out a slab of clay between ½-inch and ¾-inch thickness and smooth with a rib. The slab must not be too wet or it may stick to the stamp and you won't get a good impression. Stamp more images than you need and decide which ones to use. Let the clay firm up just enough so it won't distort when removing it from the worktable. Take a wide putty knife and cut around the edges of the stamped pattern and remove the extra clay. Slowly and carefully, run the putty knife under the clay to release it from the work surface, again being careful not to distort the edges of your pattern.

Using a small looped carving tool, carefully create grooves in the back of the pattered slab, similar to the back of commercial tiles. This makes it lighter and also serves to score the back of the clay.

Place the stamped slab over the area on your pottery where you want to apply it. With a needle tool, trace a light line around the outside border. Remove the slab and generously slip the back of the stamped image. Then, working within the tracing that you made on your pottery, score and slip that area as well (figure 3). Press the image to the clay, beginning gently at the center of the stamp and working out towards the edges. Be sure that your edges are tightly adhered to the surface of the piece or it may peel away during firing (figure 4). Remove any excess slip from the edges with a small paint brush and carefully smooth the area.

Direct Application

Directly applying the stamp to a piece is much more complicated as you risk distorting your piece or weakening a wall. Try applying the stamps to clay slabs that have been placed in a mold or directly apply the stamp to a slab and use this to create pattern pieces to be assembled. Block printing stamps can be cut so that when used in multiples they can form creative patterns (figure 5). I created four of these textured slabs (figure 6), cut them into squared pattern pieces and assembled them into a Victorian box with a lid.

Carving & Etching

SURFACE ETCHING: WATER AND WAX

by Ryan McKerley

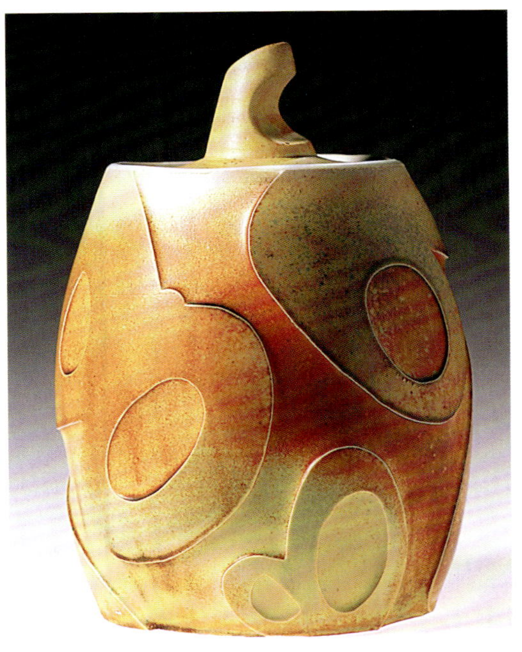

Jar, 12 inches in height, thrown and altered porcelain, with resisted surface, soda fired.

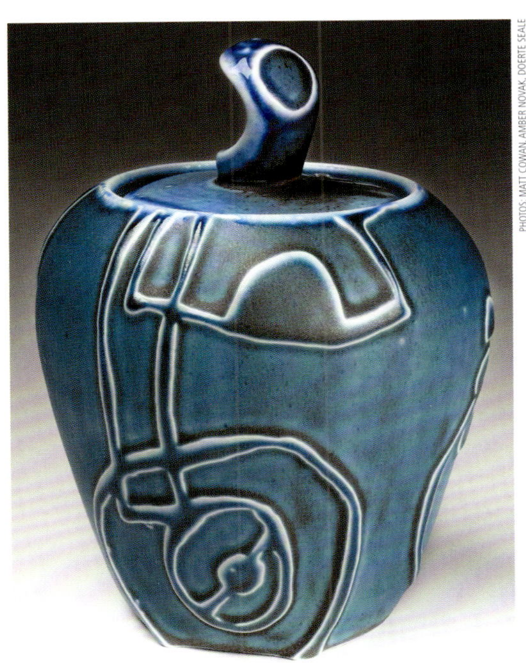

PHOTOS: MATT COWAN, AMBER NOVAK, DOERTE SEALE

Jar, 9 inches in height, porcelain, with resisted relief, soda fired.

These pots are not carved in the traditional sense. The patterns are created by painting melted Gulf Wax (parafin) onto the surface of a bone dry vessel. I then scrub the unwaxed areas with a very wet sponge. The exposed clay erodes away as it is scrubbed, leaving a smooth depression. As I am scrubbing, I use a caliper to periodically check to make sure the wall isn't getting too thin. This body of work is thrown with Coleman porcelain. This clay body doesn't mind big differences in wall thickness.

I add a small amount of motor oil to the wax to help it flow off the brush. Too much oil will make the wax soft causing it to wash away with the clay. If the wax goes somewhere I don't want it to, I carve it away with a metal trimming tool.

Soda firing highlights the edges of the patterns and alters the glazes from side to side. The recessed areas of the surface receive less soda glaze, which creates further contrast. Copper glazes surprise me every firing, adding a little chance to this tedious process.

Carving & Etching

SURFACE ETCHING: RESIST AND MIST

by Roger Graham

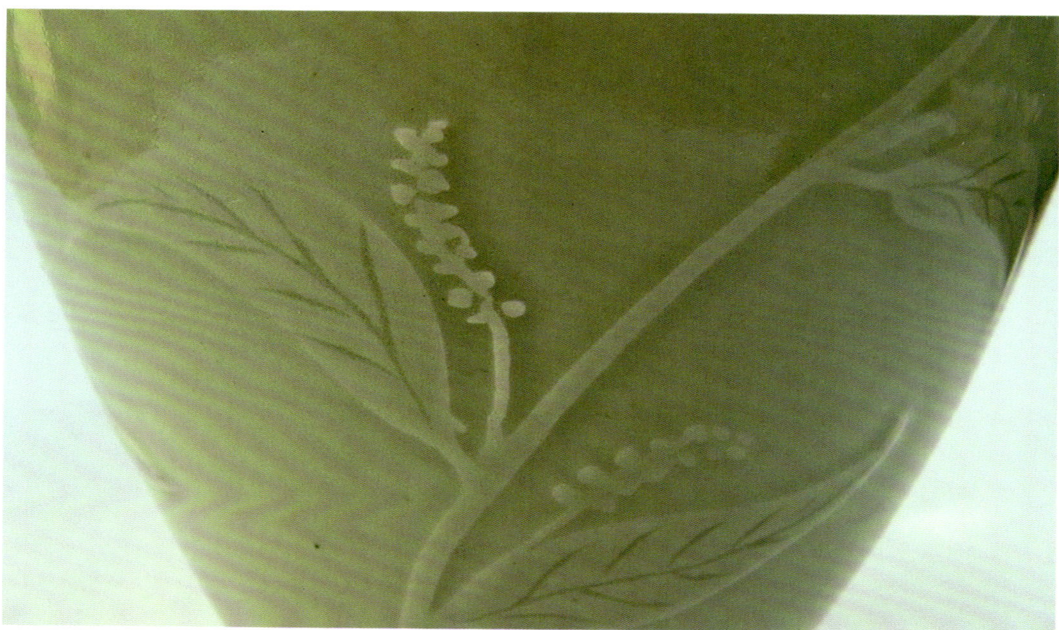

While traveling, I bought a delightful porcelain pot with a delicate raised pattern on the outside, carved with infinite patience, or so I thought. "Not at all," the potter informed me, "It's water etching." Then he gave me a brief outline of how it's done.

Back home in the studio, I followed up on his technique. It opened up a whole new realm of possibilities, and some pleasant surprises. The process is so quick and the unprotected clay washes away so fast, that it's possible to etch to a depth of a millimeter or more in less than a minute and follow a wax outline precisely.

What kind of water spray you may ask? I use the ordinary gravity-feed spray gun used for applying glazes, but wound up the air pressure to about 100 psi instead of the usual 40. It was adjusted for a fine wide-spread spray and held about 2 inches from the pot. All of this was done on a banding wheel in a spray booth, but you could go outside and use a garden hose adjusted to a fine mist. Truly, it's as easy as that.

While you may expect the water spray to undercut the wax—just as sandblasting undercuts a stencil—the pattern remains crisply defined; even thin, fine lines survive undamaged. You might also expect the constant water spray to reduce the unfired clay to a soggy mess, but this hasn't been a problem, even with thinly thrown delicate pots. If you work swiftly, the whole procedure takes only a minute or two and the lower edge of the inverted pot, which would soften first, needs only a gentle blotting with a soft sponge.

Produce work for this process using smooth, fine-grained clay. Allow it to dry to the bone-dry stage. Paint a design on the pot using wax resist

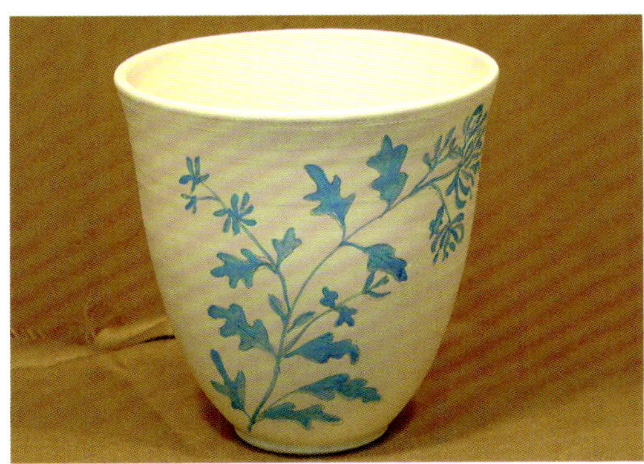
1. Adding food dye to wax resist makes it easier to see where you've carved.

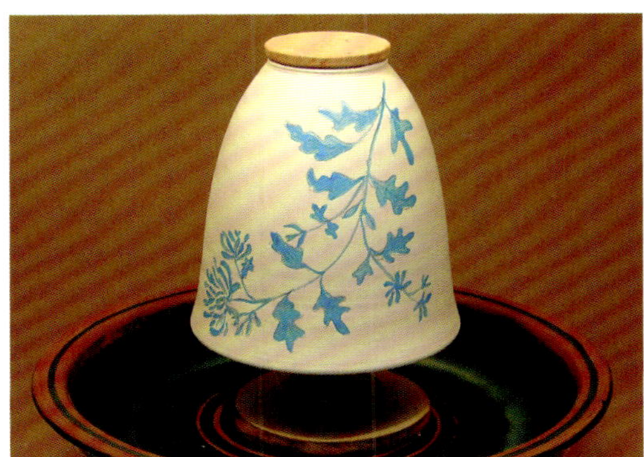
2. Invert the pot over a basin which will catch the water.

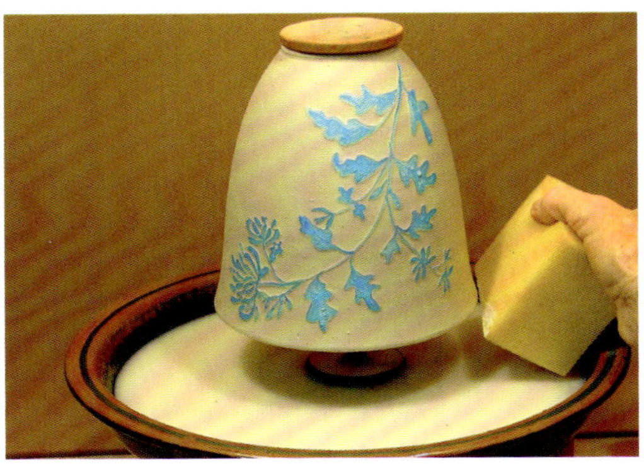
3. Apply a fine mist then gently blot away water droplets from the rim.

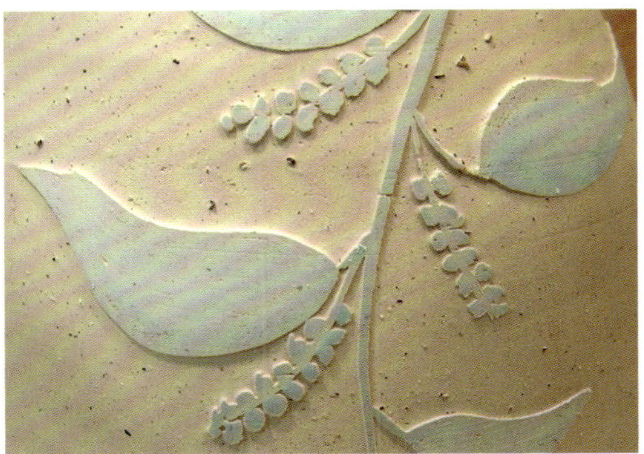
4. Once the surface has dried, carefully refine the details as needed.

and a fine brush. Adding food dye to the wax makes it easier to see where you've been (figure 1).

Invert the pot and suspend it on a pedestal or chuck. The rim of the pot needs to overhang the pedestal so water can drip into a catch basin (figure 2).

This pot was given a smooth, even coat of blue slip (1.5% cobalt oxide), just enough to cover the area where the design will go. The simple plant motif was painted on, using wax emulsion heavily loaded with dye so the narrow brushstrokes were easy to see.

Apply a fine spray of water. The water will wash away clay that is not protected by the wax. Gently blot away water droplets from the rim with a soft sponge (figure 3) to prevent the rim from disintegrating. Warm air from a hair dryer speeds up the return to crisp dryness.

Note: When using colored slips, don't forget that the rinse water is now contaminated with the slip's colorants, so dispose of it accordingly.

When the pot is dry again, or nearly dry, you can pick it up and refine the details if necessary. These details are easily added by hand with a pointed tool after the water-etched pattern has dried. If you're not satisfied with an outline of part of your design, just scrape it away. It's easy to make minor repairs, just don't get carried away (figure 4).

The edges of the pattern remain sharp and jagged lines can be touched up with a pointed tool if deemed necessary. Extra details like leaf veins can be drawn now, while the pot is still a bit damp, so the scriber makes a smooth clean line without breaking out little chips and crumbs.

If bits of grog or grit create an uneven surface, use porcelain or a very smooth, clean stoneware.

Carving & Etching

SURFACE ETCHING: SHELLAC AND WATER

by Jim Gottuso

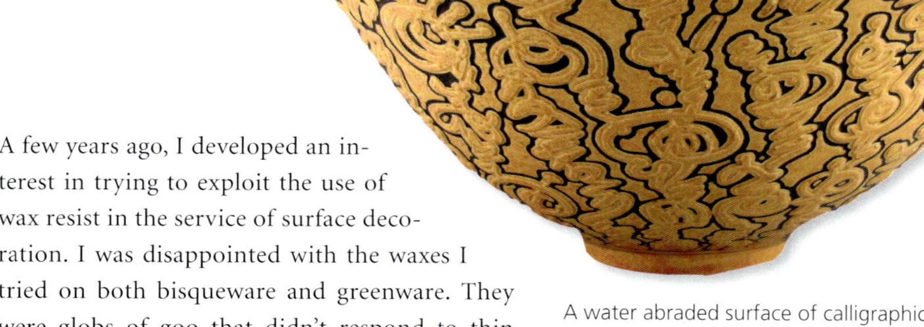

A water abraded surface of calligraphic lines decorates the surface of Jim Gottuso's clean-lined forms.

A few years ago, I developed an interest in trying to exploit the use of wax resist in the service of surface decoration. I was disappointed with the waxes I tried on both bisqueware and greenware. They were globs of goo that didn't respond to thin brushes or delicate application.

At the same time I happened upon the work of Arne Ase whose work absolutely floored me, especially after unsuccessfully trying wax, paraffin, and acrylic medium on greenware in an attempt to etch the unprotected areas and create depth to the surface. His decorations were incredibly delicate and, of course, his use of soluble salts and translucent porcelain came together in pieces of sublime beauty. What wasn't clear was what he used for a resist. It turns out that Arne had written *Water Colour On Porcelain,* which has been described as the definitive book on soluble salt use and the secret ingredient had to be in that book. Unfortunately it is out of print, but the library managed to find a copy, and the book revealed the ingredient as shellac.

Fellow blogger, Michael Kline, says that at Penland the process of using a resist and dissolving the exposed unfired clay was referred to as "hydro-abrasion". After a couple of years trial-and-error and evolving a personal visual vocabulary, it turns out that this process dovetails very nicely with what appeals to my sense of design, form, and aesthetics. I've always loved what happens when a brush, pen or pencil makes contact with another surface, and using shellac as a resist on dried, unfired clay allows the surface to be etched without losing the immediacy and spontaneity of such brushwork.

Materials

For this technique, you will need shellac, denatured alcohol, brush, sponge, water, and an OSHA approved respirator.

Shellac thickens when exposed to air and loses its ability to soak into the clay body thoroughly. It can be thinned with alcohol, but over time it loses its viscosity and eventually needs to be discarded. Avoid the waste by decanting only what you need into a small lidded jar.

Thinking in Reverse

Begin with a bone dry, trimmed piece. Since my pieces are typically about ¼-inch thick, tapering to $^{3}/_{16}$-inch at the rim, I'm careful not to put a strain on it. This process requires a bit of thinking in reverse. Protect the parts of the piece that are not to be altered. The first layer of shellac resist applied to the piece, because it covers the clay before any abrasion takes place, ends up being the

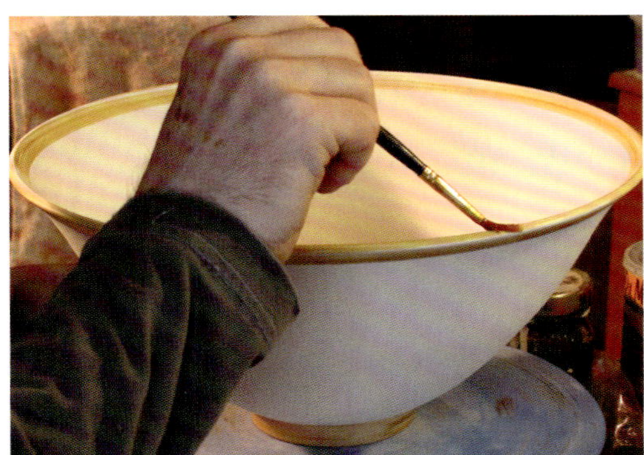

1. Apply resist to both the foot and rim to preserve their integrity throughout the process.

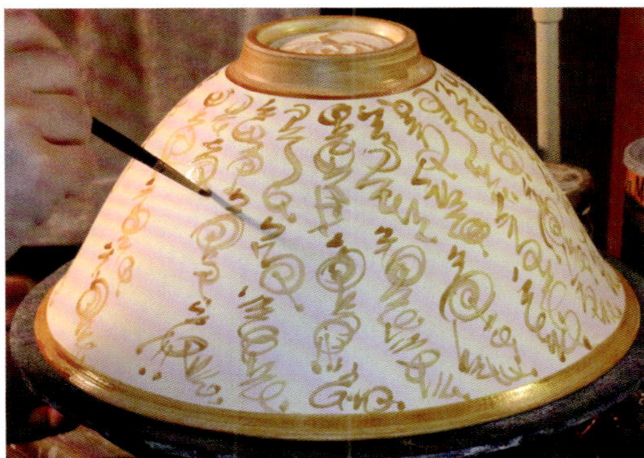

2. Apply the first (and ultimately foreground) layer of resist for your chosen design.

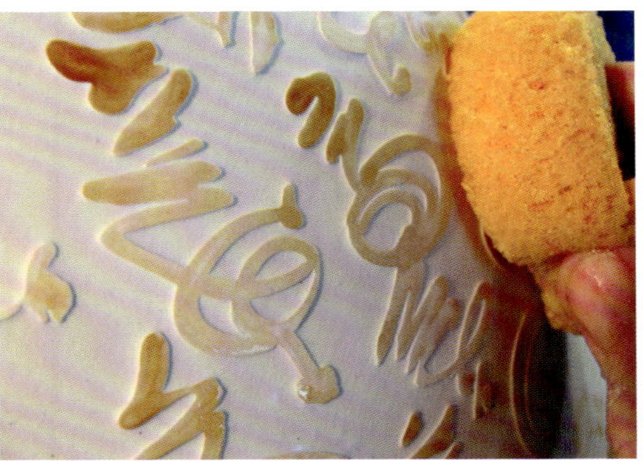

3. Allow the shellac to completely dry and remove clay from the exposed areas using a damp sponge.

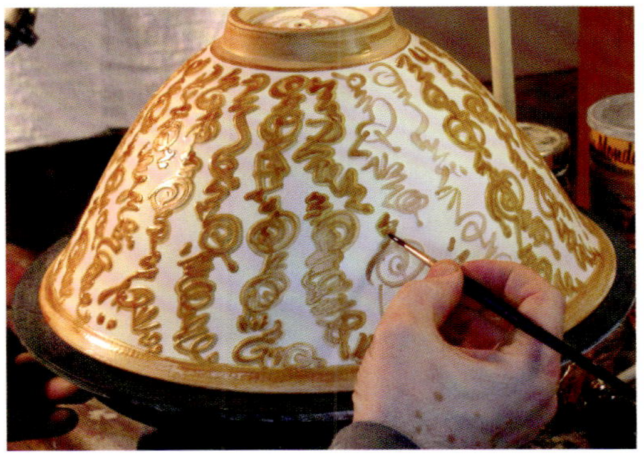

4. Apply shellac over the top of the first layer, making this second layer extend about 1/8 inch past the edge.

topmost layer, or highest relief area at the end of the process. Since I don't want the rim or foot to be etched, I apply resist to both to preserve their integrity (figure 1).

Defining the Foreground

The next step is to apply the first layer of resist that creates the decoration and results in the top or foreground layer of the final design (figure 2). Imagine writing your name with the shellac then etching the un-shellacked areas. If, after that another layer of shellac was applied in a grid pattern over the name and etched again, the result would appear as your name hovering over the grid, even though the applications were done in reverse. For the finished piece here, the first layer is a series of vertical calligraphic marks that go from the foot to the rim.

Abrading the Clay

Allow the shellac to dry completely (24 hours), then start abrading the exposed areas with a damp sponge (figure 3). If you intend to preserve what's been laid down in shellac without degradation, jettison the idea of abrasion, and think of your goal in the process as more like dissolving the clay, even though that's not technically what's happening.

Abrasion occurs when the water between the sponge and the surface collects dislodged clay particles in it and creates a localized slurry, which gets thicker and thicker as you go. Do not leave this thick slurry between the sponge and the pot. When the sponge has lots of clay on the surface and little water left in it, you're likely to eradicate your image along with the unprotected areas as the particles on the sponge move across and scratch into the surface.

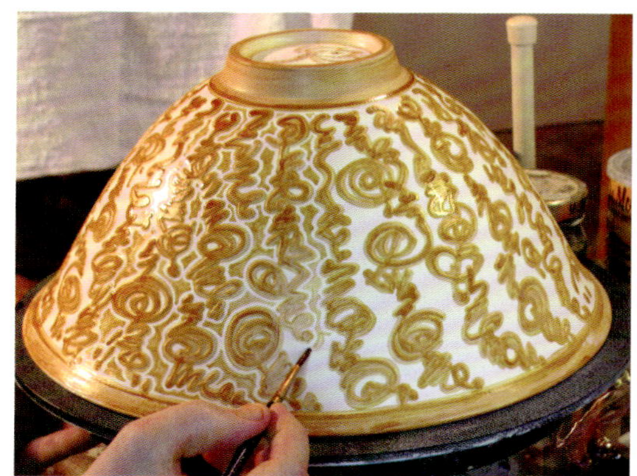
5. Brush shellac in the remaining unprotected areas, leaving a small gap between the two covered areas.

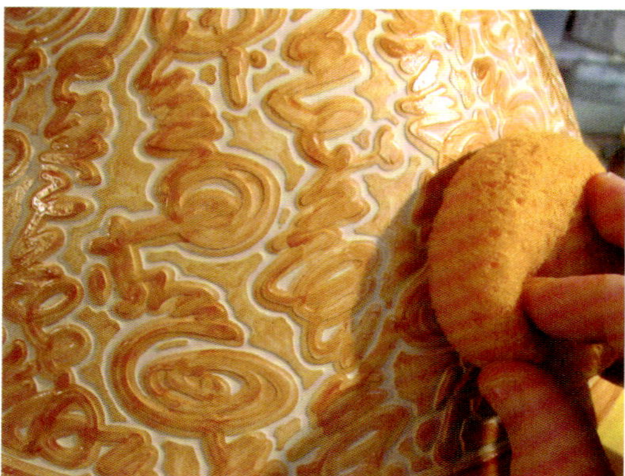
6. Allow the piece to dry again and repeat the etching process. Continue these steps until you are satisfied.

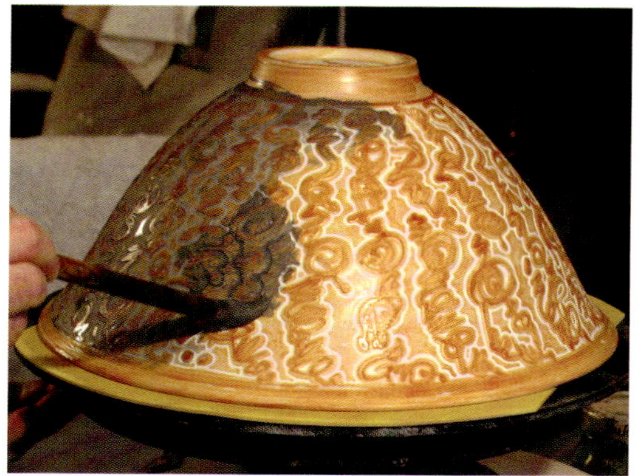
7. Brush a black slip that is suitable for use on greenware over the entire surface of the outside of the bowl.

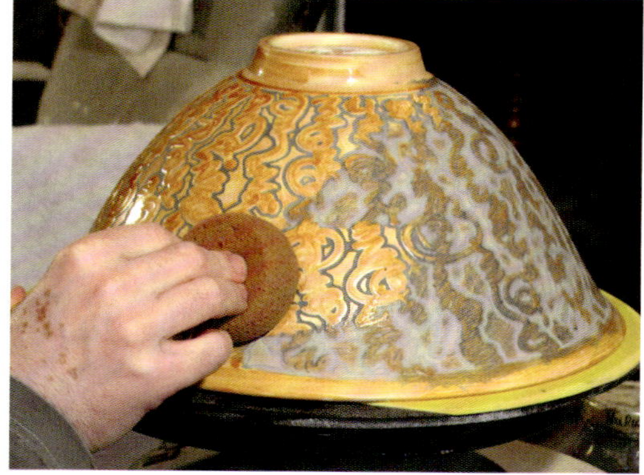
8. Use a sponge to wipe off any black slip that is not in the etched lines.

To avoid this, load a sponge with water and wipe the surface of the pot until the slurry starts to form, then rinse the sponge thoroughly in your bucket of water and repeat. In this early stage, with large unprotected areas of clay, this means you're having to rinse out the sponge frequently, sometimes after only two swipes across the clay.

Defining the Middle Ground

After allowing the piece to completely dry again apply a second layer of shellac. I'm trying to create the appearance on the final bowl of a thin brush stroke that's hovering or sitting on top of another, slightly wider, brush stroke. I apply shellac over the top of the original shellac lines and make this second layer extend about ⅛ inch past the edge of that first layer (figure 4).

Adding Linear Elements

On this particular bowl, my goal is to have a linear reinforcement of the negative space that's created by the slightly widening brushwork. To achieve this, apply shellac in all the remaining unprotected areas, leaving only a small (1/8–3/16 inch) gap of bare clay between the two covered areas (figure 5).

Allow the piece to dry and repeat the etching process (figure 6). When you notice a slurry developing, rinse the sponge to avoid abrading the edges of the resisted areas, otherwise your lines may have jagged rather than crisp edges. Since the area being dissolved now is linear as opposed to large planes, moving in a circular motion with the sponge aids in getting a uniform depth to the etching. It can be particularly difficult to gauge how

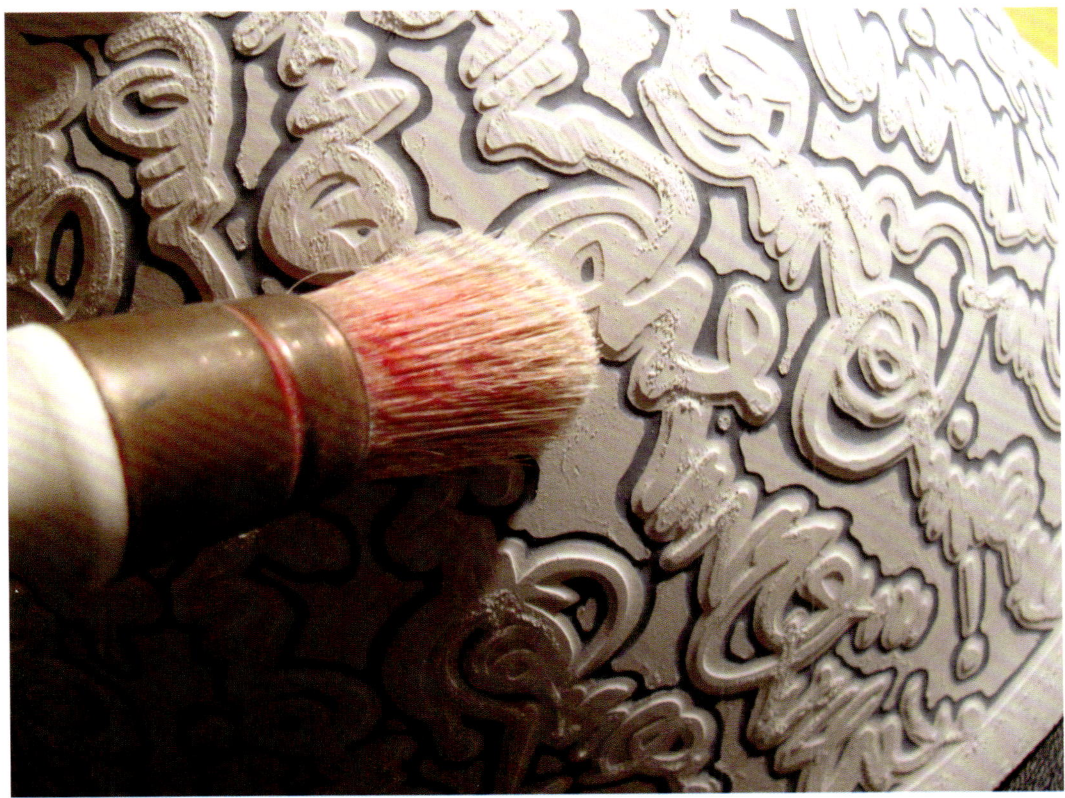

Go over the entire surface with a stiff brush after the bisque firing to clean off the shellac residue.

deep the etching is now because the layers of shellac have some thickness or depth themselves. The shellac will eventually burn out in the bisque and only then is the depth and uniformity of the etching revealed.

Adding Color

Let the piece dry completely then brush on a black slip over the entire exterior of the bowl (figure 7). My black slip is made from throwing slip reclaim and 35 grams of Mason stain #6600 black added per 2 cups of slip.

Wipe off any slip that is not in between the etched lines before it dries (figure 8). If you accidentally take too much slip off and there are unprotected areas that are now back to bare clay, it's easy to reapply more slip immediately to that area and try again allow it to dry.

Glazing Strategies

When the bowl is bisque fired, you'll finally be able to see how the decoration looks, from the subtleties of the etched layers to the contrast between the dark and light tones of the slipped and bare areas. If a flaky residue is present from the shellac, brush the entire surface with a stiff brush to clean it up (figure 9) or it will wreak havoc.

When glazing, I dip my pots but spraying, pouring and painting the glaze also works. Of course, in order to accentuate the subtle differences in relief, transparent or translucent glazes, or glazes that break over texture and edges, works the best. If the colored slip is dark (like this black one), a darker glaze cuts way down on the contrast. Note: Since the relief is low, a thin glaze application works better since a thicker glaze on the finished piece will soften the etched effect.

Carving & Etching

EXPANDED FACETING

by Hank Murrow

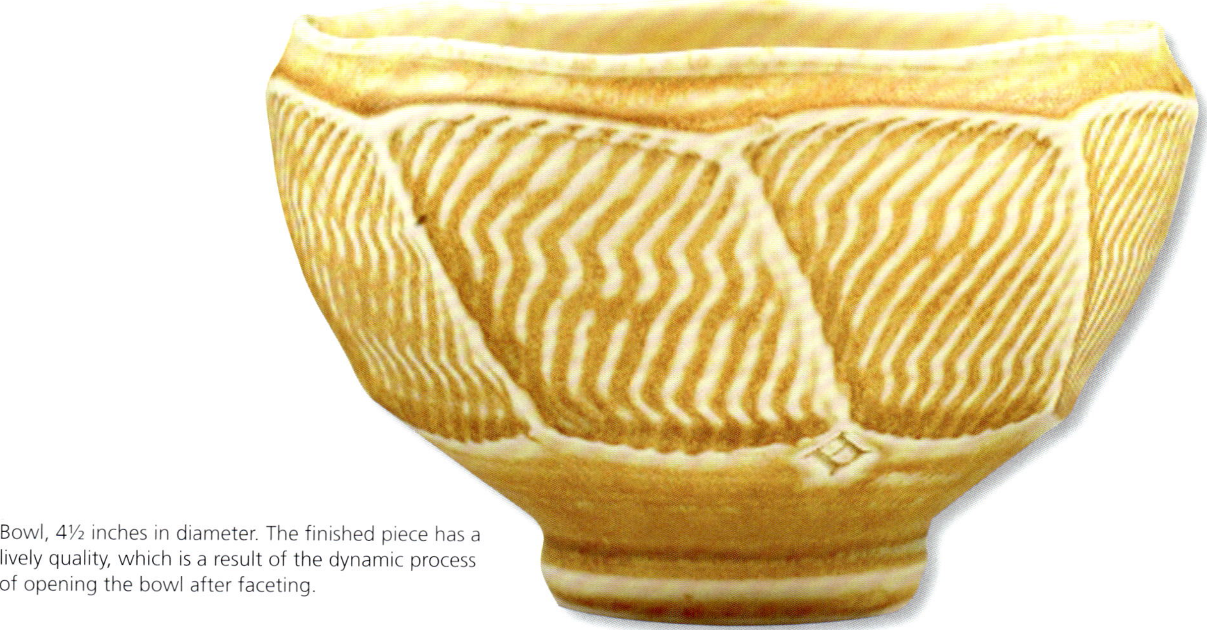

Bowl, 4½ inches in diameter. The finished piece has a lively quality, which is a result of the dynamic process of opening the bowl after faceting.

Faceting a pot—slicing clay from the form using a fettling knife, wire tool, or sometimes a Surform tool—is usually done at the leather-hard stage. Several years ago I saw Joe Bennion facet bowls while they were still wet—just after the initial form was created—then continue to throw to create a stretched facet. Through experimentation, I created my own version of this process, as well as a wire tool with interchangeable wires to achieve different surface effects.

To make a faceted bowl, begin with 2½ pounds of clay and open the form like a bowl, ribbing the bottom so you don't have to trim too much clay later (figure 1). The bowl is kept to a cylindrical shape, keeping the wall thickness to about a ½ inch or a little more. I rib the inside as well to eliminate finger marks, and then give the rim a beveled profile with my chamois or rib.

The first cut with the wire tool trims away about a third of the wall and is cut parallel to the wall profile (figure 2). Turn the wheel 180° and make the second cut, then 90° for the third cut and another 180° for the fourth. Cut the facets between the first four cuts (figure 3) and smooth the edges with a wet finger.

Use a dull wooden rib and dry fingers to open the bowl, stretching the wire cuts and dropping the rim (figure 4). It takes about three passes to develop a full bowl shape. When the bowl has half-dried, turn it over and place on a sheet of foam rubber to protect the rim.

When ready to trim, place the bowl on a damp clay chuck and use a small piece of plastic as a bearing surface for the finger while trimming the outside. Follow by trimming the inside and finishing the foot with the chamois.

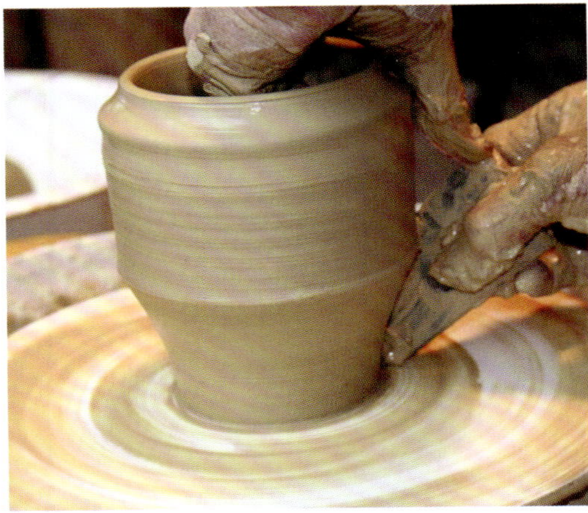

1. Throw a bowl with cylindrical shape, keeping the wall thickness to about a ½ inch or a little more.

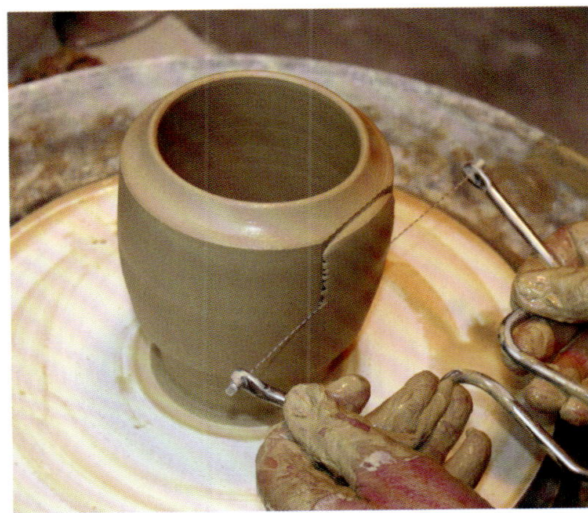

2. The first cut with the wire tool trims away about a third of the wall and is cut parallel to the wall profile.

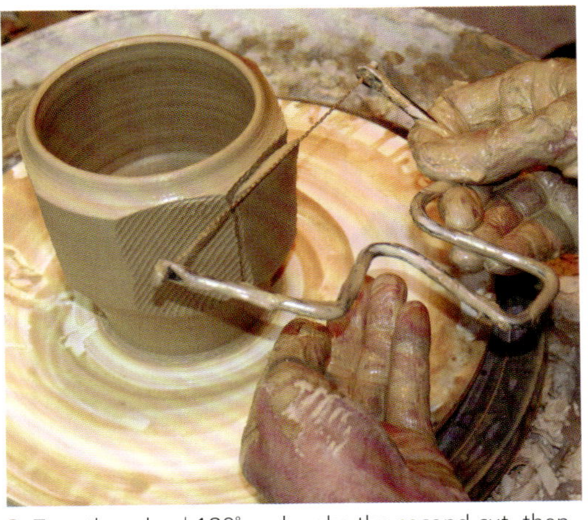

3. Turn the wheel 180° and make the second cut, then 90° for the third and fourth then between these cuts.

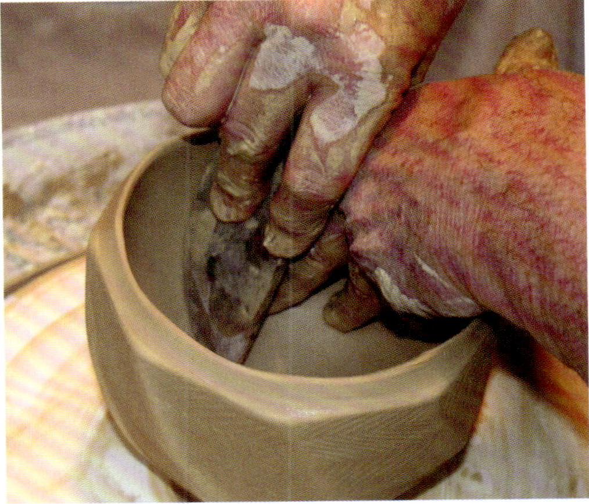

4. Use a dull wooden rib and dry fingers to open the bowl, stretching the wire cuts and dropping the rim.

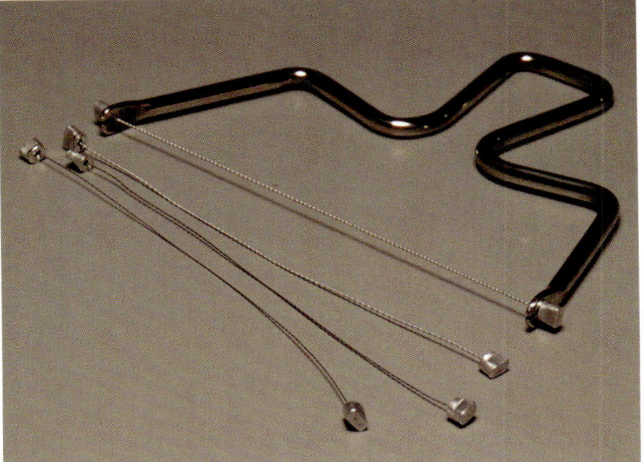

Hank's WireTool with interchangeable wires. Search "Hank's Wire-Tool" on the Internet for more information.

Carving & Etching

HOW TO MAKE A PRECISION CARVING TOOL

by Adam Field

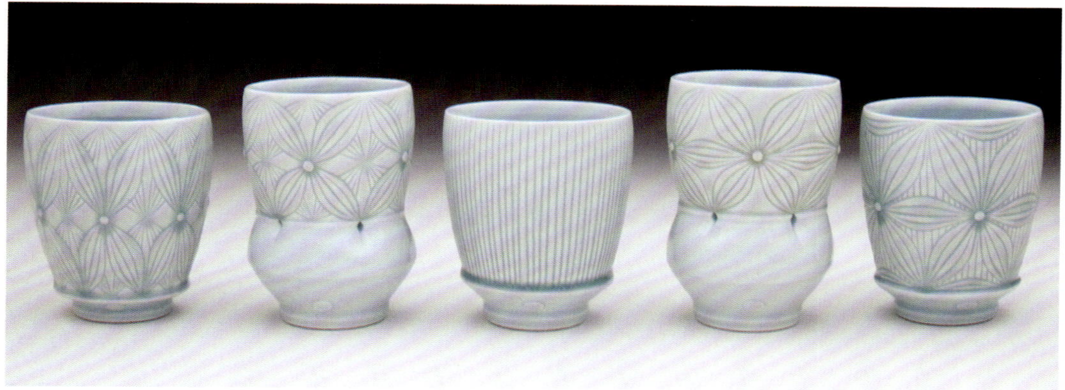

Finished cups carved with a *sanggam kal*, a carving tool used in Korea for inlay in the celadon tradition.

Carving precise lines into a smooth clay body definitely takes a steady hand and a lot of practice, but having the right tool will give you just the edge you need.

Making the Tool

The tool I use for carving is called a *sanggam kal* and is used in Korea for inlay in the celadon tradition. I make these tools using a specifically cut piece of spring steel. While I am still searching for a good local source for this type of steel, the best source I know of currently is in Korea. You may be able to find the same type at a sheet metal supplier and if so, they should be able to cut it to the specs you want.

I use ¼-inch, 18-gauge pieces of spring steel (figures 1–2). You can also use a hacksaw blade, but because the hacksaw blade has been hardened during its manufacturing, you will need to heat it with a torch before you bend it.

To sharpen the steel, fit an angle grinder with a steel grinding flap wheel— a bench grinder works well too. This will cut through the material quickly and give you the specific shape you desire. Caution: Always wear both eye and ear protection when working with power tools.

Turn the grinder on and begin to taper one end of the steel piece into a point. Grind a bevel on all four edges of the newly shaped tip from where the steel piece starts to taper all the way to the tip and into a fine point (figure 3).

Next, refine the ground end to remove any burrs. Do this by rubbing the beveled edges against a wooden table.

To form the carving hook, grip the tool and press the tip against the table to create a sharp, hair-pin, almost U-turn-like bend (figures 4–5). This is easier to do on a wooden surface where the tip will stick a bit while you bend it and not slide or slip.

I find that the tool doesn't yield the greatest quality lines until it has been broken in and used a little bit. I often break the tool in by using it like a trimming tool on a piece of firm leather-hard clay for a few minutes.

Using the Tool

Grip the tool so that the hook has its sharpened side pressed up against the leather-hard clay. If the clay is too wet, it will be difficult to get a pre-

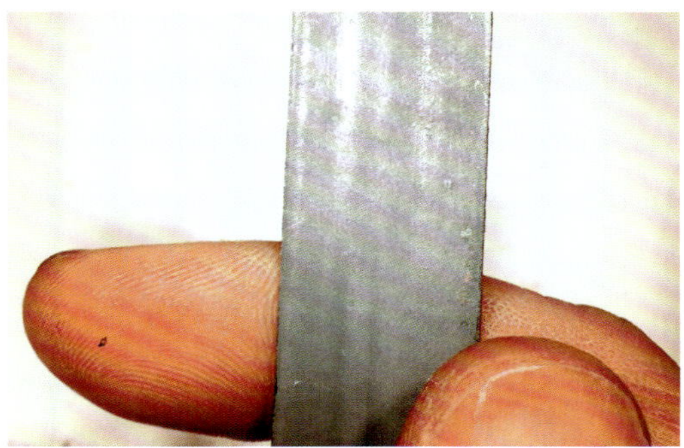

1. Use ¼-inch wide, 18-gauge pieces of spring steel for a carving tool.

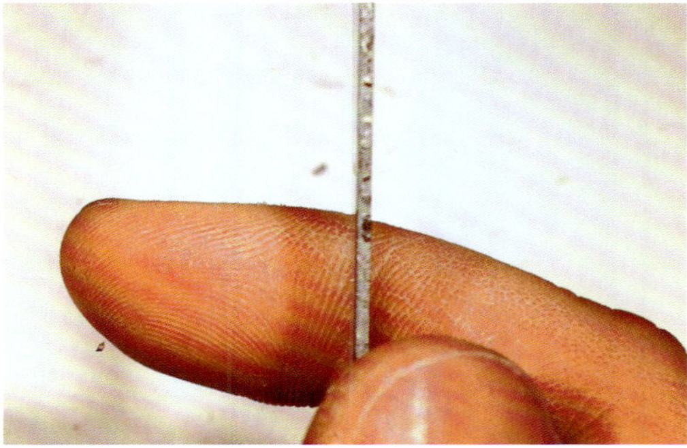

2. You can also use a hacksaw blade, but you will need to heat it with a torch before you bend it.

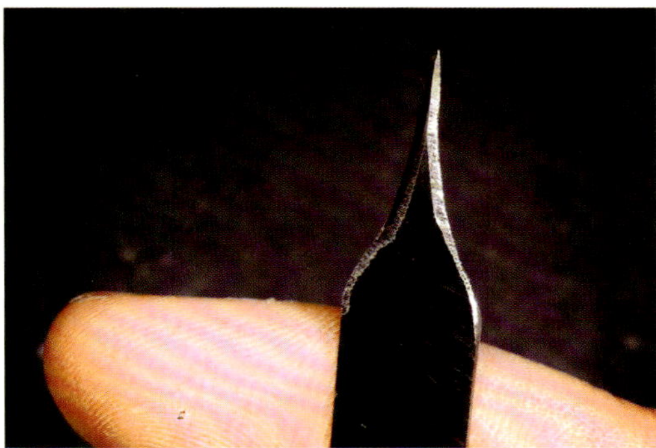

3. Grind a bevel on all four edges from where the steel piece starts to taper to the tip.

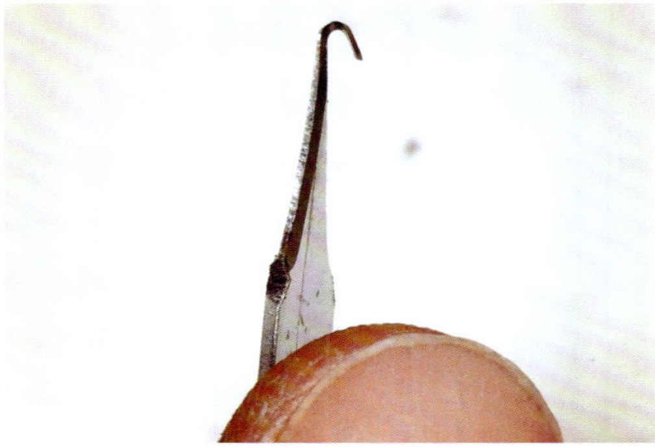

4. Grip the tool and press the tip against the table to create a sharp, hair-pin-like bend

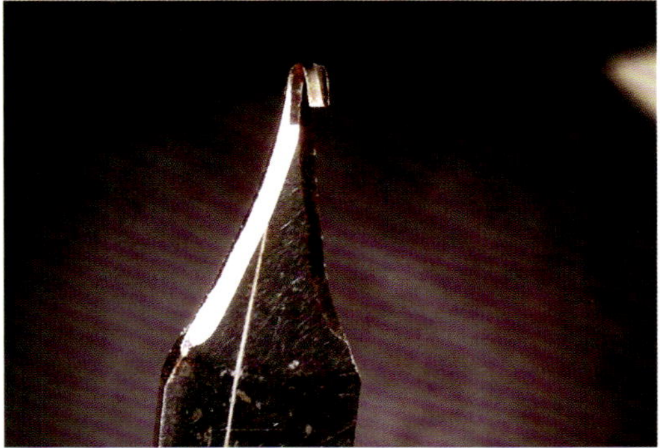

5. Bending the tip is easier to do on a wooden surface since it will not slide or slip as you bend it.

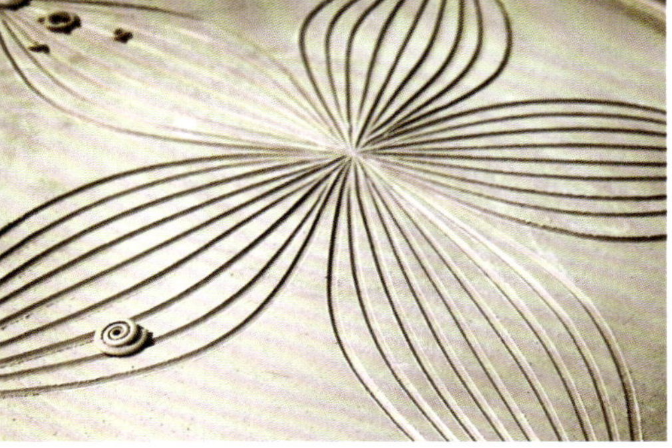

6. Pull the tool down, allowing the hook to remove material as you draw a line.

cise line. Pull the tool down, allowing the hook to remove material as you draw a line (figure 6). Use more or less pressure depending on how accentuated you want the line to be. Clay may build up in the hook and need to be wiped clean periodically. As you clean it, remember that the hook is sharp.

The tools last (and continue to get better) until they break off. The amount of time depends on the character of the clay body being carved (soft vs. hard, smooth vs. grogged, etc.). I'll usually go through a carving tip with every kiln load. The number of times I can re-grind the tip depends on the original length of the steel piece. I generally start with a piece that is about 10 inches long and can get 15–20 new tips out of that piece before it is too short to use.

Carving & Etching

A GUIDE TO SGRAFFITO

by Wayne Bates

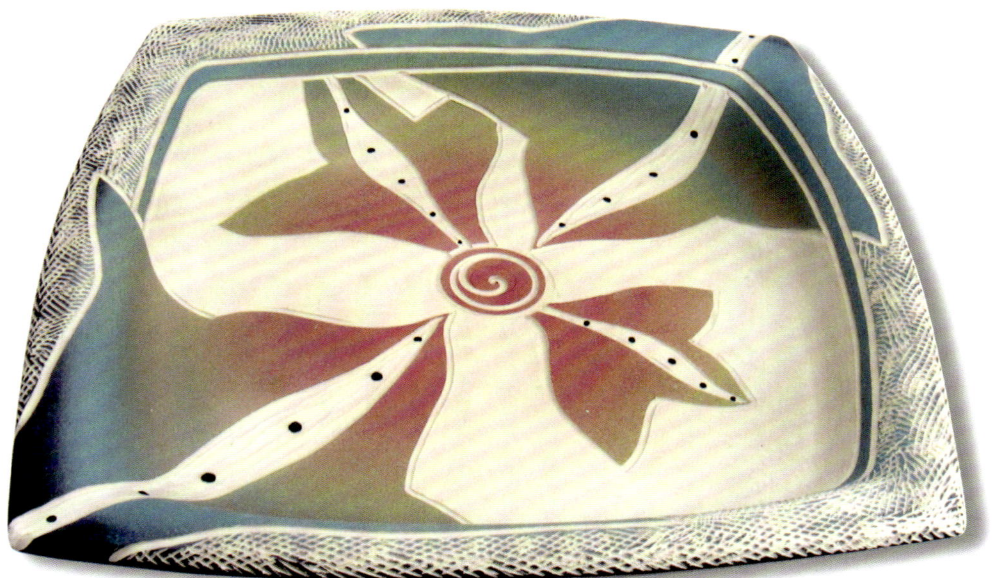

Plate, 10 inches square, sgraffito decoration with clear glaze fired to cone 5.

The word sgraffito is derived from the Italian word graffito, a drawing or inscription made on a wall or other surface (graffito also gave us the word graffiti). Graffito is past participal of sgraffire, which means "to scratch." So the word sgraffito basically means to scratch and create a graphic or an image. In ceramics, sgraffito is a technique of ornamentation in which a surface layer is incised to reveal a ground of contrasting color.

I use sgraffito to get a clean line without masking or rulers, and I do more cutting than scraping. I use a handmade tool that is thin and cuts smoothly. I cut when the piece is stiff leather hard, which makes straight lines possible. If the piece is bone dry, the cut will be jagged and brittle. If the piece is too soft, the tool raises the edge of the cut and makes a higher ragged edge.

If your clay has grog in it, or anything coarser than fine sand, you won't get a smooth cut. I use a rubber-tipped air tool and a soft cosmetic brush to blow or brush off the cuttings. The cut pieces are still moist enough to stick if you touch them to the surface, so they should be removed frequently. You can use a thin coat of wax resist to protect light-colored areas from dark cuttings. The wax resist will burn off in the bisque.

Ball clays are used for engobes because they are the most plastic clays and shrink the most allowing more room in the recipe for non-plastic color, frit, modifiers and fillers. Frit is used to bind the coating to the surface and to increase the interface with the pot and the glaze. Wollastonite is used to add calcium so the chrome-tin colors will work, and flint is used as a filler and stabilizer for colors that flux the mix. I mix the engobes thoroughly and screen them through an 80-mesh sieve. Most of my colors come from commercial glaze stains although not all commercial stains will work, but

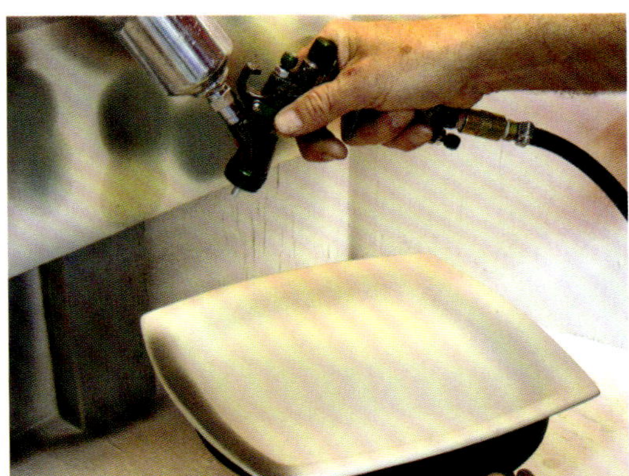

1. I use an automotive-detail-type spray gun to apply engobes and glazes.

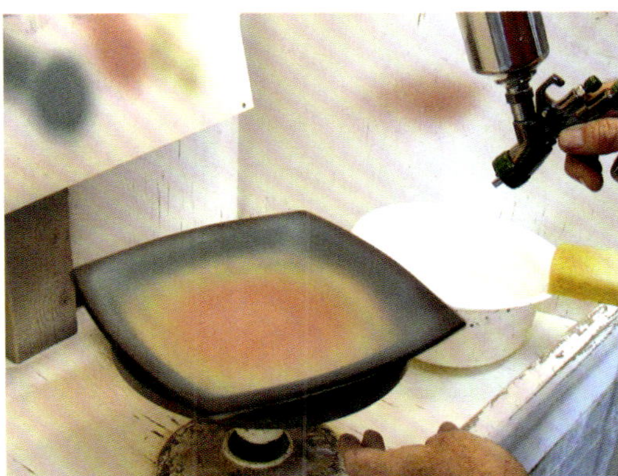

2. This detail gun has a smaller fan size than the full-size gun, has good volume and faster than an airbrush.

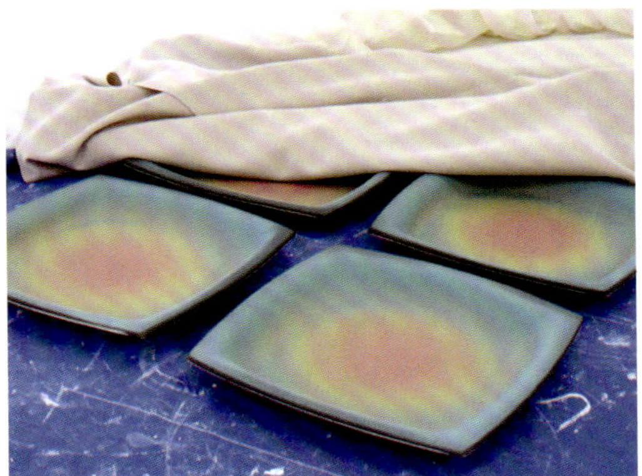

3. Platters ready for sgraffito. I use a large HLVP spray gun for the cover glazes because of its high volume.

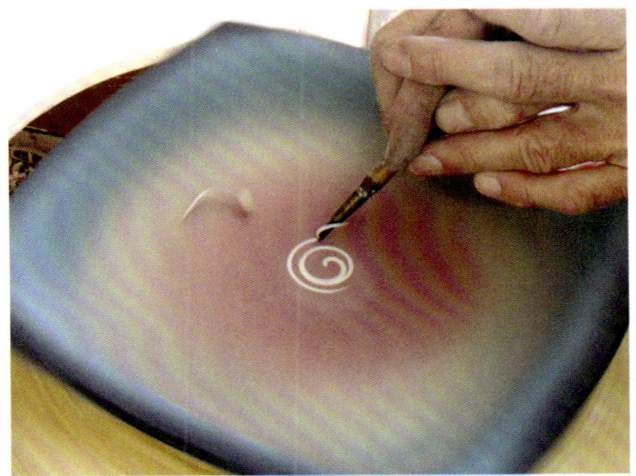

4. Place the platter on a foam rubber chuck on the wheel and create the center spiral as the wheel turns.

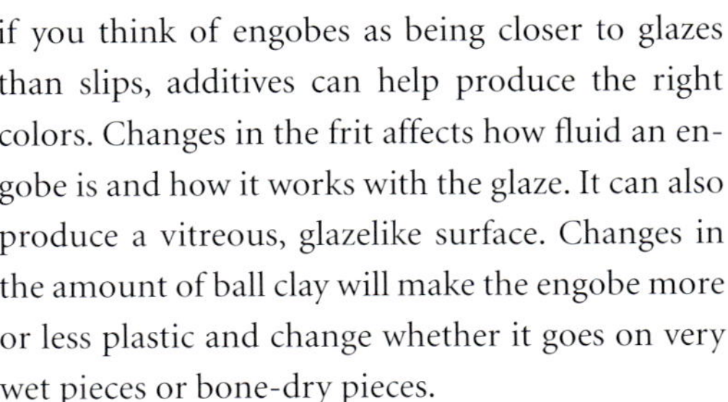

if you think of engobes as being closer to glazes than slips, additives can help produce the right colors. Changes in the frit affects how fluid an engobe is and how it works with the glaze. It can also produce a vitreous, glazelike surface. Changes in the amount of ball clay will make the engobe more or less plastic and change whether it goes on very wet pieces or bone-dry pieces.

I use a matt and a shiny glaze to cover the engobes on the face of the pieces and these two glazes are what I call "color friendly." To get as many colors as possible, they have to work with the chrome-tin colors, i.e., the reds, pinks and purples. The molecular recipe has to have three times more calcium than boron for these to work. They have that ratio and will produce the right color with all my engobes. I do use barium for what it does for the colors and for the matt. The potential problem with it has to do with the heavy metals and the possibility of leaching. From what I can find out, if a glaze has less than 15% barium in the percentage composition, it will not promote leaching. From the tests I have done, the glazes that I now use do not promote leaching when used over the engobes. I do use a liner glaze for liquid containers and I don't use the solid color glazes on eating surfaces.

I spray very wet, as if I'm pouring on a small stream of the glaze or engobe on the piece. The engobe sets quickly because the leather-hard piece can absorb some water, but too much engobe and the piece can collapse. If the engobe is too thick, it makes the color and the glaze crawl. Set the fan for a tall oval and overlap the spray by 50% with the piece on a banding wheel turning smoothly

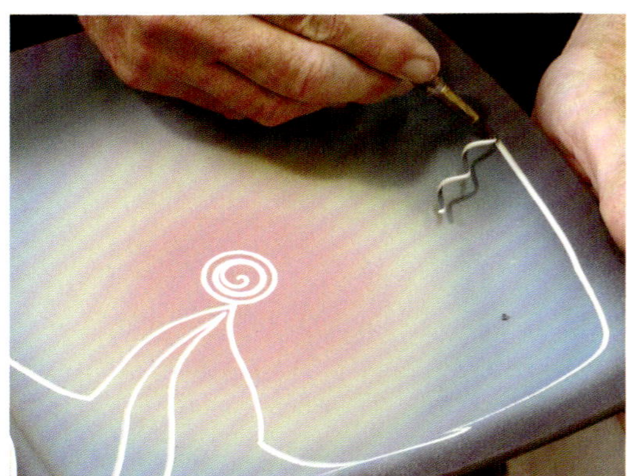
5. Do freehand work with the piece on a banding wheel.

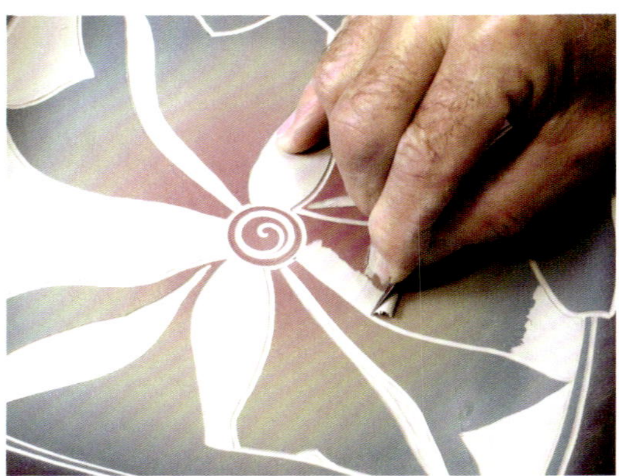
6. Scrape off large areas last using the flat side of a rib.

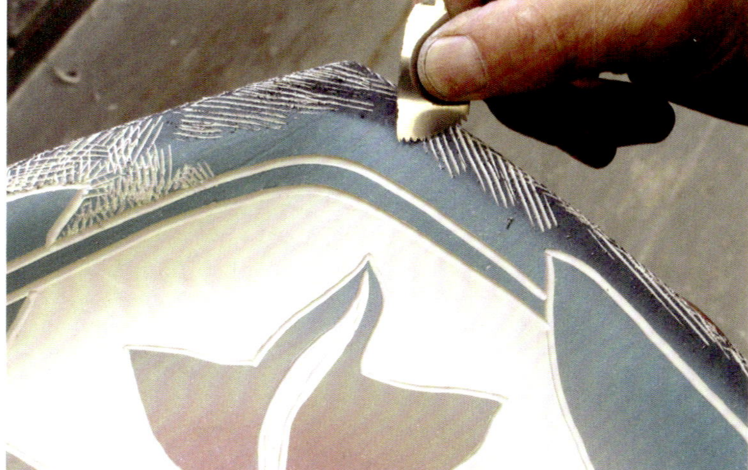
7. Cross-hatching is done with a serrated tool.

through the spray. Practice spraying with paper plates so you can cover the plate smoothly with no bare spots or dusty areas.

The four colors of this color set are Black, French Green, Chartreuse and Crimson and are applied from dark to light (figures 1–2). The spray adds water to the piece and it must dry to the leather hard state before it can be carved. When dry enough, store the pieces on cloth on top of plastic, and and place cloth over them to prevent condensation from the plastic marring the color (figure 3).

First I create the center spiral and circle using a foam rubber chuck on the wheel (figure 4). All the other lines are done freehand on a banding wheel (figure 5).

The scraping of the larger white spaces is done last, when the piece is even harder. I try to take off only the layer of color (figure 6). I use the the tool tip to make a sort of ditch that you can scrape to or from to make the larger white areas. I use the flat side of a rib to make the larger cuts.

There will be some edges that can be felt, and glazes will break away from these edges, but the glaze will fill in to make it smoother than when cut. Small nicks and cuts can be patched, but the spray overlaps are very hard to color match, so it is best to avoid mistakes! When almost bone dry, use 0000-grade steel wool to lightly smooth some of the cuts and to remove small bits of color.

Cross-hatching is another way of exposing the white of the porcelain and is done with a serrated-edge tool (figure 7). I add black dots of engobe when all the carving is done. The piece is air-dried, then bisque fired, then a clear satin matte or a shiny glaze is sprayed on the front and solid color glazes on the back.

Tools

My sgraffito tool tips are made from the main spring of a pocket watch. The spring metal is thin and strong, doesn't have to be sharpened and keeps the same feel as it wears away. To make the tip, cut a piece of spring, heat it with a small torch and bend it to the shape you want. A small rounded point is used for the line cutting tips, and a broader rounder tip for large cuts. Glue the tip with Elmers glue into the brass ferrel of the trimming tool and allow it to harden. Lightly heating the ferrel softens the glue and the ferrel can be removed and another tip glued into the tool. For ribs, cut them with tin snips from sheets of metal and flatten the edges, making two square edges for scraping (do not sharpen the edges). You can also cut serrated-edge ribs with the snips.

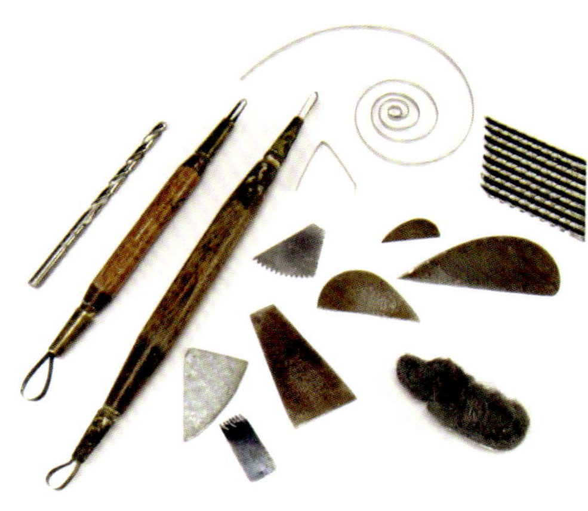

Assorted tools used in sgraffito.

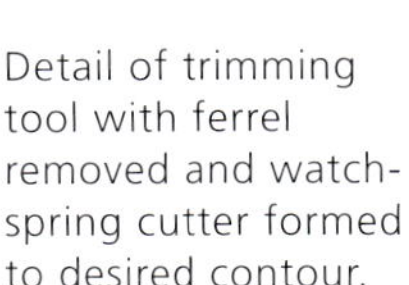

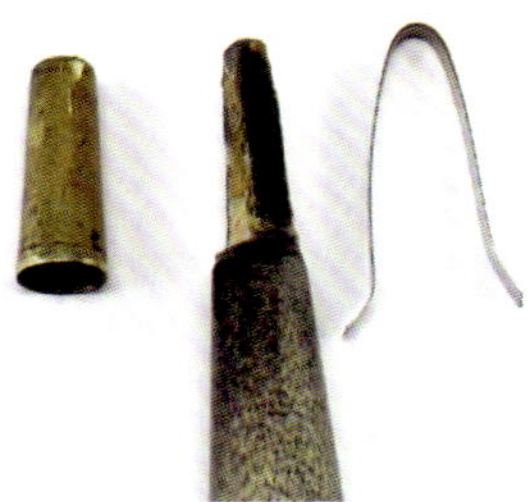

Detail of trimming tool with ferrel removed and watch-spring cutter formed to desired contour.

Engobes

Sgraffito techniques can be a lot of fun, especially with a large color palette of engobes. Most of my colors come from commercial glaze stains. Frits, fillers and retardants are added, depending on the colorant used. The following engobes are mixed with Mason stains.

Note that C&C clay is a ball clay. If not available, another ball clay may be used, but the results may vary. Although formulated for cone 6, many of these will work at higher and lower temperatures.

UBL-45 BLACK

C&C Clay	50 %
Ferro Frit 3195	20
Black #6600	30
	100 %

UR-31 CRIMSON

C&C Clay	50 %
Ferro Frit 3134	20
Wollastonite	10
Crimson #6006	20
	100 %

UG-35 FRENCH GREEN

C&C Clay	50 %
Ferro Frit 3134	15
Wollastonite	10
French Green #621	25
	100 %

UG-41 CHARTREUSE

C&C Clay	50 %
Ferro Frit 3134	20
Chartreuse #6236	30
	100 %

UB-18 TEAL BLUE

C&C Clay	60 %
Ferro Frit 3134	30
Teal #6305	10
	100 %

UG -69 TURQUOISE GREEN

C&C Clay	50 %
Wollastonite	10
Ferro Frit 3134	20
Turquoise #6393	20
	100 %

UBL-41 LIGHT BLUE BLACK

C&C Clay	60 %
Nepheline Syenite	10
Wollastonite	10
Silica	10
Black #6616	10
	100 %

UBR-17 SEAL BROWN

C&C Clay	40 %
Nepheline Syenite	20
Wollastonite	10
Seal Brown #6153	30
	100 %

UR-28 DOT RED

C&C Clay	50 %
Wollastonite	20
Ferro Frit 3134	10
Crimson #6006	20
	100 %

UBL-46 BLUE BLACK

C&C Clay	50 %
Nepheline Syenite	10
Silica	10
Black #6616	30
	100 %

UB 22-TURQUOISE BLUE

C&C Clay	50 %
Ferro Frit 3134	10
Wollastonite	10
Zircopax	10
Turquoise #6390	20
	100 %

UY-38 HOT YELLOW

C&C Clay	50 %
Nepheline Syenite	10
Ferro Frit 3134	10
Wollastonite	10
Yellow #6481	20
	100 %

UW-1 WHITE

C&C Clay	30 %
Nepheline Syenite	20
Ferro Frit 3134	10
Wollastonite	10
White #6700	30
	100 %

UP-49 HOT PINK

C&C Clay	40 %
Ferro Frit 3134	40
Pink #6020	20
	100 %

UP-34 CORAL

C&C Clay	50 %
Ferro Frit 3134	10
Wollastonite	10
Coral #6090	30
	100 %

UGR-10 SILVER GRAY

C&C Clay	60 %
Ferro Frit 3134	10
Silica	10
Silver #6530	20
	100 %

UPR-32 DEEP ORCHID

C&C Clay	50 %
Nepheline Syenite	10
Deep Orchid #6303	30
Wollastonite	10
	100 %

UB-7 PEACOCK BLUE

C&C Clay	40 %
Nepheline Syenite	10
Peacock Blue #6396	40
Wollastonite	10
	100 %

UPR-31 PANSY PURPLE

C&C Clay	50 %
Nepheline Syenite	10
Wollastonite	13
Pansy Purple #6385	27
	100 %

Glazes

The following glaze recipes can be used over the engobes, but they can also be tinted with stains.

R-1030 SATIN MATT*
Cone 5

Barium Carbonate	11 %
Wollastonite	15
Ferro Frit 3134	19
Nepheline Syenite	33
EPK Kaolin	16
Silica	6
	100 %

Similar to R-1015 but lower temperature. Will go shiny if fired higher. Top of my kiln.

FROSTY MATT
Cone 6

Barium Carbonate	22 %
Lithium Carbonate	5
Nepheline Syenite	60
EPK Kaolin	8
Silica	5
	100 %

High alkaline, distinct color characteristics, crystalline sugar like surface, turns copper turquoise, brightens most colors.

Contains barium. Can produce leaching when used with heavy metals. No claims made for success or safety.

R-1012 SATIN MATT*
Cone 5

Barium Carbonate	11 %
Whiting	12
Ferro Frit 3134	17
Nepheline Syenite	44
EPK Kaolin	7
Silica	9
	100 %

Similar to R-1015 but lower temperature. Middle of kiln.

R-1015 SATIN MATT*
Cone 6

Barium Carbonate	16 %
Wollastonite	15
Ferro Frit 3134	13
Nepheline Syenite	33
EPK Kaolin	14
Silica	9
	100 %

G-19 SHINY CLEAR
Cone 6

Wollastonite	30 %
Ferro Frit 3195	30
EPK Kaolin	20
Silica	20
	100 %

Color friendly base, will produce shiny versions of most of the Mason stain colors. Can be used as a liner glaze, unlikely to produce leaching.

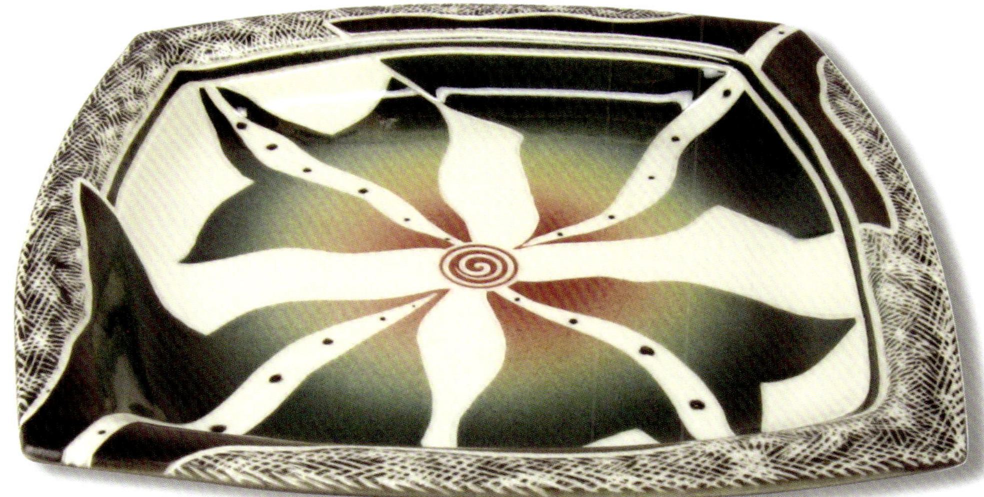

Plate, 10 inches square, sgraffito decoration with clear glaze fired to cone 5.

Carving & Etching
DECORATING WITH SGRAFFITO

by Lyla Goldstein

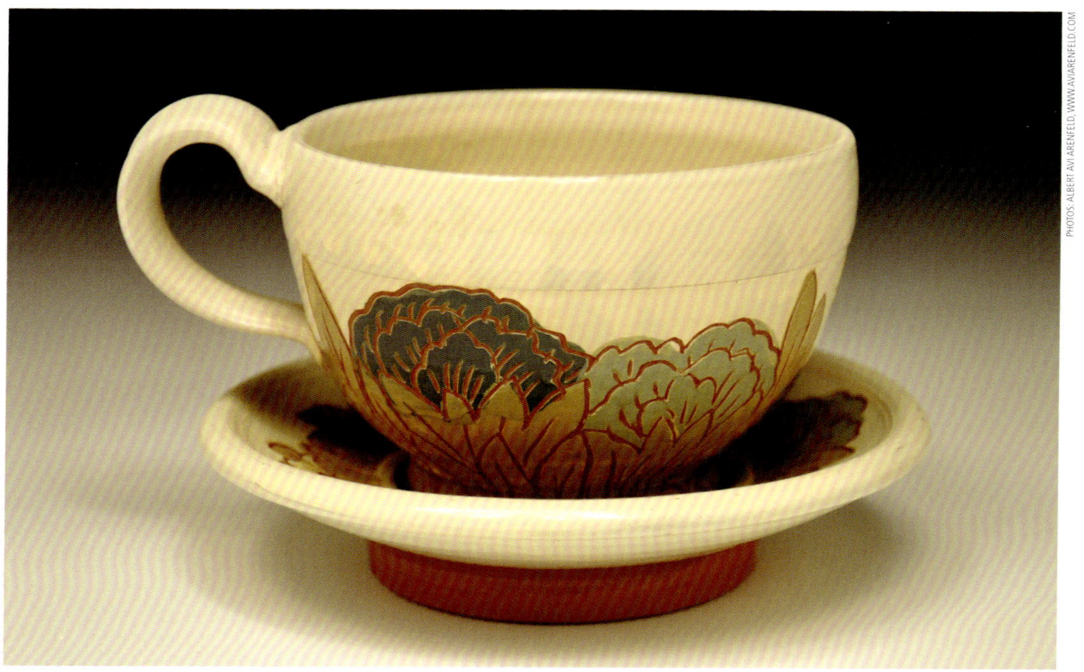

PHOTOS: ALBERT AVI ARENFELD, WWW.AVIARENFELD.COM

Cup and Saucer, 5 in. (13 cm) in height, wheel-thrown earthenware, slip, glaze, fired to cone 1 electric.

The act of drinking from a cup with a saucer is a different experience than drinking from a cup alone. It can be slower and more contemplative. The saucer enhances the significance of the cup by elevating it off the table and giving it a place to return to. My cup and saucer forms reference cups and saucers that became popular in 17th and 18th century Europe. I enjoy making these pots that can function independently, and come together to form a relationship.

My pieces contain an ongoing investigation of decoration. Through the use of color and line, the cup is united to the saucer through shared decorative patterns that convey a sense of movement. I incise drawings of plants and flowers through brushwork on the outside of my cups and saucers. Layering the pieces with colorful slips and glaze adds depth to the surface.

Slipping the Pieces

Slipping your pieces successfully depends upon the thickness of the slip and the dryness of your pieces. I slip my pieces when they are nearly dry but still have some moisture in them. You can also experiment with different thicknesses of slip. A skim milk consistency will break on edges and lines on the piece. A heavy cream consistency will cover more of the red clay body. Be careful because a thick application of slip means more water and a higher chance of your piece caving in or cracking.

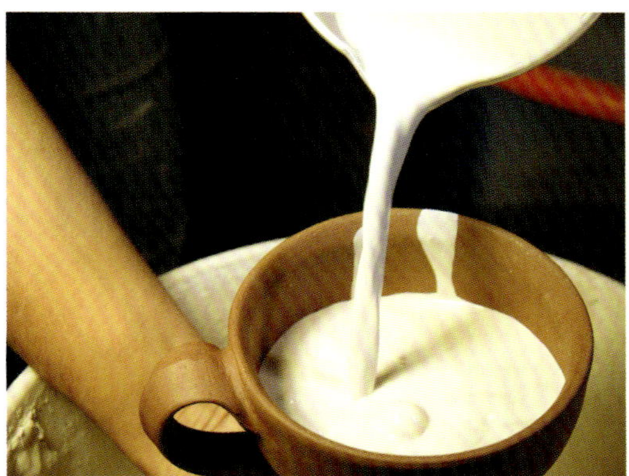
1. Pour white slip into the cup.

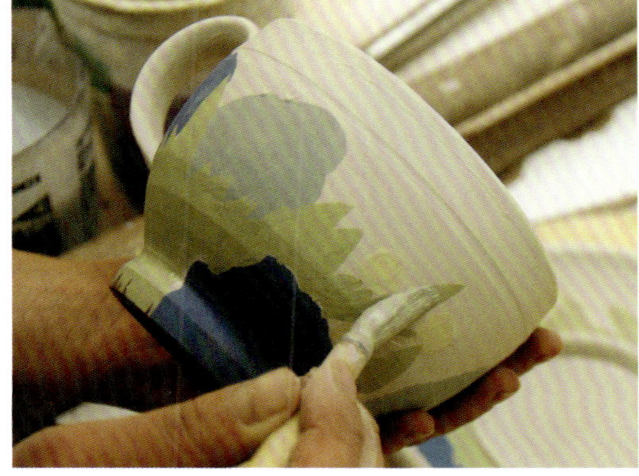
2. Paint colored slips on the surface.

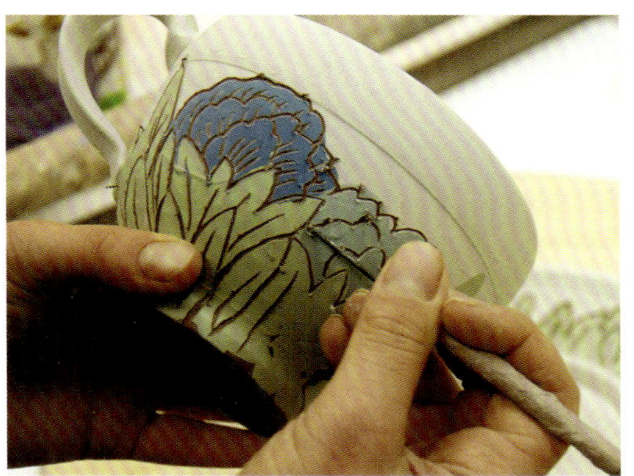
3. Use a dull needle tool to incise a drawing through the layers of colored slip, revealing the clay body.

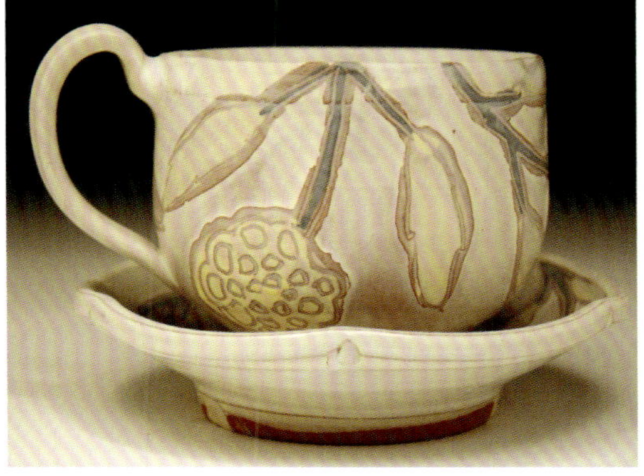
Cup and Saucer, 5 in. (13 cm) in height, wheel-thrown earthenware, slip, glaze, fired to cone 1 electric.

Hold your cup in one hand and, with a measuring cup, pour slip into the interior of the cup (figure 1). Rotate your hand and wrist as you pour the slip back out. Hold the cup by the foot and dip it into the slip bucket to coat the outside. Hold for three seconds, pull it out and carefully set it to dry. To slip the saucer, hold it by the foot vertically in one hand. Use the measuring cup to pour slip in one spot on the saucer as you rotate it with your other hand. When the saucer is lined, dip it into the slip bucket to coat the back.

Decorating the Surface

Decorate with colored slips when the white slip has set up and is no longer tacky (figure 2). For my colored slips, I mix Mason stains in the white slip base at approximately two percent by weight. Mixing different colored satins, varying percentages, and experimenting with other pigments can also be great ways to acquire a palette of colors that are specific to your needs. Consider how the decoration and color choice can unite the cup and saucer. Use a brush to paint a pattern or image onto your cup and saucer.

Let the piece soak up the slip, and then use a dull needle tool, pen, or carving tool to carve a line drawing on top of your painting (figure 3). After carving your lines, do not touch the piece. Wait until it is bone dry and ready for the bisque, at which point you can lightly rub the carved edges smooth. I bisque at cone 04 and apply a clear glaze then fire to cone 1.

Carving & Etching

MAKING SGRAFFITO TOOLS

by Nancy Gallagher

Clay is rough on tools. Fortunately, some of the most used tools in the box are quick and cheap to assemble right in your own studio. To make your own sgraffito and carving tools, start by gathering dowels, pencils, or brushes that can be used for tool handles. Taper the ends with a pencil sharpener just a bit so the edges don't cut into your clay surface while you're working. Drill a ¹⁄₁₆-inch hole into the tapered end.

Smaller Carving Tools

Utility staples and office staples make excellent carving loops. A straightened utility staple makes a needle-type stylus for sgraffito, which creates nicely tapered lines when the chiseled edge is held at an angle. An office staple is easy to bend into a small carving loop. Use a pair of needle-nose pliers, bend the staples to the shapes that will work best for your sgraffito work.

Put a small dab of Gorilla Glue in each drilled hole, then insert the wire shape into the hole. Note that Gorilla Glue expands while it dries. Dry the tool in an upright position for 12 hours.

Larger Carving Tools

For creating thicker lines or carving away larger areas of clay, make loop tools with spring steel from a measuring tape. Cheap measuring tapes from a dollar store work fine. Unscrew the back of the tape and slowly remove the inside tape, which is under pressure. Cut into 1-inch strips of varying widths with scissors.

Cut a ¼-inch-deep slit into the end of your dowel. Loop your strip of steel tape so the ends meet, dip the ends in Gorilla Glue, and place them into the slotted end of your dowel. Let the tool dry upright for 12 hours.

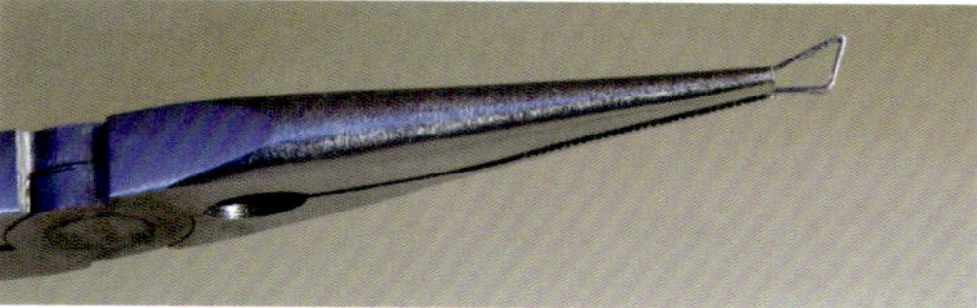

Bend staples to the shapes that will work best for you.

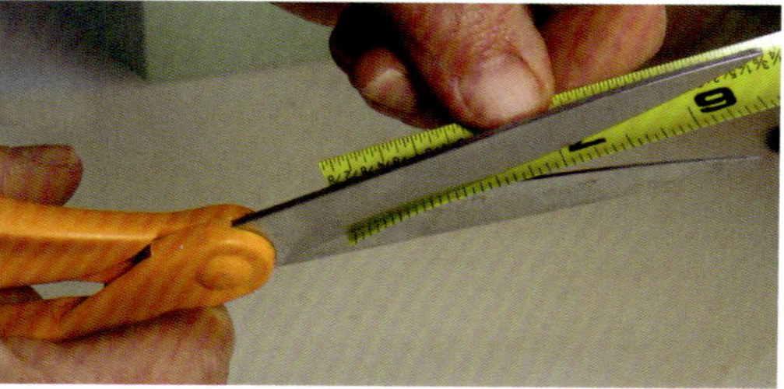

Scissors easily cut cheap steel measuring tape.

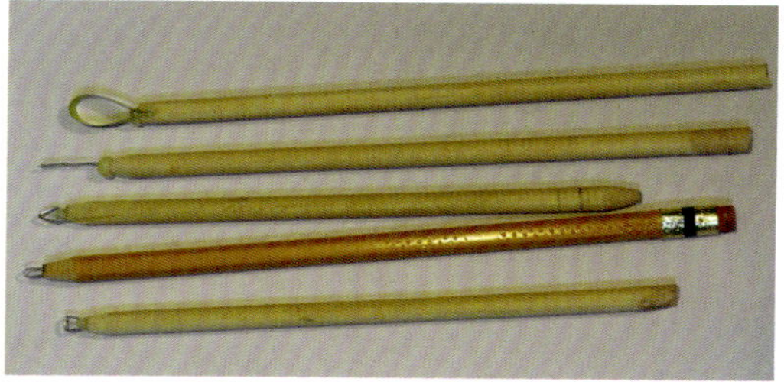

Assorted handles fitted with various metal tips.

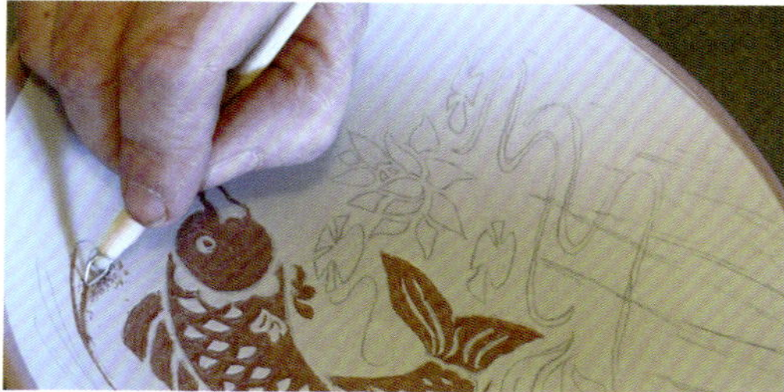

Bent staples carve lines of varying width.

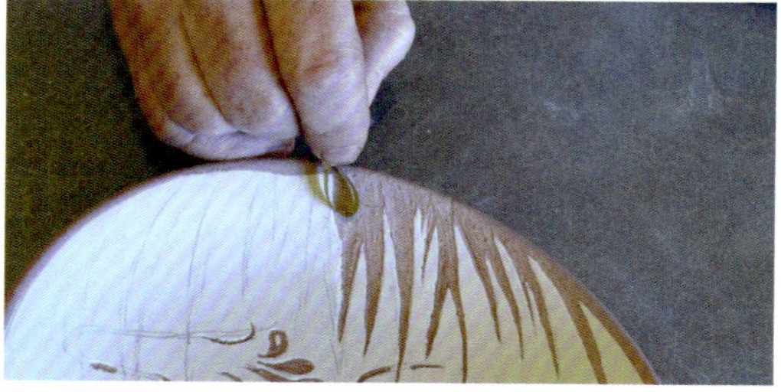

Steel loop tools work well for thicker lines and carving.

Carving & Etching

SGRAFFITO WITH INLAYS

by Ben Krupka

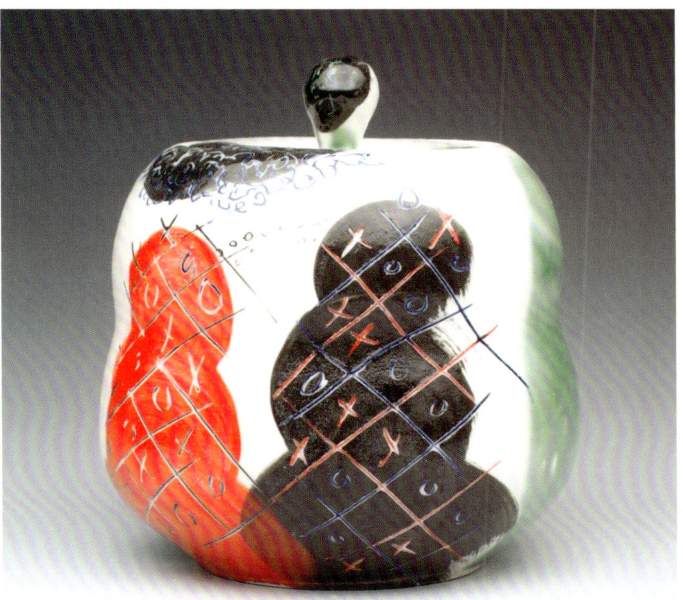

Ben Krupka carves through wax-resist-covered slips to create a playful Oribe-inspired surface on his porcelain jar.

As a maker, I remain dedicated to the evolving conversation with material, aesthetic ideals, and function. I work within the parameters of aesthetic functionalism while striving to build pots that feel full of volume, look soft and fresh, and tell a story, while maintaining a historical reference. The work shown here references the experimental and playful feel of Oribe-style ceramics, but through a contemporary lens, both in pattern and narrative themes as well as in form, which is influenced by how I eat and drink. The work uses abstract cloud forms to reference an intangible dream state and fuzzy communication that are depicted in unframed floating spaces. Pattern is used to define place and divide space.

The majority of my work begins on the wheel. I find this tool to be the simplest way to connect curves and create not only physical volume, but also a visually suggested sense of volume.

Slip Decoration

It's important to have a vision for your finished piece in order grasp the steps and work backward. I find it helpful to sketch my ideas on paper prior to applying slip to the surface of the pot. Once the pot is on the dry side of leather hard, begin to apply colored slips by starting with the darkest color, in this case black. After allowing the black slip to dry, apply the next color of slip—I used Amaco Velvet Underglaze V-388 Radiant Red.

Once the slips are dry, cover the entire pot with wax resist and allow it to sit overnight so the wax hardens (figure 1). The longer you let the wax dry, the easier it will be to draw clean lines.

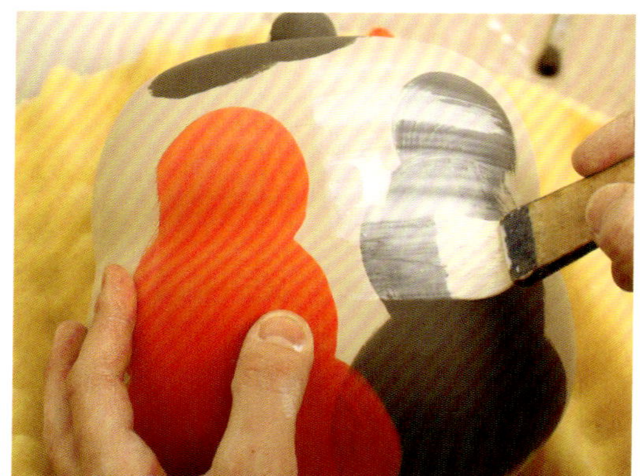

1. Apply colored slips. After the slips are dry, cover the entire pot with wax resist and allow the wax to harden.

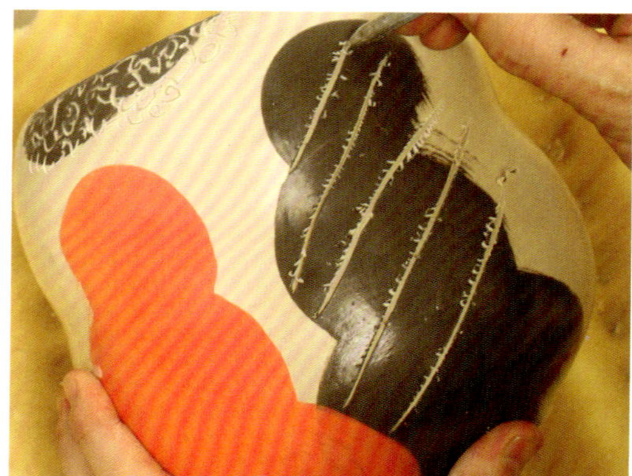

2. Use a pointed tool to draw through the wax and slip creating lines. Avoid brushing burrs into the lines.

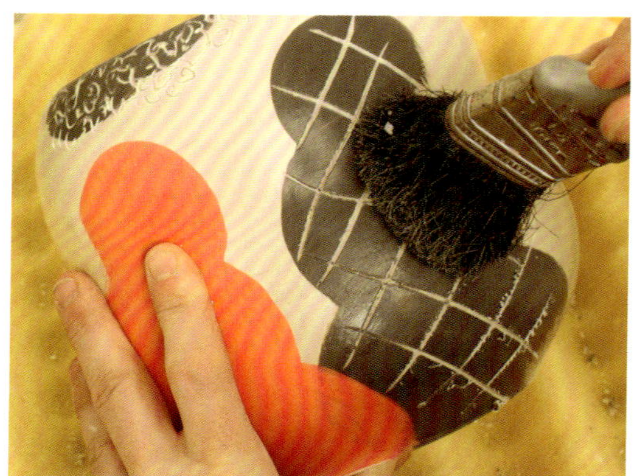

3. Use a soft brush to remove the dry burrs of wax and clay that peel up as you draw.

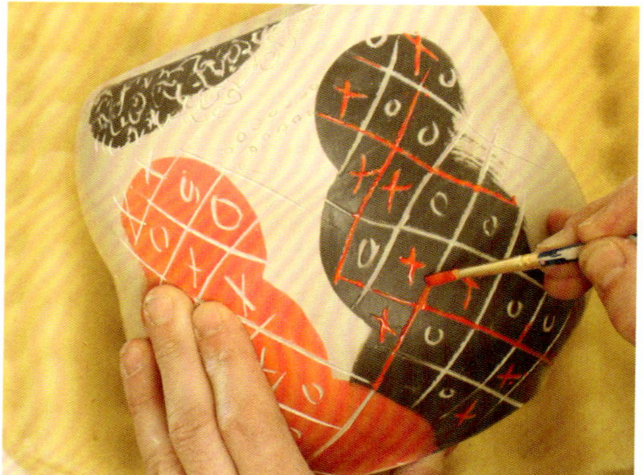

4. After the drawing is complete, use colored slips to fill the lines.

Incising and Inlaying

Use a tool with a point that gives the line quality you desire—anything from a ballpoint pen to a needle tool will work. Another contributing factor to line quality is the moisture content of the clay. The drier the pot, the sharper the line (figure 2).

Throughout the drawing process, pause occasionally to brush off the burrs of wax and clay that peel up as you draw so they don't accidentally get pushed back into your lines. Be patient and wait as long as it takes for the burrs to dry. The drier the burrs are when you brush them away, the cleaner the line will be (figure 3).

Once the drawing is complete, use colored slips to fill in the lines (figure 4). After each color is applied, sponge away what doesn't adhere before

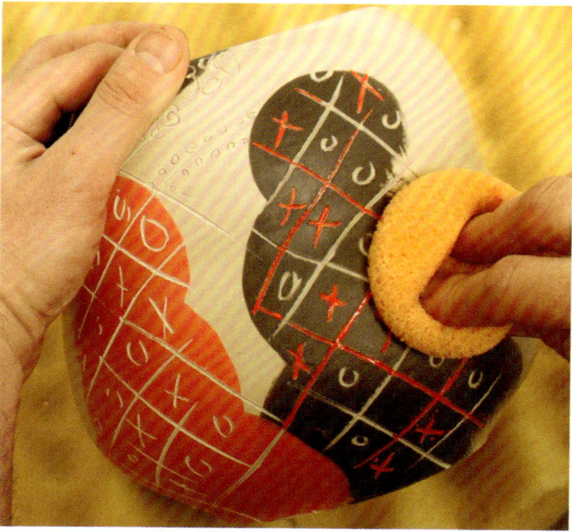

5. Sponge away what doesn't fill the lines before applying the next color.

applying the next color (figure 5). The overlying color should wipe away easily due to the layer of protective wax resist still on the pot.

Glazing

After bisquing the pot, use a damp sponge to clean the surface before applying glaze. This removes any dust that developed from the wax burning off in the kiln and allows for a consistent and clean coat of glaze. Apply areas of colored glaze (figure 6), allow them to dry, then apply a thin layer of clear glaze on top of the entire pot (figure 7). Wipe the bottom clean, allow the glaze to dry, then fire it to temperature.

SLIP BASE
(VAL CUSHING-VCHF1)
Cone 6

Nepheline Syenite	10 %
Ferro Frit 3124	10
EPK Kaolin	30
Grolleg	10
OM4 Ball Clay	30
Silica	10
	100 %
Add: Zircopax	5 %
Bentonite	3 %
For black: Mason Stain #6666	10 %

17K CLEAR
Cone 6

Lithium Carbonate	5 %
Wollastonite	20
Ferro Frit 3124	35
EPK Kaolin	18
Silica (325 Mesh)	22
	100 %
Add for green:	
Copper Carbonate	5 %

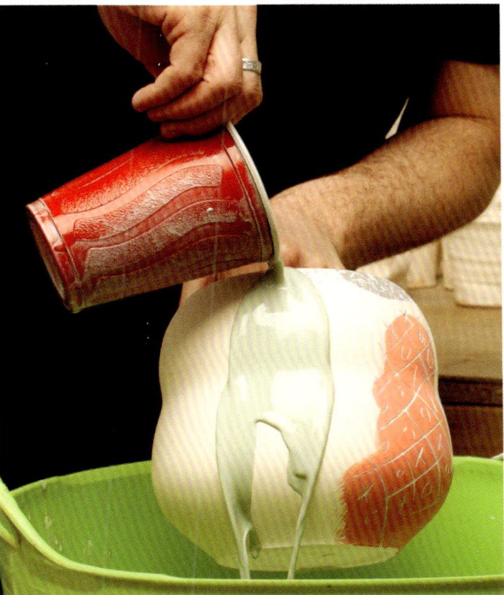

6. Apply a colored glaze in sections around the exterior.

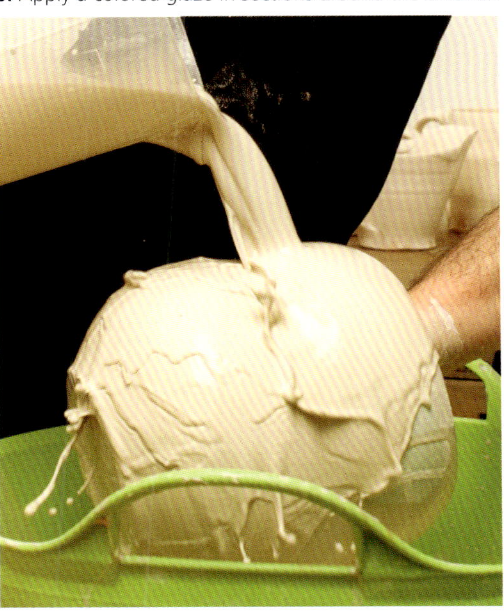

7. Apply a thin layer of clear glaze on top.

Following page: Vase, 9 in. (23 cm) in height, porcelain, slips, glazes, sgraffito and inlays, fired to cone 6 in an electric kiln, by Ben Krupa..

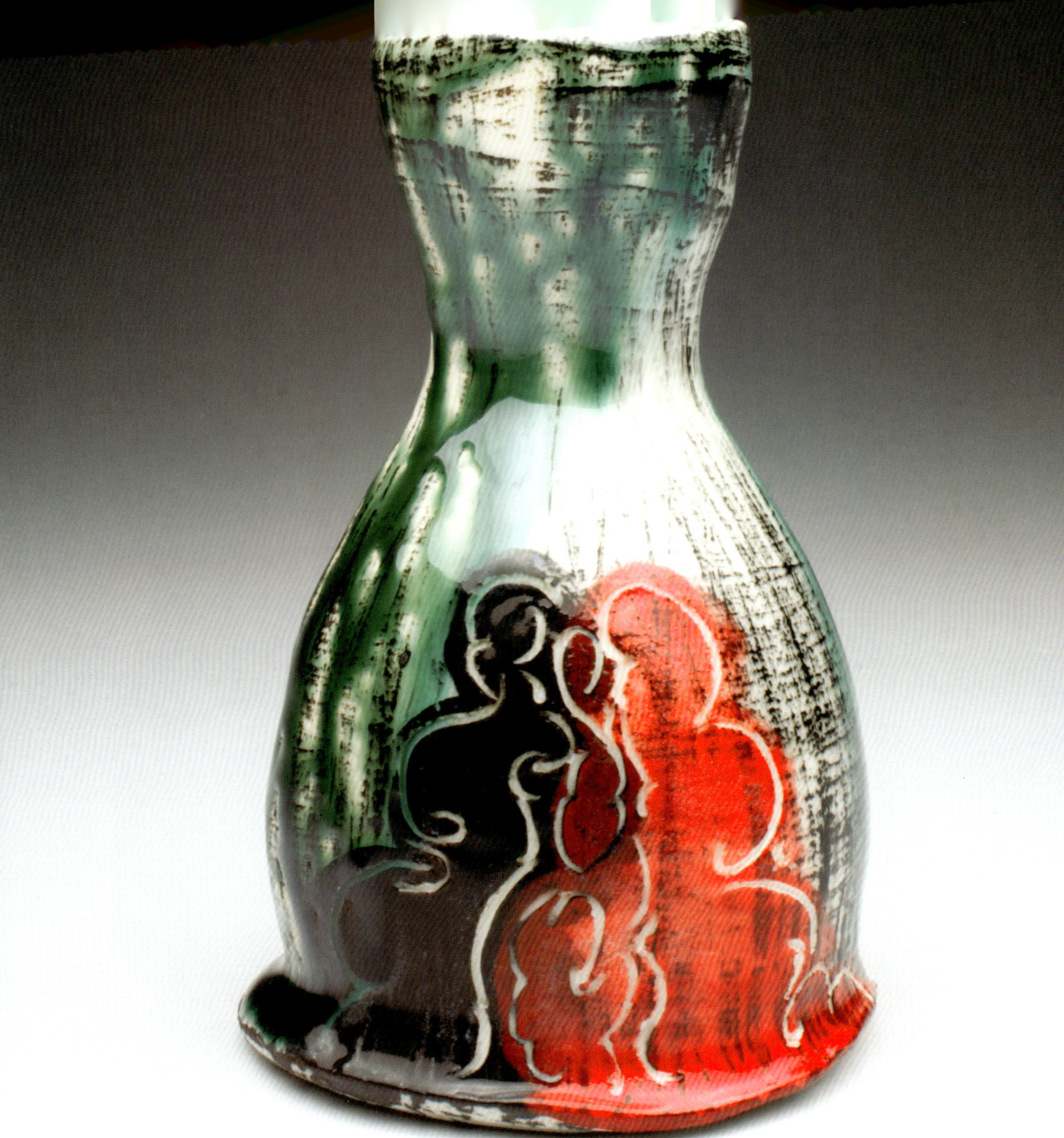